THE *"Infamas Govener"*

SIR FRANCIS BERNARD

THE
"Infamas Govener"

Francis Bernard and the Origins of
the American Revolution

COLIN NICOLSON

Northeastern University Press

Boston

Northeastern University Press

Copyright 2001 by Colin Nicolson

Library of Congress Cataloging-in-Publication Data

Nicolson, Colin.
The "infamas Govener" Francis Bernard and the origins of the American Revolution / by Colin Nicolson.
p. cm.
Includes bibliographical references and index.
ISBN 1-55553-463-5 (acid-free paper)
1. Bernard, Francis, Sir, 1712–1779.   2. Governors—New Jersey—Biography.
3. Governors—Massachusetts—Biography.   4. New Jersey—Politics and government—To 1775.   5. Massachusetts—Politics and government—To 1775.
6. United States—History—Revolution, 1775–1783—Causes.   I. Title: Infamous Governor Francis Bernard and the origins of the American Revolution.   II. Title.

F137.B47 N53   2000
974.4'02'092—dc21
[B]   00-033234

Designed by Christopher Kuntze

Composed in Caslon by Coghill Composition Co., in Richmond, Virginia. Printed and bound by Edwards Brothers, Inc., in Ann Arbor, Michigan. The paper is Edwards Brothers Natural, an acid-free sheet.

FRONTISPIECE
Sir Francis Bernard, aged c. 60 years. By John Singleton Copley, c. 1772. Christ Church College Library. By permission of the Governing Body, Christ Church, Oxford.

MANUFACTURED IN THE UNITED STATES OF AMERICA
04   03   02   01   00   5   4   3   2   1

Contents

Illustrations

Acknowledgments

I gratefully acknowledge the following sources used in preparation of this book. Excerpts from Thomas Hutchinson's Correspondence, the Governor's Executive Council Records, and the Suffolk Registry of Deeds appear by courtesy of Massachusetts Archives. Extracts from Henry Hulton's Account of the Proceedings of the People of New England are published with permission of Princeton University. The Bernard Papers were used extensively with the permission of the Houghton Library, Harvard University, together with the Hulton Letterbooks, the Franklin Letters, and Papers Relating to New England. The permission of the Trustees of the National Library of Scotland was given to quote from Nathaniel Coffin's letters in the Charles Steuart Papers, National Library of Scotland. The Wentworth Woodhouse Muniments were cited with the permission of Olive Countess Fitzwilliam's Wentworth Settlement Trustees and the Head of Leisure Services, Sheffield City Council. The House of Lords Main Papers were used by permission of the Clerk of Records. Massachusetts Historical Society kindly gave me permission to quote from its fecund manuscript collections.

My gratitude to Robert Spencer Bernard for permission to quote from the Spencer Bernard Family Papers at Nether Winchendon House, Aylesbury, and the Spencer Bernard Papers, Buckinghamshire Record Office. I am delighted that I was able to include, with permission, hitherto unpublished photographs of family portraits held at Nether Winchendon. My thanks to Charles Crisp Photography for the reproductions.

It has been a long journey. Along the way, I have benefited from the advice and the encouragement of academics and nonacademics in Great Britain and the United States. I am particularly indebted to Robert and Kate Spencer Bernard for their generosity and hospitality, and to fellow residents of Beacon Hill Friends House. My numerous inquiries to libraries and archives were always cordially treated. I am especially grateful to Peter Drummey, Librarian, and Virginia Smith and Jennifer Tolpa, reference librarians, Massachusetts Historical Society; Barbara DeWolfe, Curator of Manuscripts, William L. Clements Library; Bill Lucas, Burlington Historical Society; Stephanie Philbrick, Maine Historical Society; Hugh Hanley, County Archivist, Buckinghamshire Record Office; Judith Curthoys, Christ Church Library; Adrian Wilkinson, Archivist, Lincolnshire Archives; William Bell, Archivist, Sheffield City Archives; and Alan Dell, Buckinghamshire Family History Society. I must, however, single out Gordon Willis and Linda Cameron of Stirling University Library for their unfailing professionalism. My colleagues in the History Department at Stirling have been similarly supportive of this project over the last seven years, not least by fostering an excellent research environment. Research for the book was generously supported by the Department, the Faculty of Arts, and the Carnegie Trust for the Universities of Scotland.

The manuscript was carefully read by several historians, and the book is all the better for their comments and suggestions. My sincere thanks to professors William Pencak, George C. Peden, and David Bebbington, and to Malcolm Freiberg, Owen Dudley Edwards, Frank Cogliano, and my sister Meg McCall. John W. Tyler of the Colonial Society of Massachusetts and Conrad E. Wright, Director of the Center for the Study of New England, have both been inspirational. My thanks also to the publishing team at Northeastern University Press, especially John Weingartner and Emily McKeigue, and to Jennifer Wilkin for her splendid copyediting. Needless to say, whatever errors remain are mine alone.

Historians neither live nor work in isolation from the world around them. My students will recognize, I am sure, some of the ideas that have enlivened our seminars on the American Revolution. Friends too will no doubt recall how often our conversations on quite different topics, sometimes in the unlikeliest of places, would veer toward the Revolution. For that I do not offer an apology but an appreciation; my thanks to you—Drew, Gary, Graham, Ian, and Jane. I wonder, sometimes, whether or not this book would have appeared without my family's assistance. My mother Sarah Nicolson, and Janet and David Hay sustained the venture when help was needed. Most of all, it is for you, Catherine and Catriona, that I am eternally thankful.

Parts of chapters 2, 3, 4, 7, and the conclusion were previously published in Colin Nicolson, "Governor Francis Bernard, the Massachusetts Friends of Government, and the Advent of the Revolution,"
Proceedings of the Massachusetts Historical Society, 3d ser., 101 (1991):
24–113; and Colin Nicolson, " 'McIntosh, Otis & Adams are our
demagogues': Nathaniel Coffin and the Loyalist Interpretation of the
Origins of the American Revolution," *Proceedings of the Massachusetts
Historical Society*, 3d ser., 108 (1996–97): 73–114. They are included
here in an updated and revised form with the permission of the Massachusetts Historical Society.

THE *"Infamas Govener"*

INTRODUCTION

The *"Infamas Govener"*

THE FUTURE seemed bright for the English-born governor and onetime canon lawyer, when, on a cold Saturday afternoon in February 1763, he walked onto the small balcony of the Boston Town House. He read aloud a brief statement, a royal proclamation: the longest war in the history of the province of Massachusetts Bay was over. Governor Francis Bernard politely took his leave of the cheering crowd. The following Tuesday, 8 February, he celebrated with the province's "principal gentlemen" at the Concert Hall, and after toasting the king's health, reported one newspaper, a "general Joy was difused thro' all Ranks" of townspeople. The province legislature could not have been more fulsome in praising Governor Bernard: "We sincerely wish that you may long be continued at the Head of the Government, promoting that interior Peace, upon which our Prosperity so much depends."[1]

Only for the most pessimistic of New Englanders were the signs ominous. One participant in these proceedings was a brilliant lawyer who had lately astonished the governor with his audacity to challenge in a colonial court the legality of a vital instrument of royal government. James Otis Jr. often confounded his many admirers with his vivacious talk but of one thing he had never been more certain: the cessation of the struggle against the French promised to awaken dormant conflicts of interest between the king's American subjects and an imperial government in London unappreciative of the many sacrifices that the colonists had made.

Otis was particularly concerned at the role that royal officials like Francis Bernard might play in Britain's modernizing plans. Bernard encouraged the colonists to revel in their British identity, but his every word seemed mindful of Britain's postponed intention of bringing the colonies under stricter metropolitan control. The commonwealth had resisted imperial intrusions before and must remain vigilant, Otis chided, for the "Jealousies" of "weak and wicked" officials were fermenting "in the Blackness of Darkness." Oxenbridge Thacher had also succumbed to the pessimism that visited his colleague: "We seem to be in that deep sleep or stupor that Cicero describes his country to be in a year or two before the civil wars broke out."[2]

The "interior Peace" that prevailed in the early 1760s, the colonists claimed, was disrupted by a conspiracy of Catilinarian proportions. Governor Bernard, his deputy Thomas Hutchinson, and certain British ministers aimed at nothing less than the destruction of colonial rights and liberties.[3] John Adams, the future U.S. president, confided in his diary that "The Enmity of Govr. Bernard" and his cabal "to the Constitution of this Province is owing to its being an Obstacle to their Views and Designs of Raising a Revenue by Parliamentary Authority, and making their own Fortunes out of it."[4] It was Bernard who was blamed for the province's failure to avert the introduction of parliamentary taxation in 1765, which ignited the flames of protest. It was Bernard who brought British troops to Boston in 1768 as an army of "occupation" to quell a conscientious and loyal people. It was Bernard who was largely responsible for persuading the king, his ministers, and Parliament that Massachusetts was on the brink of revolution. And it was Bernard who besmirched as rebels the Patriots who answered their country's call: Otis, the brace of Adamses, Hancock, Warren, and all.

In the spring of 1769 Samuel Adams, the clerk of the House of Representatives, published copies of Bernard's letters to British ministers, which he believed provided incontrovertible evidence of the governor's treachery. The assembly petitioned for Bernard's removal, but rather than punish the errant governor, King George rewarded him with a title. When Sir Francis Bernard left Massachusetts, nine years to the day of his arrival, Bostonians reaffirmed their loyalty to the Crown but likened their governor's recall to the expulsion of a tyrant. The town batteries were fired intermittently from morning until sunset, deafening those who cherished the harmony of the church bells. The flag of St. George was hoisted on the Liberty Tree and unfurled on Hancock's wharf, while a party hack hurriedly issued a series of turgid odes marking the deliverance from this English Cataline, "rob'd in Smiles, the Villain's worst disguise."[5] Another colonist etched a simple, more enduring message in a windowpane:

August 2d 1769
The infamas
Govener left
our town.[6]

Francis Bernard's infamous reputation rests upon his part in undermining British-colonial relations on the eve of the American Revolution. Few colonial governors were spared the ribald invective that
enlivened political debate in the colonies, where partisanship was
highly personalized, but Bernard is historically important more for
what he did and what he attempted than what he represented and
what the colonists supposed he was capable of. There was no conspiracy to deprive Americans of their rights and liberties involving
Bernard and other members of the British imperial elite who occupied senior Crown-appointed positions in the colonial governments,
the customhouse, and the army; however, their determined efforts to
get the colonists to obey imperial laws exacerbated disputes over parliamentary taxation and the reform of the trade laws, and also over
wider issues concerning parliamentary authority and royal prerogatives. Bernard was an intelligent and scholarly man, headstrong and
impetuous, but he was no tyrant. Behind the tyrant's mask of revolutionary iconography, there was a keen mind intent on finding a solution to imperial controversies. Bernard was an imperial reformer
caught in the cross fire between Britain and the colonies. Unlike
some other governors, however, he chose to confront colonial radicalism rather than acquiesce in its emergence. He urged the British
to undertake a sweeping reform of colonial government in order to
strengthen the power of the Crown and the authority of Parliament.
Few colonists were prepared to tolerate Bernard's strictures. To a
large extent the colonists' demonization of Bernard served to rationalize the escalation in opposition, which by 1769 had begun to desta-
bilize royal government. At the same time, Bernard's hostile reports
on the situation in Massachusetts and his influence on British policymakers opened a chasm in British-colonial relations that by 1774 was
virtually beyond repair.

This book is a political biography, not a personal biography like
the recent crop of books on colonial governors;[7] nor is it a study of
the "politics of reputation."[8] Political biography has been criticized
for perpetuating leadership-centered interpretations of the origins of
revolutions, but it is not my intention to attribute to individuals the

"robust processes" that bring about revolution—disequilibriums in states' power, social and economic dislocation, internal elite conflicts, and mass mobilization against the apparatus of the state.[9] Conjuncture is not the only justification for reexamining Governor Bernard's administration in Massachusetts (1760–71); we need to know more about Bernard's failure to sustain royal government if we are to appreciate the radicalism of the American Revolution. My aims are to reconstruct the political processes that led the colonists to justify their opposition to Britain by excoriating Bernard as a tyrant and that prompted the governor to denounce colonists like Samuel Adams and James Otis as revolutionaries. Bernard's political relationships with the colonial elites and his influence on British colonial policy-making reveal why royal government was so weak in Massachusetts and why, long after Bernard had left the province, counterrevolutionary activity was so short-lived.

*   *   *

The Revolution, which grew out of a crisis in British imperial authority and encompassed a colonial war of independence and a civil war, gave three million colonists living on the fringes of the transatlantic world a newfound sense of common identity as Americans. It is in the nature of revolutions, which irrevocably change people's lives and perceptions, that the victors are eulogized by their descendants and the losers denigrated. The demonization of Crown officials like Francis Bernard was as much an essential item of early Americans' cultural baggage as the deification of the Founding Fathers. Such an interpretation flourished in the first patriotic histories of the Revolution, which peddled the doctrine of American exceptionalism to explain the colonists' success. It has also been a centerpiece in most popular histories that reproach the tyrannical British for provoking the Revolution.[10] More than one nationalist historian, however, was astonished by how quickly the colonists' discontent with Britain grew after 1763, when, as George Minot put it, the colonists were denied a "new charter of civil and religious privileges." Bernard's aberrant "Personality," Minot admitted, may have "accelerated or retarded" the colonists' disenchantment, but of more significance, he argued, was Bernard's inept showing as a party manager.[11]

The difficulty of gaining access to Bernard's state papers in Britain's Public Record Office limited the scope and substance of most other historical inquiries, however. Few Americans, save the prolific

Harvard professor Jared Sparks, showed any interest in writing about the Revolution from the governor's perspective. Sparks was editing the *Library of American Biography* series when, in 1848, he purchased from a "gentleman of Providence" for six hundred dollars thirteen volumes of Bernard's letterbooks. Sparks failed to persuade the Massachusetts Historical Society to buy Bernard's papers, and he bequeathed them to the Harvard University library; but he never found the time to write about Bernard.[12]

The process of demonizing Bernard reached its apogee in George Bancroft's influential *History of the United States*, which nevertheless tried to find the source of Bernard's antipathy toward the colonists. Bancroft argued that the mutual antagonism between Bernard and the New Englanders was rooted in cultural differences. Colonial Americans' half-formed sense of national identity could be measured by what it was not—English arrogance exemplified by Bernard. The governor was a product of the ancien régime, toppled by revolution, republicanism, and democracy in America and Europe, who desired nothing less than the Anglicization of colonial life and the Anglicanization of colonial religion.[13]

Historians who were discomfited by the radicalism of their own times offered a more favorable account of Bernard. Samuel Adams's biographer, James K. Hosmer, presented both Adams and Bernard as "honorable and well meaning" patriarchs unsullied by the grubby business of politics. Bernard was "by no means wanting in ability," but while he fought his corner with "courage, persistency, and honesty . . . the traditions of English freedom had become much obscured in his mind" by Toryism and high Anglicanism.[14] British historians such as George Otto Trevelyan did nothing to demystify Bernard, who was portrayed as an exemplar of the corruption that ate at the heart of eighteenth-century government.[15]

Bernard has had his apologists. Most Loyalist historians had something to say about the governor and his administration, even if it was, like Peter Oliver, to chide him for being "more open in his Declarations than was perhaps consistent with political Wisdom. . . . His Reasons were just & solid, but Truth, it is said, is not to be spoken at all Times."[16] Thomas Hutchinson, Bernard's deputy and successor, was more understanding. "No governor, before Mr. Bernard, had been obliged to propose measures against which not only the people of his own government, but of every other government on the continent, were united." The strong, independent-minded ways of the Massachusetts legislature and towns were too much for even the most dedicated official to withstand.[17] A biography of the governor by his son Thomas was published soon after the Revolution, but neither it nor the worthy family history by Mrs. Higgins analyzes the governor's political and policymaking roles in a sustained fashion.[18] The only modern biography is an informative if flawed study of an inflexible "civil servant."[19] It is anachronistic, however, to judge Bernard by the standards of modern bureaucracies, for professionalism was in its early stages of development. Moreover, because of his office Bernard found himself at the center of an imperial crisis so serious, he believed, that it could only be put right by extraordinary responses both from himself and from colonial policymakers in London.

Bernard's role in the coming of the American Revolution has long been awaiting reappraisal. Modern historians have largely accepted the Patriotic view of Bernard as a venal officeholder and ambitious parvenu bereft of tact and diplomacy. (The one major exception is Bailyn, who describes Bernard as a "decent man who had simple, uncomplicated desires.")[20] The radicalization of Massachusetts politics certainly owed something to Bernard's personality, but far more, of course, to the imperial controversy that precipitated lengthy confrontations between Governor Bernard and the Whigs who led the colonial protest movement. The treatment afforded Bernard, however, has often been cursory.[21] More recent studies have shown that Bernard's fragile ideological and political relationships with the friends of government, proto-Loyalist colonists who criticized the radical Whigs, were a major factor in the declension of royal power and ultimately in the failure of the Loyalist counterrevolutionary movement.[22] This book, then, empathizes more clearly with the governor's predicament in order to demonstrate why the political bases of royal government eroded so quickly during the 1760s and early 1770s.

*   *   *

The British colonies on North America's eastern seaboard were flourishing communities when Bernard first crossed the Atlantic in 1758. The 1.25 million colonists were largely of English descent, although by the end of the Revolution, two-fifths were immigrants and one in five a black slave. The colonists had a complex sense of identity. They were subjects of the king, but they lived in distinct and separate polities, each with its own government and legal system, and were subject to imperial laws. British visitors such as Bernard were impressed by how different the white Americans appeared in their dress, mannerisms, social attitudes, and speech, and how they seemed to enjoy longer, healthier lives, but the colonists left visitors in no doubt that they considered themselves to be British. Allegiance to the Crown was not the only reason. The colonies were now a vital market for British goods, receiving around one-third of all British exports, and had contributed hugely to Britain's campaigns against the French during King George's War of 1740–48 and the French and Indian War of 1754–63.

There were nine royal colonies on the mainland whose governing institutions derived their authority from a royal charter. Paradoxically, royal government in Massachusetts had its origins in revolution. In 1684, the future James II revoked the first royal charter and reorganized Massachusetts, her neighbors, and New York into the Dominion of New England. Hitherto Massachusetts was a corporate colony, which elected its own governor and legislators, and in 1686 was forced by King James to accept a Crown-appointed governor, Edmund Andros. In 1689, when William of Orange ousted King James, the colonists sent Andros packing. It is little wonder that the sense of dislocation that these changes wrought, together with costly conflicts with Native tribes, found an outlet in the hideous deeds perpetrated at Salem village in 1692.[23] The witch trials reinforced the stereotypical view of Puritan intolerance held by Britons like Bernard, but also their conviction that royal authority was the principal foundation of stable government.[24]

Royal government was established in Massachusetts by a charter issued by William and Mary in October 1691. The charter recognized the corporate institutions established in the mid-seventeenth century: the towns, which ran local affairs, and the General Court, which made laws affecting the province. The General Court comprised the governor, the House of Representatives (the lower chamber), and the Governor's Council (the upper chamber and an advisory body to the executive). The principal difference under the new charter was that the royal governor, his deputy, senior law officers (the attorney general and the solicitor general), and the Superior Court judges were appointed directly by the Crown.

A royal governor was the king's representative, his captain general and vice admiral, and exercised by proxy the king's prerogatives in colonial government and imperial administration. With respect to the former, the royal governor was the colony's chief executive, in which capacity he issued warrants, addressed the House, presided over the Governor's Council, and administered the provincial executive.[25] With respect to imperial administration, the governor was obliged to familiarize himself with Britain's complex and lengthy trade laws—the Navigation Acts—in order to protect the preferential system from infringement by the colonists.[26] This never seriously irritated the colonial merchants until the early 1760s.

A governor's principal political function was to mediate between London and the colonies in imperial matters. Governors were obliged to send regular reports to the secretary of state for the Southern Department—the British minister responsible for colonial affairs—to whom governors were directly accountable. In turn, they communicated to the legislatures royal instructions from London, the most controversial of which were requisitions to be made on the legislature or directives to enforce specific acts of Parliament and orders-in-council. Failure to act on these instructions could result in dismissal. Until 1766 governors were also obliged to keep the Board of Trade up-to-date with colonial affairs. The Board was an advisory body to the secretary of state and the Privy Council's committee on plantation affairs, and wielded considerable influence in policymaking. Bernard's reports were usually considered once or twice a year; however, during the Stamp Act crisis they were required every two months or so. But the slowness of transatlantic communications often undermined his attempts to keep abreast of developments in London. Letters could take between six weeks and several months to cross the Atlantic and were usually sent in triplicate by different ships. Communication between governors and ministers was not significantly improved until the creation of a single colonial secretary in late 1767.

The relationship between "King and People," Richard L. Bushman has shown, was an integral feature of colonial government. The king was the people's protector, the guarantor of their rights and liberties, and because of such was due and received the colonists' allegiance. It was a role to which all but the most obtuse governors aspired.[27] In retelling the story of Andros the colonists shied away from justifying the right of rebellion against governors as a last resort largely because they never needed to justify it. A truculent governor could often be silenced by a refusal to pass the annual salary bill. The king was never assailed in the public prints or in the debating chamber until 1774 or 1775—that would have destroyed the symbiotic relationship; instead, it was the governor who bore the brunt of the colonists' anger.

Royal governors in theory had considerable powers, but in practice these were counterbalanced or outweighed by the General Court. Their powers of patronage were never so extensive as to enable them to pursue a brand of Walpolean politics. A governor could veto any legislative bills that "impaired" the collection of revenue or discriminated commercially in favor of the colonists, but disallowance was not commonplace. Colonial complaints about unscrupulous governors were legion, however, although rarely did they lead to a recall, for governors invariably could rely upon friends in high places. Argument rather than confrontation typified relations between governors and the General Court.

War had an unsettling effect on governors' relationships with the colonial legislatures. Governors spent much of their time persuading the assemblies to meet Britain's requisitions for men and money. For the most part the colonists contributed generously, and at a considerable cost to the well-being of their public finances. Britain's military successes did not lead its ruling elite to accept colonial Americans as equal partners in the British imperial state, however. Imperial administration had tended to be pragmatic and reactive and at worst haphazard;[28] but with victory in sight, the British began reinforcing the mercantilist system by improving the regulation of the trade laws. The imperial reforms pursued by successive ministries in the 1760s, which bolstered parliamentary authority, did not, however, address Bernard's concerns that the colonists exercised an unacceptable degree of de facto self-government, which exposed royal governors to popular pressures.

These tensions were manifest in the first significant political realignment of Bernard's administration. In the mid-1760s, there emerged in all the colonies popular protest movements, which challenged the constitutional premises and economic bases of British colonial policies. These were not revolutionary movements, though they became such between 1774 and 1776. The colonists' conceptual understanding of political revolution was much narrower than ours is today. A revolution meant change at the highest political levels, such as the coup d'état that removed Andros, that did not disturb the foundations of institutions. Civil war, such as those that racked Britain in the mid-seventeenth century, was an altogether more terrifying prospect. Colonial Americans, it was once said, did not imbue revo-

lutions with an aura of "irresistibility" or endow them with a power
to change human history, as they did after 1776 and 1789.[29] But that
was not how they viewed the Glorious Revolution of 1688–89. The
leaders of the colonial opposition propagated the fallacy that by establishing a limited constitutional monarchy in Britain, the Glorious
Revolution had secured for the colonists the full constitutional rights
of Englishmen commensurate with the emergence of a "balanced"
government in each of the colonies. The New Englanders considered
themselves to be good Whigs—contractarians in the Lockean tradition—and demanded that society's governors respect the liberties of
the governed. The declivity in parliamentary legislation with respect
to the colonies between 1720 and 1750—the period of "salutary neglect"—gave credence to the Whig interpretation, but it was the consolidation of the colonies' self-governing institutions during the
eighteenth century that gave substance to their arguments. By 1750,
Jack P. Greene observes, the colonies had met all the prerequisites of
self-governing states.[30]

The Whigs were a well-organized faction. Their views on the issues of the day covered a spectrum of opinion from radical to moderate and conservative. Bernard attributed his declining influence and
his own misfortunes to the machinations of a dozen men, including
James Otis Jr. and Samuel Adams, "whose own ruined or insignificant Fortunes make the destruction of their Country a matter of indifference to 'em."[31] Among the merchants for whom Bernard
promised much and delivered little were James Bowdoin, the scion of
a fine family, who harmonized with Adams's opposition in the Governor's Council and the House of Representatives; and John Hancock, the prince of Beacon Hill, who dissipated his fortune on
politics before beckoning Americans to strive for independence with
an elegant pen. "Men of a lower Rank of Life" also came to the fore,[32]
including the physician Joseph Warren, whose political career began
with a flourish in the pages of the *Boston Gazette* and ended tragically
at Bunker Hill; the distiller Thomas Chase, one of the secretive
Loyal Nine, whom Bernard accused of sedition; Dr. Benjamin
Church, who delighted Americans with his skits on Bernard only to
betray the cause for pelf; William Palfrey, a mechanic's son and a
partner of Hancock, who alerted the English radical John Wilkes to
Bernard's heady disregard for American liberties; and Harbottle
Dorr, a Boston shopkeeper, whose collection of annotated newspapers identifies for posterity the authors of scurrilous attacks on royal

officials. There were countless others—artisans, women, caulkers, shipwrights, and laborers from Boston's wharves and ropewalks—who found good reason to despise Bernard for the contempt in which he held them.

The Whigs' initial aims were largely to protect the autonomy of colonial institutions and to persuade the Crown and Parliament to recognize what the colonists had long taken for granted—that, as one veteran explained succinctly, "we always had governed ourselves and we always meant to." Where this left royal authority no one was quite sure. The Whigs seemed to be saying that because the prerogatives of the Crown and the establishment of colonial institutions antedated the charters, the charters had "confirmed and legalized" colonial rights of self-government.[33] Parliamentary authority in America was circumscribed by a Lockean "compact" between the colonies and Britain, enshrined in the royal charters, that neither party could justifiably alter without the other's formal consent. Subsequently, the Whigs maintained that parliamentary taxation transgressed natural law by denying the colonists an opportunity to voice their consent or dissent. Other colonists, however, were more circumspect, believing that the imperial Parliament did not have to exercise supremacy in order to maintain its sovereignty to levy any kind of tax.

The second major realignment of Bernard's administration comprises the ideological and political fissures within the Massachusetts elite, which the governor aimed to exploit. Colonists became "Whigs" or "friends of government" depending on how they responded to matters of British colonial policy and how they viewed Governor Bernard. The bulk of scholarship on prerevolutionary Massachusetts has tended to concentrate on Bernard's relationship with the Whigs rather than the friends of government. The friends of government, who were erroneously derided as Tories by the Whigs, were the embodiment of antirevolutionary opinion and included luminaries such as Thomas Hutchinson and Jonathan Sewall, and merchant families such as the Amorys, the Ervings, and the Coffins. They were an amorphous group of some 727 elite colonists—councilors, representatives, officeholders, Anglican clergy, merchants and shopkeepers—whose antirevolutionary views were formed in the hurly-burly of town meetings, legislative chambers, and counting-houses. They became hostile to the radicals after 1765 for exacerbating disputes with Britain, yet were also critical of both Britain and Bernard for failing to resolve the imperial crisis. They refused to believe that there was a conspiracy in London to deprive them of their liberties and came to see in the colonial protest movement the seeds of what Janice Potter has called a "democratic tyranny."[34]

When the political process denied Bernard the chance to compete on level terms with the Whigs, he took another more dangerous path. Bernard's startling reports on crowd action influenced the cabinet's decision to send regiments of British troops to Boston to maintain law and order and to protect officials.[35] A full assault on the autonomy of Massachusetts's institutions did not come until 1774, however, when the administration of Lord North endeavored to punish the town of Boston for its outrageous Tea Party. Parliament revoked, in ways and by means that Bernard had advocated, Massachusetts's corporate privileges. By centralizing power in the royal governor's office, Britain provoked the insurrection that Francis Bernard had supposed would be the price of Britain's neglect to undertake root and branch reform.

The polarization of Massachusetts politics that occurred during Bernard's administration to a large extent foreshadowed the emergence of Patriots and Loyalists when the war began in 1775. A great deal has been written about the Massachusetts Loyalists but little attention has been paid to their prewar political behavior.[36] Bernard's fragile relationship with the friends of government was the most important factor in undermining the Loyalists' potency on the eve of the Revolutionary War. Few colonists retained any confidence in the provincial executive: those who did were friends of government only vaguely in a partisan sense and more decidedly friends *to* government in an ideological sense. Although the ideological bases for a counter-revolutionary movement emerged in Massachusetts during Bernard's administration and those of his successors, its political form never fully developed.

CHAPTER ONE

"An Oxonian, A Bigot, A Plantation Governor"
Bernard's English Origins

*B*ERNARD'S FORMATIVE YEARS in England and his motives
for coming to America indubitably influenced his later responses to colonial Americans. Bernard left behind a vibrant society,
but he saw in the American colonies an opportunity of sorts to find
his own peace and security. Bernard belonged to the emerging professional elite, who extolled the virtues of British imperialism, but he
was largely ignorant of the colonists' situation and their different
ways of life. New Englanders knew enough about Bernard to view his
connections with the British political elite and his nationalism with
considerable suspicion. James Otis attributed Bernard's arrogance
and acquisitiveness to his "defects of rank, family, fortune or ability,"
and described him as an *"Oxonian, a bigot, a plantation governor,"*
whose "favourite plans" were "filling his own pockets at all hazards,
pushing the prerogative of the Crown beyond all bounds, and propagating high church [of England] principles among good peaceable
Christians."[1]

Francis Bernard was forty-six years old and in his prime when he
came to America in 1758. He was a stoutish man of medium height
who enjoyed "robust health" until his latter years. Though "not tall,"
his daughter Julia recalled that his governor's robes lent him a "dignified and distinguished . . . appearance and manner."[2] He was an accomplished lawyer, restless in his pursuit of office, and generally
more forthright than mendacious in his conduct of business. A colonial governorship was the principal achievement of his career. Bernard never coveted higher office, and planned to retire to an estate in
England or America. His Anglocentric sense of British identity,
which irritated colonial Americans, was defined as much by his own

career progression as by his understanding of history and his staunch Anglicanism. Bernard was sixty years of age when, in 1772, Copley depicted him as the epitome of the English ruling classes: confident, dignified, and full of face, wearing a barrister's short periwig. The prepossessing mien, offset by blue-green eyes and a thin upper lip, also distinguishes the earliest known portrait of Bernard, commissioned sometime after his marriage. Bernard had good reason why, on the threshold of his thirties, he should appear so satisfied with the world.

Eighteenth-century England was a relatively integrated society of elites and nonelites, yet far more hierarchical than colonial America. The English elite was relatively stable, comprising some two hundred peers, between six and seven hundred baronets, and some fifteen thousand gentry, whose badge of status was a country estate or manor. There was some upward social mobility for nouveau riche merchants and professionals, who readily embraced what the Stones have called a "homogenized culture of gentility."[3] As in America, vertical relationships between elites and nonelites were regulated by deference and clientage, which in Bernard's case aided his advancement.

*   *   *

Francis Bernard was born sometime in July 1712 for he was baptized on 12 July in the parish of Brightwell, Berkshire, in the heart of rural England.[4] His father, Francis Bernard (1660–1715), was the local rector and a magistrate. His mother, Margery Winlowe, was a squire's daughter from the neighboring parish of Lewknor. When they wed on 13 or 17 August 1711,[5] Reverend Bernard was fifty-one years old— Margery twenty-one years his junior. Francis was the only child to bless the union of this genteel couple who had married rather late in life. An American once quipped that Francis was "the chance production of some am'rous spark,"[6] but his was an auspicious start in the world.

Marriage and fatherhood ideally complemented Reverend Bernard's standing in his local community, but they had been a long time in coming. He was born and raised in St. Mary's Parish, Reading, Berkshire, and was educated at the local grammar school before receiving a scholarship to St. John's, Oxford, in 1677. The college register describes him as a "plebeian," a label assigned to some 12 percent of Oxford matriculants, but which is not a clear indicator of lowly

The Reverend Francis Bernard (1660–1715), the governor's father. Artist un-known. By permission of Robert Spencer Bernard, Nether Winchendon House. Photograph by Charles Crisp, A.B.I.P.P.

social origins.[7] Bernard was descended from a cadet aristocratic fam-ily of Norman ancestry, although the fortunes of the Reading Ber-nards had long since declined. They were down-at-heel parish gentry, the poor relations of their cousins the Bernards of Abington, Northamptonshire, who owned the bulk of the family estates. By the time Bernard obtained his bachelor's degree in 1681 and his master's four years later, his father and grandmother—the family matriarch—

were dead, whereupon his association with Reading appears to have ceased.[8]

Bereft of patrimony, Bernard relied upon patronage for advancement. Like many such graduates, he viewed Oxford as a gateway to preferment in the Church of England, and proceeded to take the Bachelor of Divinity degree. In 1690, he was made a proctor, a senior officer in the university administration responsible for the enforcement of regulations. The first benefice he obtained (in 1692 or 1698) was within the patronage of St. John's—the rectory of Codford, St. Mary's, Wiltshire, on the edge of Salisbury Plain. A former rector of the parish and past president of St. John's—Dr. Peter Mews, the Tory bishop of Worcester—presented Bernard to Brightwell in 1702.

Brightwell was a good living for a forty-one-year-old cleric. The parish nestled in the lee of the Chiltern Hills close to Oxford, and was less than a day's journey from London. There had been a chapel there since Norman times, although the rector's church had been built mostly in the fifteenth century.[9] Brightwell and the county were never far removed from the great events of English history. A few miles from Brightwell is Chalgrove Field where, in 1643, the parliamentarian leader John Hampden, revered for his stout resistance to Charles I's ship-money tax, was fatally wounded. (How Governor Bernard must have winced when James Otis adopted "Hampden" as a pseudonym.) Secure and respected, though not wealthy or perhaps even contented, the rather stern-looking rector would have mixed socially with the affluent parish gentry of local notables. After nine years at the rectory, his betrothal to Margery Winlowe, a beautiful coheiress, sealed his good fortune.

Margery's father Richard Winlowe died in 1709, though what happened to his estate is uncertain. The bulk of the estate may have passed to her older sister Mary and her husband John Tyringham or been divided equally among his three daughters. The Tyringhams already possessed the manor of Nether Winchendon, a 122-acre estate near Aylesbury, Buckinghamshire. Their daughter Jane and her husband William Beresford eventually inherited the manor and possibly Lewknor too. The youngest of the three Winlowe girls, Sarah, also married a more substantial man than Reverend Bernard—Moses Terry, LL.B., a church lawyer; it is they who introduced the rector and the spinster. When their assistance was needed most, Margery's wealthy relations—the Tyringhams, the Beresfords, and the Terrys—

Margery Bernard (née Winlowe) (c. 1681–1718), the governor's mother. Artist unknown. By permission of Robert Spencer Bernard, Nether Winchendon House. Photograph by Charles Crisp, A.B.I.P.P.

did all they could to help the rector's young son make his way in the world.

Reverend Bernard died on 14 December 1715, a few days short of his fifty-fifth birthday, leaving his thirty-four-year-old wife unsure of her future. Margery was still living at the rectory when Bernard's replacement arrived. It was of course a very difficult time for her. She

was probably making plans to return to Lewknor when she established a rapport with the new arrival. A courtship soon commenced.

The Rev. Anthony Alsop was a comforting if not an alluring suitor
for a grieving widow. He was a forty-three-year-old bachelor, chubby
but physically imposing, witty, and scholarly. Originally of Darnley,
Derbyshire, he was a graduate of Christ Church, Oxford, where he
tutored and called himself a doctor. He probably knew Reverend
Bernard from Oxford and may have been a trusted family friend. He
had held several benefices before coming to Brightwell, and had won
the favor of the controversial Tory bishop of Winchester, Sir Jonathan Trelawney, one of seven bishops whose arraignment for sedition
was a major factor in the movement to depose James II. Alsop had
published a collection of Aesop's fables, *Fabularum Æsopicarum delec-
tus*, in 1698,[10] whereas his original work, epistolary odes mainly, was
published posthumously in 1752 by Francis Bernard. According to
one scholar, Alsop's poetry reveals that his love for Margery was deep
and sincere; he emerges as a "genial, loveable Oxford don and country rector" with a "slightly Pickwickian" character.[11] Despite his af-
fectations, Alsop was one of the finest exponents of Latin poetry in
what was England's golden age of classicism. The literary movement
to which he belonged centered on a group of scholars and professionals educated at Westminster School and Christ Church, institutions
that were at the forefront of classical studies, and included Robert
Freind, the Tory headmaster of Westminster (1711–33), and his
brother John, a London physician, who was related by marriage to
the circle's leading patron—Francis Atterbury, dean of Christ
Church (1711–13) and bishop of Rochester. Other patrons included
the young duke of Newcastle.[12]

Shortly after Alsop began his courtship of Margery Bernard, Margery's mother Jane Winlowe died of smallpox. Having lost her husband and her mother within a few months of each other, it is
understandable why Margery should be attracted to this bookish,
middle-aged man. She and Alsop married sometime in 1716, possibly
no more than six months after Reverend Bernard's demise. It might
have been a marriage of convenience for Margery, though not for
Alsop. He appears to have abandoned another woman to be with
Margery, and was pursued for two thousand pounds for breaching a
promise of marriage. In 1717, Alsop fled to Holland to avoid impris-
onment, and it took two years for the parties to reach a settlement.

The Reverend Anthony Alsop (1672–1726), the governor's stepfather. Artist unknown. By permission of Robert Spencer Bernard, Nether Winchendon House. Photograph by Charles Crisp, A.B.I.P.P.

Meanwhile, in May 1718 Margery was taken by smallpox, leaving Alsop to grieve his loss and folly for the rest of his life.[13]

Francis Bernard was not yet six years old. In the space of just two and a half years, he had lost the two most important people in any young child's life, and had seen his father's place taken by a man he probably barely knew. It would be foolish to dismiss as insignificant the impact of bereavement on the development of his personality, though we cannot document the emotional turmoil he must have endured. Margery at least would have been able to explain his father's death, but when she died Alsop was probably absent in Holland and Francis in the care of the Terrys.[14] Bernard, however, believed that he emerged unscathed from the tragedy that blighted his childhood. Bereavement, he once reflected, was less a time for morbidity than "an easy determination of a well spent Life . . . if it was not for the pain which the separation gives the relatives left behind."[15] Known long-term effects of loss in one so young, such as depressive illness, are far from obvious in Francis's case. Like many such unfortunate infants he probably adjusted well in time. Bernard's own son Thomas dismissed any suggestion that his father was left "embittered" by trauma.[16] However, Bernard's aspirations toward social mobility were rooted not only in socioeconomic factors but also in a personal search for fulfillment and stability. On hearing of what was his wife's eleventh (and last) pregnancy he proudly exclaimed that " 'till Nature sets bounds to the Number of my children, (which is not done yet) I know not how to limit my wants or desires."[17]

When Alsop returned to Brightwell, he took full responsibility for raising Francis, and appears to have overcome any resentment the young boy may have harbored. In 1725, when Francis was thirteen years old, Alsop sent him to Westminster School, England's oldest public school, which in reputation and size rivaled Eton, Harrow, and Winchester. Bernard received a king's scholarship and was able to make friends with the sons of the aristocracy, people to whom he might look for patronage in adulthood. Sadly, however, Alsop was drowned at Brightwell the following year.

Francis went to live with the Terrys at Lincoln Close in the east Midlands. They were just as important as Alsop was in guiding him through life's tribulations. Here, Francis established one of his few lifelong friendships, not with the Terrys' only daughter Jane, who was two months younger than him, but with his other cousin Jane Tyringham, whom he later described as his most "intimate friend & Relation."[18] She had been living with the Terrys since the death of her mother (Bernard's aunt Mary). Jane Tyringham was ten years older than Francis and indubitably understood the pain he had suffered. Their friendship was akin to that between an older sister and a much younger brother. Jane married William Beresford (then in his forties) in 1722, and lived with him for nine years at Long Leadenham, Lin-

Jane Beresford (née Tyringham) (c. 1702–71), Bernard's cousin and lifelong friend. Artist unknown. By permission of Robert Spencer Bernard, Nether Winchendon House. Photograph by Charles Crisp, A.B.I.P.P.

colnshire, before moving to Nether Winchendon, her family home. She was a handsome, kindly-looking woman, but she never remarried and returned to Lincoln around 1740 following the death of her only son. It can be assumed that Francis expected to inherit Nether Winchendon manor, although twenty-two years were to pass before Jane made a will confirming Bernard and his heirs as her successors.

Christ Church, Oxford, Alsop's alma mater, was a natural progression for Francis. Alsop's connections with the college and his
friendship with the Westminster headmaster, Robert Freind, ensured
that Francis was elected to a Westminster Studentship by the dean,
although he would also have had to pass an examination. Such favor-
itism was rife and studentships were highly coveted because an Oxford education was particularly expensive for someone of limited
means. Whereas fees, accommodation, subsistence, and servants
would have cost Alsop sixty pounds per year, Francis's annual outlay
would have been nearer to one hundred pounds. Westminster Studentships were in theory reserved for former pupils without income
from estates. In practice, the majority of recipients were sons of
prominent clergymen, prosperous lawyers, and the gentry, but as
many as one-third were of humbler origins, mainly sons of the parish
clergy such as Bernard. Studentships were held for life and were relinquished only on marriage, preferment, or by a failure to take a degree. The students were a mixed bunch, from sons of the aristocracy
and gentry to impecunious scholarship students, for it was not until
the 1760s that the universities became more elitist.[19]

When he matriculated on 12 June 1729, Francis was obliged to
swear that as a foundation scholar, he possessed neither an estate nor
a pension and that he would faithfully uphold the doctrines of the
Church of England. The colleges were originally intended as semi-
naries for the church and student life was highly regulated. Students
were rarely harshly punished though, and regularly frequented Oxford's taverns and coffeehouses; in Bernard's day one of the most
popular student associations was John and Charles Wesley's Method-
ist Holy Club.[20] For Bernard, Oxford was an essential rite of passage
to preferment, which in turn affirmed his loyalty to the established
church and to the established social order.

The academic environment, however, was far from inspiring, if
the complaints of disenchanted alumni are to be believed. Latin was
the language of the classroom and undergraduates followed a course
of lectures, private study, disputations, and examinations. At the end
of each term they were prescribed oral tests or "collections." Bernard's tutor was one Oliver Battely, whose students read in their first
year grammar and rhetoric and in subsequent years logic, moral philosophy, geometry, and Greek. Homer, Virgil, Cicero, and Euclid
were among the set texts, although Locke and Newton were also
widely read, alone it seems among the progenitors of the Enlighten-

ment.[21] Little else is known about the quality of Bernard's academic work, or whether he was regarded as an intellectual by the dons. The new dean, John Conybeare, was a noted teacher and respected theologian, and he made a favorable impression on Bernard. Bernard possessed Conybeare's most important publication, which was a retort to Matthew Tindal's Deism. Conybeare left in 1756 to become bishop of Bristol whereupon Bernard maintained a brief and respectful correspondence with his former teacher.[22]

Scholarship students like Bernard invariably took their degree, unlike many of the aristocratic rakes who frittered away their time. Bernard, it may be presumed, had passed the requisite examinations—which were never rigorously administered—when he graduated with a bachelor of arts degree in 1733. His master of arts degree, which he received in 1736, supposedly entailed a further three years' study of geometry, astronomy, metaphysics, natural philosophy, ancient history, Greek, and Hebrew. (That Bernard had already entered the Middle Temple to study law suggests not only that the residential requirement for a master's degree was not enforced, but that he may not have had to do much academic work at all.)

Most graduates still looked for positions in the church, though many had started looking elsewhere—to law, the army, or government. Law was a conventional career path for the son of a beneficed clergyman such as Bernard, more so for one whose guardian, Moses Terry, was a church lawyer. Lawyers, of whom there were around twelve thousand by 1759, were among the eighteenth century's most successful professionals. Their technical expertise brought many a decent income and some considerable wealth, while the market revolution and the enclosure movement kept lawyers everywhere busy. At the top of the profession were the barristers—350 in 1783—who could plead in the high courts in London and who earned around one thousand pounds per year. At the bottom were the solicitors and attorneys, excluded from the high courts, who subsisted mainly on fees from conveyancing and commissions; in the middle were the provincial lawyers (including some barristers such as Bernard), who also prospered from moneylending and property speculation, earning between eighty and a hundred pounds per year.[23]

Most common lawyers began as apprentice clerks to an attorney or barrister, but the more ambitious or those with a university degree attended one of the four Inns of Court in London. Bernard entered the Middle Temple on 22 October 1733. His annual expenses were

around three times what they had been at university, but the quality
of his education was not much better. Students were largely self-
taught: clerking and attendance at court were obligatory, but reading
in chambers was not common until much later. The law books at
Bernard's disposal, such as Sir Matthew Hale's *History of the Common Law* (1713), did not provide a comprehensive coverage of the
common law. In spite of all this, the Inns in the 1730s attracted earnest young men of different social backgrounds and, like the universities, did not become more exclusive until much later.[24] The
required period of study averaged seven years, but Bernard was evidently an able student for he was called to the bar after just four
years, on 29 April 1737.[25]

It was a significant juncture in Bernard's life. His career prospects
were brightest if he remained in London, where business abounded
and offices were easier to come by. Any thoughts he had of one day
becoming a King's Counsel depended on finding patrons in the government. A second option was the Church of England, and the most
aspiring ecclesiastical lawyers proceeded to study civil or canon law in
Doctor's Commons. Bernard's third and perhaps predictable choice
was to return to his surrogate family in Lincoln. Moses Terry was
now a prebendary in the diocese and a clerk of the dean and chapter,[26] and thus able to help procure Francis a position. Bernard arrived in Lincoln sometime in 1738, and in December was admitted as
a notary public in the Prerogative Court of the Archbishop of Canterbury, the superior probate court of England and Wales.

Later, Bernard spoke of having been invited to return to Lincoln
by William Gylby, the town recorder, who would have been well
known to Moses Terry. Gylby promised Bernard three vitally important things: a position, an introduction to "His Friends" among the
local elite, and, when he retired or died, control of his "business" (by
which he may have meant both his public duties and his private ven-
tures). Lincoln Common Council was one of several hundred char-
tered corporations that ran the affairs of English towns, and the
recorder was usually the most important salaried officer, providing
legal advice to the town council and the borough court of quarter sessions.[27] Gylby was Bernard's first patron and provided access to some
of the county's powerful magnates.

Lincoln, an ancient market town of some three thousand persons,
had grown up around a steep hill that dominated the flat countryside.
"Abovehill" were the cathedral and the close, a walled enclosure of

Sarah Terry (née Winlowe), Bernard's maternal aunt and guardian. She and her husband Moses, a canon lawyer, cared for young Francis after his mother's death and in Alsop's absence. Artist unknown. By permission of Robert Spencer Bernard, Nether Winchendon House. Photograph by Charles Crisp, A.B.I.P.P.

residences on the east side of the medieval bail owned by the dean and chapter and outside the jurisdiction of the town council. The gentry of the close, noted one visitor, entertained little "curiosity for anything out of their own circle"; social intercourse was confined to "three things, eating, going to Church, and card playing." "Below-hill" were the crowded, pungent streets lined with wooden buildings

Moses Terry, LL.B., Bernard's guardian. He helped advance Francis Bernard's career in the law and the church. Artist unknown. By permission of Robert Spencer Bernard, Nether Winchendon House. Photograph by Charles Crisp, A.B.I.P.P.

and artisans' workshops.[28] Bernard lived in the close, where he was one of several lawyers competing for work generated by the church and the town council. Justices of the peace or the lord lieutenant also sent business their way, as did local magnates who used lawyers as election agents, among other things.[29] Bernard obtained his first significant office in 1739 or 1740 when he was made commissioner of bails for the Midlands Assize circuit, one of six itinerant Crown circuits. Court proceedings were mostly related to the laws of crime and property, but the records of the Midlands Assize are long since lost.[30] Afterward, Bernard's acquisitiveness was temporarily thwarted when Gylby retired because of ill health.

The new recorder elected by the Common Council was Charles Monson, a lawyer by profession and the local Member of Parliament. The Monson brothers were Whigs and firm allies of the duke of Newcastle, for which they were rewarded with several positions.[31] For that reason Bernard brashly asked Charles Monson to employ him as a deputy, a common enough practice. His letter to Monson, however, hints at pressing financial problems.

> *My only Sollicitude about the Recordership has been in regard to my Business. For if Honour and Authority had been the only Advantages of the Place, I should not have presumed to have been so troublesome as I have been. But as I was encouraged to settle here upon the View of Succeeding Mr. Gylby in his Business, & upon the assurance of his Recommendation . . . I should think myself unfortunate, now that I am fixed here, to have a Stranger come and interfere with me, in the little Business this place affords.*[32]

Although Charles Monson was agreeable to Bernard's proposal, his older brother, the baron John Monson, had other ideas and persuaded the council to elect one Thomas Vivian. Vivian's local contacts were better than Bernard's,[33] but Bernard was also too closely identified with the dean and chapter to be acceptable to the council.[34] Bernard aimed to address these particular weaknesses when he purchased the freedom of Lincoln in 1744, a year after Vivian, which was a prerequisite of conducting business in the town itself, holding office in the council, and voting in parliamentary elections. Subsequently, Bernard was able to advise the council in its attempt to persuade Parliament to legislate against hawkers and peddlers who were making unwelcome inroads in the local market.[35]

Bernard had to wait until 1754 for his first municipal position,[36] when he was appointed deputy recorder to the corporation of Boston, a small market town some thirty miles southeast of Lincoln. The recorder was Jonathan Mitchell, a gentleman with whom Bernard enjoyed a good relationship. (Mitchell later became mayor and married

Francis Bernard, shortly after his marriage to Amelia Offley. By Richard Phil-
lips, c. 1741. By permission of Robert Spencer Bernard, Nether Winchendon
House. Photograph by Charles Crisp, A.B.I.P.P.

into the prominent Fydell family.) The minutes of Boston corporation shed little light on Bernard's involvement in local affairs, however. Once, he advised on the revision of a bylaw concerning the
town's butchers, which had to be redrawn because of new legislation,
in which matter he sought the opinion of his friend, King's Counsel
John Eardley Wilmot.[37]

Long before he obtained the Boston post, Bernard concentrated

his efforts on the Church of England. Ecclesiastical offices in much
of the east Midlands were under the patronage of the bishop of Lincoln and the archdeacon, George Reynolds. Bernard quickly made
himself known when he and Moses Terry advised the archdeacon on
routine legal procedures. Bernard later spoke very warmly of Reynolds,[38] for within a few years he had acquired several church offices.
Bernard's ordination in 1741, probably as a deacon, was a necessary
precondition for entering church administration (and retaining the
Westminster studentship).[39] On 16 September 1745 Bernard was appointed receiver general for Lincoln Minster, in which capacity he
maintained the cathedral's accounts and finances and was responsible
to the dean and chapter.[40] This position, which he could hold for life,
was unsalaried, but it enabled Bernard to take on lesser posts that
yielded a modest income. Between 1745 and circa 1751 Bernard was
deputy registrar both to the archdeacon and to the bishop, and, con-
currently, clerk to the common chamber of the dean and chapter.
The office of registrar was a sinecure, and it was Bernard who supervised the clerks and administered the receipt of fees paid to the
church for, *inter alia,* searching records, registering wills, issuing
marriage licenses, and carrying out sequestrations. He was entitled to
one-third of some 248 pounds in fees his office gathered each year.
(The registrar took two-thirds—one for the bishop and one for the
archdeacon.) However, payment was erratic and nonpayment very
common. Bernard's duties entailed accompanying the archdeacon on
visitations throughout Lincolnshire—round-trips of 140 miles undertaken twice yearly.[41]

Bernard's role as a church accountant did not preclude his participation in the ecclesiastical courts. Indeed, these early positions provided Bernard with essential experience in church administration.
On 24 April 1750 Bernard was admitted as a procurator general in the
Consistorial and Episcopal (or bishop's ecclesiastical) Court of Lincoln. Bernard's main function was to represent persons appearing in
court, whether as plaintiffs or defendants, much as a barrister would
do in the common law courts. Matters that demanded his attention
included the recovery of freehold property and the settlement of title
deeds.[42] In 1756 Bernard was made a "Commissary of their Peculiars"—an ecclesiastical judge—in the counties of Oxford, Buckingham, and Northampton.[43] The peculiars were areas within these
counties that were exempt from the bishop of Lincoln's jurisdiction

and were the responsibility of the archbishop of Canterbury, whom Bernard formally represented.

By the early 1750s Bernard had a visibly significant role as an adviser to the Lincolnshire elite. Between 1745 and 1752 he was the principal agent for the twenty-six proprietors of the Lincoln assembly rooms, who included the dukes of Ancaster and Buccleuch and local dignitaries such as the Monsons and the Whichcots. Bernard did not subscribe to the scheme to provide Lincoln with an important civic amenity, probably because of the cost but also because of his professional involvement: he audited the accounts; supervised the construction of the grand building; arranged for the payment of masons, bricklayers, and other tradesmen; and organized the grand society balls when everything was ready.[44] In September 1756 Bernard organized the county assemblies for the local races: he drew up the concert program, had the tickets printed, and ensured that Ancaster's Lincoln apartment was properly aired when he arrived.[45]

By his own admission, Bernard made "several . . . valuable friends" in the legal profession before he left England.[46] Sir William Lee, chief justice of the King's Bench (1737–54), was a bencher at Middle Temple when Bernard was called to the bar; his brother Sir George Lee was dean of the Court of Arches. The Scots-born solicitor general, William Murray, who eventually succeeded Lee as chief justice and became the first earl of Mansfield, probably knew Bernard when the latter was called to the bar. These men were of aristocratic origins. Bernard respected them, but must have felt ill at ease with his dependence upon their favor. Barrington, curiously, once remarked to Bernard that he had "never . . . observed anything in you which made me conceive you were fond of Titles."[47]

Bernard's more intimate friends were commoners and lawyers. One elderly patron was Randle Wilbraham, a counsel to Oxford University, a bencher of Lincoln's Inn, and a Member of Parliament.[48] Another friend was William Fitzherbert of Tissington Hall, Derbyshire, who spent seven years at the Board of Trade.[49] The best-known of the lawyers Bernard met on the Midlands circuit were Edward Thurlow, who was appointed solicitor general in 1770, and John Eardley Wilmot, the chief justice of the Common Pleas court who presided over the famous Wilkes libel case. The "Wilkes and Liberty" controversy touched the lives of nearly everyone connected with government and for lawyers of Bernard's generation raised many uncomfortable issues. Bernard's friends in law were not amused by Wilkes's salacious libels, but they worried about the freedom of the press and the legality of search warrants. We do not know what Bernard's views were on these particular issues, for his defense of search warrants in the colonies was colored by a different set of circumstances. Bernard's best friend, Welbore Ellis, was a placeman (political appointee) and the antithesis of the Wilkesites, who, because he was the son of a bishop, rose very quickly to high office after leaving Christ Church.[50] Bernard's abilities were recognized by his profession when he was invited to join the bench of the Middle Temple, its governing body, on 26 January 1770, and when he became a reader shortly before his death. On 2 July 1772 he was awarded the honorary degree of doctor of law (DCL) by Oxford.

Business apart, Bernard was an engaging man—a patron of the arts interested in science, literature, music, and architecture, and an accomplished horseman to boot. Whatever else the colonists said of him, none could deny that he was possessed of "his full Share of Learning & good Sense."[51] Dr. William Warburton, a friend of Dean Conybeare and a future bishop of Gloucester, described Bernard as "a man of unusual honor and sentiments of friendship in his commerce of the world."[52] Bernard accumulated a "very large and valuable" library, which was auctioned in Boston, Massachusetts, in 1773, and collected another on his return to England.[53] The 215 books he donated to Harvard University in 1764 were mainly concerned with theology and religion; their publication dates, with some twenty-five exceptions, predate Bernard's birth, which might suggest that they once belonged to his father and/or his stepfather. The subject matter reveals a mind interested in the great religious and political controversies of the late seventeenth and early eighteenth centuries. High Church Anglicans figure prominently among the list of authors, including Archbishop Laud and Bishop Thomas Sherlock; but so also do Dr. Edward Stillingfleet and Bishop Symon Patrick, who advocated unity with nonconformists and took the oath of allegiance after the Glorious Revolution; and the latitudinarian or Low Church scholar Bishop Benjamin Hoadley.[54] If this was Bernard's standard fare, it contrasts with the works of Puritan theology and English radicalism consumed by his contemporaries in New England.

Bernard's associates in law and the church helped him at various stages in his career, but none was as important as his wife, Amelia Offley. She was the second daughter of Stephen Offley, a Presbyterian squire of Norton Hall, Derbyshire, some four miles south of

Sheffield, an emerging industrial town of twelve thousand inhabitants in the neighboring county of Yorkshire. Offley was high sheriff of Derbyshire, and his family was long established in that county and in Staffordshire, although other family members were traders out of London who figured prominently in the affairs of the Merchant Taylors Company. Amelia's mother, Ann Shute, was Stephen Offley's second wife. The Presbyterian Shutes were Irish peers and had risen to prominence through their loyalty to the Hanoverian kings. Ann's brother, Samuel Shute, had been rewarded with the governorship of Massachusetts in 1716 but was one of the most unpopular men ever foisted upon the Yankees. Another brother, John, was the first Viscount Barrington. Amelia's parents were both dead, however, by the time she met Francis, and she lived with her stepbrother Joseph Offley.[55]

Amelia was a fine catch, and probably first met Francis through John Eardley Wilmot at one of the Sheffield or Derby assemblies sometime in 1741. She was twenty-four years old, pretty and slender, five years younger than her future husband and probably slightly taller. The courtship lasted at most six months, for in October Bernard spoke of his delight at her stepbrother's "generous and kind reception" to his "sudden declaration" of intent to marry Amelia.[56] Joseph was probably anxious that his stepsister should find a husband, and was unperturbed by the couple's denominational differences. (Amelia became an Anglican.) Francis and Amelia were wed in December, probably at Norton, whereupon Bernard returned to Lincoln and Amelia temporarily to her stepbrother.

Married life for Amelia entailed a more modest standard of living than that to which she had been accustomed at Norton Hall.[57] She and Francis lived in or near Lincoln for the next sixteen years, possibly at Nettleham Hall, a country house on the northeast side of Lincoln in the demesne of the bishop of Lincoln. Amelia was everything that society demanded of a woman of her station: dutiful, graceful, and exceptionally fertile. Her first child, Francis Jr., was born on 27 September 1743, and over the next sixteen years she produced ten more children, who, with one exception, survived infancy. Such a large family was not unusual, though it was a punishing achievement that left Amelia "tender in her make, & so sensible in her feelings."[58] Amelia and Francis were rarely apart during thirty-seven years of marriage and "experienced," Francis wrote, "the happiness of the marriage state for so many Years."[59]

Amelia Bernard (née Offley) (1719–78). By Richard Phillips, c. 1741. By permission of Robert Spencer Bernard, Nether Winchendon House. Photograph by Charles Crisp, A.B.I.P.P.

All things considered, the early years in Lincoln were a promising time for Francis Bernard. The annotations in his prayer book reveal a steely character and an ambitious personality. After expressing regret for the time he had "lost in loving the World and the Creatures," he concluded " 'tis time that I begin to employ my hours about that for which they were Designed."[60] Preferment and marriage had brought him to the attention of the Lincolnshire elite, though several years were to elapse before Amelia's aristocratic connections brought a major reward. In the meantime, Bernard embraced the ideology of the established elites.

*   *   *

Talented professionals of Bernard's generation—"superior flunkeys" as British historian Roy Porter called them—exuded an arriviste pride not only in their own attainments but also in the consolidation of the British state and the growth of the empire.[61] The Glorious Revolution of 1688–89 was the most important political event in the lives of Bernard's parents. Also, five years before Bernard was born, the Act of Union, which joined Scotland and England under one parliament and one flag a century after the Union of the Crowns, laid the foundation of the British state. It was many years, however, before political stability was assured.

As a child, Bernard was exposed to Tory influences which, though not parochial, were at odds with the wider changes occurring in British political life. The college his father attended, St. John's, was notably Tory, while the political views Alsop expressed in his poetry mark him out as an "ardent jacobite."[62] Few such Tories subscribed to Charles I's notion that kings were divinely ordained, but viewed James II's deposition in the Glorious Revolution as unlawful. The central doctrine of Tory ideology was that no subject could depose the monarch and defender of the established church, whose hereditary right to the throne was "indefeasible." Neither Reverend Bernard nor Reverend Alsop, however, would have contemplated insurrection in favor of a Stuart pretender. Their Toryism was less in keeping with Jacobitism than with Oxford University's reputation for high Anglicanism, the zenith of which was during the reign of Queen Anne (1702–14).

Political realities and the government's skillful management of university patronage circumscribed the Toryism of Alsop and his friends. Although they insulted the Georges with impunity, Tories learned to accept the Hanoverian succession; very few sided with the Tory party of Henry St. John (later Viscount Bolingbroke) and Robert Harley (later first earl of Oxford); fewer still became rebels during the Jacobite Rebellions of 1715 and 1745. In 1723, however, Atterbury, Trelawney, the brothers Freind, and others were arraigned for treason by Walpole's government. The show trial was a lesson that anyone connected with Alsop's learned circle was unlikely to forget. With

Atterbury deprived of his offices by his peers and banished into exile, the Freinds—perhaps Alsop too before his death—deftly changed political allegiance, professing to be loyal Whigs and Hanoverians.

The Toryism Francis Bernard encountered at university in the 1730s was less prevalent than when his father and stepfather were students. Christ Church, if not the entire university, was moving toward a more solid Whig position. With the onset of the Whig domination of Parliament and government in the 1730s, Toryism was confined to the fringes of national political life, though perhaps not as much as scholars once thought, and resurfaced in the early 1760s.[63]

As an Anglican, Bernard was committed to maintaining the unity of church and state. The test oaths, which he was obliged to swear, required officeholders to pledge allegiance to the king and to the liturgy of the Church of England. (The law requiring university graduates and ordinands to subscribe to the Thirty-Nine Articles was not changed until 1779, and the Test and Corporation Acts remained in place until 1828.) By the oath of abjuration, Bernard swore "to disclose and make known to his Majesty and his successors, all Treasons and traiterous Conspiracies which I shall know to be against Him."[64] Never in his life did Bernard question these principles or his loyalty to the Crown. However, as Linda Colley has argued, an ecumenical version of Protestantism provided an intellectual "framework" in which Britons defined loyalty to the imperial state.[65] Bernard was no bigot. By "religious liberty," he once explained, he meant toleration of nonconformity and freedom of worship. Because he was married to a Presbyterian, it is hard to see this protestation as anything other than sincere. Bernard could barely contain his rage when the Massachusetts Congregationalists suggested otherwise. The only documentary record of Bernard's ever referring positively to "natural rights," a term he considered a byword for rebellion, was his accusing the New Englanders of turning a sensitive political issue into a "religious Concern" because of his Episcopalianism.[66]

There were two major rebellions in Bernard's lifetime: the Jacobite Rebellion of 1745 and the American Revolution thirty years later. The Midlands had been rent asunder during the English Civil War when Lincoln, a royalist stronghold, fell to the Parliamentarians.[67] In 1745, the Midlands again faced a marauding army. There was little support for Charles Stuart's Jacobites in the region, but the advance to Derby sent the government into a panic. Lincoln was one of fifty English communities that raised a Loyalist militia between September and

December 1745, and among more than two hundred that issued loyal addresses to King George II before Prince Charles's army retreated northward on 6 December.[68] Bernard was one of 137 subscribers who raised nearly six thousand pounds to fit out and maintain for eight months a regiment of 260 men, mostly farm laborers and artisans, commanded by the duke of Ancaster. (The twenty pounds pledged by Bernard was a substantial sum, worth twelve hundred in today's money.) Although this regiment never engaged the Jacobites in battle, it joined the duke of Cumberland's pursuit of the pretender as far as Newcastle and was disbanded in June 1746, two months after the Jacobites' defeat at Culloden.[69] The aftermath was a telling example for Bernard of how rebels should be treated. Bernard's mentor, Sir William Lee, presided over the trials, which sent 120 Jacobites to the scaffold and hundreds more into exile; their leaders lost their heads and their estates.

The Lincoln subscription is the first piece of political evidence indicating Bernard's association with local Whig magnates. It is a fair bet that he also approved the congratulations offered the king in 1745 for the capture of the French fortress of Louisbourg, Cape Breton Island (though he would learn later that the victory owed everything to the bravery of the New England troops). Britain declared war on France again in 1756, and imperial matters intruded even in the affairs of small provincial towns like Boston, Lincolnshire. One of Bernard's last acts as deputy recorder was to assist in the production of an address to George II, in November 1756, which expressed common fears of a French invasion and urged that the militia be reestablished. This time the militia was not to be used to harry rebels but to curb riots, which were endemic in times of economic crisis.[70] Lincolnshire had escaped a spate of food riots in 1766, but in 1757 there were popular protests by the rural populace against the militia draft, which did not involve civil disorder or destruction of property.[71]

Bernard's political ideology reflected the values of the British elite, who equated civic virtue with the possession of land and property and their domination of government with the defense of the commonwealth. Bernard was not a krypto-Jacobite and purveyor of the doctrine of passive obedience as his American critics alleged later. He was a conservative Whig who readily synthesized Whig and Tory principles. Like most Englishmen, Bernard lauded the Glorious Revolution for establishing a balanced constitution with a limited monarchy. Although he adhered to the Whig principle of resisting arbitrary power, from whatever source it came, Bernard embraced a neo-Tory interpretation of the Lockean concept of contractual government, which stressed the obligations of subjects and deference to entrenched authority over any revolutionary right to make and unmake governments.[72] His sense of British identity, moreover, was manifest in chauvinistic hostility toward the French and his unwavering Anglocentric belief in parliamentary supremacy, the central tenet underpinning the government of the United Kingdom of Great Britain.[73] It was natural that Bernard should wish to transpose these views onto American affairs.

Bernard was to be profoundly unsettled by the spread of political radicalism in Britain and America. He despised, for example, the "insolent" practice of public assemblies being held for the purpose of petitioning the king about parliamentary reform. Whether it was in England or Massachusetts such innovations were breeding grounds for demagogues, he thought, and ought to be prosecuted as "tumultuous assemblies."[74] Bernard missed the Wilkes and Liberty controversy of the 1760s, which had a considerable impact upon the American revolutionaries, but saw for himself in colonial Boston what politicized crowds might achieve. Elite dominance in Britain was often legitimized by crude appeals to history and by patriotic iconography, but in Massachusetts the radicals assayed the reputations of Loyalists without fear of redress. Bernard once likened Boston's Liberty Tree to the "Oak of Reformation" sported by Jack Cade and his followers during the English peasant rising of 1450.[75]

> Surely so daring an *Assumption of the royal Authority was never practised by any City or Town in the British Dominions even in the Times of greatest Disorder; not even by the City of London when the great Rebellion [the English Civil War] was at the highest, and the Confusion arising from thence most urgent for some extraordinary Measures.*[76]

When Bernard helped bring British regulars to Boston there were few gray areas in his "schemata" of how Britons of his rank should respond to any hint of social leveling.

Money worries, arising from the birth of four children between 1752 and 1757, prompted Bernard to seek an appointment in the American colonies rather than wait for a senior position in the legal profession to become available.[77] It might be supposed that the trou-

bled administration of Amelia's uncle, Samuel Shute, ought to have
dissuaded Bernard from supposing he might prosper in America.
Colonial service, however, was never more attractive to career-
minded Britons like Bernard; noblemen and military men had once
dominated the governorships, but lawyers, merchants, and native-
born Americans had largely replaced them.[78] Bernard was now
middle-aged and had been patient long enough. With the aid of
well-placed friends and patrons he was able to acquire the colonial
governorships of New Jersey and Massachusetts.

Lincolnshire had strong connections with the American colonies,
dating back to the settlement of New England. The county is on the
fringe of that swath of southern England—East Anglia, Essex, Kent,
and London—from which, in the 1640s, there came between thirteen
thousand and twenty thousand emigrants; Lincolnshire accounted
for 3 percent of the total migrant population. Emigration perhaps
dissipated opposition to Charles I, for the Puritans and Parliamentarians attracted the most support in small towns like Boston.[79] The
colonial capital, of course, was named after the Lincolnshire town,
but it is extraordinary that four seventeenth-century governors of
Massachusetts were previously recorders or deputy recorders of the
Lincolnshire Boston.[80] Bernard, then, was not short of role models.

Two Lincolnshire men—the Pownall brothers—probably first
kindled Bernard's interest in the colonies. The Pownall family, like
Bernard's natural father, belonged to the "poorer English gentry,"
and possessed a "modest" estate at Salfleetby on Lincolnshire's
northeastern coast. John Pownall entered the Board of Trade as a
clerk, a middle-ranking official, and in 1745 became its secretary, the
most important colonial administrator in Whitehall. When he was
appointed undersecretary of state for the American Department in
1768 he was earning from his several offices and commissions some
five thousand pounds per year—the kind of income Bernard desired.[81] John Pownall's success in the home government was matched
by that of his younger brother Thomas in America. Bernard and
Thomas Pownall probably met for the first time in 1745 when they
subscribed to Lincoln's Loyalist association; their paths would also
have crossed at the Lincoln assemblies. They were both scholarly
men. Pownall, like Bernard, published his first work in 1752, a theo-
retical treatise on government titled *Principles of Polity*, from which
Bernard later adapted the title for his own paper on imperial reform.
Pownall's letters to Charles Monson, written between 1754 and 1756,

offer a highly optimistic account of a governor's life in New Jersey, where a "man may live like a Prince" and luxuriate in a peaceful existence.[82] Although he was ten years younger than Bernard, Thomas Pownall preceded him as governor of both New Jersey and Massachusetts before returning home in 1760 and entering Parliament. Thereafter, Pownall and Bernard were friendly rivals for ministers' attentions.[83]

The parallel careers of Bernard and the Pownalls provide some insight as to the role of "superior flunkeys" in imperial administration. All three were extremely able men, but they were not civil servants in any modern sense. John Pownall is the nearest approximation to a professional government official in that he held office not through the favor of a magnate, as did Edmund Burke for example, but because ministers had full confidence in his abilities.[84] The same cannot be said of either his brother Thomas or Bernard, who both needed the favor of powerful men (and the assistance of John Pownall, as well) to achieve what they did. John Pownall was able to alert Charles Monson and Bernard to the vacancy in New Jersey created by his brother's promotion to Massachusetts. Pownall could also have brought Bernard to the notice of his superiors: George Montague Dunk, earl of Halifax and president of the Board of Trade, who appointed governors; and Thomas Pelham-Holles, duke of Newcastle and joint leader of the government with Secretary of State William Pitt.[85]

It was one thing for Bernard to express an interest in an American office but quite another to persuade ministers to show faith. For this he was indebted to a man five years his junior, William Wildman Barrington, the second Viscount Barrington and Amelia Bernard's cousin. Barrington was close to his cousin and godfather to her first son. He was also the rising star of the Pitt-Newcastle government, though many thought him a myopic office-seeker, and had the requisite influence with Halifax and Newcastle to advance Francis's career. He knew little of colonial affairs, although he had once discussed with Halifax a radical proposal to appoint a single governor for all the British colonies on the American mainland, with himself as the first.[86] Barrington was to hold a cabinet post, as chancellor of the Exchequer, only briefly (March 1761–May 1762), after which he gradually lost interest in high politics. But he always did what he could to help Bernard.[87]

The governorship of New Jersey was a relatively minor favor for

Barrington to have asked of Newcastle. The profligate duke had managed American affairs for thirty years as a secretary of state, but now that he was first lord of the Treasury he technically no longer had the authority to make colonial appointments. His reputation as the "great dispenser" of patronage for political ends went before him, however. His recommendations were normally rubber-stamped by Pitt and Halifax, and nobody at the Board of Trade ever seemed to question the appointees' fitness for office. It was more common than not for Newcastle to give American posts to loyal Whigs, and to use colonial patronage to support his influence in Scotland, Nottingham-shire, and Sussex.[88] There is evidence, however, to associate Bernard with the duke's political interest. Bernard's collection of Alsop's poetry (1752) was sycophantically dedicated to the duke. Although a Cambridge graduate, Newcastle had close connections with Christ Church, and looked favorably on the many requests for preferment coming from other Westminster old boys. What did Newcastle hope to gain? Presumably, he had no wish to offend Barrington or Halifax, but it is possible that his favor to Barrington had some local political significance. Newcastle was one of the largest landowners in Lincoln-shire, and the offices occupied by Bernard were in the lordship of the duke's nephew, the earl of Lincoln (a relation of George Clinton, a governor of New York).[89]

It is likely that by the beginning of Newcastle's second ministry in 1757, Francis Bernard was considered a Whig worthy of promotion to colonial office. Bernard was appointed to the governorship of New Jersey by order-in-council on 27 January 1758. Bernard met Newcastle, probably for the first time, at Newcastle's London residence a few days before he left for New Jersey.[90] The duke described him much later as a "very ingenious" and "very honest" lawyer of good "reputa-tion."[91] For better or worse, the duke's protégés—Thomas Pownall, Francis Bernard, and others—left an indelible mark on colonial America.

*   *   *

Colonial service nevertheless presented its own set of financial and personal problems. Bernard spent several weeks in London waiting to receive his governor's commission, for which he had to pay £400. Another £600 went for the "trapings of government," including his robes and a portrait of King George II; together with the cost of pas-sage and incidental expenses his total outlay was £1,600. Barrington probably helped him, but, without an independent income, Bernard was obliged to recoup this hefty sum in the colonies. A governor's annual salary was on average £1,500 currency (about £1,000 sterling, the equivalent of £60,000 or $90,000 today). In New Jersey and Massachusetts, his salary was paid by the colonial assembly, which often threatened nonpayment in order to influence governors. Other emoluments included lawful shares of fees paid on the issuance of government documents and, controversially, from Crown prosecutions in colonial courts.[92]

Disgruntled Americans later viewed Bernard's financial dependency as one source of their mutual antagonisms. But from what little he knew of the colonies, Bernard was confident that he could endure such sniping and got on with the business of preparing his family for their life in the New World.

The Bernards left Portsmouth for America in April 1758 on board the HMS *Terrible*. It was an arduous voyage at the best of times, but particularly hard on Amelia, who was pregnant. The stress of spending eight weeks in the cramped quarters of a British warship, wrote her concerned husband, was relieved only by the captain's exceptional "civilities."[93] When they stepped ashore at Perth Amboy, New Jersey, on the evening of 17 June, whatever trepidation this English provincial lawyer may have felt was banished by a comforting prospect: with only seventy houses and a handful of public buildings, the port resembled an "elegant" English village.[94] Four days later he undertook a grueling six-day tour of the province, covering 140 miles on horseback.

New Jersey offered few of Lincoln's material comforts. There was no spacious governor's mansion, such as the Bernards were to enjoy in Boston. Francis bought a two-story brick mansion, with an orchard and large garden; his plans to extend the two wings, he boasted, would make it the "best house" in the province.[95] It was a convenient arrangement, though Bernard was to be absent for weeks at a time when the assembly moved to Burlington in the west. While he disparaged the colonists for their ignorance of the arts and sciences, Bernard thought them "polite & friendly" and professed to enjoy a "reasonable abundance of social pleasures." Francis and Amelia were never happier than they were in Perth Amboy.[96] Bernard often regretted leaving New Jersey when Boston's severe winters depressed him and government business intruded upon his family life.

New Jersey was socially and culturally more diverse than the English Midlands or Massachusetts. There were Dutch Calvinists, Quakers and Anglicans of English descent, Scottish Presbyterians, Lutheran Swedes, Methodists, Moravians, Baptists, and Roman Catholics, but very few Congregationalists, who were to make his life in Massachusetts so troublesome. Bernard's Anglicanism was not a political issue as it would be in Massachusetts, mainly because of the decline of group cohesion along denominational lines.[97]

Bernard's two-year sojourn, nonetheless, was a tough apprenticeship. He was preoccupied with persuading the colonists to part with money and men to fight the French and their Native American allies, in which he largely succeeded. In 1758, he helped to negotiate the Easton Treaty with the Delaware Indians that brought a respite in raids on outlying settlements and allowed the assembly to divert more resources for the campaigns against Quebec and Canada. Bernard's second test was to prevent the assembly from funding provincial regiments with currency. He engineered a short-term compromise whereby Britain modified its policy of restricting the issue of currency, and the assembly agreed to issue bills of credit under specific restraints. Bernard's administration is historically important for his success in resolving the competing demands of policymakers in London and vested interests in the province.[98]

It could be said that Bernard had scarcely had time to make enemies before he left for Massachusetts, and that fiscal uncertainty on both sides of the Atlantic rendered the Pitt-Newcastle ministry more amenable than usual to compromise on matters of policy.[99] Bernard was a pragmatic man, however, who learned the necessity of assuaging popular anxieties and of cultivating allies, as he did with the Quakers. "The Greatest Satisfaction" he "received [was] from the very good understanding that has prevailed between me and the People & in Consequence of it between the Council & Assembly." Bernard was an altogether more self-assured figure than when he first arrived, boasting that in his dealings with the assembly "never was so great an harmony known before."[100] Bernard ultimately attributed his success to the "openness, integrity, disinterestedness & affability" with which he conducted government, and to remaining free of partisan entanglements. These were not self-serving vaunts, as his success in New Jersey attests, and they became his guiding principles in the early part of his administration in Massachusetts.[101]

Bernard's attempts to persuade the British to find him a more financially rewarding province quickly bore fruit. On 15 February 1760

Bernard learned that he was to be moved to Massachusetts to replace Thomas Pownall, who was returning to England. Once more he was indebted to Barrington's influence with the earl of Halifax, now secretary of state for the colonies.[102] He was keen to be on his way. Boston, he had heard, was the most "polished" of American towns, and although it had no theater, it had its fair share of dancing masters, concert halls, and "tolerable" music.[103]

Bernard's ambition was not without cost: the separation of the family unit. When Francis and Amelia came to New Jersey they brought with them only their four youngest children: baby William, thirteen-month-old Frances Elizabeth, four-year-old Amelia, and six-year-old Shute. Two others were born in the colony—Scrope on 1 October 1758 and Julia, their last child, on 19 November 1759. Their four siblings remained in England, under the guardianship of Jane Beresford, ostensibly to complete their education: Francis Jr., the oldest; John, who was aged twelve when his parents left; Jane, aged eleven; and Thomas, aged seven. Francis, John, and Thomas joined their parents in Boston, but the whole family was not reunited until 1771.

The needs of his family never seemed so pressing as when Bernard was preoccupied with the affairs of state. Unsettling as it was, the long separation and the move to Massachusetts did not arrest the children's development.[104] However, the anxiety it aroused in their parents was manifest in earnest attempts to guide their offspring. The Bernard infants were taught by tutors and never attended a colonial school (though William and Scrope were later sent to Harrow before entering Christ Church). By the time the family had moved to Boston, Amelia was better placed to attend to their education herself, as was increasingly the case with genteel mothers in England. "No school, no governess," Julia recalled, nothing "ever wearisome or unpleasant. . . . No childish books, no fatiguing tasks." She had an education "of ideas not words": Milton, Shakespeare, and journals like *Tatler*, as well as the Bible; politics, geography, foreign languages, music, history, philosophy, and the sciences as well as the classics. Each night her father helped the children with their lessons and read to them from "the best plays and amusing interesting books."[105]

Bernard's relationship with his older sons was more conventional than the fine education he and his wife provided for their daughters. Having decided that John, his second son, had obtained at Lincoln Grammar "as much School learning as the way of live [life] he is designed for will require," Bernard placed him with a merchant house in Boston before helping him to establish his own business in 1765. His third son, Thomas, a "very good Classick Scholar," was sent to Harvard, where in 1770 he graduated with a master of arts degree and "entertained" the commencement with a thesis in the arcane Chaldaic language, reputedly the "first of the Kind exhibited in America."[106] Thomas was closer to his father than any of his siblings and became his stenographer.

Frank, the eldest son, was eager to see the world beyond England. His father, however, who soon regretted his son's "abundant curiosity," tried to impress the scholarly Benjamin Franklin by describing Frank as an "uncommon schollar" who had "master[ed]" Latin, Greek, and Hebrew "to a greater perfection" than other boys his age, and who dabbled in Newtonian physics.[107] Frank Bernard was certainly a bright young man. Viscount Barrington enlisted the support of the duke of Newcastle to get Frank a Westminster scholarship at Christ Church, where he flourished in his first two years.[108] Thereafter, Bernard's insistence that after university Frank should pursue a career was a source of much friction. Frank had everything that Bernard had had and more—above all the stability and peace to develop his intellect and take stock of his prospects. But his son's "precipitate desire of hurrying into the Study of Life and manners" gradually disturbed his father.[109]

Like most young men of his age and status, Frank yearned to see something of the world. A head injury he suffered at Westminster, shortly before his parents left for America, may have been the root cause of Frank's excitable disposition and rebellious attitude toward his father, though the injury was not considered serious at the time. Equally, the parental guilt the separation induced probably accentuated Bernard's overprotectiveness.

Bernard was fast becoming a distant father to his sons, and his paternal influence was irrevocably weakened by their three-year separation. In 1761, a year before Frank's majority, Bernard insisted that Frank interrupt his studies and come to Boston in order to "settle the future plan of his destinations." The "interview," as Bernard called it, was anything but successful.[110] Frank arrived safely in October 1762 but alarmed his father with a story of how he was obliged to change ship at Madeira after the captain had lodged him in the steerage, where his belongings were stolen.[111] Such effrontery aside, Frank, it seems, knew nothing of his father's plan to get him appointed Naval

Officer at Boston, one of the few positions to which Bernard had the sole right of making recommendations to the Board of Trade.[112] Ignoring "all kinds of Offers of employment," Frank refused to return to Oxford.[113]

Bernard could be just as stubborn as his son when crossed. After a bitter row with his father in October 1763, Frank and a companion left Boston for Philadelphia, and traveled two hundred miles to Fort Pitt on the Ohio River frontier. His first communication came some six weeks later from a tavern in Alexandria, Virginia, where he remained for two months, subsisting on credit. Bernard was grateful for Benjamin Franklin's assistance in returning Frank to Boston,[114] and viewed his son's return to Christ Church to complete his degree as "a Term of Probation" that might afford "some kind of Proof that he might be trusted in another Station."[115]

The "Instructions" Frank received spoke of Bernard's disappointment in having to "dictate . . . with the Authority of a Father" instead of "concerting" with him as a friend. Frank was forbidden to go to London during vacations, given a strict allowance of seventy pounds, and ordered to send progress reports. Bernard was clearly nonplussed by Frank's individualistic streak, but his correspondence also alludes to his son's errant or possibly aberrant behavior—"vicious habits" that were eroding his "religious & moral" principles. We can only speculate as to what these "habits" were—womanizing, homosexuality, or gambling, perhaps—but they were the basis of some "extremely disagreable [sic]" reports concerning subsequent misdemeanors at Christ Church,[116] which were "sufficient to show the Necessity of removing him from College" before he was disciplined by the dean.[117] Bernard was loath to commit his own son to "perpetual disgrace & probable ruin," but he resolved to get him out of England, and asked Barrington to find him a commission in the army.[118] Eventually, Bernard relented, and sent his son a heartfelt plea for reconciliation that is the most affectionate letter he has left to posterity. "As soon as you come here," Bernard promised, "whether we are to agree or disagree, things shall be settled in the best manner they can. For I will not live in continual altercation with one I love."[119] Frank took his degree in 1766, the same year that Britain approved Bernard's scheme to have him succeed Benjamin Pemberton as Massachusetts's Naval Officer,[120] which position he held jointly with Pemberton until his untimely death in 1770.

*   *   *

New Englanders never warmed to Francis Bernard, thinking him vain and arrogant and too easily offended. Bernard was all of these things. But he was also a dutiful father, a benign patriarch with an authoritarian streak whose career ambitions were driven by the simple desire to provide his children with every possible advantage in life. Bernard certainly owed his appointment as a colonial governor to his connections with Whig politicians, but he was manifestly an able administrator. The colonists never forgot that Bernard had powerful friends but they too readily supposed that he lacked experience in public administration. Bernard drew heavily on these experiences in the colonies. In New Jersey, he strove to represent the colonists as best he might, and was more successful than the vociferous criticism he later attracted might suggest. In Massachusetts, a more fractious polity, Bernard encountered a far more challenging set of problems, and a people wary that he might just as easily turn his noble patrons against them.

CHAPTER TWO

"Harmony between the King and People"
The Governance of Empire, 1760–1764

$\mathcal{B}$ERNARD'S ARRIVAL in Massachusetts in the summer of 1760 was a choreographed celebration of royal government. Bernard delayed leaving New Jersey until 28 July, ostensibly to await his replacement, Thomas Boone, but also to ensure that the departure of the popular outgoing governor, Thomas Pownall, did not cast a shadow on his enterprise. Pownall and Bernard had met secretly in New London, Connecticut, in early April to discuss affairs of state and possibly Bernard's idea for a grand entrance. Pownall left for England on 3 June with the colonists' praises ringing in his ears, accompanied by the young John Hancock, a nephew of a close friend. Bernard had none of Pownall's connections and was determined to make an impression by being the first governor since William Burnet in 1728 to enter Massachusetts by land.[1]

Bernard issued careful instructions but left Massachusetts's senior executive officers to make the arrangements so that he "mayn't appear to have been a mover in this business" lest any penny-pinching colonist object.[2] The province sloop, the *Prince George,* left Bernard and his wife at Newport, Rhode Island, on 30 July. They were welcomed by the province secretary of Massachusetts, Andrew Oliver, and lodged with the Newport collector before taking a boat to Providence. On Friday, 1 August, they set out by coach for Wrentham, Massachusetts, where they were met by a troop of the governor's horse guards and the county sheriff, Stephen Greenleaf. The party moved on to Boston the next day, by way of Dedham, and on the twelve-mile journey were accompanied in "a very Magnificent Manner . . . by a multitude of gentlemen in their coaches and chariots." Bernard was greeted at the Province House, the governor's official residence, by a coterie of eminent citizens and escorted on the half-mile walk to the Town House by the Company of Cadets, an honorary bodyguard. King Street was lined with people, and the Boston militia saluted Bernard as he entered the redbrick building. Upstairs in the council chamber, Bernard received his royal commission from a committee of the province legislature and took his oath of office before the acting governor, Thomas Hutchinson. As he moved outside onto the small balcony overlooking King Street, the townspeople and the soldiers shouted three huzzahs, and a thundering cannonade rang out from the town batteries and the Royal Navy warships anchored in the harbor. That night Bernard dined with the town's finest at Faneuil Hall. His children arrived a few days later, and he received the customary round of welcoming addresses from the municipal authorities, the province clergy, and the Boston merchants.[3] It was a promising beginning.

Within three weeks, Bernard had addressed the General Court and received his salary and removal expenses in an atmosphere of "uncommon unanimity."[4] Thirty years earlier, Governor Belcher's first words were of providence and his Puritan heritage;[5] Bernard's were of empire and the colonists' secular obligations. His "Inclination as an Englishman" was to preserve both the colonists' "general Rights as British Subjects" and the "particular Priviledges" conferred on them by the Charter of 1691. The colonists were never easily impressed, but they welcomed Bernard with grace and good humor, noting that he seemed "perfectly well acquainted with the Rules of civil Policy and the Laws of the Land." Bernard's "wise and good conduct" in New Jersey also drew particular praise.[6] Thus Bernard supposed that "Harmony between the king and people" would prevail in the governance of empire.

The encomiums, which reaffirmed the colonists' loyalty and reiterated the governor's vice-regal responsibilities, papered over conflicts of interest between the Crown and the legislature, but the installation of a new governor was a rare opportunity for all citizens to celebrate their British heritage. Bernard was blessed with several such moments, including the accession of George III later that year and the victory over the French in 1763.[7] Bernard was never so ready to defer to the colonists' sensibilities as he was during these nervous early encounters. The goodwill he experienced on the road to Boston did not last long, though he expended considerable effort in trying to persuade the British to be more tolerant of the colonists and the colonists to remember their obligations to the Crown.

*   *   *

Before politics intruded upon his reverie, Bernard was content with life in Boston, a seaport of sixteen thousand inhabitants. He moved his family into the Province House, an elegant three-story mansion, situated in the heart of the town. Bernard found much to like about his new abode. Cocooned from the bustle of the town, the children played safely in the gardens, where Bernard tended a greenhouse and an orchard. The family was attended by "a great number of servants" paid for by the province, including Cato, a black cook and probably a slave, who returned with them to England.[8] As winter approached, however, Bernard found that he had to order his own coal (from the Cape Breton mines) and replace the stoves and grates in many of the rooms.[9] He also began redecorating at his own expense the public and private rooms, some of which were already wood paneled. From the items that the Bernards sold at auction when they left Boston, Higgins deduced that the house was comfortably but not grandly furnished: there was a set of three tables that fit together to form a horseshoe around the main fire in the great room during winter evenings; a mahogany four-poster; rich curtains of crimson damask and blue and white chintz; a "great variety" of china, silver cutlery, gardening tools, and "Sundry Mathematical instruments"; a library; the contents of a wine cellar; plus mundane items like bedding.[10] The Bernards' standard of living was not as sumptuous as that of English county gentry, but the items listed on the bill of sale, which were probably also collected from Bernard's house at Jamaica Plain, were commonplace in the mansions of Boston's richest merchants, though not in the room-and-parlor homes of the provincial elite living elsewhere. Similarly, Bernard possessed his own carriage (probably a four-horse coach), the likes of which was a rare sight in Boston's uncobbled, crowded streets. (It would have had to have been imported from England unless it was commissioned from Adino Paddock, Boston's chaisemaker.) The province also maintained smaller carriages for his family's use.[11]

A public day was scheduled each week at the Province House, when Bernard conversed and dined with provincial dignitaries, but he was soon obliged to hold meetings most afternoons. On these occasions, recalled his daughter Julia, Bernard "dressed superbly" in his regalia of office, yet seemed uncomfortable with the "parade of Government & the great concourse of company." It was a "peculiar state of intercourse," she noted, with "everybody coming to us, and we going to nobody."[12] Bernard was a gregarious man but he cherished his privacy. At Amelia's request, he refurbished the apartments at Castle William, out in the harbor. The family spent most summers there, and for the children swimming and sailing rather than lessons were the order of the day. Bernard enjoyed excellent health, but the same could not be said of his wife, who was "much weaken'd" by winter fevers.[13] Despite her ailments, Francis consulted Amelia on matters of state—though how often and to what effect is impossible to say—and she devoted her time to educating the children.

An Englishwoman once remarked that "All the Luxury & Elegance . . . is confined to Boston, & twenty miles around, if you travel further it is necessary to carry your Provisions with you."[14] To some Bostonians, Bernard and his family may have appeared just as aloof, but Bernard was no snob where food and drink were concerned. The recipes, such as for elder wine and green-pea soup, that he gave his cousin Jane Beresford reveal a taste for wholesome country cooking.[15] In New Jersey, he had developed a liking for Swedish pickled salmon, cider, and caviar, and later sought the advice of the polymath Benjamin Franklin with respect to the merits of establishing his own sturgeon fishery.[16] Bernard loved Madeira wine and red port as much as the colonists, but these items were subject to heavy import duties. His personal supplies were smuggled "by way of Falmouth" on the northeastern coast. He regularly obtained other delicacies such as hams, onions, plums, and lemons, packed as ships' stores to fool customs, plus seeds of several varieties of shrubs and trees for his garden.[17] These were supplemented by consignments of old English cheeses.[18] His voracious appetite for young cod—the food of Boston's common people—was ridiculed as unbecoming to his station.[19]

Bernard enjoyed the company of the province's cognoscenti. He helped Harvard professor John Winthrop, one of the few American members of the Royal Society, to obtain funding from the General Court for his expedition to Newfoundland to observe the transit of Venus.[20] He learned tales of exploration in the New World from the British army surveyor Francis Miller and something of colonial history from Thomas Hutchinson. Bernard impressed with his mastery of Latin and Greek and his recitations from Shakespeare, and was a welcome dinner guest of merchant princes John Rowe and John

Hancock.[21] His fastidiousness could be irritating, however. He scolded friends for misspelling his surname *Barnard* though that was how he pronounced it in his English upper-class accent, emphasizing the first syllable and elongating the vowel; in the Yankee dialect it would have sounded harsher to him, like "B'naad" or "Birnäd" with the emphasis on the second syllable.[22] Conversely, Bernard probably found the Puritanism of men like Dr. Charles Chauncy rather stifling, though he dutifully issued royal proclamations against vices such as gambling. The imperial controversy drove a wedge between Bernard and the gentry of Boston and Cambridge, and by the mid-1760s he had restricted his companionship to fellow members of the Anglican King's Chapel and the Boston Episcopal Charity Society.

"We have not made a bad exchange," Thomas Hutchinson told his Harvard classmate Col. Israel Williams. Swallowing his pride at being passed over for the governorship, Hutchinson got on with the business of helping Bernard and his family to settle in. But he stopped short of briefing Bernard about colonial politics until he knew more of what Pownall had told the new governor.[23] Bernard, however, supposed he might repeat Pownall's successes and looked forward to a "quiet & easy administration."[24] He trusted that he was about to "enter upon the Government, without any party being formed against me."[25] It was a privilege denied virtually all his predecessors.

In his quest to win New Englanders' confidence, Bernard faced numerous obstacles—some political, economic, and social, others personal. Perhaps the most basic of these was his metropolitan prejudice. Bernard supposed that Americans wanted, or ought to want, much the same things as Britons: victory over the French, political stability, and economic growth. These aims were not antithetical to colonial interests, of course, but were often presented in such a way as to dismiss the distinct and often divergent aspirations of the peoples of the Atlantic fringe—Americans, Scots, Irish, and Welsh: to put it bluntly, British imperialism was invariably English nationalism writ large.[26] The capture of Montreal in September 1760 and the reduction of Canada, which Bernard proclaimed England's "greatest prize" since the medieval "Conquest" of France, was an enormous boost to his self-confidence.[27] When Bernard met the General Court for a second time on 17 December, his optimism was infectious. He foresaw the "firm establishment of the *British* Empire in *North-America* and [the] Superiority of It's Power" offering new beginnings:

the "connexion between these Provinces and their Mother-Country is now well understood and put upon the best Footing, that of filial obedience and parental protection mutually promoting each other."[28] The General Court's reply contained none of the antagonistic language that typified later exchanges and put great store in the continuation of royal government.[29] One colonist thought that Bernard talked "like a weak honest Man," a view the young John Adams dismissed as a "silly thoughtless Repetition of what he had heard others say." Adams was less judgmental than he would be in 1765, seeing "no Marks of Knavery" and several "marks of good sense" despite several grammatical "Inaccuracies."[30]

The good feelings that distinguished the early years of Bernard's administration owed much to the fact that victory over the French was now in sight. The colonies had been at war since 1754, and before the peace was concluded between 15,000 and 20,000 Massachusetts men served in the provincial and British regiments. Over 10,000 recruits were called up in Massachusetts in 1759 and 1760, and saw service mainly in Nova Scotia, at Louisbourg, in Quebec, and at Crown Point in upper New York. Three-quarters of Massachusetts's 245,000 inhabitants lived and worked on the land, and it was they who swelled the ranks of the British and provincial regiments.

The militarization of colonial society, however, accounted for much of the colonists' assertiveness. Daily contact between colonial and British soldiers raised awareness of basic differences that was occasionally expressed in quasi-nationalistic terms. Bernard had little contact with these Yankees but knew enough of military affairs from New Jersey to be wary of dismissing their complaints about discipline, poor provisions, and the profanity of the British. Fortunately, he was able to choose the provincial officers, and, in consultation with the provincial commanders, he selected officers on merit—a practice alien to the British army.[31] He was pleased by the overall quality of the provincial recruits and deeply impressed by their stoic patriotism. "The common People," he told his superiors in London, "seemed to be animated with the Spirit of the General Court, and to vie with them in their Readiness to serve the King."[32]

It would be disingenuous to say that Bernard was able to raise colonial regiments with little fuss each spring until the very eve of peace.[33] The main cause of friction was the desire of the British commander, Gen. Jeffery Amherst, to deploy some of the colonials to the disease-ridden Caribbean and the insistence of the General

Court that the recruits should not be sent "south of Albany."[34] Bernard could hardly refuse to tell the recruits where they were going if any regiments were to be put in the field in 1761. "Tho the Assembly were not entitled to these Assurances, yet the men, who are all to be Volunteers, are."[35] Persuading the British to respect the colonists' sensibilities was never easy.

Amherst was five years Bernard's junior, a man of middling origins like Bernard who had risen far in the service of his country. They had met two years before at Bernard's home in Perth Amboy in what was probably their only encounter. Some of Amherst's military colleagues thought him lethargic,[36] but it was the general's obstinacy that Bernard found hard to take. Amherst showed little understanding of Bernard's predicament—of how he had to negotiate with between twenty and thirty representatives who, if they wished, could easily get the House to trim the military budget or cut the enlistment period.[37] Amherst dismissed the assembly's arguments as "frivolous pretences," yet eventually accepted the General Court's conditions of service.[38]

Amherst had also been urging Britain to put the provincials in the regular regiments, and in 1762 the colonies were asked to raise fourteen thousand soldiers for the provincial regiments and another four thousand to serve with the regulars. Massachusetts contributed about a quarter of the eight hundred troops she was asked to provide for the regulars. It might have been more, Bernard thought, were it not for the unnecessarily strict regulations on the height and age of recruits, and the Yankees' "great shyness" at serving under British officers.[39] Amherst, however, rejected Bernard's proposal that they be formed into separate provincial companies.

When a French fleet took the Island of St. John's in Newfoundland in 1762, a diversionary action to Britain's Caribbean campaign, Massachusetts had nearly exhausted its manpower resource. All Bernard could send the province governor by way of assistance at short notice was fifty men from the recruiting service. Although fishing and commerce along the northeastern coast were disrupted, he offered that it was not "in his power to raise Men for this purpose, unless the Danger was more urgent."[40] Bernard was shocked when, after the Council appropriated five hundred pounds to refit the province sloop for the St. John's campaign, he was criticized for usurping the House's control of the purse. The House had never been slow to protest any infringement before, but Bernard did not spare the members with his "hard words." James Otis, the Boston representative, responded with an influential essay decrying executive infringements to the House's legislative privileges.[41] Despite the bickering, some five hundred Massachusetts soldiers served with distinction when St. John's was recaptured in October.[42] These men did not forget the arrogance of Amherst's officers when, thirteen years later, they turned out against the redcoats. The sturdy yeoman farmer of revolutionary iconography, ready to defend his liberty at a moment's notice, was no myth.

Despite his upbeat approach to military affairs, Bernard was pessimistic in his assessment of the war's impact upon Massachusetts's economy. Economic growth had been steady if uneven for most of the century, with the colonies experiencing alternate periods of boom and stagnation. The French wars enriched many a colonial trader, preeminently wholesale merchants like the Hancocks and the Ervings who won supply contracts. It also fueled demand for British goods, which in consequence, as Bernard observed, led to an expansion in the numbers of importing shopkeepers. Less than 3 percent of the colony's population made a living from commerce, but by the mid-1760s about 11 percent of adult males in Boston were traders.[43] Another issue was that colonial indebtedness to British houses and banks reached disturbing levels (£1.28 million by 1772). Traders operating with extended lines of credit were extremely vulnerable to fluctuations in European exchange rates, so much so that the 1764 credit crisis in Amsterdam led the colony into an economic depression.[44] Partly to relieve their predicament and partly to realize their "expansionist" designs, colonial merchants began to argue for unfettered access to British and foreign markets. This was the underlying issue of contention, when instead of relaxing the trade laws Britain began to shore up the mercantilist system.

The war had also put Massachusetts's public finances under severe strain. Massachusetts spent £490,000 on the war effort, on top of £108,000 required for government. She received £328,000 in compensation from Britain, but struggled to meet the shortfall.[45] The problem was particularly acute because of the shortage of specie. The Land Bank scheme of 1739, which aimed to issue paper money backed by mortgages, had collapsed when Governor Shirley and the province's hard-money merchants marshaled British opposition. Parliamentary legislation of 1751 restricted the issue of bills of credit as a circulating medium, ruining hundreds of colonial debtors—farmers, artisans, and small traders mainly, including the father of Samuel

Adams. The currency debate was revived in 1762 when Thomas Hutchinson, an expert on public finance, proposed reducing imports by devaluing the Massachusetts currency, which was based on silver, by introducing a gold standard.

James Otis championed the colony's debtors, but Bernard instinctively and in line with British policy sided with the hard-money men. He reluctantly assented to a bill that backed currency with both silver and gold, which reduced the price of goods in the long run and benefited the province by improving the balance of trade.[46] Bernard refused the province agents permission to lobby for the right to print currency and, with the Council's agreement, urged Britain to resist the temptation to repeal the prohibition on currency emissions. Paper money, he once wrote, was the "Negative Power of Riches. . . . It at first occasions all the Specie in the Country to be carried out of it; and afterwards it creates a Want of an extraordinary Quantity of Specie to pay the Debts of which it bears the Testimony."[47]

Fiscal conservatives warmed to Bernard's appeal to adopt a "Spirit of Industry, Frugality and Oeconomy." From 1763, Bernard, the provincial treasurer, and the General Court aimed to reduce the province debt to £160,000 by June 1765, excluding interest, and to discharge the entire sum by 1769. This was funded by increasing provincial taxes to £100,000 per annum, never a popular course of action, but to which the Massachusetts elite was now largely reconciled; by sinking £40,000 or £50,000 each year the debt was reduced to £40,000 by 1771.[48]

The British government in London was not really interested in whether a colony's financial problems made a governor's life more difficult, provided public finances were kept in order. To the British, a governor's main job was to keep the empire working, by compromise and persuasion, and not a little cajolery. That was how governors had managed in the past to deal with colonial complaints about the Navigation Acts, currency regulation, or the resourcing of the regiments. To the colonial elites, however, an accomplished governor devoted his time and energy to promoting colonial interests. New Englanders, Bernard once wrote, will not "allow a Governor to be neutral in their Disputes with Great Britain, but expect that he shall Side with them in their Pretensions against the Parliament."[49]

Bernard knew enough about the colonists' reverence for the Charter of 1691 to understand why they resented metropolitan interference. The Privy Council overturned, upon the recommendation of the Board of Trade, less than 5 percent of all colonial legislation largely because governors were able to veto offensive acts.[50] Even so, Bernard told the Board of Trade, the colonists regarded the Privy Council's superintending authority as a real threat to the integrity of colonial self-government.[51] Effective royal government, Bernard soon realized, rested not only upon Crown prerogatives but also on the full cooperation of colonial institutions.

Only occasionally was the Massachusetts elite called upon to consider imperial issues, and the main function of the House of Representatives was to attend to provincial affairs in a corporate fashion, acting in conjunction with the Council and the governor. For governors, the most worrying political development in the eighteenth century was the success of the provincial assemblies in extending influence over royal officials. Bernard could not fail to have been concerned by the fate of Amelia's uncle, Samuel Shute, whose "Political Error," he believed, "was making too many Concessions in hopes of Peace." With the colony facing the threat of a French invasion, Shute had contested the right of the House to elect its own speaker. The underlying issues were Shute's request for a permanent salary and the governor's authority to control where and when the House would meet—Shute lost on both counts, but when he returned to England in 1723, the Privy Council issued an additional charter recognizing the House's privilege of choosing a speaker subject to the governor's approval.[52] Payment of the governor's salary was a perennial issue of contention, for the General Court had successfully resisted governors' demands to legislate permanent salaries, for the governor, his deputy, and the senior judges, who were paid by annual grants. The dependency of royal officials was a common refrain in Bernard's reports.

Cooperation between the governor and the House was often problematic, for the representatives were primarily agents of the towns, which generated most legislative business. Written instructions from constituents, as some representatives now called their electors, were not common until the mid-1760s, but representatives had to account for their actions on Election Day. On average, about 40 percent of the House was replaced each year. The most influential were the representatives with the longest service or those who enjoyed the confidence of their neighbors and colleagues.[53]

Bernard accepted that corporatism and localism were twin pillars of royal government, but found the democratic aspects of colonial

politics and egalitarian social attitudes very disturbing. He was appalled to learn that in Boston and most other towns a majority of
adult males were voting in elections, despite property restrictions.[54]
Many years later he wrote that

> *so uniform a System of bringing all Power into the Hands of the
> People has been prosecuted without Interruption & with such
> Success, that all that Fear Reverence, Respect & Awe which be-
> fore formed a tolerable Ballance against the real Power of the
> People, are annihilated & the artificial Weights being removed,
> the royal Scale mounts up & kicks the Beam.*[55]

To all intents and purposes, the town meeting was a forum for white
male democracy. Because of deference,[56] however, colonists consistently limited their choice of town officials and representatives to
"leadership pools" made up of wealthy and long-established local
families, or men with extensive political or military experience. Boston's leadership pool never exceeded 1 percent of inhabitants, while
those elsewhere were generally around 6 percent.[57] In the towns of
the Connecticut River valley, the so-called "River Gods" dominated
local and county affairs as much as any English squire.[58]

Massachusetts's political leaders were not an oligarchy but an elite
that enjoyed broad-based popular support. Local and provincial government were conducted not only by the wealthiest members of the
community but also by the "middling sort"—a large proprietorial
group of yeoman farmers, professionals, craftsmen, and traders of
one sort or another. Around 10 percent of the population were artisans, some of whom confused the British by adopting the title of
"gentleman." Subsistence-farming communities were the most socially homogeneous of all communities. However, in ports such as
Salem, Gloucester, and Marblehead wealth and power were concentrated in the hands of relatively few property owners and creditors.

Social inequality was most pronounced in Boston. Per capita income levels for England and New England were roughly similar, and
the town's merchants were among the wealthiest in America, as prosperous as the Virginia planters and the upper echelons of English
gentry. The opulence of someone such as Nicholas Boylston, which
no doubt impressed Bernard as it did the young John Adams, was the
consequence of Boston's emergence as a major entrepot at the center
of transatlantic commerce. For all their gentility and pride, the mer-

chants were enterprising and pragmatic. The Boylstons were among
the first Americans to trade with Russia, and before he died Nicholas
Boylston bequeathed fifteen hundred pounds to Harvard to endow a
chair.[59] The merchants' conspicuous consumption never blinded
them to social or political realities. A third of Boston's adult males
were propertyless. In spite of the contempt that men of his back-
ground held for society's lower orders, Bernard was distressed by
their suffering after the Great Fire of 1760, which destroyed nearly
one-third of the town's buildings and left hundreds destitute.[60] His
compassion soon evaporated when some of the protests against British policies bore the hallmarks of social conflict. Political radicalism
was never as extreme as in Europe's much larger urban centers,
largely because of the wider distribution of property and greater opportunities for social mobility.

The British, however, always regarded Massachusetts as a fractious polity. The factions that made a governor's lot so difficult were
not organized parties but amorphous groups bound by kinship and a
sense of public duty as much as by competition for offices and ideology. Their community of feeling was durable, even though they
formed short-lived coalitions in response to particular issues.[61]

The "court" faction was not solely a party of officeholders and governor's friends as the term suggests. If defined by denomination and
status, Anglicans, wealthy merchants, and well-to-do farmers pre-
dominated. Most were fiscal conservatives and represented the more
prosperous commercial-farming towns of eastern Massachusetts.
The Bostonians among them had long since moved out of town, to
tranquil towns like Milton, Medford, Roxbury, and Cambridge.
What coherent leadership there was came from Thomas Hutchinson, Andrew Oliver, and Col. Israel Williams, the "monarch" of
Hampshire County.

The country faction contained more representatives from subsistence-farming towns, mainly yeoman farmers, who spoke out against
the plural officeholding of the Hutchinsons and Olivers and favored
an inflationary financial policy. In Boston, the popular party, based
on the town's "caucuses" and merchants' committees, was a particularly formidable association. Worried by the concentration of power
in the hands of the Hutchinson-Oliver clique, these men gravitated
toward popular leaders such as Samuel Adams who brought to local
politics the communitarianism associated with the Puritan covenant-
ing traditions.[62]

Hard-money merchants and court faction leaders like Hutchinson were committed mercantilists, although like most colonists they would have liked to have seen lifted many of the restrictions placed on colonial commerce. Country leaders such as the Otises and many of the merchants who led the opposition to Britain were ultimately more confident of America's future prosperity without the protection afforded by Britain's imperial might.[63]

However much Bernard thought his prospects seemed promising he had to be wary of alienating both main factions. The executive officers and judges who were elected to the Council were invariably political allies of the governor. But a governor could easily offend these men if he exercised his veto over councilors or colonial legislation carelessly. There did not exist in the General Court or any other colonial legislature a substantial body of placemen, unlike the imperial Parliament where half the members could be "King's Friends."[64] Governors' independent powers of patronage were limited and of little use in tempering dissent; virtually all appointments required the assent of the Council, which could never be taken for granted, and confirmation by the Crown, which might take several months. Governors, then, had few legitimate political tools at their disposal, and persuasion rather than coercion was their rule of thumb in dealing with the General Court.

Bernard's sociability and legalistic mind were useful assets in confronting the challenges that awaited him. So too was his connection with the British political elite. Bernard counted among his patrons one secretary at war—Barrington—and three secretaries of state—the duke of Newcastle, the earl of Halifax, and the earl of Hillsborough. The most successful governors, however, were those who had friends among the colonial elite. Some such as William Shirley and Thomas Pownall had also managed to appeal to the colonists' economic interests and cultivate friends among leading merchants, despite bitter wrangles over currency policy and military affairs.[65] Bernard had few of the advantages of his predecessors. Shirley, Massachusetts's longest serving royal governor (1747–57), was born in England, but had spent many years in Boston as a lawyer and officeholder, and was well connected to the provincial elite. Under Shirley the court faction flourished. His thirty-eight-year-old successor, Thomas Pownall, had a predilection for informality in both his dress and the conduct of business, which attracted some adverse comment, but he was widely respected for his erudition, and later wrote extensively on a range of subjects from imperial administration to geography and economics. John Adams once described Pownall as "a friend of liberty," largely on account of his later criticism of Bernard, but also perhaps because as governor he aligned himself with the country faction. By the time Pownall entered the House of Commons in 1767 and made a name for himself as a commentator on American affairs, the New Englanders had come to regret ever setting eyes on his replacement.

*   *   *

It was not what Bernard had to say on imperial affairs so much as his lack of political sagacity that first irritated the colonists. Bernard's ignorance of the nuances of Massachusetts politics was never more evident than in the first significant controversy that dogged his administration—the appointment of a chief justice of the Superior Court in succession to Stephen Sewell, who died in September 1760. Most members of the General Court were officeholders at one time or another, and rivalry for provincial offices was a major cause of partisanship.[66] The personal animosities between Hutchinson and the Otises, arising from the competition for the vacant chief justiceship, made their political rivalries more intense. For Bernard it was a rude introduction to colonial politics.

Bernard knew little of the man whom many regarded as the ideal candidate. Col. James Otis was a successful lawyer from one of the colony's most socially mobile families. As a leader of the country faction in the General Court, his political realism oiled the wheels of colonial government; his power base, such as it was, rested with the provincial farmers. Governor Pownall warmly approved Otis's election as House Speaker, and appointed his son James deputy advocate-general of the Vice Admiralty court. With the Otises on his side Pownall thought he would be more able to counter the designs of his deputy, Thomas Hutchinson. Pownall also reiterated a promise first made to Otis by Governor Shirley: that he would appoint the colonel to the Superior Court as soon as there was a vacancy. It would be a fitting honor for this seasoned public servant. Pownall's replacement, however, was bound by no such pledge.

Bernard's views on the affair are for once obscure though his motives were entirely political. It is most unlikely that, when Bernard and Pownall met in New London, Pownall would have spared Bernard his views on either Otis or Hutchinson. At first, though, Bernard tried to keep an open mind. Hutchinson refrained from badgering the governor—his friends did that for him—perhaps because he was beset by a rare moment of self-doubt; alone among the likely candidates (councilor William Brattle and Superior Court justice Benjamin Lynde were the others) Hutchinson had no legal training. Colonel Otis, meanwhile, genuinely believed that Hutchinson would champion his candidacy. According to Hutchinson, however, Bernard resolved not to appoint Otis irrespective of whether or not Hutchinson wished to be considered for the position; only then did he offer to make Hutchinson chief justice. Bernard, it seems, was obliged to make a straight choice: between Otis, a stolid lawyer and reliable legislator well versed in the mechanics of provincial politics, and the urbane Hutchinson, who knew more about the dynamics of royal government than anyone else in the province. This did not mean, as historians once supposed, that because of the looming controversy over the enforcement of the trade laws, Bernard had already made up his mind. Whatever he did, one of the principal candidates would lose face. It did not take Bernard long to decide that he could least afford to alienate Hutchinson. Much later Bernard apologized to Lord Justice Mansfield for getting Hutchinson appointed, but never seriously regretted this decision.[67]

Hutchinson and Bernard were roughly the same age, and although they freely exchanged views on colonial politics and British policies in the years to come, they approached these subjects from different vantage points. Hutchinson, a moderate Congregationalist and scion of one of Massachusetts's first families, had succeeded in the confines of a provincial world that Bernard had stumbled into. Leaving his sons to run the family business, Hutchinson devoted his time to public affairs and completing his magnum opus, a three-volume history of Massachusetts. He succeeded Bernard as governor in 1771 having served him loyally, despite, Bailyn notes, having good cause to resent him both "personally and politically."[68]

Hutchinson and Bernard did not so much like as tolerate one another, though in time they came to respect each other. They disagreed privately many times during the imperial controversies of the 1760s, in matters of both style and substance. By disposition, Hutchinson was a pragmatic politician, but never pedestrian, always preferring diplomacy to confrontation. Hutchinson was a "much prudenter man than I ever pretended to be," Bernard once conceded, though always a "fair dealing Man."[69] Bernard needed Hutchinson for his influence with leading colonists as much as his leadership qualities. Hutchinson, on the other hand, liked to suppose that away from the public gaze the roles were reversed: that he was the diligent and cerebral magistrate whose sufferance was the foibles of an insecure and irresolute Englishman. Bernard seemed restless and impatient in high office, too "open in his behaviour," Hutchinson once recalled, "regardless of mere forms, and inattentive to the fashionable arts of engaging mankind."[70] Many times Hutchinson criticized Bernard for lacking political acumen, but he could not afford to alienate Bernard if he wanted to succeed him as governor.

Bernard was never indifferent to the price he had to pay for securing Hutchinson's loyalty. His own unpopularity was to some extent a reflection of his association with Hutchinson. Colonel Otis did not endure slights easily. Neither did his gifted, impetuous son, James Otis Jr., who resigned from the administration when Hutchinson became chief justice. For now at least, the Otises spared Bernard the anger they vented at Hutchinson. But it was the end of Bernard's honeymoon period as governor. The reverberations of the Otis-Hutchinson feud in a few months prompted Bernard to take a more politically proactive role, but in truth there was little Bernard could do to extricate himself from the imperial controversies he encountered in his first year as governor.

The dispute over the enforcement of the trade laws began in earnest before Bernard's arrival, when the British tried to reverse decades of neglect in combating the colonists' illicit trade with the French colonies in the West Indies. For the first time in sixteen years the customhouse initiated prosecutions in the Vice Admiralty court against several colonial merchants, the most prominent of whom was John Erving, a member of the Governor's Council, whose vessel was confiscated and sold. Bernard was the nominal head of the Massachusetts Vice Admiralty court, one of eleven such courts, but naively told the British there was no evidence in the court records of smuggling and blamed instead the merchants of Connecticut and Rhode Island. Bernard was not easily persuaded that otherwise reputable men were determined lawbreakers.[71]

Two things changed his mind. Bernard learned from Charles Paxton, the surveyor and searcher at Boston, and the British government that collusion between customs officers and colonial merchants was the main reason why the revenue collected from trade duties was so low. When Bernard tried to assist Paxton and his colleagues to up-

Thomas Hutchinson, Bernard's erudite deputy and successor as governor. By Edward Truman. Courtesy of the Massachusetts Historical Society.

hold the trade laws, he was accused of having a vested interest in seeing smugglers brought to book. That was true enough: as the law stood, Bernard was entitled to a one-third share of the profits arising from seizures; one-third was reserved to the king for the province's use, from which informers were paid, while the remaining third went to the officer who brought the case to court. Bernard had not come to Massachusetts with a preconceived plan to prosecute smugglers for

his own pecuniary gain, although that was what he was accused of
when the British took steps to improve law enforcement.

In December 1760 the Boston merchants and the General Court
claimed that admiralty court officials had misappropriated moneys
from the province's share of seizures since 1753 and made illegal pay-
ments to informers, a total sum in excess of five hundred pounds.
Bernard had no desire to be dragged into the affair, and reluctantly
agreed to a bill instructing province treasurer Harrison Gray to sue
for the recovery of the money (*Gray v Paxton et al.*). The Superior
Court deemed the suit technically invalid, but another was brought
in the name of the province, which was successful. Potentially more
damaging to the customhouse, as Bernard reported, was the case of
Erving v Craddock, by which Erving and his fellow merchants aimed
to prove that in making seizures customs officers were liable for trespass and damages. Erving was awarded five hundred pounds by the
Massachusetts Superior Court, which the customhouse appealed to
the Privy Council. Erving withdrew his action in March 1761 only because of the expense involved. Bernard was shocked by Erving's
openness and the jury's bias against the customhouse, as reputedly
were also representatives from the eastern ports, but these men were
in the minority.[72]

In February and April 1761 Bernard participated in an inquiry
headed by Judge Chambers Russell of the Vice Admiralty court into
the activities of a disaffected customs official, Benjamin Barons. Barons was suspended from duty in December 1759 when Charles Paxton
accused him of corruption. A detailed report was sent to London.
Bernard found some disturbing evidence of a well-organized illicit
trade between the New England colonies and New Orleans in skins,
indigo, molasses, and Dutch tea mainly, and set his heart on exposing
the Bostonians involved. The French smugglers he interrogated, if
not working with the tacit support of Barons, who had been temporarily reinstated, had certainly benefited from the collector's studied
negligence; they also took advantage of Bernard's leniency by ab-
sconding from parole.[73]

Bernard's use of troops to seize one vessel provoked an extraordinary outburst from Barons. The collector interrupted Bernard while
he was at lunch to demand for himself and his men a share of any
profits arising from the condemnation of the vessel. When Bernard
refused, Barons claimed to know that Bernard was soon to be replaced.[74] Bernard drew no credit from the contretemps. "Self-inter-

John Erving, Sr. By John Singleton Copley. Courtesy of Smith College Museum of Art, Northampton, Massachusetts, bequest of Alice Rutherford Erving.

est," he confessed, "made it necessary for me to accuse" Barons and support Paxton.[75] He was pleasantly surprised, however, when the House of Representatives refused to consider Barons's request of 2 February 1762 to investigate Paxton's accusations, but it is otherwise difficult to identify support for Bernard on this issue among the court faction. Eighteen days later Bernard learned that Barons had been dismissed for good. Thereafter, the merchants and the Boston repre-

Charles Paxton. By Edward Truman. Courtesy of the Massachusetts Historical Society.

sentatives left the former collector to his fate, having used him well in mobilizing opposition to the writs of assistance.

The equanimity that had distinguished Thomas Pownall's administration and that Bernard tried to capture began to unravel when, on 24 February 1761, James Otis Jr. represented the Boston merchants in the most celebrated case ever to come before a colonial court. Many Patriots retrospectively traced the origins of the Revolution to Otis's unsuccessful attempt to overturn the legality of the writs of assistance—royal search warrants issued to customs officers. Otis was an expert "popularizer" of ideas, and drew upon an eclectic list of sources—from law, history, and political theory—which delineated colonial liberties and "natural rights." His argument was based upon a solid proposition, however: that because such writs were no longer used in England they were ipso facto invalid in the colonies. Hutchinson adjourned the court until word arrived from England temporarily confirming the legality of the writs; in the meantime surveyor-general John Temple procured writs for Paxton and several other officers.[76]

Bernard has left few clues as to what he thought about Otis's performance in trying to overturn the writs of assistance. In an oft-quoted phrase, Bernard exclaimed that it was Otis's desire to avenge the slight to his father that "set the whole province in a flame."[77] He subsequently scolded the House for paying undue attention to "Declamations tending to promote a suspicion of the Civil Rights of the People being danger. Such Harangues might suit well in the Reigns of *Charles* and *James,* but in the time of the GEORGES they are Groundless and unjust."[78] (From this statement alone, Bancroft rather oddly concluded that Bernard admired Stuart absolutism.) Privately, Bernard described Otis as "a Gentleman of great Warmth of Temper & much indiscretion."[79] Once, Otis stormed out of the House of Representatives and threatened to resign when the members had the temerity to be more fulsome in their praise of the governor than he thought proper. Otis was never obsequious, yet on this occasion it was he who had proposed the motion to grant Bernard his salary as a goodwill gesture.

Otis's tantrums caused him to stutter and left him flailing for breath, and his incessant caviling unsettled the governor. Bernard never came close to understanding this talented thirty-five-year-old lawyer or his complex, contradictory character, though few of Otis's friends ever did either. Otis was classically educated, like Bernard, and was a fine scholar of Latin, law, and history before turning his attention to imperial issues. Behind the frenzied outbursts he witnessed, Bernard could see at work a mind sharper than his own. Bernard labeled Otis an "incendiary," but could not deny that he was the "best writer in Boston" and a "first rate politician."[80] The logic of where his inquiries into the imperial system and colonial government might lead tormented Otis—as it did many an American racked by an inner conflict over loyalty—and was a principal cause of his con-

tradictory arguments on parliamentary authority. Attacking royal officials was the most obvious means whereby Otis channeled his anger
and frustration.[81]

Bernard's subsequent efforts to placate the Otises and the Otises'
intermittent approaches to Bernard should not be dismissed as half-
hearted gestures. It was not inevitable that Bernard would cast Otis
as an enemy of royal government after the fiasco over the chief justiceship. But he lost patience with Otis long before his rival was beset
by mental illness. Bernard's respect for Otis was dissipated by his fre-
quent twists and turns: Bernard never understood why, having vehemently criticized his administration, Otis could voice his support six
months later.

*   *   *

Bernard found his growing unpopularity a "very odd experience" indeed.[82] But he realized early on that any attempt to use patronage to
create a government party to fend off the Otises and their supporters
would be fraught with problems. The legislature was never going to
tolerate any sustained effort to pack offices. Hutchinson apart, Bernard avoided making any remotely controversial appointment, nor
any unnecessary changes to senior or junior positions when the death
of George II necessitated the renewal of all Crown commissions.
When the grace period for officeholders ended, Bernard twice re-
newed the commissions of all incumbents, first on 25 October 1761 for
six months, and then on 25 April 1762 until further notice.[83]

Between 1760 and 1762, Bernard tried to establish in Massachusetts what the duke of Newcastle had called a "broad bottom" administration, wherein patronage was distributed freely, in order to
discourage.

> *I have long thought that in general Governors have greatly im-
> paired their own authority by interfering too much in the pro-
> vincial Councils; & have thereby been obliged to resort to man-
> agement and Intrigue to do that, for which they might have had,
> by a more open way of acting, the Voice of the people. I wont say
> that this observation will hold everywhere; but it is . . . the policy
> for this Country. The People here are loyal & public spirited, but
> jealous of their liberty (of which they form high & sometimes un-
> constitutional ideas) to a great degree and therefore the appear-
> ance of treating them as Independents . . . in politicks . . . is Very*

agreeable to them. And in doing so It seems to me that I am strengthening myself; Whilst I am giving them credit for their independency I have an [sic] right to insist upon my own. . . . It has been the principal object of my politicks, since I arrived here to place myself on a bottom of my own, I had no other choice: When I came here I found the province divided into parties so nearly equal, that it would have been Madness for me to have put myself at the head of either of them. I have nothing to do but keep myself to myself & maintain my own Dignity.[84]

Bernard probably discussed these issues in his secret meeting with Thomas Pownall, and reiterated his quest for nonpartisanship in a cathartic speech of 29 May 1761, at a point where disputes over plural officeholding and the trade laws had left him drained. Bernard appealed to the General Court to "Lay aside all Divisions and Distinctions" and follow the "example" set in the reign of King George II when British administrations were established "on as broad a Bottom as may be." "Party Divisions," he observed, seemed to prevail longer in the colonies than at home where "Party is no more. It is resolved into Loyalty. Whig and Tory, Court and Country are swallowed up in the Name of *Briton;* a Name which has received an additional honour" by George III's "public assumption of it." With the new king appealing for an end to party strife in Britain, Bernard pledged to leave "the Way to Honour and publick Employment . . . open to every one who has Merit."[85]

Bernard's patriotic rhetoric echoed the sanguine hopes of Britons and colonists alike that George III's accession might usher in a new era. These expectations took a long time to dissipate, particularly in the colonies, where the king's proclamation extolling "the Name of Briton" was well received. George III was just twenty-two years old when he ascended the throne: he was a diligent, conscientious young man when it came to the affairs of state, though he rarely interfered in the making of colonial policy.[86] His aspirations to be a "patriotic" king—the father of the nation, untrammeled by the grubby machinations of politicians—disturbed many a doughty Whig who suspected he had absorbed too much of Viscount Bolingbroke's Tory treatises on patriotism and monarchy.[87] A "new toryism," drawing inspiration from King George's celebration of "Britishness," had begun to modify what Brewer has called the "ubiquitous whiggism" of high politics. The King's Friends and independent Members of Parliament

applauded the king's attack on intrigue and corruption, and were
ready to assist him in reasserting the royal prerogative.[88]

Bernard redefined his governor's role in the name of the patriotic
young king, promoting himself as an enlightened civic magistrate.
His appeal to "the people" sprang from a genuine desire for congeni-
ality and cooperation: to grace colonial politics with the governor acting in lieu of the king, or, according to Bolingbroke, as head of "a
patriarchal family . . . united by one common interest, and animated
by one common spirit."[80] This can explain why Bernard created an
unprecedented number of justices of the peace. In his first two years
in office, Bernard, with the Council's approval, appointed 462 justices
of the peace (117 in Boston and Suffolk County alone) comprising approximately 1 percent of adult males in the province. Absolutely and
proportionately, this figure exceeds the number of justices for English counties like Buckinghamshire, Essex, and Hampshire, and was
only some forty short of Middlesex, the most populous county. Between 1761 and 1765, nearly two-thirds of Massachusetts representatives were justices.[90]

Justices were officers of the county, not of the province or the
towns, and less exposed to Massachusetts's democratic tendencies
than the representatives. New Englanders had long regarded the justice of the peace, the epitome of English local government, as a royal
imposition, unsuited to a polity where power was decentralized. By
accepting the unpaid commission, a justice committed himself to extensive public service duties, which often drove a wedge between him
and his fellow townspeople.[91] Was this Bernard's unspoken purpose?
Probably not. It is not possible to reconstruct the political loyalties of
the majority of justices appointed by Bernard. Justices who were
House representatives had in the past tended to vote with the court
faction, but Bernard would not have known very much about any of
these men. Bernard's principal criteria for selection were probably social status and membership in leadership pools, for appointees generally belonged to families who held local office already. Those who did
not attracted the condescension of Judge John Cushing, who complained of a "Spirit of Levillism" being introduced by Bernard when
he unwittingly promoted "persons of neither Honour or honesty,"
many "Scandalous" and others "unfit," and neglected "friends of government" like Col. Josiah Edson of Bridgewater.[92]

Cushing was right on the second point, at least. Bernard made relatively few exclusively political appointments between 1760 and 1765

compared to Hutchinson when he became governor. On the whole, Bernard was unwilling to reward his friends if that was likely to incite partisan criticism, as had happened with Hutchinson. Only when his political influence was compromised, beginning in 1764, did Bernard find offices for his "inner cabinet" of confidants, including Timothy Ruggles, Robert Auchmuty, and Jonathan Sewall.[93]

Bernard's future remained buoyant for as long as the Otises and their friends concentrated on undermining Hutchinson, and there were signs too that Bernard and the Otises could put their differences behind them. On 19 February 1762 Bernard assented to legislation reducing Hutchinson's salary as chief justice. Otis wrongly supposed that Bernard was ready to abandon the lieutenant governor, when instead he thought it prudent to give way to the opposition for the first time.[94] On 22 February Otis introduced a very popular bill to replace the writ of assistance with a toothless provincial warrant. It passed both houses quickly, requiring only Bernard's assent to become law.[95] It is possible that the House of Representatives' unexpected resolution of 27 February, granting Bernard Mount Desert, an uninhabited island lying off the coast of Maine, was intended as a sweetener for the bill on provincial warrants. The grant was made ostensibly in consideration of Bernard's "extraordinary services" to the province. Bernard had no inclination of what the House intended and guessed that the island, some one hundred square miles, was worth around a thousand pounds sterling. Such largesse was not uncommon, though governors were expressly forbidden to accept gifts. Both parties maintained that the grant was compensation for the six hundred pounds Bernard had spent refurbishing the apartments at the Province House and Castle William, although Bernard never petitioned the assembly for recompense.[96]

If Otis, who warmly approved the governor's grant, supposed it would make Bernard more amenable to the campaign against the writs, then he was sorely disappointed. Bernard simply prorogued the General Court. His subsequent consultations with the Superior Court, on whether the bill contravened an act of William III, were a charade to buy time until word arrived from England. Otis knew full well that Bernard could not approve any provincial legislation that was questionable on a point of law.[97] If Otis aimed only to demonstrate the strength of colonial feeling against the writs, then he succeeded: writs of assistance were again issued after the failure of the merchants' court case and Otis's bill, but subsequent legal and political developments cast doubt on their validity.[98]

The land grant was an incentive, but one that transcended the feud over the writs and was consistent with the expansionist views of many colonists. Mount Desert was located in the region of Sagadahoc, the territory lying between the Penobscot and St. Croix Rivers, where jurisdiction was disputed by Massachusetts and Nova Scotia. If Bernard wished to develop the island then he was obliged to push Britain to recognize Massachusetts's claim, established by Governor Pownall in 1759. Discussions between Massachusetts and Nova Scotia had been ongoing since May 1762 though Bernard was not a participant. Just one week before the Mount Desert grant, the General Court issued grants to some 352 investors with a view to establishing twelve townships on the east side of the Penobscot River.[99] The "tacit consideration" in these proceedings, Bernard admitted, was "that I should give my utmost assistance towards obtaining the Kings approbation of the grants of the Townships, which I should have thought it my duty to do if I had not been paid for it."[100]

Bernard's first eighteen months in post was a confusing period. His path of good intentions was strewn with hazards, yet his most scathing detractor had delivered a prize of land that he did not expect. Otis's criticism of Bernard originated in a feud with Hutchinson, but his political aims throughout Bernard's early years were clear enough: to establish the preeminence of the country party over Hutchinson's faction and to protect the liberties and interests of the colonial merchants. Attempts by Otis to deprive Hutchinson of his dual executive and judicial responsibilities failed, however, as did a more popular bill to change the tenure of Superior Court justices to "good behavior" as in England and to exclude them from the Council.[101] Bernard understood the motives if not the man himself, supposing that if he himself curried favor with the silent majority he might nullify those who protested most loudly. The Otises were little impressed, however, when Bernard elevated Colonel Otis to the bench of a probate court in February 1764. They never succeeded in legislating against plural officeholding, although in 1766 they managed to remove Hutchinson and his allies from the Council democratically. They also succeeded in making Bernard's life a misery.

The power of the Puritan patriarchs may have waned, but their descendants and heirs who watched their new governor struggle to adjust viewed his staunch Anglicanism with trepidation. Antago-

nisms between Massachusetts's leading Congregationalists and Anglicans had been simmering for some time. Bernard's predecessors
Pownall and Shirley were also Anglicans, but they were largely spared
the furor that greeted the revival in 1758 of plans by leading Anglican
clerics to establish an American episcopate with power to ordain colonial priests. The episcopacy dispute politicized the Massachusetts
clergy like no other issue. The Anglicans, who were the second-
largest denomination in the colonies, had but ten congregations in
Massachusetts, including King's Chapel, where Bernard and his wife
worshipped. In resisting Episcopalianism, the Congregationalists,
the Presbyterians, and the Quakers all defended religious pluralism
against the integration of church and state on Laudian lines.[102]

The problems that the episcopacy controversy created for Bernard
might not have been so acute had the contenders not drawn so extensively on sectarian paradigms from the religious and civil conflicts of
the seventeenth century.[103] The Reverend Dr. Jonathan Mayhew,
pastor of Boston's Congregational West Church, had once warned
fellow dissenters that high Anglicanism was associated with "unlim-
ited submission" to the king, thus equating "ecclesiastical tyranny"
with "civil tyranny." He never tired of reminding governors of his
Whiggish views. Mayhew's exchange of pamphlets with Anglican
clerics Henry Caner and East Apthorp between 1761 and 1765 rekin-
dled denominational disputes. Archbishop of Canterbury Thomas
Secker also joined the fray to propose a solution: the American
bishop should be invested not with full episcopal authority but that
of a commissary, a subordinate official; nor was he to be supported
by taxes, as the colonists feared, or any system of canon law courts.[104]
Another point of contention was the assistance given the Church of
England by royal governors. Theoretically, Bernard was a defender
of the faith by proxy. In practice, he was supposed to see that the
Book of Common Prayer was adhered to, that the sacrament followed church rites, and that the missions established by the Society
for the Propagation of the Gospel (SPG) had their full complement
of priests.[105] Bernard carried out these tasks faithfully.

Similarly, he forwarded to London the Congregationalists' address
to the king of 27 May 1761, which protested against giving the Anglicans a portion of the taxes paid by the Congregational churches and
denounced plans for an American bishop.[106] Initially, Bernard was
anxious not to appear too close to Caner and his colleagues. When
Caner's associate, Rev. Edward Bass, demanded that he evict a dis-

senting congregation from a chapel at Newbury, Bernard refused, declaring that "Accommodations are Very common in many parts of Europe between communions of different religious persuasions."[107]

Bernard, it has been suggested, was an "unwitting *agent provocateur*" for an American bishop,[108] but on several occasions he irritated the Congregationalists. He appointed an inept Anglican chaplain to attend the Passamaquoddy Indians, who were nominally Roman Catholic, without even considering sending a Congregational pastor.[109] He also refused to approve the General Court's bill of February 1762 to incorporate a Congregationalist missionary society, the Society for Propagating Christian Knowledge (SPCK), whose patrons included Mayhew, James Otis Jr., and Samuel Adams. He argued that any such bill required royal assent, a view that was upheld by the Privy Council in May 1763.[110] The Congregationalists presumed that Bernard the lawyer was hiding behind the law, and he wished only to give the SPG a monopoly.

Bernard was not entirely familiar with what English churchmen thought of the proposed episcopate, with the exception of Archbishop Secker, the bishop of London Richard Terrick, and possibly John Green, the bishop of Lincoln.[111] He was not unwittingly drawn toward the episcopacy scheme, nor did he blindly urge the British to press ahead regardless. On this occasion he kept his thoughts to himself, waiting for an appropriate moment to discuss his ideas with friends in England.

"A Plan for appointing a Bishop," found in Bernard's letterbooks, is a copy of a document composed probably in the early 1760s at the height of the episcopacy controversy or in 1766 when the Anglican clergy of Massachusetts arranged their first convention. This short paper reflects the frustration of the Massachusetts Anglicans but also the caution of England's leading churchmen. Like Secker, Bernard favored appointing a suffragan or assistant bishop acting under the jurisdiction of the bishop of London, in whose diocese America fell. Instead of taxing the colonists,[112] he proposed that the episcopate be supported by specially reserved benefices in England, and opposed "the Exercise of any coercive Jurisdiction" through ecclesiastical courts.[113] The Congregationalists' distaste for pomp might be assuaged if the new bishop was "settled with as little Shew & Parade as possible" in a place such as Perth Amboy, New Jersey, where the new governor's house would make an ideal official residence. In spite of its conciliatory overtones, Bernard's plan echoed the ennui of clerics such as Caner. He too dismissed the "pretended Jealousy" of the Congregationalists, and claimed for the Anglicans "no greater Priviledges than what the Dissenters in America of all Denominations enjoy themselves, namely a Power of continuing the Succession of their Ministry within their own Country, & of using the religious rights which belong to their Church."[114] Bernard wisely refrained from publishing the plan, however.

The Congregationalists probably knew nothing of this document when, in April 1762, Mayhew claimed Bernard was "deep in the plot" to establish a bishop. Mayhew's suspicions were based on snippets of information about Bernard's career as a church lawyer, which he received from Thomas Hollis in London.[115] Mutual antipathy also played a part, for the previous December Bernard threatened Mayhew with a libel action after the pastor allegedly accused him of defrauding an Indian from Martha's Vineyard who was petitioning the General Court. Mayhew was subjected to a humiliating dressing-down in the Council chamber, where Bernard scolded him for associating with admirers of Oliver Cromwell. Mayhew protested that his right to free speech was being violated, and afterward delivered to the governor a masterly character assassination: "your Excellency may be pleased further to know, that those persons, whom I make my friends and companions, are of such an irreproachable character, that it would be no disgrace even to your Excellency, to be sometimes, or often, seen in such *honest* company." Neither man ever disclosed the contents of this letter or referred to the altercation in their subsequent disagreements, but they remained bitter enemies until Mayhew's death in 1766.[116]

As the episcopacy controversy raged, Otis and the Congregationalists tried to stay abreast of developments in London and concentrated their efforts on gaining control of the province agency. The colonial agents, of whom there were eighteen by the mid-1760s, were the prime advocates for their respective colonies. The agent was normally appointed jointly by the governor and the General Court, but his election was always a partisan affair. Otis and Mayhew were determined to replace the incumbent, William Bollan, a son-in-law of William Shirley, with Jasper Mauduit, an elderly and sickly London wool merchant but, most importantly, a dissenter. Bollan, an Anglican, had held the post for nearly twenty years and had performed competently enough; his finest triumph was his and other agents' persuading Britain to reimburse the colonies after King George's

War. Bollan's contribution was quickly forgotten. Although Otis had deputized for Bollan as advocate-general of the Vice Admiralty court, neither he nor his associates believed that any friend of Hutchinson's could be trusted. Bollan had seen his three-hundred-pounds salary reduced by one-third and had survived two previous attempts to oust him when, on 19 April 1762, Otis's supporters mustered sufficient votes to carry a motion that he be removed from office. The debate, observed Bernard, was "carried on with great heat and impetuosity" in the House, and the Council concurred by a majority of one.[117] To add insult to injury, Otis insisted that the province claw back over twelve hundred pounds in commissions Bollan had rightfully taken.[118]

Bollan was expendable to Bernard, who now promoted his own candidate for the agency. King's Counsel Richard Jackson was a forty-one-year-old Anglo-Irish barrister and patron of the SPG. He was an erudite man, much admired by the celebrated English scholar Samuel Johnson. Jackson's connections and experience made him an ideal candidate for the Massachusetts agency: he was a solicitor to the Board of Trade and had performed extremely well as agent for Connecticut for several years. Jackson was a close friend of the Pennsylvania agent Benjamin Franklin, and had been recommended to Bernard by Thomas Pownall.[119] Bernard's interest in Jackson was distinctly personal. Bernard probably knew him when he was an aspiring barrister at the Inner Temple. Now, as the Board's solicitor, Jackson would be asked to advise the Board on Massachusetts's boundary disputes with Nova Scotia, in which case his opinion would be crucial in determining whether or not Bernard received confirmation of his Mount Desert land grant. Of course, Jackson was also in a position to assist confirmation of the General Court's Penobscot land grants. Bernard did not brief Jackson fully until July, though he may have approached him as early as March, a few weeks after the land grants had been made and before Bollan's removal; either way Jackson became Bernard's personal agent for the Mount Desert grant and aided the province in its dispute with Nova Scotia over Sagadahoc.[120] (Jackson's advice was also to prove instrumental in persuading the Board to retract a censure issued Bernard.)

Bernard's designs to get Jackson appointed agent were complicated by Thomas Hutchinson's interest in the agency. Despite Hutchinson's growing unpopularity in Boston, many representatives in the House supposed he would make an ideal agent. In what was the first of many slights, Bernard refused to grant Hutchinson leave from his official duties. Otis believed that Bernard did not trust Hutchinson, fearing that on arriving in England he would make a bid for the governorship.[121] He was probably right: Jackson's candidacy came unstuck when Hutchinson got his friends to vote for Mauduit. Bernard had no choice but to accept Mauduit as agent, though, for what it was worth, he obtained Otis's agreement that Jackson should act as Mauduit's solicitor—initially in an unpaid capacity—on the understanding that he would succeed Mauduit.[122]

A subsidiary factor in Bernard's deteriorating relationship with Otis's faction was the ardent anti-Catholicism of the New Englanders. In the summer of 1762, five boatloads of French-speaking Catholics or Acadians—one thousand adults and children in total—who had been expelled from Nova Scotia, sought asylum in Massachusetts. A few families had already found shelter in the province, but it was reported that such a large influx of immigrants would "lower the price of labour" in Boston.[123] The refugees' plight pricked his conscience, but Bernard was not prepared to overrule the General Court in permitting them to land.[124] He was also forbidden by the British to return the Acadians to French jurisdiction. When the war ended, the refugees were relocated to the French island of St. Pierre in the St. Lawrence River, and to Hispaniola, where many perished from disease. The sympathy that the Anglicans evinced for the Acadians was evocative of their own minority status in New England.

Congregationalists never regarded the Church of England as a benign presence, however, particularly when Anglicans were making inroads in the colonial universities. Congregational Harvard and Presbyterian Princeton were the only dissenting universities largely untouched by Anglican influences. Bernard was genuinely interested in education, and had no grand plan to turn Harvard into a seminary for the Church of England, but his interference in Harvard's affairs was both culturally arrogant and politically inexpedient.

Wishing to "change the internal Discipline" of an institution he thought "too much narrowed by . . . old prejudices,"[125] Bernard urged the university president, Edward Holyoke, to adopt Oxford's example in commemorating the accession of George III with a series of poetical tributes. The Reverend East Apthorp, a Cambridge cleric, had already irritated the overseers by proposing the introduction of Anglican services, and it is thus understandable why the Congregationalists should be suspicious of their governor. Bernard probably supposed that because Holyoke was a liberal Calvinist, he might be more amenable to the proposal (although that other liberal, Reverend Mayhew, rarely spared the governor). With twenty-five years' experience behind him, Holyoke knew better than to offend a governor who might yet prove useful. After "some difficulty," Bernard reported, Holyoke agreed to commission the tributes. Thirty-one poems were published in 1761. Bernard haughtily insisted on composing not only the dedication but nine of the tributes when the quality of the early contributions disappointed him.[126]

More provocative to Harvard was Bernard's apparent support of Col. Israel Williams's proposal to establish a rival college in Hampshire County. The colonel aimed to make full use of a kinsman's generous bequest, but the Governor's Council rejected his petition to charter Queen's College in February 1762. Bernard may have been fulfilling a promise to Williams when he subsequently issued a royal charter. On 1 April, however, after protests from the Council and the Harvard overseers, he suspended the charter. Bernard's primary concern may have been to placate his eastern critics at the expense of western interests.[127] But he was also concerned to avoid further criticism of his right to issue charters, having denied the General Court the right to establish the SPCK.[128] Williams must have looked warily upon a governor whose word was not his bond. When Bernard needed Williams most, during the Stamp Act crisis, the colonel was conspicuously absent from most Council meetings.[129] (It was another generation before a college was established in western Massachusetts, in the town of Amherst.)

For all his faults, however, Bernard was a useful patron to Harvard. The conflagration that destroyed Harvard Hall on the night of 24 January 1764 upset Bernard as much as anyone, for it was he who had summoned the General Court to meet there when smallpox broke out in Boston. For upwards of two hours, the governor and members of the General Court carried water to the fire wagons while a snowstorm raged and the library went up in flames. Bernard was one of several donors who helped to replace the five thousand books that were lost, valued at three thousand pounds, together with the teaching apparatus. Many of the two hundred or so books he took from his personal library were of a High Church stamp, which he doubtless hoped would prove instructive to the dons and students. He also elicited contributions from the archbishop of Canterbury and the SPG.[130]

Afterward, Bernard, who was a competent draftsman, was invited by the General Court to draw up architectural plans for Harvard Hall. It was a courteous and politic gesture. The reconstruction of the library and new student residences was supervised by Capt. Thomas Dawes, a master mason, and funded by a public lottery. Bernard's main contribution was to persuade Britain to lift its objections to lottery funding.[131] The Harvard students, who were overwhelmingly Whig, quickly forgot their governor's largesse when, in 1768, frightened by the arrival of British troops, they vandalized a portrait of Bernard hanging in the new library by cutting out his heart.[132]

*   *   *

The image that Bernard presented to the colonists was an incongruous construction that reflected the dual nature of royal government: that of a loyal minister striving to remain faithful to a liberty-loving people while also serving a patriotic royal master. As the war drew to a close, he basked in the illusion of a "most perfect harmony."[133] Despite victory over the French and a judicious use of patronage, Bernard struggled to maintain harmony. The first major political realignment of his administration was the emergence of a "confederacy," as he called it, of merchants, lawyers, and Congregationalists, concerned by Britain's efforts to enforce the trade laws and by creeping Anglicanization.[134] They watched his every move as the dispute over the episcopacy unfolded. Bernard himself was depressed by these tussles. It was easy then to convince himself that Otis and his adherents were determined "to get me removed."[135]

CHAPTER THREE

A "System Maker Full of Vanity and Prejudice"
Bernard and Reform, 1763–1765

T HE ROOT CAUSE of the colonists' desire to get Bernard recalled was the governor's interest in reforming colonial government. Bernard's basic ideas were developed in an essay composed in the summer of 1764, "The Principles of Law and Polity," which he distributed to ministers and friends in England. It comprises ninety-seven "propositions" on taxation, commerce, constitutional law, and politics, and was published in 1774 as an appendix to *Select Letters on the Trade and Government of America*. Bernard argued that the peace was an opportune moment for Britain to establish not a single government for all the colonies but a uniform system. His central proposals were that all the provinces should be made royal colonies and that the power imbalance in the governors' relationships with the legislatures should be redressed. His most crass proposal was the creation of an American pseudonobility. His most controversial was that Parliament should revoke the Massachusetts Charter.[1]

Historians have largely forgotten that Bernard conceived his plans as a constructive contribution to debates in London.[2] Bernard was determined to make a name for himself as a reformer—a "System Maker" who thought he could bring a sense of urgency to colonial policymaking. Thomas Pownall waited until he had left office before promoting his schemes. Bernard did not because, he confessed, his "Vanity" and "prejudice" led him to suppose that he could find a solution to the problems that beset imperial administration.[3] When Bernard found himself thwarted he became truculent and impatient with both the Americans and the British. Arguably, his fits of pique left him unprepared to cope with a looming crisis in British-colonial relations.

Bernard's interest in imperial reform was genuine, but the stimuli were as much personal as political. "Preferment," Bernard once wrote, had come "too fast upon him,"[4] leaving him "more in want of money than fine things."[5] His main source of income was his governor's salary and fees, but he often groaned that "there is no-one so ill paid in all America."[6] Between April 1758 and January 1761 his total income was £2,700 sterling. Of that he spent £2,400, including £400 for each of his three commissions. Bernard was barely solvent when he delivered a highly unusual request to the Treasury to reimburse him for at least one of the commissions. It was rejected, despite the intercession of Barrington and Newcastle.[7] By 1763, his annual income was £1,100, some £300 more than what it had been in New Jersey, and reached a maximum of £1,400 in 1765.[8] Bernard could only dream about the riches he had heard that Lord Clive, the celebrated nabob, had found in India,[9] and was less well off than Massachusetts's merchants, including his deputy Thomas Hutchinson, who was worth some £15,000.

Land speculation was one means of raising money. Bernard's largest acquisition was a share in a Crown grant of one hundred thousand acres of virgin land in Passamaquoddy Bay, Nova Scotia. His partners included Benjamin Franklin, Richard Jackson, and Thomas Pownall.[10] In November 1763 the Kennebeck Company awarded Bernard five hundred acres in Pownalborough, possibly as an incentive to win his favor in the company's legal disputes with Chief Justice Hutchinson.[11] Bernard also acquired cheaply lots in several Massachusetts townships and seven others in New Hampshire.[12] Speculators made money by reselling, leasing, or mortgaging such acquisitions, but Bernard regarded his as minor investments from which he made little if any profit.[13]

Mount Desert Island, however, offered Bernard a chance to provide his family with an estate. His "Great Object" was to establish a community of tenant farmers and fisherfolk, similar to the manor of an English squire or a New York grandee. Bernard undertook three voyages to the island and supervised the surveying teams, who included the talented British cartographer Lt. Francis Miller. On the first voyage, in the autumn of 1762, he reconnoitered the uncharted coastline of Penobscot and Mount Desert's interior. On the second and third voyages, in 1763 and 1764, he conducted thorough surveys at the province's expense marking out sites for a township and a country house, and erecting two small houses, a sawmill, and a jetty. Attracting settlers was more difficult. He spoke of getting sixty families, a minister, and a merchant to populate the island, and succeeded in relocating a party of eight families from Gloucester, Massachusetts, forty-seven people in all, including three newborn babies. How long they remained is unclear. He also failed to entice a party of German emigrants.[14] Other projects intended to sustain the community came to naught, including the production of hemp,[15] used in the manufacture of clothing and rope, and potash, commonly used in soap making, at which colonial Americans had become particularly adept.[16] Altogether, Bernard spent fifteen hundred pounds trying to develop the island.[17]

The venture was doomed to failure so long as Britain refused to recognize Massachusetts's title to Sagadahoc. It was an awkward situation: having been enlisted as an advocate for the province, Bernard worried that his personal interest would deter recognition of both claims. He secretly asked John Pownall at the Board of Trade whether the linkage between the province's claim and his own could be broken.[18] But on 15 April 1763 he received a censure from the Board of Trade accusing him of improper conduct in accepting a grant of land in a territory over which jurisdiction was disputed. He was sufficiently concerned to think that Pownall's superiors had lost confidence in him.[19]

The province agent Jasper Mauduit had already alerted the General Court and the Penobscot speculators to Bernard's duplicity. They retaliated by attacking Bernard's personal agent, Richard Jackson. At Mauduit's behest, Otis tried to persuade the House to remove Jackson from his unpaid position as solicitor to the agent and replace him with Mauduit's brother Israel. While Otis's efforts were temporarily defeated, Jackson was in a strong position to make demands of Bernard and threatened to resign if the province did not pay him for advising on the Penobscot grants.[20] One solution Bernard considered was getting the Council to appoint Jackson as its own agent.[21] (This had been done before, but it is ironic that Bernard later charged the Council with acting unconstitutionally when it appointed Bollan its sole agent.) It was another two years before Bernard had enough support in the House to get Jackson elected agent. His politicking, however, sent a clear signal that his strictures on partisanship were being compromised by his pressing desire to address his own predicament.

Bernard worried that he was failing his wife and family, such was his disappointment at his own modest achievements. He immersed himself in preparing documents protesting Massachusetts's title to Sagadahoc[22] and drafting a formal statement by the General Court.[23] His sterling efforts paid off. The Board of Trade retracted the censure and praised the "zeal and capacity" with which he had explained the complexities of the boundary dispute. However, when the Board recommended that the Privy Council confirm the Mount Desert grant it said nothing on the vexed question of the boundary line between the two colonies.[24] Later, when the Board drafted instructions for the governor of Nova Scotia, it also fudged the question of jurisdiction.[25] When Bernard realized that confirmation of the Mount Desert grant would take a while, he affected indignation at "all the encouragement" he had had "to consider" Mount Desert as his "own."[26] A refusal now, he told John Pownall, would "break my Spirit." The Privy Council did not decide in Massachusetts's favor until December 1769, and Bernard's Mount Desert grant was not approved until 1771.[27]

Before the bouts of self-pity consumed him, Bernard recast himself as an imperial reformer in an attempt to revive what seemed like a flagging career. Shortly after arriving in America, he opened a lengthy correspondence with the earl of Halifax, president of the Board of Trade, in which he offered some "immature" thoughts on colonial government.[28] When, in the spring of 1761, Bernard received a request from the Board of Trade for information on provincial administration, he began to think more deeply about the governor's role.[29] One of his early reports reviewed the General Court's power to incorporate new towns. Thirty-nine new towns were formed during Bernard's administration, more than in previous administrations, largely because of demographic changes and local disputes.[30] In 1761, 170 towns were entitled to send at least one representative to the General Court, though only 68 percent did so that year. No governor should ever think he could "manage" such an unwieldy body, Bernard concluded. Several towns already jointly maintained representatives on account of the expense involved, but Bernard urged the British to think about introducing legislation to limit the number of towns entitled to send representatives to the General Court in the manner of the Scottish boroughs that combined to elect Members of Parliament.[31]

As he waited for confirmation of the Mount Desert grant, Bernard hypothesized that his predicament could be resolved by redrawing

provincial boundaries. He learned from Richard Jackson that ministers had been discussing the constitution and boundaries of the several New England colonies. New Hampshire and Rhode Island,
Bernard supposed, might be easily incorporated with Massachusetts
to create a "Union" of New England. A new colony of "Main and
Sagadahock" could be established with himself as governor. The
more Bernard thought about the scheme the more attractive it
seemed, despite the fact that during the war, the British had abandoned discussions on reforming the colonial governments or unifying
the colonies under one single administration. Benjamin Franklin's
Albany plan for a colonial union had failed to win much support
from anyone but the governors in 1754. Any such initiative would also
suffer invidious comparison with James II's Dominion of New England.[32] In the years ahead, Bernard delivered equally controversial
proposals for supporting the governor: that royal officials should receive Crown salaries and that the Crown should assume the right to
appoint the Governor's Council.[33] Unsurprisingly, he never discussed
these sensitive topics in public.

*   *   *

There was no political will in London to redraw provincial boundaries, let alone to undertake to reform the colonial governments,
when the Pitt-Newcastle ministry collapsed in 1762. Newcastle, who
criticized the peace negotiations in Paris, and more than fifty of his
henchmen were purged from office in the colonies and Britain.[34]
New factions were emerging—around George Grenville, William
Pitt, the marquis of Rockingham, and Lord North—all of whom, in
due course, formed administrations. Bernard's difficulty in promoting his reform plans arose not from the fact that Newcastle or Pitt
were opposed to reform, but because there was a hiatus in colonial
policymaking that momentarily sidelined the imperial reformers.

Bernard knew he had an audience among the imperial reformers,
though he was uncertain as to how his reform ideas would be received. Reformers Halifax and Barrington survived Bute's purge and
the elevation of George Grenville to First Lord of the Treasury. Bernard was delighted when Grenville appointed Halifax secretary of
state for the Southern Department in the late summer of 1763. He
had simpered that there could be no "finer field" for the peer "to exercise his abilities and virtues upon" than reforming colonial government and imperial administration.[35] Bernard resumed his private

correspondence with Halifax in which he proffered ideas untamed by a public arena. "Perhaps," he admitted to Pownall, such an "open way of writing, where it is well intended, is fitter for information than greater precision."[36]

The correspondence that Bernard maintained with Viscount Barrington over many years is an excellent chronicle of the governor's efforts to influence from afar deliberations in London. As secretary at war, Barrington met the king and cabinet ministers on a regular basis to discuss military issues. Barrington's deep affection for his cousin Amelia ensured that he read, though not always attentively, what her husband had to say about colonial affairs. When Barrington left the Exchequer and the cabinet in May 1762, after just thirteen months as chancellor, he seemed destined for obscurity. But he returned as Grenville's secretary of the navy. Barrington was an able minister, and though ignorant of colonial affairs and later more interested in reforming the British army,[37] he did not lack influence. He described Halifax and the new First Lord of Trade, Wills Hill, the earl of Hillsborough, as "the most intimate friends I have in the world."[38]

There were few others whom Bernard supposed might be sympathetic. Charles Townshend, Newcastle's brother-in-law, was an unknown quantity to Bernard, despite having served on the Board of Trade. Townshend showed more interest in what Bernard had to say about the Massachusetts–Nova Scotia boundary dispute than colonial government. He lost interest in American matters until his appointment as chancellor in 1767. Bernard also contacted the earl of Shelburne, who briefly succeeded Halifax as president of the Board of Trade, but he was unresponsive. When Shelburne became a secretary of state in 1766, he regarded Bernard's plans with some suspicion.[39] Bernard's old friend Welbore Ellis, who in 1761 had replaced Barrington as secretary at war, was potentially another point of access to ministers,[40] but much less important than John Pownall, the secretary to the Board of Trade.

John Pownall's principal function was to administer the affairs of the Board of Trade. He regularly met with colonial agents, corresponded with governors, and advised ministers on all aspects of colonial affairs.[41] The continuity he provided as ministers came and went was invaluable to Bernard, particularly when Bernard lost faith in the province agents. The agents, Hutchinson once remarked, were "more strongly attached to me than they are to [Bernard]."[42] Only Richard Jackson, who was appointed agent in January 1765, showed any interest in Bernard's reform plans, but indifference rather than warmth distinguished their relationship when the General Court dispensed with his services in February 1767.

In formulating colonial policy, the Grenville ministry (April 1763–June 1765) had more pressing concerns than the ambitious plans of a colonial governor. The most basic problem was to get the colonists to pay for the upkeep of ten thousand British troops—one-third of Britain's peacetime army—stationed in North America at the close of the war on the insistence of John Stuart, the earl of Bute, and the king. Grenville, who succeeded Bute, gave little thought to the political consequences of shifting onto the Americans some of the annual costs, estimated at £350,000. The remonstrances variously proffered by governors, agents, and assemblymen could not compete with harsh financial realities: British per capita tax burdens were now twenty-five times greater than the colonists', while the national debt, estimated at £130 million in 1765, had increased 43 percent since the start of the war. The Revenue Act of 1764 and the Stamp Act of 1765 were expected to raise £150,000 annually from the colonies.[43]

Initially, however, Grenville concentrated on improving the enforcement of the trade laws, when he discovered that the molasses duty raised no more than two thousand pounds in a good year, which was insufficient to pay one-quarter of the costs of collection. The importation of molasses was a significant adjunct to New England's exports of lumber and fish. Most of the molasses used in the colonial distilleries came from the French West Indies, and under an act of 1733 was subject to a duty of six pence per gallon. This was too high to make legal trade profitable, and most molasses was imported illegally. Smuggling made economic sense, and expanded considerably during the war when, Bernard observed, the merchants seemed "less disposed to obey the Laws of Trade." In many areas, the customhouse was moribund and in the whole of New England there were only ten full-time customs officers. After the writs of assistance controversy, customs officers rarely pursued smugglers with conviction—with the notable exception of two of Bernard's friends, James Cockle and Charles Paxton.[44]

The British responded by ordering the customhouse to be more vigilant in tackling smuggling and governors to give officers their full support.[45] Shortages in personnel were addressed by appointing in 1763 the first of twenty-five new comptrollers. By January 1766 there were well over a hundred customs officers working in the continental colonies.[46] New legislation empowered officers of the Royal Navy to apprehend smugglers and to retain one-half of the profits arising from seizures. In due course, the Board of Customs Commissioners deputized some fifty-three Royal Navy ships and 112 officers.[47]

It was difficult for Bernard to persuade British policymakers to address the reform of colonial government when their attention was focused on improving imperial administration and raising revenue. He empathized with the colonial merchants when in July 1763 he learned that the British were reviewing the operations of the customhouse as a prelude to legislating a new molasses duty.[48] The colonial merchants argued for a reduction in the six-pence duty, to one-half or one and a half pence, though most were prepared to accept two. The West Indies merchants in London, however, who stood to benefit from a higher rate, lobbied for four pence.[49]

Bernard's views on Grenville's imperial reforms were much closer to those of the colonists than has been supposed. A duty of one and a half pence, Bernard told Jackson, was not so high as to make smuggling worthwhile and would still yield a net revenue, as ministers wished.[50] This premise was the basis for a memorandum that Bernard sent the Board of Trade in September,[51] and a more substantive letter on the proposed revenue bill that he forwarded in November.

> *The Question seems to be whether It [the bill to renew the molasses duty] should be an act of prohibition or an Act of Revenue. It was originally, I believe designed for the former; & if it shall be thought advisable to continue as such, it will want no more than to be fully executed. But if it is meant to be an Act of Revenue, the best means to make it effectual, that is, to raise the Greatest Revenue by it, will be to lower the Duties in such proportion as will secure the entire collection of them & encourage the importation of the goods on which they will be laid.*

It followed that Britain ought "to encourage a trade between North America & the foreign Plantations under Proper restrictions," a view that did not really take account of the merchants' deep concerns.[52] The announcement in January 1764 by surveyor-general John Temple that the customhouse intended to enforce the trade laws rigorously "caused greater alarm," Bernard famously observed, than the capture of Fort William Henry by the French in 1757.[53]

Grenville's Revenue Act, which received royal assent in April 1764, was a compromise of sorts. Although it reduced the molasses duty from six to three pence, the revised rate represented between 25 and 30 percent of the wholesale price of one gallon of molasses, leaving New England merchants with the prospect of having to sell up to one-third more goods in the West Indies in order to maintain the same value of imports for sale in the colonies. Moreover, the enumerated list of taxable and nontaxable commodities was extended, with the intention of redirecting much of the colonies' trade with Europe to Britain. Bernard was less concerned by the act's other provisions relating to law enforcement, which confirmed the contested right of informers and customs officers to share the profits from confiscated property and excused them liability for trespass and damages. Officers were also empowered to pursue smugglers in either the juryless Vice Admiralty courts or the provincial courts.[54]

Bernard tried to link Grenville's revision of the molasses duty to his own agenda for reforming the colonial governments. He asked Jackson not only to lobby on behalf of the merchants, but also to press upon ministers his proposals for Crown salaries, which he suggested might be maintained from the customs revenue.[55] Before the colonists found out, Bernard's position as a provincial advocate was already being undermined by his responsibility to assist the customhouse in apprehending smugglers.

Bernard's vociferous defense of the "governor's third" embroiled him in an unseemly competition with Admiral Lord Colville, the British naval commander, at the same time as the colonial merchants were complaining of Grenville's reforms. Bernard contested the right of Colville's officers to a share of seizures in a lengthy, articulate paper that he submitted to John Pownall on "behalf of the North American Governors." He claimed that the empowerment of Royal Navy officers for the more "effectual prevention" of smuggling (2 Geo. 3) contravened the governor's prerogative, which had been written into one of the earliest of the Navigation Acts (15 Car. 2) and subsequent trade laws. The ministers and officials who drafted the 1763 act appeared to be ignorant of this.[56] Bernard asked Pownall to present the document to the Board of Trade only if Grenville decided to question his prerogative or if Colville had the matter raised in Parliament.[57] Neither happened, although when Colville reported Bernard's opposition to the Lords of the Admiralty, Bernard contacted Halifax. There were two possible solutions, he told Halifax: either introduce new legislation to clarify the situation or compensate governors by giving them Crown salaries. The failure of the Board of Customs Commissioners in London to resolve the dispute was not unexpected, since the Board had no wish to upset the navy.[58] Bernard's attempts to link the reform of colonial government to the Revenue Act failed, however. In July 1764, the Treasury notified Bernard that Colville's claim to a share of seizures could only be settled in a court of law. The matter was still unresolved when he left the province five years later.[59]

Bernard was little troubled by what the colonial merchants thought of his defense of the governor's third, or of his friendship with zealous customs men such as Charles Paxton.[60] "Strange People!" he arrogantly exclaimed, when he heard that some merchants wanted him replaced, "who can think that a Governor respected by evry order of men through the Province, except the Smugglers, & offensive to them only by his doing his duty & paying obedience to his general & special instructions, should be removeable."[61] Bernard may have been foolish to dismiss the merchants' criticism, but it is unlikely that he was profiting as much from seizures as some claimed.[62] Hutchinson's recollection that Bernard made a "profitable" income from the pursuit of smugglers requires some qualification.[63] Exactly how much Bernard made from seizures is uncertain. Bernard estimated that between 1760 and 1765 he amassed seventeen hundred pounds,[64] though surveyor-general John Temple later claimed it was twice as much. Bernard's profits dropped by around 37 percent when the number of prosecutions fell dramatically during the Stamp Act crisis.[65] Even so, Bernard's profiteering helps explain why politically moderate merchants never really warmed to him.

It also partly explains why Bernard alienated John Temple, the fastidious head of the customhouse in the Northern District. Temple was only twenty-eight years old when he was appointed surveyor-general in 1760, having been lieutenant governor of New Hampshire. The Boston-born Temple was by far the best connected of the governor's many adversaries. He was a brother-in-law to William Pitt and a kinsman of George Grenville, but it was his connections with Bostonians such as James Bowdoin, whose daughter he married in 1767, that unsettled Bernard. Temple was no idler but an eager policeman, hard on smugglers and hard on anyone—the governor included—who questioned his judgment. Before their personal relationship degenerated into "inveterate hatred,"[66] their professional relationship was severely strained by a vehement disagreement over the modus

operandi of prosecuting smugglers. Temple disliked using informers
to gather evidence for prosecutions because of the resentment it
aroused. He also distrusted the practice of customs officers compounding with merchants arraigned for smuggling, for it left his officers open to bribery and allowed smugglers to pay but a part of the
trade duties to which their cargoes were subject. He estimated that
the Treasury was losing some 80 percent of its revenue because of
this, while the governor's profits were largely unaffected.[67]

Bernard was just as concerned as Temple at the merchants' growing discontent when, in March 1764, Grenville announced that stamp
duties, similar to those operating in England, might also be imposed
upon the colonists. A parliamentary bill was not presented for another eleven months while officials gathered information from the
colonies and Grenville toyed with the idea of letting the colonial assemblies levy the stamp duties. Consultation was very limited: apart
from the agents and merchants in London, the government relied
mainly on the customhouse, but not, strangely enough, the governors. Had they been asked, Bernard and his colleagues would have
advised against introducing any tax by an act of Parliament.

The response of the colonists turned not only on economic issues
and the governor's profiteering, as Bernard supposed it might, but
also on the momentous question of whether the imperial Parliament
could impose taxes on a people who were not directly represented in
that august body. The General Court's instructions of 13 June to the
province agent Jasper Mauduit explained the likely impact of the
Revenue Act on commerce and the fisheries, but pledged that "no
taxes or duties will be laid upon the colonies whilst they remain unrepresented in Parliament." In May, the Boston town meeting presented its four representatives with comprehensive instructions on
how to vote on matters relative to colonial rights and British colonial
policy, a practice soon adopted by many other towns.[68]

With the benefit of hindsight, Bernard and several other royal officials lamented that Britain badly miscalculated the depth of feeling
aroused by parliamentary taxation. Bernard's views on the stamp tax
are not cogently expressed in any one particular document dating
from 1764 or 1765. It is evident that his criticism of the tax stemmed
as much from the difficulties it caused him as from its provisions. At
no point, of course, did he question Parliament's right to levy any sort
of tax.[69]

Bernard also tended to relate disagreements over taxation to the

wider issue of reforming colonial government. He wrote "The Principles of Law and Polity" in some "haste" shortly after the General
Court instructed Mauduit and James Otis published an influential
analysis of colonial rights, *The Rights of the British Colonies*. Bernard
was surprised that the pamphlet was so "temperate & decent." This
was an oblique acknowledgment of how moderate Otis's position on
colonial rights actually was.[70] Otis had produced a lengthy exposition
of the colonists' legislative rights, which denied the legitimacy of Parliament's right to tax so long as the colonists were unrepresented in
Parliament: he did not repudiate parliamentary supremacy. Otis's
outbursts in the House were more discomfiting than his pen. In a
speech of 8 June Otis did openly challenge Parliament's authority to
tax the colonists, and called for a congress of all the colonies to debate
the issue.[71] In every colony, debates on British policies were being
dominated by "Pamphlets on the popular Side,"[72] but Bernard knew
better than to engage Otis in a public debate, and addressed his comments to ministers instead.

Bernard's "Principles of Law and Polity" was a manifesto for
strengthening the royal components of colonial government. Bernard
described his first set of propositions (nos. 1-14, pp. 67-73) as "self-
evident" principles governing British-colonial relations. Like that of
most British commentators, Bernard's examination sprang from the
premise that the fundamental constitutional principle governing the
expansion of the British Empire and the growth of the British state
was parliamentary supremacy. Parliament's sovereignty was indivisible and inviolable, he baldly stated. Anything else would be to admit
the illogicality of an *imperium in imperio*. In his early speeches to the
General Court Bernard had spoken of the colonists' rights and their
mutual contractual obligations, but there is nothing in "The Principles of Law and Polity" to indicate that he sympathized with the colonists' objections to the principle of parliamentary taxation.
Expediency and common sense, he mused, would restrain Parliament
from adopting injurious measures. Bernard's jejune evaluation was
typical of British imperialists who adhered to the Aristotelian con-
ception of empire as a conglomeration of "perfect communities"
under metropolitan control.[73]

Bernard's second set of propositions (nos. 15-54, pp. 74-77) sought
to delineate those legal rights of the colonists that were "capable of
positive proof." Irrespective of whether colonial liberties originated
in positive law, as with the royal charters, or in custom, they were, he

maintained, ipso facto derivative; thus their continuation depended upon the grace of the king-in-parliament and were not in any sense "natural" rights. From this premise, Bernard defended Grenville's assertion that only residents of Britain possessed the right to consent to taxation; no subject was at liberty to make their loyalty to the Crown or Parliament contingent upon their consent. Other passages, however, again questioned the expediency of taxing the colonists by a Parliament in which they were not directly represented.

Bernard stressed that he was looking for some means of reconciling "British dominion with American liberty, on terms of compact, beneficial to both parties" (p. 78). If Grenville went ahead with the stamp tax, then he hoped that the revenue would be applied solely for the defense and support of the American colonies. An attractive alternative to direct taxation, he suggested, was that the provincial assemblies be allowed to levy the stamp duties themselves, as Grenville had hinted. Such disputes might also be avoided by allowing the Americans direct representation in Parliament (p. 80). Bernard remained a firm advocate of colonial representation in Parliament.[74] It was an altogether moderate if ultimately impractical scheme, but one that enjoyed considerable credence in the colonies in 1765, even with Otis.[75] It is wrong to think of Bernard as a centralist reformer wholly inimical to the colonists' interests, as Otis did, but though he recognized colonial liberties he evidently could not equate them, as Otis did, with any natural right to consent to Parliament's laws.

Bernard's paper complemented the efforts of Thomas Hutchinson, who sent Richard Jackson an insightful essay on the tensions in imperial relations caused by taxation and trade regulation. Bernard praised his deputy's enterprise, though only a few months previously he had again refused Hutchinson leave to go to London. Hutchinson composed his discursive essay sometime between May and early July—before Bernard completed "Principles." He urged Jackson to publish it in the London newspapers, which he never did because of Hutchinson's critical tone: it was not so much the amount the colonists would have to pay that concerned Hutchinson so much as the precedent that was being set. In this respect, as Bernard well knew, there was nothing to separate Hutchinson from the Boston town meeting.

Hutchinson's main target was also James Otis, but his exposition of colonial rights and liberties was in many respects closer to Otis than to Bernard. Whereas Bernard was dismissive of Otis's appeal to natural law, Hutchinson supposed the British ought to defer to colonial sensibilities in the question of parliamentary taxation. Hutchinson was puzzled as to why Bernard and Jackson, like many British conservatives, might think they could placate the colonists by making a distinction between "internal" taxes, such as stamp duties, and "external" taxes, which were defined as duties on articles of commerce; as British subjects the colonists were entitled to enjoy the same rights as "Englishmen." Hutchinson proceeded to demolish the proposition, from which Bernard did not depart, that the colonists were "virtually" represented by British Members of Parliament; there was no such thing as tacit consent, he warned, before finishing with an appeal for Britain to pull back from taxing the colonists.[76] Unlike Otis, Hutchinson was always ready to defer to Bernard and, if the provincial interest required it, to suppress his convictions. Hutchinson never again delivered such a forthright defense of colonial legislative authority, not because he abandoned these principles, but because of the radicalization of both the colonists' claims for legislative self-government and Bernard's advocacy of sweeping reform.

The third set of propositions in the "Principles" (nos. 54-97, pp. 78-82), which Bernard deemed more hypothetical than the rest, set him far apart from Hutchinson. Here Bernard proposed what elsewhere he called a "general Reformation of the American Governments." This might entail Parliament legislating the abolition of the corporate colonies, Rhode Island and Connecticut, and introducing Crown salaries for royal officials. For the first time Bernard proposed that the charter right of the General Court to elect a new council be revoked and that the Crown appoint councilors by a writ of mandamus.[77]

In the "Principles" at least Bernard gave no thought as to how the New Englanders would react to these proposals, no doubt because he had no wish to discourage ministers. However, it was an act of folly on Bernard's part to imply later that the colonists were little concerned. "It requires no arguments to show that . . . for the Peace & Order of this Government . . . the royal Scale should have its own Constitutional Weights restored to it & thereby be made much more equiliberal with the popular one. How this is to be done, whether by the Parliament or the King's Bench, or by both, is a Question for the Administration to determine; the Expediency of the Measure is out of Doubt."[78] Any delay on Britain's part to address points of friction over constitutional and economic issues, Bernard argued, would inevitably contribute to the radicalization of colonial politics. That sense of crisis inhibited Bernard's thinking on the colonists' problems and led him to concentrate on the problems attendant to his own manifestly weak position.

In contrast, Thomas Pownall, unshackled from the business of government, was able to produce a more rounded and deeper analysis of British-colonial relations. Several editions of Pownall's *Administration of the Colonies* were published in the 1760s, beginning in 1764. Bernard probably read the first edition of this treatise, and certainly read with interest the much-expanded 1768 edition. Pownall ranged widely over commerce, currency, trade regulation, Indian affairs, colonial expansion, and military matters, whereas Bernard was more narrowly focused on colonial government and imperial law. It was galling for Bernard to hear colonists regret Pownall's departure while criticism of his own administration mounted, and then to hear Pownall praised for his treatise. When Pownall returned to England Bernard probably did not contact him until March 1766, in order to congratulate him on his recent marriage. Still, he agreed with Pownall on many things, not the least of which was the conviction that imperial reform required Britain's urgent attention.

Both men offered, as they saw it, some practical suggestions rather than the theories and speculation which, until Adam Smith's *Wealth of Nations* (1776), characterized a great deal of British writing on imperial reform.[79] Bernard and Pownall were mercantilists yet both were concerned that the trade laws unnecessarily restricted the colonies' opportunities for commercial expansion. Bernard's views on the merchants' problems, however, were developed more fully in his correspondence with ministers than in "Principles of Law and Polity." Bernard was also pleased by Pownall's advocacy of a more streamlined administration, through the creation of an American department, and by his observations on how the governor's power had been gradually undermined by the Massachusetts General Court. Both men were in complete agreement that a compromise had to be reached with the colonists on basic constitutional principles, though Pownall, unlike Bernard, did not make any specific suggestions in the 1764 edition (save recommending the reform of the colonial judiciaries).

Pownall did not share Bernard's overriding concern, which was to establish clearly and exactly the extent of colonial subordination to the imperial Parliament. In his letter to Pownall of 1766, Bernard

talked of the necessity of rooting out the "disease" at the heart of colonial government and of "administer[ing] remedies which shall not
only cure it for the present but prevent its ever returning."

> *I dont see how the Parliament can now avoid disclaiming their
> being bound by establishments made by the King only [the prov-
> ince charters]: taking the Governments of America into their own
> hands; & new forming them upon true constitutional principles
> of British Liberty: at the same time ascertaining & declaring, by
> a kind of local Magna Charta, the rights of the Americans & the
> essential Nature of their dependance upon Great Britain. For
> these, Ireland, except in the one circumstance of distance affords
> a precise precedent.*[80]

Bernard's reformism offered a complete rewrite of the constitutional
relationship between the colonies and Britain. Although the bias was
in favor of centralizing authority in royal officials, Bernard was convinced that colonial grievances and aspirations could be resolved by
Parliament enacting an American bill of rights. This proposal excited
many writers on imperial affairs and was taken up by Joseph Galloway at the Continental Congress on the very eve of the Revolutionary
War. Be that as it may, Bernard presupposed, unlike Galloway or
Pownall, that it was necessary to revoke the colonial charters of government as a prelude to instituting an American parliament or a bill
of rights.[81]

Bernard's proposal for a unitary American assembly subordinate to
the British Parliament also came with a caveat. The model he had in
mind was the Irish parliament, whose powers were limited by a British declaratory act, and whose legislation, under the notorious Poyn-
ing's Law, required prior approval by the Crown.[82] The Irish model
was never likely to appeal to the colonists. The troubled history of
that island, which Americans knew so well, spoke of British oppression. Ireland was a subjugated colony, where the lord lieutenant never
balked, as Bernard and Hutchinson did, from turning the military
against protestors. Bernard was captivated by the power of the British
establishment in Ireland because, as J. P. Reid has shown, it did not
place the same legal constrictions on the lord lieutenant's powers as
the "conditions" of law placed upon the imperial elite in the American colonies.[83]

Thomas Pownall recoiled from Bernard's draconian proposals, and by 1768 was able to reflect on the growth of colonial opposition to British policies. When he proposed a union of Britain and the American colonies he envisaged a union of equal partners similar in law to that between England and Scotland. In effect he was recommending the creation of an imperial federation. Pownall also strongly urged the British to show a "constant regard" for American objections to Parliament's legislative supremacy because of the "spirit of suspicion and alarm" that pervaded imperial affairs. He broadly hinted that this had more to do with colonial governors like Bernard than any other factor.[84] Later, however, Pownall saw some worth in Bernard's proposal for an American Magna Carta, an idea that he presented as his own in a letter to the Reverend Samuel Copper.[85]

Bernard's ideas on a British-American union fell a long way short of Pownall's or Galloway's. He favored an incorporating union (as happened with Ireland in 1801) rather than a confederation or a devolution of powers to a unitary American legislature.[86] He never, for example, explored the possibility that an American assembly could be a useful counterweight to the colonial assemblies, though he might have moved in that direction. In Bernard's defense, it might argued that he was not the only official or colonist who, before the prospect of war sharpened his senses, lacked the imagination to suppose that a division of powers between the center and the periphery could form the basis of a decentralized union or a confederation.

Bernard forwarded to ministers copies of "The Principles of Law and Polity" with a note disingenuously claiming that his ideas had considerable support among officials in the northern colonies. Barrington also discussed Bernard's paper with Halifax.[87] Bernard had no intention of publishing the "Principles" in Massachusetts, and asked Jackson to arrange publication anonymously in London. Unlike Hutchinson, however, Bernard would not publish unless his ideas were, as he told John Pownall, "agreable to the P[lans] which the Ministers have allready formed."[88] If such came to pass, then he would get the credit for pinpointing the structural and political weaknesses of royal government in the colonies. Bernard promised John Pownall that in time he would produce more "Exoterick & . . . Esoterick" commentaries[89]—a promise that he had cause to regret when his ruminations inexplicably became the talk of Boston. It was not the last time that Bernard's enemies were privy to his correspondence with Britain.[90]

The Grenville ministry, however, showed no interest in Bernard's proposals and never sanctioned the publication of his paper, probably because of his criticism of the Revenue Act. Hutchinson's essay, by contrast, inspired several Members of Parliament who later spoke in favor of repealing the Stamp Act. The inertia that Bernard believed stifled his initiative was indicative of the ministry's need to evaluate information from several sources: if not directly from Hutchinson, then certainly from the colonial agents and the assemblies, Members of Parliament, the Treasury, and British merchants.[91]

*   *   *

While he waited for news from London, Bernard did not seek to obstruct the colonists' protests but to temper them. He refused to allow the House an opportunity to finish a petition protesting at Grenville's reforms, and prorogued the General Court over the summer months. What was to be gained from confrontation with Britain, he asked the Boston representatives, when the Revenue Act was a fait accompli? "There can be no doubt" that the ministry intended to let colonies tax themselves, as both he and Jackson had argued. Consequently, they should all await instructions as to how to proceed.[92]

These were not bland assurances or a willful attempt to mislead. Neither Bernard nor anyone else as yet knew whether or not the ministry would impose parliamentary taxation. However, even if Bernard was not aware of Grenville's intentions, the colonists could ask with some justification why he made no attempt to ascertain ministers' views when in August he sent the Board of Trade the lists of provincial fees it had requested.[93] The General Court did not meet until 18 October. Meanwhile, Bernard took off for Mount Desert on 27 August, leaving behind a town seething with indignation.[94]

The most serious accusation leveled at the governor was not duplicity, however, and it came not from the colonists but from another imperial official. With Bernard out of the way, surveyor-general John Temple complained to the Treasury that

> *Governor Bernard's insatiable Avarice has led him into all Quarters, and into all Departments for money, in a way that is Realy a disgrace to his Appointment, and This Gentleman Interfering with me in Office (regardless of the Kings Instruction to the Contrary) weakens my Power and Influence over the Officers, disconcerts me in the Vigorous measures I am desirous of taking for the Security of the Revenue, and Renders me very unhappy*

in an Employment; in which I think I could get some Reputation
if I was not so Interrupted.[95]

Bernard responded to Temple's outburst on 29 September, shortly
after returning from Mount Desert.

It will give me an opportunity to free myself from the difficulties
I have laboured under for some time, in endeavouring to make
obedience to the orders of my Superiors & to the dictates of my
own Sense of my duty reconcileable with the desire I have had to
maintain a friendly intercourse with you.[96]

Temple, however, had spent the previous month gathering evidence
against Bernard, and on 3 October accused the governor of being
privy to fraud and of bending the law for his own benefit.[97]

Bernard's alleged accomplice was James Cockle, the Salem collector. He was a zealous and successful officer, hated and feared in equal
measure by the colonial merchants. Temple suspended Cockle on 28
September after investigating the complaint of four Salem merchants, the owners of the *Gloucester,* that the collector had extorted
fifty pounds from them.[98] Cockle had the temerity to offer Temple a
seven-hundred-pound bribe to ignore the transgression. Coming just
one day before the Revenue Act took effect, Cockle's suspension was
celebrated in Boston with "bonfires, entertainments, &c." Temple
himself was "much applauded by the merchants."[99] The Board of
Customs Commissioners in London dismissed Cockle on 30 October for these "Notorious breaches" of duty.[100]

While investigating the *Gloucester* affair, Temple discovered that
Cockle had withheld from him information about a more serious
matter, possibly on Bernard's say-so. On 23 August the collector had
received a letter from the governor of Anguilla in the Caribbean
warning that ships bound for Massachusetts were carrying forged
clearance papers. This was a common method of misleading the customs officers who inspected cargoes for taxable goods at the port of
entry. Cockle alerted Bernard on Saturday, 25 August, before con-
tacting Temple. On the Monday morning prior to Bernard's departure for Mount Desert, Cockle brought *in personam* prosecutions in
the Vice Admiralty court against fourteen captains found in possession of the forgeries. On 12 September Bernard's wife Amelia agreed
to a composition with the shipowners for her husband's share.[101]

Temple supposed that Cockle and Bernard aimed to profit from their knowledge of the Anguilla forgeries. It was relatively easy for them to identify the false clearance papers and for Cockle to persuade the shipowners to compound for the return of their vessels; both the collector and the governor were entitled to retain one-third of the fines. The speed with which Bernard and Cockle registered the libels led Temple to suspect that they had been colluding in such schemes for a while. Temple's personal audit of the customhouse records revealed that between March and September 1764 an inordinate amount of molasses for such a small island as Anguilla—nearly two thousand hogsheads—had been entered at Salem duty-free. Temple estimated that nearly five thousand pounds in duties ought to have been received during this period. The money accrued from compounding with libeled merchants was twenty-four hundred pounds, of which Bernard and Cockle each took eight hundred pounds.

Temple was reluctant to concede that compounding was technically legal, but personal animosity mixed with a genuine desire to do his job properly drove him to accuse Bernard of improprieties. The avarice of Bernard and Cockle, Temple argued, and their exploitation of compounding were positively detrimental to the collection of revenue and the enforcement of the trade laws.[102] In spite of his own family's influence, Temple was wary that Bernard's connections with Halifax and the Board of Trade would count against him. Thus he carefully apprised the Board's solicitor, Richard Jackson, of his discoveries, adding the frisson that Bernard was "quite a different man" from when Jackson knew him.[103]

A deposition taken from Sampson Toovey, a tidewaiter and Cockle's subordinate, seemed to implicate Bernard. Toovey claimed to have been the "Negociator" in a scam whereby Salem merchants delivered to Bernard casks of wine, fruit, and oils in return for Cockle accepting part payment of import duties. Petty corruption of this kind was commonplace. When Temple interviewed Toovey a second time, he found that at Cockle's house on 10 October Bernard had tried to persuade one of the owners of the *Gloucester* to attest that he had always expected Cockle to return to him the fifty pounds he had illegally retained. This merchant corroborated Toovey's testimony when pressed by Temple, who viewed Bernard's intervention as a botched cover-up.

Historians who have judged Bernard by the standards of modern bureaucratic government have been far too hasty to condemn him. The most detailed study of the affair accepts uncritically most of what Temple had to say.[104] The concept of a disinterested or apolitical public official, however, was only half-formed in Britons' minds accustomed as they were to purchasing offices and relying upon patronage. Bernard's behavior was rather typical of eighteenth-century colonial governors, who fully expected to exploit their position for material gain. As Thomas Hutchinson sensibly noted, Bernard's notion of "incorruption" was relative: he may have been receptive to the occasional gift, but that did not compromise his authority or mean that he "took any improper steps" to line his pockets.[105] Political opponents and ambitious rivals such as Temple chose to view such behavior very differently.

The narrative that Temple forwarded to his superiors in London was highly selective in its reconstruction of the sequence of events concerning his investigation of Cockle's links with the governor. Bernard was certainly remiss in failing to discuss the Anguilla forgeries with Temple before he left Boston on 27 August. That does not mean, as Temple claimed, that Bernard and Cockle connived to keep this information secret. Cockle wished to prosecute the merchants as quickly as possible in the Vice Admiralty court, but both Bernard and advocate-general Robert Auchmuty refused to proceed until the collector could prove that the governor of Anguilla was right about the forgeries. Cockle's own explanation is also worthy of consideration: any delay, he said, might allow the merchants to sue the customhouse for damages, as had been tried before.[106] After compounding with the merchants, Cockle and Bernard were not then obliged to sue for the payment of duties in full, as was soon explained to Temple.[107] (The Revenue Act, which permitted Temple to seize the vessels for nonpayment of duties, did not take effect until 29 September.)[108]

Bernard's association with Cockle is less puzzling than it might appear, however. Temple supposed that if he had accepted instead of rejecting Cockle's bribe he would have "Secured Govr. Bernards friendship as Well as Cockles future Obedience."[109] This was for Grenville's consumption. James Cockle and Francis Bernard were in fact old friends. Cockle's father was an alderman of the Lincoln Common Council, while Cockle and his brother had run a business in Lincoln. When the partnership folded, James was left holding the debts, and absconded to America sometime in 1760.[110] His appointment to the customhouse probably owed something to Bernard's influence, and Cockle's indebtedness certainly explains why he exploited his position as collector. In 1763, however, Cockle and Bernard began to concert their efforts. Bernard, it seems, urged the collector to initiate prosecutions in the Vice Admiralty courts whenever possible, for the simple reason that in these courts, unlike the common law courts, smugglers could not rely on a sympathetic jury to acquit them. Because Cockle saw himself as the governor's adviser, he saw no reason subsequently to justify his actions to Temple.[111]

Although Cockle's friendship with Bernard would appear to strengthen Temple's case against Bernard, it nonetheless reveals why Temple was so angry with the governor for interfering in the customhouse. Temple was an empire-builder who prided himself on being able to rid the service of the "Super Annuated Cripples" who seemed to hold so many positions.[112] Cockle, as the governor's "dupe," had to go.

Bernard's intercession could not save Cockle, but he offered the disgraced collector some support in his hour of need. Bernard asked Richard Jackson to get him a good lawyer when Cockle insisted on making a personal appeal to the Board of Customs. Pursued by his debtors, however, Cockle fled to France or Holland. Cockle's disappearance reflected badly on the governor, yet in spite of this Bernard promised him "asylum" in Nova Scotia as a surveyor.[113] Bernard temporarily lost touch with Cockle, but later promised to "procure an Enquiry" that might vindicate him. Nothing happened, and with Bernard preoccupied with answering other, more important accusations brought against him, he warned Cockle to stay away.[114]

Temple's allegations of corruption against Bernard failed to impress the governor's superiors, although the Board of Customs Commissioners upheld the assertion that Bernard had been negligent in his duty to aid the surveyor-general.[115] Temple pleaded with undersecretary Thomas Whately that "Mr. Grenville must surely see by the Evidence I send him that Governor Bernard and myself cannot both (consistent with the Welfare of the Public Service) remain in our present Stations." Grenville was unmoved, and the Privy Council cleared Bernard of any wrongdoing.[116]

Grenville had no wish to make the conduct of British officials the subject of interdepartmental disputes, yet it was foolish to ignore the political connotations of the Temple-Bernard affair. For sure, no one in Britain anticipated how the colonists would react to the Revenue Act and the stamp tax, but ministers ought to have reviewed how the colonial merchants would take to the customhouse and the Vice Admiralty courts being vested with greater powers, and to governors such as Bernard who made no secret of their association with unsavory officials.

*   *   *

Bernard's vociferous defense of his right to profit from the enforcement of the law and his recalcitrance in allowing the General Court the chance to petition Parliament about the Revenue Act and the stamp tax won him few friends. Otis's proposal that the House suspend payment of the governor's salary if the stamp tax were ever introduced was only narrowly defeated; no one apart from Bernard supposed that this insult might strengthen the case for Crown salaries.[117] When the General Court convened on 18 October, Bernard urged "Unity, Prudence, and Moderation" in the business of preparing the petitions, and boasted to Halifax that his plea had "considerable effects" on what transpired, but it took all of Hutchinson's political skills to prevent confrontation with Britain over the question of taxation.[118]

Hutchinson persuaded the Council to reject the House's petition to the House of Commons and chaired a joint committee whose watered-down version was accepted and delivered to London. According to Bernard,

> The Grand point which was the Chief matter litigated thro' the whole of this Affair was, whether they should assert their exemption from Parliamentary taxes as a right, or only insinuate it in the way of praying a continuance of that favor & indulgence which they had hitherto experienced.[119]

Largely at Hutchinson's request, all references to colonial "rights" were omitted from the petition and "liberties" inserted instead. It was not a semantic distinction. Whereas many colonists rejected the wisdom of parliamentary taxation, Hutchinson and his "moderate" friends on the joint committee stopped well short of accepting the radicals' contention that the authority to tax rested solely with the General Court. Their prime consideration was to persuade the British to compromise over the stamp tax. The final version of the petition delivered mainly economic arguments against Grenville's reforms that, as John W. Tyler has shown, echoed those made earlier by the Boston merchants.[120]

Bernard was pleased when the General Court asked him to support the petition, and was supremely confident that with Hutchinson's help he could settle the disputes over trade regulation and taxation once and for all. He told Richard Jackson that the General Court was "convinced of the expediency of moderate & united Councils upon this occasion." In forwarding the petition to Halifax, Bernard rightly observed that its supplicant tone was owing to the influence of "Moderate men and friends of government." He also made it clear that, while he could not abide by any challenges to Parliament's legislative authority, he shared the colonists' apprehensions as to the economic impact of British legislation. On these issues Bernard's views differed markedly from his superiors in London. His criticism of Britain was also an insurance of sorts against criticism by the House, for on 12 November he answered Halifax's request for a "list of instruments" used in the province courts that might be subject to stamp duty.[121] However, Bernard's assurances that the petition and his letter to Halifax would carry "great Weight" in London sounded hollow. "We hope," the House warned in its published address, these "are not times of Distrust," though "we distrust not the Wisdom and Goodness of Parliament."[122]

One promising development was that Bernard was able to push for the appointment of Richard Jackson as province agent after Mauduit's hapless performance. Jackson was now Grenville's private secretary, but it remained to be seen whether he would use his position to promote colonial interests.[123] With the popular faction promoting the candidature of Mauduit's brother Israel, and others proposing Thomas Hutchinson, the London merchant Sir William Baker, and Thomas Pownall, Bernard's "first Care," he told Jackson, "was to prevent the friends of government being divided"; his second was to make the election "a contest between the Government and the opposition."[124] Baker, he knew, had publicly declared against accepting the agency over a year ago. However, he would have been glad to accept Pownall instead of Israel Mauduit. This time Bernard did not rule out sending Hutchinson home as a special agent but managed to persuade him to get his supporters to vote for Jackson; it was not too difficult, given Hutchinson's admiration for the man. Jackson won the election by just four votes in the House, but not before James Otis had tried unsuccessfully to impose a time limit on his commission. Jackson had no trouble in winning the Council's approbation.[125]

The contest illustrated the polarization that was occurring in colonial responses to British policies. In the House, the friends of government comprised between forty and forty-five representatives; bad weather and sickness accounted for more than twenty others Bernard reckoned were on his side. Thus, Bernard suggested that perhaps three-fifths of the General Court were friends of government, a figure that subsequent roll calls suggest was exaggerated but not greatly. The popular faction comprised about one-third of the members when, in February, their motion to deprive Hutchinson of his chief justice's salary lost by just one vote.[126] Bernard came to regret not sending Hutchinson to London, for the agents' influence on subsequent developments was minor. They did not offer any sustained criticism of the constitutionality of the measure, which the General Court had attempted in a moderate fashion, and which the Virginia House of Burgesses would do more vociferously. When Jackson, Franklin, and the other agents met Grenville on 2 February, they failed to dissuade him from presenting the stamp tax bill to Parliament four days later.[127]

*   *   *

As 1764 drew to a close, the reciprocity that Bernard deemed essential to a harmonious working relationship with the General Court was being progressively eroded, not only by political disputes but by his own frustrations and a growing sense of powerlessness at being able to influence policymakers in London. Bernard struggled to separate projects that would benefit him and his family from those in which he had no personal stake: it became harder to make any such distinction when his interest in the enforcement of the trade laws was attacked from all sides. Bernard's interest in reforming the colonial system exposed his penchant for self-aggrandizement, and he succeeded only in presenting himself as an obvious target for an aggrieved community. The energy Bernard expended in promoting "The Principles of Law and Polity" might have been better spent in repairing his relations with the General Court.

Had Bernard shown more concern for the colonists' anxieties over the stamp tax as well as the Revenue Act and worked closer with them he might have been spared the opprobrium he endured in coming years. It is doubtful, however, whether a more forceful intercession by the governor would have made any appreciable difference to Grenville. If Bernard supposed that he could garner all the credit for persuading the colonists to accept taxation pro tempore as a prelude to the reform of colonial government and imperial administration, in which their grievances would be attended to, he was woefully out of touch with developments both in London and in the colonies.

It is a harsh judgment that exaggerates the differences between Bernard and other imperial reformers and ignores the simple fact that Bernard, like the colonists, was never given a hearing by the Grenville ministry. British enthusiasm for Bernard's root and branch approach to the reform of colonial government was at best sporadic and short-lived. Ministers and officials really had no reason to listen to what Bernard had to say irrespective of Temple's criticism, for they regarded the Revenue Act and the stamp tax as innocuous financial expedients. Britons likewise saw little worth in James Otis's radical declamations of colonial rights and liberties. They were "not well timed," one Bostonian reported from London: "the present Sentiments of the Ministry are such that they will not be bullied into Opinions contrary to their own."[128] Similarly, Hutchinson's subtleties in steering a middle course in the General Court were wasted on the Board of Trade and Privy Council who regretted the "indecent disrespect" with which the House of Representatives claimed the right of exemption from parliamentary taxation.[129]

As events unfolded in Boston and elsewhere, they reinforced Bernard's conviction that only by extending metropolitan authority could the American Question be put to rest. The Revenue Act proved a dismal failure, raising no more than four thousand pounds before it was substantially revised in 1766.[130] Conflicts between royal governors and senior customs officers, as between Bernard and John Temple, may have contributed to the inefficiency of the customhouse, although not greatly perhaps. It became more difficult, however, for Bernard and Hutchinson to defend parliamentary supremacy while arguing against the impropriety of taxation. Bernard consoled himself by blaming Otis and his cabal of smugglers and pastors for his predicament. He was delighted when Otis began to contradict his early denials of Parliament's right to tax the Americans and voted to increase Hutchinson's chief justice's salary, which had previously been cut in half. Bernard often misunderstood Otis's clever politicking: Otis had no intention of becoming a government man, but he realized that the assistance of both Hutchinson and Jackson were invaluable if the stamp tax were to be averted at this late stage. Bernard was not far off the mark with the jibe that Otis was repentant in "sackcloth & ashes." James Otis was no fool though he was a "recreant": like many Whigs he awaited with trepidation Britain's response to their assertions of colonial legislative rights. Otis's waning influence in Boston was temporary, however, and before the momentous year of 1765 was out he had retaken his place in the Whig leadership.[131] History, Otis once wrote, demonstrated that when governors "deviate from truth, justice and equity, they verge towards tyranny, and are to be opposed."[132] Had Otis chosen to ignore his conscience, the course of American history might have been very different. The Stamp Act crisis boosted the failing reputation of Otis in Massachusetts and of Bernard in London, and confirmed the fears of both men that royal government rested on uncertain foundations.

CHAPTER FOUR

"Anarchy and Confusion"
The Crisis of Authority, 1765

*T*HE SPRING OF 1765 was the last time Bernard enjoyed anything approaching the peaceful existence he desired when he
came to Massachusetts. When the Stamp Act received royal assent
on 22 March, the "common talk" in Boston was of conspiracies in
London to deprive Americans of their rights "as Englishmen" to
consent to acts of taxation.[1] The governor faced a seemingly impossible task in persuading the colonists to tolerate what they regarded as
an unprecedented change in their legislative relations with Britain
and as a threat to their traditions of self-government. How could he
reassure the colonists that their grievances would be attended to
when their complaints had hitherto been ignored? Should he now
supplicate himself before the General Court or tackle the extremists
whose words and deeds challenged parliamentary authority? Bernard
struggled to comprehend the radicalization of colonial politics
brought on by the Stamp Act controversy, but had no intention of
sacrificing his career by doing nothing. But when he spoke not of
protecting colonial liberties but of accepting Parliament's supreme
authority to do what it liked, he firmly established in American
minds what Benjamin Franklin later called "the Grenvillian Notion
of a necessary Connexion between Subjection and Taxation."[2]

Few colonists took kindly to being lectured to—especially the
somber and plainly dressed former tax collector who entered the
House for the first time on 27 September, two days after Bernard had
delivered the most important speech of his career. Good fortune had
long deserted Samuel Adams. He was forty-three years old, ten years
younger than Bernard, but had enjoyed little of the governor's good
health and fine living. His father's merciless creditors had eaten up

his modest patrimony, and his maltster's business was failing by the time Adams made his mark on provincial politics. Three of Adams's five children had died in infancy; he had been a widower and single parent for seven years when he remarried in 1764. To his friends, Adams was stoic in the face of adversity, a model of provincial integrity and of New England Calvinism. He was austere, his admiring cousin John wrote, but was always polite and agreeable; he was a man of "soft and delicate" political talents, and selflessly devoted to the "Cause" of liberty.[3] To his enemies, Adams was a bitter, resentful man who deceived colleagues into believing that Bernard and Hutchinson were intent on subverting colonial government.

Samuel Adams distrusted any Englishman who might presume to tell him what to do or think. He did not see himself as a natural opponent of government so much as its protector, dedicated to exorcizing the corruption that endangered the liberties of his countrymen. He was a "classic radical" who lamented the waning of Massachusetts's communitarian ideals. His mission in 1765 was to revitalize the commonwealth of incorporated towns as a bulwark against British tyranny, whereas James Otis was more "anglocentric" and legalistic in his analyses of the imperial relationship.[4] Along the way, Adams encountered an English governor who seemed to epitomize the worst aspects of imperial administration and a native-born deputy he believed was betraying his countrymen. Bernard was not the first governor to suffer Adams's wrath, but he was the first to be destroyed by the political machine that he had helped to create.

*   *   *

Adams's elevation from town to provincial politics coincided with the birth of a popular protest movement that challenged both the principles and propriety of British colonial policy. Adams was not the rabble-rousing leveler that Bernard claimed he was in some of his wilder outbursts, although Adams often ran ahead of public opinion. As J. P. Reid observes, everyone—Bernard, the British, and Adams—understood fully "that the authority to legislate was the [fundamental] issue in controversy, even when that issue was not directly asserted by the colonial whigs." Whigs consistently argued that Parliament's legislative supremacy was in law and in fact constrained by obligations to respect the colonists' self-governing institutions: Parliament had no right to legislate in respect of taxation. It was not

Samuel Adams. By John Singleton Copley, c. 1772. Deposited by the City of Boston. Courtesy, Museum of Fine Arts, Boston. Reproduced with permission. Copyright 2000 Museum of Fine Arts, Boston. All Rights Reserved.

until the colonists were provoked by the Coercive Acts in 1774 that the Whigs publicly carried the argument to its logical conclusion.[5]

The Whigs were gentlemen like Adams, lawyers like Otis, but also farmers, women, merchants, clergymen, artisans, and craftsmen. They were supremely effective propagandists, but their influence generally derived from the coordination of opposition in the legisla-

ture and in the towns, where support for the Whigs grew steadily between 1765 and 1774. Nongovernment opposition to British colonial
policy was sustained by political clubs such as the Sons of Liberty,
socially inclusive demonstrations and boycotts, and special committees of correspondence operating at provincial and interprovincial
levels.[6] The sense of purpose that radicals such as Adams brought to
provincial politics echoed the crusading zeal of the Puritans and the
Covenanters during the Great Rebellion of the 1640s. Otis too
preached unity in the face of adversity, and advocated the isolation of
the fawning "tories"—"low, rascally, artful and designing dogs"—
who dared profess loyalty to a "petulant and domineering governor."[7]

The friends of government were the mainstay of antirevolutionary
opinion in Massachusetts before the emergence of the Loyalists in
1775. First, they came to dispute the radicals' interpretations of American constitutional rights and the restrictions they placed on the
scope of parliamentary authority in the colonies. Like Adams and
Otis, they professed to uphold the constitutional arrangements settled by the Glorious Revolution and the province charter. In terms of
political ideology, the friends of government were mainstream
Whigs, but in terms of political strategy were far more cautious than
the leading Whigs.

They rejected outright the means employed by radicals to defeat
British policies—a strategy based on conventional constitutional
methods and extralegal protests. The preferred method of safeguard-
ing fundamental liberties was for the colonists to endure hardship
temporarily while the General Court and Governor Bernard negoti-
ated relief with the British government. It was how things had always
been done. Prominent friends of government like Attorney General
Edmund Trowbridge and the judge Peter Oliver warned of reprisals
should the General Court fail to include in its petitions explicit ac-
knowledgments of Parliament's sovereignty. More typical, however,
was the position taken by representatives such as Timothy Ruggles,
Gen. John Winslow, and Dudley Atkins who, according to John
Adams, supported calls for a repeal of the Stamp Act with pointed
criticism of the radicals. Only a few friends of government saw any
virtue in the Stamp Act itself, such as the Reverend Henry Caner and
James Murray, a recent arrival from North Carolina.[8] Nor was there
any enthusiasm for the doctrine of virtual representation as developed
by British placemen such as Thomas Whately and favored by Ber-

nard.[9] Most friends of government shared the Whigs' conviction that the right to tax lay firmly with the provincial assemblies.

It is difficult to estimate the numerical strength of the friends of government during the Stamp Act crisis because they did not create political associations until the 1770s. Around seventy, however, have been positively identified for 1765 and 1766, and another 116 during the remainder of Bernard's administration. The friends of government were in the majority in the Council, and during the 1764 and 1765 sessions comprised approximately 30 percent of the House. In twenty-five cases, they represented "court" towns with established political links to the royal governor.[10]

They included some of the province's most experienced public figures such as Israel Williams. Another such veteran of the French wars was Col. Richard Saltonstall of Essex County, who considered the Stamp Act "unwise but not illegal." Both men hailed from fine colonial families. Col. John Murray, who was sent to the House by the citizens of Rutland every year between 1751 and 1774, was by contrast a self-made man. He was an Irish immigrant who, from humble beginnings as a storekeeper in the frontier town of Rutland, amassed realty and personalty worth over twenty-one thousand pounds and married into the prominent Chandler family of Worcester.[11] Bernard's most important ally in the western counties was Timothy Ruggles, a lawyer by profession and a rival of the Otises before he was given command of provincial regiments in the French war. Ordinary people, observed John Adams, approached the brigadier general with "Dread and Terror" on account of his "conscious Superiority," but he was widely praised for the "quickness of his apprehension, Steadiness of . . . Thoughts and Expressions, [and] strict Honor." Ruggles was a critic of parliamentary taxation, but he was also among the most vociferous of James Otis's detractors.[12] These were self-important men who accepted deference as their due and treated governors as their equals.

They treasured their loyalty to Britain, but understood how the exigencies of war and the vicissitudes of peace were changing colonial politics and Britain's relations with the colonies. Woe betide any governor or minister who took their loyalty for granted. The friends of government were discomfited by Bernard's call for a "respectful submission" to the Stamp Act when, by late May, they knew how little impression the governor and the agents had made on ministers. Some may have joined the Whigs in trying to prevent Andrew

Oliver's election to the Council, after receiving news of his appointment as stamp distributor for the province. They would have succeeded but for the fact that Otis also tried to get rid of Hutchinson,
who could still count on his many admirers. On 6 June the friends of
government joined the moderate and radical Whigs in calling for a
congress of all the colonies, a proposal that had originated with James
Otis a year before. Otis, Ruggles, and Oliver Partridge were appointed Massachusetts's delegates to the Stamp Act Congress, which
met in New York in October.[13]

It was, as Bernard rightly observed, a groundbreaking experiment
in intercolonial opposition to Britain. One British historian has suggested that the British might have tempered the colonies' enthusiasm
for the congress by enacting Bernard's proposal for a Crown civil
list.[14] The opposite seems more likely, however, for in Massachusetts
at least the proposal for the congress was also a vote of no confidence
in the governor's ability to resolve their differences with Britain. Bernard was powerless to prevent the assembly sending delegates to the
congress, although he was subsequently able to brief Ruggles. Ironi-
cally, what made Bernard's situation all the more embarrassing was
that Massachusetts was by no means the most extreme of the colonies. Virginia, Connecticut, and New York all claimed for "the People" a right to "resume" a power to reject the Stamp Act, whereas it
would be several years before the General Court formally assumed a
sovereign power to nullify parliamentary legislation.[15]

The influence of the Massachusetts radicals should not be over-
stated. Samuel Adams enjoyed considerable acclaim in Boston,
where the friends of government had little influence in local offices
generally.[16] Adams was fully aware of matters farther afield, particularly the reluctance of western towns to follow Boston's lead. Adams
frequently criticized rural voters for choosing moderates such as Si-
meon Strong of Hadley, who was being "led away" by the "POPERY"
of the friends of government as to be "but a step from a total APOS-
TACY [sic]."[17] Moderate Whigs were lukewarm to Adams's robust
leadership and effusive protestations of colonial rights, and though
they occasionally voted with the friends of government they were also
critical of the governor.

The only group solidly behind Bernard was the Anglican clergy.
Bernard would have agreed with the Reverend Henry Caner when he
claimed, with little regard for history or politics, that the Church of
England was "the only religious Profession among us that sincerely

cultivates the Principles of Loyalty and obedience to the British Crown and Government."[18] Peter Oliver, an Anglican, famously accused the "Black Regiment" of Congregationalist clergy of fomenting rebellion from the pulpit,[19] but denominational affiliation never solely determined political allegiances. The Anglican laity of Boston and Cambridge were wealthy men, and though they became Loyalists they were not firm supporters of the governor. Twelve prominent Anglicans were Whigs before they became friends of government, including, for example, George Bethune, who was a member of the merchants' pressure group, the Boston Society for Encouraging Trade and Commerce.[20] In other towns, the Anglicans were drawn from a much broader section of the population and, as it transpired, were much divided in their political views.[21] One Anglican merchant regretted that only in England the Episcopalian "mingles in Acts of Friendship" with dissenters, yet he was more perturbed by the economic aspects of Grenville's reforms than the church's failure to get an American bishop.[22] It was the same even for Henry Barnes, a wealthy merchant of Marlborough and one of the few laymen to embrace the campaign for a bishop.[23]

With few exceptions, the colonial leaders could claim descent from the settlers of the Great Migration,[24] but in the absence of extrainstitutional associations some thirty-three extended family groups helped to provide leadership and foster group identity among the friends of government. They included the Amorys, the Ervings, and the Coffins of Boston, as well as the better-known Hutchinsons and Olivers, the Chandlers and the Putnams of Worcester County, and the Pickmans of Salem. The Coffins were numerically the largest of these families. No fewer than seventeen of merchant William Coffin's sixty children and grandchildren became Loyalists, five of whom were active friends of government before the war. Nathaniel Coffin, the oldest son, was a merchant who married the daughter of Henry Barnes. Nathaniel's sisters both married Anglican merchants— Thomas Amory and Gilbert Deblois—who, though moderate Whigs, in the late 1760s came to question the expediency of crowd action and a unilateral boycott if the Townshend Acts were to be repealed. Nathaniel Coffin was ambivalent toward politics until the controversy over the Stamp Act, and like many friends of government was well connected to both local Whigs and government officials.[25]

Bernard still thought the political situation in the early summer of

1765 "generally favorable to Government" despite the General Court's refusal to channel its grievances through his office.[26] When Grenville resigned in July, Bernard could be forgiven for supposing that Massachusetts's citizens would "submit . . . to the Stamp Act without actual Opposition." New Englanders' enthusiasm for Virginia's radical assertion of colonial rights was waning.[27] No one expected that royal officials would fall hostage to some of the most violent riots in the colony's history.[28]

*   *   *

On the morning of Wednesday, 14 August, an effigy of Andrew Oliver, the stamp distributor, was found hanging from a tree near the busy intersection of Essex and Orange Streets in Boston's South End. A large crowd dissuaded sheriff Stephen Greenleaf from removing the effigy; he and his men withdrew, Bernard reported, thinking they were in "imminent Danger of their Lives."[29] The crowd grew to some five thousand by the afternoon, thronging Boston's narrow streets. Sightseers from the country, workmen, craftsmen, women, and children flocked to observe and join the processions that wound their way through the streets, decrying infringements to their liberties.

In the early evening a mob some one thousand strong carried Oliver's effigy to the Town House, where Bernard and the Council were sitting. They "gave three huzza's by Way of Defiance & pass'd on." On hearing "Bombs bursting and canons firing," reported one citizen, Bernard and the Council took "to their Heels as fast they could." Under the leadership of Ebenezer MacIntosh, a cordwainer, the mob proceeded to demolish Oliver's unfinished storehouse on Kilby Street, where it was rumored that the stamps to be used on colonial documents were being kept. The timber fed a bonfire on Fort Hill. Oliver was not at home when, later that night, the mob broke into his home, flattened his garden, and vandalized his furniture and other valuables. The next day Oliver promised to resign his distributor's commission.[30]

Governor Bernard spent an anxious night at the castle, staring across the harbor to the glimmering lights on Fort Hill. He was profoundly disturbed by the day's proceedings, which he reported "exceeded all others known here both in the Vehemence of Action and Mischeivousness of intention."[31] He found the ambivalence of the Council puzzling: some councilors were too quick to dismiss the effigy as the work of "pranksters," whereas, by the afternoon, others were warning that the demonstrations were "a preconcerted business, in which the greatest part of the town was engaged."[32] Any attempt to disperse the crowd, they said, would invite retribution, far worse than the shower of stones that greeted Thomas Hutchinson when he ventured to stop the mob from vandalizing Oliver's home. Bernard learned shortly that when the crowds gathered on Fort Hill a few hotheads proposed tracking down Oliver and Hutchinson, but the justices of the peace and the selectmen talked them out of it. The crowd seemed content with breaking the windows of Hutchinson's fine mansion the next day, which were decorated with crowns.

On the evening of Monday, 26 August, however, angry mobs took to the streets once more. At a prearranged signal, the crowd marched to the rented home of the hated customs official Charles Paxton, who managed to escape before it arrived. The crowd proceeded to ransack the home and office of William Story, deputy register of the provincial court of Vice Admiralty, and burn court records. Next in line was the comptroller of customs, Benjamin Hallowell. The militia officers refused Bernard's request to call out Boston's four companies, many of their drummers having already joined the mobs.[33] While Bernard skulked at the castle, Hutchinson refused to leave his home, bravely awaiting a mob now animated by punch and an "evil spirit." Hutchinson fled at the last possible moment, responding only to the desperate pleas of his daughter Sally, and was eventually brought to Castle William in Bernard's barge. Bernard thought his deputy would have been lynched had he remained behind. Between thirty and forty people, many of the "lowest" sorts, proceeded to loot and vandalize Hutchinson's possessions. They spent the night diligently removing the cupola, exposing part of the roof; only the thickness of the walls prevented them from demolishing the building. The next morning the streets were littered with money, silver plate, and scraps of Hutchinson's manuscript collection. Hutchinson estimated his losses at around £2,218 sterling.[34]

The composition of the mobs drew particular comment from Bernard. He was shocked by how "many Abettors of Consequence" there were. Before he fled the town on 14 August, Bernard claimed to recognize "fifty Gentlemen Actors" disguised in trousers and jackets (though he did not name them), "besides a much larger Number behind the Curtains." These gentlemen, he admitted, had a restraining influence on the lower orders, for they "proceeded no further than

burning the Effigy & then departed & had no hand in Storming [Ol-
iver's] House"; it was they who, along with the justices and selectmen, persuaded the mobs to refrain from physical attacks.[35] In short,
the "Abettors of Consequence" gave crowd action a political direction, which it otherwise might have lacked, and helped to contain
lawlessness.

The Boston riots were anything but spontaneous. They were
probably organized by the Loyal Nine, a committee of artisans, small
businessmen, and shopkeepers associated with Samuel Adams and
the town's caucuses who were the core of Boston's Sons of Liberty.
Smugglers and land speculators "elated" by old grievances "as fresh as
if it had been a Business of yesterday," noted Bernard, might also
have lent a hand; their resentment of Hutchinson was more personal
than political and was "the Principal if not the Sole Cause of the second insurrection." The demonstrators may have included such
wealthy merchants as John Rowe and Solomon Davis, who wrongly
suspected Hutchinson of having sent to England sworn affidavits accusing them of smuggling.[36] The identities of only a handful of rioters are known from court records pertaining to their subsequent
arrest. Other such records, however, suggest that the majority of rioters were manual laborers, shipyard workers, and artisans.[37]

One thing is certain: the mobs' targets were carefully chosen; Oliver, because he was to be principal administrator of the hated stamp
tax, and Hutchinson, because as chief justice he was responsible for
its enforcement. The plural officeholding of Hutchinson and Oliver
was also cited by the likes of John Adams and the Boston town meeting as a major reason why they had incited resentment, though the
Whigs were genuinely distressed by the methodical destruction of
Hutchinson's property.[38]

Demonstrations against the Stamp Act occurred in several colonial towns and succeeded in forcing nearly all the distributors to resign, but none were so violent as those in Boston and New York. The
Boston rioters were neither rebels nor levelers, however, and had
taken to the streets as a *posse comitatus* in defense of the commonwealth. Crowd action was a traditional mechanism of social and political protest, a form of extralegal political action that Governor
Bernard never fully understood because it legitimized the intimidation of government officials. When the conventional processes of
averting parliamentary taxation appeared to be exhausted, the Whig
leaders in Boston transformed the crowd into what William Pencak

has called "a quasiinstitutionalized instrument of the popular party."[39]

To be sure, the "Abettors of Consequence" Bernard decried were unable to control every move of their social inferiors—skilled and unskilled workers, women, "boys," and "negroes" who swelled the crowds. It is generally agreed that the desecration of Hutchinson's mansion is the most important instance of when a colonial crowd got out of hand, where reason and moral authority gave way to pent-up emotions and resentment at Hutchinson's wealth.[40] Bernard knew this, but, because he was not a witness to the sorry spectacle, he supposed that MacIntosh's superiors had acquiesced in the attack on Hutchinson's house only to see their influence called into question by the violence that ensued. "Great pains," Bernard wrote, "are taken to separate the two riots; what was done against Mr. Oliver is still approved of, as a necessary Declaration of their Resolution not to submit to the Stamp Act . . . but it has been publicly hinted that if a Line is not drawn between the first Riot & the last, the civil Power will not be supported by the principal people of the Town, as it is assured it shall be now." Having "raised the Devil" of mob rule and the specter of a "War of Plunder" between "rich and poor," the colonists would have a devil of a job in putting them to rest.[41]

Bernard was mightily relieved that he "had no share in this resentment," noting that "during the whole disturbance no personal insult was directed at me."[42] No recent Massachusetts governor had been mishandled by a mob, but it was evident from what happened to Hutchinson that Crown office in itself did not confer immunity from attack. It is possible that the mob turned on Hutchinson because Bernard had already fled to the castle when it came calling at the Province House on 15 and 26 August to shout abuse. Although that scenario seems unlikely, given that resentment toward Hutchinson had been simmering for some time, it should not be entirely discounted. Another more plausible reason why Bernard was spared was that he had no property in the town. Thus, any moves against the governor would necessarily involve the crowd surrounding a public building—the Town House or the Province House—or manhandling the governor in the street. Either way the colonists would run the risk of appearing as seditious rebels.

The Stamp Act riots were Bernard's first encounters with instances of prolonged civil disorder, and they appeared all the more frightening because of this. His first shot in trying to persuade British

ministers that resistance to the Stamp Act was seditious came on 16
August when he made the startling claim that any "Man who offers
a Stamped Paper to sell will be immediately kill'd."[43] Law enforcement, Bernard asserted, had temporarily broken down in Boston.
Such a perception was an issue of contention between Bernard and
the Whigs for the remainder of his administration, as historian J. P.
Reid has shown. But this was not Bernard the lawyer talking so much
as Bernard the governor, tortured by his failure to enforce the law. In
other letters he speculated whether the riots were a prelude to a coup
d'état. Even if that were not the case, it was reckless of Britain to have
attempted to tax the Americans against their wishes when it was evident that royal government was ill equipped to compel submission.
Bernard was aroused to a state of intense alarm by the painful realization that ministers were patently unaware of his predicament—that
royal government faced an unprecedented crisis of authority.

> To introduce Parliamentary Taxations into America before the
> Establishment of a Power sufficient to enforce Obedience to them
> is . . . beginning at the Wrong End. The People know at present
> they may chuse whether they would be taxed or not; & in such a
> deliberation it is easy to say what their Choice will be. . . . Surely
> it is not known in Whitehall how weak & impotent the Author-
> ity of the American Governors is in regard to popular Tumults.[44]

Bernard was proved wrong with respect to his claims about law and
order and the colonists' plans to seize power. Subsequent events,
however, exposed his powerlessness to enforce imperial law against
the wishes of the commonwealth—not only the populace but the
House, the Council, the magistracy, and the militia: that, by the governor's reckoning, constituted rebellion.

Bernard's initial and perhaps instinctive reaction was to seek a military solution. But the Council, having earlier refused to establish a
town watch, on 28 August refused to join Bernard in asking General
Gage, the commander in chief of Britain's North American forces, to
send British regulars to Boston, on the grounds that troops would
only inflame the populace. The Council records reveal that both
moderate Whigs and friends of government voted down the proposal, possibly Hutchinson and Oliver too. Bernard legally required
the Council's consent to make any such application, and sensibly let
the matter rest for the moment.[45] So long as the threat of reprisal re-

mained, Bernard resolved to make no such application on his own authority.[46] He was bemused by the Council's recalcitrance, however, which he attributed to a "Timidity . . . which persuades People to keep out of the Way of Resentment," although many councilors were "in their hearts well wishers to Government & ready to support it, when they can do it with safety."[47]

The Council was more pragmatic in its response to crowd action and law-and-order issues than Bernard was ever wont to admit. The Council approved Bernard's proposal that the militia companies of nearby towns—Roxbury, Cambridge, and Charlestown—be called to alert. On 27 August the Council recognized Bernard's concern about the unreliability of militia when it was rumored that the customhouse and up to fifteen more houses were to be attacked the following night. Three hundred men normally excused service in the militia—the Company of Cadets, customs officials, gentlemen, and merchants—were formed into a volunteer guard to protect property and patrol the town's streets under the command of the colonel of the militia Joseph Jackson. Similar associations were formed in the towns of Plymouth, Salem, and Marblehead.[48]

While Bernard acquiesced in the Council's opposition to using British troops, the report that he sent General Gage in New York on 27 August was worded as to encourage Gage to make military preparations, which the general was entitled to do without the authorization of the civil government if he believed the situation in Boston warranted it. When the mobs appeared "all civil power ceased in an instant. . . . [He] had not the least authority to oppose or quiet the mob." The "commotions" of Boston, he also warned Admiral Colville, "are got to such a pitch, that it is now in an actual State of Rebellion. . . . ev'ry Person having command under his Majesty should contribute every thing in his Power to preserve this place from utter ruin from a merciless Mob."[49]

Gage appreciated why the governor "seemed to wish for troops, tho' afraid to demand them."[50] He did not doubt that if Bernard could convince the British of his situation he would eventually get the troops he wanted. Gage did not act hastily, though, and placed the Twenty-ninth Regiment at Halifax, Nova Scotia, on a state of alert. He also sent Bernard a trusted officer to help him prepare for a retreat to Castle William.[51]

If there was to be an insurrection Bernard and Gage supposed that it would take the form of an organized assault on the castle, though that would have required the Bostonians to collect a flotilla of boats. (The Council had recommended on 21 August that when the stamps eventually arrived, they should be stored at the castle. They arrived on 23 September and were moved to the castle on 2 October.[52] Bernard had little choice but to go along with the Council lest he wish to take delivery of the stamps himself.) When Bernard learned that Gage could only spare one hundred soldiers in the first instance, he began to panic: such a small force could never patrol the town effectively, and if used to garrison the castle would surely incite the mobs.

In the meantime, Bernard did what he could to improve the castle's defenses. On 29 August Bernard asked Col. Richard Saltonstall to raise a company of the Essex militia "not tinctured by the seditious spirit" for garrison duty at the castle. Saltonstall completed his assignment, in spite of a peaceful demonstration by more than three hundred people when his company left Essex.[53] Bernard was beginning to realize just how serious the ideological divisions in the province were, but he had no real option but to accept the Council's recommendation to disband Saltonstall's company and give up plans to deploy the county militia in Boston.[54]

Bernard's attempts to apprehend the rioters were equally fraught with difficulties. His reports on the riots were prima facie evidence of unlawful and felonious assemblies to warrant investigation by the Crown; so too was the imputation that the town officials, the justices, and the militia had been negligent and at worst parties to criminal acts. Rioters could be charged with either unlawful assembly or petty treason (as were many of the Gordon rioters in London in 1780). In either case, the Crown was obliged to prove intent—that the riots were premeditated acts.[55] For that reason Bernard issued on 15 August a proclamation offering a pardon and one hundred pounds for information leading to prosecutions.[56]

On 27 August, however, Sheriff Greenleaf arrested Ebenezer MacIntosh in King Street, and over the next twenty-four hours or so six other men were taken into custody. Bernard and Hutchinson needed MacIntosh to turn king's evidence if they were ever to apprehend the organizers of the riots, and on 28 August a reward of three hundred pounds was issued for the discovery of the "directors."[57] Something extraordinary, however, had already happened that undermined all efforts to bring the rioters to justice. Shortly after MacIntosh's arrest, Nathaniel Coffin and "several other gentlemen" protested to Sheriff Greenleaf that he be set free immediately. According to Hutchinson, Coffin told Greenleaf "that it had been agreed that the cadets and many others should appear in arms the next evening, as a guard and security against a fresh riot, which was feared, and said to have been threatened, but not a man would appear unless MacIntosh was discharged." To Hutchinson's chagrin, the sheriff did not consult him before releasing MacIntosh. When Bernard refused to move for a prosecution, MacIntosh was allowed to enjoy his freedom.[58]

Coffin's intercession encapsulated the equivocal response of many friends of government to the law-and-order issues raised by the riots. Hutchinson did not comment directly on Coffin's motivation, but he criticized Greenleaf and Bernard, for he believed that MacIntosh knew the identities of those citizens who had organized the riots. But this, we may deduce, was the root of the problem from Coffin's point of view when he confronted Greenleaf: the rumor of further disturbances may have reflected pressure being brought to bear on the volunteer guard by the Loyal Nine, who feared that MacIntosh would divulge their names.[59] Bernard acquiesced in Greenleaf's decision to release MacIntosh without seeking Hutchinson's opinion, though he protested vehemently that lawbreakers were being allowed "to walk the Streets with impunity." Bernard had evidently failed to persuade any citizen to testify against MacIntosh, and thus was unable to persuade MacIntosh to turn against his abettors. Moreover, the volunteer guard was the only force available to police the town, and clearly Bernard had no wish to provoke another riot by holding the cordwainer. On 1 October MacIntosh's accomplices were rescued from the town jail with suspicious ease. According to J. P. Reid, these incidents demonstrated "that to enforce any law remotely associated with the political controversy" it was necessary "to accept whig ordained conditions. No whig rioter was again arrested in Boston."[60]

It has often been said that Grenville miscalculated when he supposed that by appointing prominent colonists like Andrew Oliver as distributors he would palliate opposition to the stamp tax. No one could have anticipated that senior officials would be so ritually humiliated by crowds or indeed that afterward the General Court would ignore a governor's pleas to obey an act of Parliament. What Bernard witnessed in August 1765 never left him: his impressionistic accounts of an unstable polity struggling to realize ill-informed directives from London was the single, enduring message in his official correspondence for years to come. Henceforth, Bernard was preoccupied with recovering his dignity and exposing those whom he believed were conspiring against royal government.

*   *   *

Bernard returned to the Province House at the beginning of September to consider what might be done to get the Stamp Act implemented on 1 November, the day it took effect.[61] He took the precaution of forming a bodyguard of militiamen under Maj. Jeremiah Green, commander of Boston's South Battery, which was to be used "where the preservation of his majesty's subjects in their lives and properties shall require."[62] Having alerted Gage to the possibility of armed resistance, Bernard now worried that the general would act unilaterally, and on 12 September rejected Gage's offer of troops. He required "fair play & a clear stage" if he was "to prevail upon the assembly to counter work the passions of the people."[63]

By the end of August at the earliest, Bernard had decided to make an appeal to the General Court.[64] On 5 September he treated the Council to a "pathetick" account of the "Miseries" that would likely follow any attempts to prevent his administration from using the stamps. Public offices including the customhouse, the law courts, and the province Treasury would simply close, for officials could not be expected to contravene an act of Parliament. "Necessity," he continued, "will soon oblige & Justify an insurrection of the Poor against the rich; those that want the necessaries of Life against those that have them."[65] The meeting ended in agreement that Bernard should summon the General Court.[66] While Bernard accepted that "civil government" was returning to "full Power," he gambled in supposing that the "prospect of . . . Anarchy & confusion" would focus minds. The members, he supposed, would be "greatly Staggered" if he were to ask them "to assist the Execution of an Act of Parliament which is opposed by Violence." Hitherto the opposition was "chargeable upon private persons only," but if the legislature refused to recommend submission to an act of Parliament or assist in its execution, all they might reasonably expect was a "forfeiture of their Rights."[67]

The gross unpopularity of the Stamp Act precluded any attempt by Bernard to seek support for British policies per se. Instead, he resorted to making what he called "argumentative speeches," whereby he reduced the complexities of political and constitutional arguments to a simple choice of principles, a kind of ideological blackmail where the colonists' response was measurable on a sliding scale between loyalty and disloyalty to the Crown. Bernard's efforts were "addressed to a particular people . . . for particular purposes"—the friends of government and the moderate Whigs, who he hoped would lead a backlash against the radicals; this might also obviate any need for the House to address the king, which the Bostonians urged their representatives to do on 13 September.[68] Bernard's timing could not have been better, for the stamps arrived at Castle William two days before he was due to address the assembly.[69]

Bernard's speech of 25 September was the most controversial of his career. It was his "last and strongest effort," he told Jackson, to have the Stamp Act implemented by 1 November. His approach, he explained to Halifax, was "to Open their Eyes in the General Court [to action] necessary to Save their country from immediate Ruin."[70] His administration could not be expected to flout parliamentary authority by allowing public offices to function without the validation of the stamps, he flatly told the General Court. Nor, he quickly added, did he alone have the requisite authority to distribute the stamps now that Oliver had resigned. The responsibility for resolving this dilemma, Bernard proclaimed, fell on the whole government of the province, not just the chief magistrate.[71] Bernard allowed no distinction between legal and extralegal protests: "Disobedience," he continued, "was productive of much more Evil than a submission to it [the Stamp Act]."

> *If the parliament declares that this right [of taxation] is inherent in them, are they likely to acquiesce in an open and forcible opposition to the exercise of it? . . .*
>
> *May it not bring on a contest, which may prove the most detrimental and ruinous event which could happen to this people?*

Anarchy, "Fraud and Rapine" would haunt the province if criminal and civil legal processes were brought to a halt. The closure of the ports would surely bring misery to those whose livelihoods depended upon commerce. And what then, he asked: "Will these people [suffer] want quietly without troubling their neighbours?"[72]

As well as submitting to the Stamp Act, Bernard suggested that the province might atone for the riots by compensating those persons whose property had been damaged, a policy later adopted by the Rockingham ministry. Britain might not punish the province, but if the assembly rejected compensation then surely Britain would exact some form of restitution. (Bernard chose not to suggest that Britain might abolish the province charter, for the prospect of direct rule from London was hardly appealing under the circumstances.)[73]

Bernard saw no reason to give the Whigs an opportunity to formulate a riposte, and prorogued the assembly as planned three days later to allow the friends of government and moderates to elicit local support for his recommendations. Bernard's speech was published and subsequently satirized in broadsheets and newspapers as the edicts of a biblical tyrant (Francis the Ruler) or Spanish Don (Bernardus Francisco).[74] It was a "wretched speech," wrote the Reverend Mayhew, that "seems to desire that the general court should assist in putting these heavy chains on themselves and the people." Bernard, observed John Adams, had "painted a dreadful picture of the times."[75]

When Francis Bernard chose to employ the imagery of social conflict and civil war, he aimed to exploit perceptions and anxieties rather than actualities. The colonial protest movement was not wholly controlled by a radical faction and the province was not on the edge of revolution, as Bernard asserted, though many colonists were clearly apprehensive about the prospect of ever changing ministers' views on parliamentary taxation after the August riots. In retrospect, however, Bernard misjudged the disposition of the legislature.

When the General Court met again on 23 October, it delivered a stinging rebuke of Bernard's schemes, in which it reaffirmed a commitment to work for an immediate repeal of the Stamp Act. The members could see no justification for Bernard's grim prognosis, and berated the governor for his thinly veiled accusations of disloyalty. They rejected out of hand the suggestion of compensating the victims of the riots. The crimes were "committed by a few individuals," and they were not "convinced" public restitution would discourage "such outrages in times to come." Bernard had never suggested that it might; thus did the House artfully twist the context in which the proposal was originally made. Instead of becoming the issue on which the representatives could unite behind his administration, compensation was made to sound ludicrous.[76]

Bernard claimed that his plans were thwarted by fears of mob intimidation, lest the friends of government's support for his administration be misinterpreted as support for the Stamp Act itself. The testaments of Bernard and Hutchinson do not overestimate the impact of the Boston riots on the thinking and actions of the friends of government. They fail, however, to acknowledge the positive reasons for their refusal to support the administration.[77] On 29 October the House unanimously adopted a declaration of "inalienable rights" held to be "consistent with a subordination to the supreme power of Great Britain." The declaration reaffirmed loyalty, recognized parliamentary sovereignty, and called for the repeal of the Stamp Act in terms that most colonists would have considered reasonable and consistent with their charter rights. One resolution, however, explicitly rejected American representation in Parliament as a proposed compromise.[78] By October 1765 more than forty towns had instructed their representatives to work for the act's repeal, including Salem, Marblehead, and Newburyport, whose representatives were noted friends of government and whose inhabitants Bernard considered generally "well disposed to government."[79]

On his return from the Stamp Act Congress in late October, Otis reassumed leadership of the popular faction in Boston, though by then Samuel Adams had made his mark. Bernard was thoroughly dispirited by developments on 30 and 31 October, when the House debated Adams's contentious resolve to suspend the Stamp Act on the grounds that Bernard had no authority to issue stamps to public offices. A joint committee of thirteen, with a Whig majority, recommended that if the public offices were not to be closed, then officials should be ordered by the province to proceed without the stamps, as had already happened in Rhode Island.[80] Only two councilors and one representative spoke in Bernard's defense when the debate turned on the question of how the governor might react to the prospect of the General Court's legislating against the execution of the Stamp Act. Adams had urged defiance, but few could yet countenance seizing such a power as they would in 1774.

The "Governor would pass it, he must pass it, he could not refuse it," Bernard reported the legislators saying.[81] However, neither the House nor the Council could agree on the substance of the resolution's preamble, and consideration by the whole was postponed until the next session in January. Some were discomfited by talk of nullifying an act of Parliament, and worried as to what might transpire if their governor were to be boxed in. Had Adams's resolve passed without amendment, Bernard would certainly have left Boston, weather permitting, for he had made arrangements with Admiral Colville for a navy ship to be on standby to take him to England.[82]

Bernard's urgency to resolve the crisis had led him to ignore warnings from his confidants—undoubtedly Hutchinson and Andrew Oliver—that the colony "would not hear of a Submission." It is likely that Bernard was urged to delay making his argumentative speech until such time as he could build up political support privately. Whig councilors would surely have alerted their colleagues in the House to what the governor had told them on 5 September, and few persons could have been expected to make their support for Bernard public when mobs had generated fear and indecision among officials. Bernard, however, had little opportunity to "sound out" actual and potential supporters before the legislature met, yet foolishly made no attempt to ascertain the views of the members in general, with the exception of Timothy Ruggles and Oliver Partridge. Without such information, he could not understand why the friends of government were so reluctant to do anything to help him.

The only evidence of support for his administration that Bernard could cite in his reports to Whitehall was Timothy Ruggles's apostasy at the Stamp Act Congress, of which body he had been elected president. Before Ruggles left for New York, Bernard asked him to consider what had been said to the General Court, and to persuade the other delegates that "a Submission to the Act for the present" was the only sensible option open to them. As it was, the Congress's petitions and resolutions were less strident than those already drawn up by colonial assemblies. The main issue of debate, according to one historian, was "whether to balance the denial of Parliament's authority to tax the colonies with an acknowledgement of what authority it did have." The Congress refused to recommend that the colonies accept the enforcement of the Stamp Act or, as Ruggles wanted, send to the assemblies for approval the Congress's address to the king. Ruggles abdicated the chair in disgust, whereupon one young radical, Thomas McKean of Pennsylvania, challenged him to a duel. The fifty-four-year-old war veteran calmly ignored McKean and returned home. Only one other delegate refused to sign the Congress's petitions on account of what they contained, although others refused because they were not specifically mandated by their assemblies to do such a thing: we can discount therefore any notion that Ruggles led a conservative clique. Ruggles was subsequently censured by the Massachusetts House, but the *crise de conscience* he experienced arose from the realization that most Americans were not represented at the Congress, and that whatever that body did it alone would never be able to persuade Parliament to repeal the Stamp Act.[83]

Bernard's predicament and the marginalization of friends of government like Ruggles were a salutary lesson for other royal governors. Discretion, silence even, might have been preferable to lecturing the colonists on their duties. "The sound of liberty was enchanting," Thomas Hutchinson later recalled in a veiled criticism of Bernard; "the terms passive obedience and non-resistance . . . were deservedly odious."[84] Gov. William Franklin of New Jersey, the son of Benjamin Franklin, supposed that the controversy would have blown over were it not for the "unnecessary Officiousness" of Bernard in Massachusetts and Cadwallader Colden in New York in refusing to accept that *ex necessitate* the Stamp Act should be regarded as a dead letter. However, it was only because, as the Morgans once remarked, Boston "set the pace" of resistance to parliamentary authority in the colonies that Governor Franklin had the luxury of being able to reflect on "what Govr Barnard . . . experienced" before acquiescing in the face of the opposition in New Jersey.[85]

*   *   *

The political iconography that emerged during the Stamp Act crisis—in riots, demonstrations, parades, celebratory dinners, ceremonies at Liberty Trees, and political writings—aimed to maximize popular awareness of political issues and to encourage participation at the expense of "Tories."[86] Bernard, however, was concerned that the street parades planned for Pope's Day, 5 November, might degenerate into violence. Rivalry between the North End and South End gangs had disturbed the previous year's festivities, when the militia were called upon to usher away the crowds.[87] On 31 October the militia warned Bernard that it could not answer another such request. The officers "assured [him] that if the Guard was dismissed the Town would be quiet, otherwise not," and that "there would be no hurt done to any one or anything."[88]

As this incident suggests, crowd action functioned within strict parameters. Boston's justices, selectmen, and merchants well understood the controlling influences of the Loyal Nine. The parades were carefully policed to ensure that the lawlessness of 26 August would never again tarnish reputations. The pageantry was symbolic of the commonwealth's determination to evoke the moral authority of the *posse comitatus* in defiance of the governor. On 1 November the *Boston Gazette* was printed as usual, but without any Crown stamp. At 2 P.M., a procession led by Ebenezer MacIntosh, the people's general as he was now being called, took to the streets. More than two thousand people joined the parade, "walking in exact order," watched by "innumerable people" who had come in from the country. There were between one hundred and one hundred and fifty stewards, as competent as a "military Corps." Equally unsettling was the sight of the elderly William Brattle, the adjutant general of the militia, walking arm in arm with MacIntosh at the head of the procession. Brattle "complimented him [MacIntosh] on the order he kept & told him his Post was one of the highest in the Government."[89] The crowd made its way to the Town House, where the General Court was in session. To Bernard's utter dismay, Brattle escorted MacIntosh into the building, and "conducted him round the Town House whilst both Houses were sitting before which regular Huzza's were made."[90]

A worrying aspect for Bernard was the tendency of moderate councilors like William Brattle to side with the radicals. Bernard was perplexed by the turn of affairs, which had brought some of the colony's first citizens—and future Loyalists—into contact with lowly artisans like MacIntosh. Brattle was not a wealthy man and his political loyalty to the government had been motivated by his personal friendship with former governor William Shirley.[91] He had not fallen out with Bernard—indeed he had been "remarkably civil" to him—but gravitated toward the popular party with the onset of the Stamp Act crisis. Lately, he had composed a set of instructions for Cambridge's representative that Bernard thought "outrageous," "indecent," and an "infamous libell [*sic*]" on Parliament.[92] The only explanation he could think of was that the old general wanted to "make . . . a merit of being an object of the Governor's anger."[93]

The governor's supporters had formed a majority on the Council since the early 1760s. That majority began to dissipate during the Stamp Act crisis. Ten councilors elected that year were Whigs, including James Bowdoin, Royal Tyler, and Col. James Otis Sr. Several others, including William Brattle, John Erving, Treasurer Harrison Gray, and Isaac Royall, considered themselves to be moderate Whigs and did not belong to any Whig organization such as the Sons of Liberty. Some radicals doubted their conviction. Brattle was known as the "weathercock," for example, and in time he and the other moderates became friends of government. John Erving's Whiggism was influenced by the politics of the countinghouse and his conflict with the administration over his family's illicit trading activities.[94] Family connections figured more prominently in determining the allegiance of Harrison Gray. John Adams described Gray as "an open and decided an American as James Otis," whose brother was married to Gray's daughter. With the death of his mentor, the Reverend Jonathan Mayhew, Gray "lapsed into a very tender mind," reluctant to confront any "Man of the other Side," lest "everybody will be against him." It was said he "hoped to prepare the Way for his Escape" by refusing a seat on the Council at the next election. He did not, however, and remained in office until 1774.[95]

However much the moderates were discomfited by the riots, they were reluctant to do anything that might actually assist in the implementation of the Stamp Act. All the moderates had rejected Bernard's suggestion that British troops might be necessary to protect government officials.[96] The Council again advised Bernard not to summon the militia for 5 November when MacIntosh's men were abroad. The "union" of the North End and South End gangs under MacIntosh symbolized the communality of the colonists' struggle against the Stamp Act.

For Bernard, however, it was a potent signal of democracy. MacIntosh was the son of a Scottish immigrant, raised in the backstreets of Boston, and had served with provincial forces in 1758. He now dressed splendidly in a colorful gold-laced coat, carrying a rattan cane and speaking trumpet "to proclaim his orders" to his officers who were dressed in red hats; "no one else had any Stick or offensive Weapon; & no Negro was suffered to appear in their Ranks." The crowd, Bernard stressed, "acted Visibly under the directions of persons much his Superiors."[97] Several "Stages with Images & popes & Devils" and stampmasters were dragged to the Town House while Bernard was nervously chairing a Council meeting. By his own admission, Bernard was the only person in the building to voice any "disapprobation" of the proceedings, yet wisely gave a donation to "the Pageants" when asked. His money went toward the cost of "a public entertainment" at a local tavern attended by two hundred people "of all sorts."[98]

The moderate councilors justified their association with the radicals by claiming that Bernard's behavior was unlikely to encourage the colonists to act with restraint. On 7 November the Council stated unequivocally that they had agreed to resource Saltonstall's regiment only because "the minds of the People were so agitated" by the riots. They never intended to assist in the execution of the Stamp Act, but acted to preserve law and order. They were "by no means fond of exercising such a Power," and assured the representatives that "the Board are embarked in the same bottom with the . . . House; we must both sink or swim together."[99] The Council's concurrence with Bernard was mitigated by its members' desire to placate the radicals in the House. In December the Council apologized to the lower chamber for having disbursed money from the province treasury to pay the garrison at Castle William before the stamps were taken there, despite acting in accordance with its emergency powers.[100] The councilors also acquiesced in the appointment of Dennis DeBerdt as a special agent to work with Richard Jackson, though the House did not consult with them. Hutchinson complained later that the "valiant Brigadier Royall is at head of all popular measures . . . and become a great orator. Erving, Brattle, Gray . . . and [John] Bradbury and [Nathaniel] Sparhawk . . . are in the same box."[101]

Bernard was now isolated from the very institutions that could resolve his predicament. He did not care to hazard any attempt to distribute the stamps when, as he told Boston customs officials, the General Court twice refused to "assist me in carrying the Act into execution."[102] On 8 November Bernard pleaded with the members to understand his predicament: that he, like the stamp distributors, was a victim of Grenville's miscalculation. "[The Stamp Act] brought upon me a necessary Duty which, it seems did not coincide with the Opinions of the People. This is my offence, but it is really the offence of my office."[103]

*   *   *

When John Adams first met Bernard in a Boston courtroom in the winter of 1765, he was a young lawyer from the small town of Braintree representing the Boston town meeting. Adams floundered, struggling to cite "analogous Cases" that might convince the governor to accede to the town's extraordinary request of 15 November that he instruct officials in the common-law courts to ignore an act of Parliament. Adams and his celebrated colleagues, Jeremiah Gridley and James Otis, argued that extreme necessity was sufficient justification. However, a "Majority of the Council," Bernard observed, "were firm against discrediting themselves by too great a Submission to the demands of the People."[104] Bernard sought refuge in the doctrine of the separation of powers to explain why the governor-in-council refused to direct the judiciary to ignore the Stamp Act. But the argument he had employed to ward off resistance to the Stamp

Isaac Royall. By John Singleton Copley, 1769. M. and M. Karolin Collection of Eighteenth Century American Arts. Courtesy, Museum of Fine Arts, Boston. Reproduced with permission. Copyright 2000 Museum of Fine Arts, Boston. All Rights Reserved.

Act—the necessity of complying with an act of Parliament—was now turned against him. As the *Boston Gazette* remarked, the governor had made a "resolution . . . that no law should be executed if the stamp act was not."[105] If then, as Bernard feared, anarchy and chaos should follow a lengthy closure of the courts and the customhouse,

John Adams. By John Greenwood. Founders Society Purchase, General Membership Fund. Photograph copyright The Detroit Institute of Arts.

then it would be Bernard whom the people would blame. Bernard was more impressed by Adams than Adams ever realized, and three years later offered him a government office.

On 19 December Bernard received orders from the Treasury to distribute the stamps in place of Andrew Oliver and to assume care of any revenue collected.[106] Two days before, two thousand townspeople stood in the pouring rain to witness Oliver publicly resigning his dis-tributor's commission.[107] Bernard was perplexed as to why Oliver should submit to the mobs until he learned of Oliver's gracious expla-nation that he had acted alone in order not to "raise a Jealousy of your Excell[y] in the People."[108]

It had been seven weeks since the customhouse shut its doors. As the new year approached, the colony's merchants instituted nonim-portation agreements to exclude British imports. With commerce al-ready at a standstill, the boycott made little difference to the merchants' purses, at least in the short term. Because of this there was little dissent or opposition to the boycott.[109] A few merchants such as John Boylston, who spent much of his time in England on business, and Joseph Green refused to subscribe until they could be sure that the smaller Massachusetts ports would follow suit.[110] Thomas Robie was the only merchant who refused to subscribe to Marblehead's agreement, whereas his neighbor, the future Loyalist Robert Hooper, worked hard to encourage subscriptions.[111] Gener-ally, merchants such as the Amorys who later broke with the Whigs wholeheartedly supported the boycott in 1765.[112] Economics was as important a factor in determining their allegiance as were their views on constitutional issues. Tom Boylston, for example, described as a "viper" by John Adams, had lately seen his brig *Recovery* seized in the Bahamas under the Revenue Act though he claimed it had left before the act came into effect. Boylston won the sympathy of Bernard, the General Court, and Samuel Adams but never obtained redress from the Vice Admiralty court. Boylston went on to serve on town com-mittees, but economics played a large part in his and others' decision to become Loyalists in 1775 following the British blockade of Boston.[113]

Whatever difficulties the customhouse's closure caused were short-lived. When Attorney General Trowbridge refused a legal opinion, John Temple and Bernard transferred the chest to Castle William. On 23 December Temple, however, allowed the custom-house to reopen on the premise that stamped papers were unobtain-able. To those who would listen, Bernard protested he "had nothing to do in this business."[114] The matter of the law courts was more problematic, however.

The General Court reassembled in January, and the House lost no time in trying to break the impasse. A resolution proposing that the General Court should order the courts to reopen was opposed on 22

John Amory. By John Singleton Copley. M. and M. Karolin Collection of Eighteenth Century American Arts. Courtesy, Museum of Fine Arts, Boston. Reproduced with permission. Copyright 2000 Museum of Fine Arts, Boston. All Rights Reserved.

January by only five representatives, including John Winslow. (Bernard, not incorrectly, attributed the overwhelming majority to the nonattendance of friends of government from the country towns, including Ruggles, though he failed again to acknowledge that friends of government such as Andrew Oliver Jr. and Thomas Clap voted against him. Even so, perhaps a majority of the House might still be counted moderates, for the radicals' motion to exclude officeholders and judges from the Council was defeated by a margin of three to one.)[115] Bernard was determined that if the Council concurred with the House he would refuse his assent. He had no intention of making the "Executive Power of this Government . . . be active against the Act of Parliament," he told Conway on 21 January, though it might, he said later, prove to be a "Signal" for the "popular Fury" to drive him from Boston.[116]

To Bernard's surprise, the Council, at Hutchinson's prompting, referred the House's resolution to the Superior Court. Hutchinson refused to be moved, and having already resigned his post as a probate judge tendered his resignation as chief justice. When Bernard refused to accept it, Hutchinson protested that the governor was allowing him "to die by inches" for James Otis's pleasure. The other justices, however—Benjamin Lynde, Chambers Russell, and John Cushing—were more disposed to accept the argument of the town lawyers that necessity justified reopening the law courts.[117] If it was hopeless to have attempted anything to try to implement the Stamp Act, it soon became pointless when word arrived that the ministry was to consider repeal. By April most public offices in the east of the province were functioning without the stamps or preparing so to open. The Superior Court successively postponed business until June, by which time confirmation of the repeal had arrived.[118]

*   *   *

In the course of two turbulent weeks in August 1765, Governor Bernard witnessed the beginning of the end of British rule in the thirteen colonies. He spoke wildly of "Anarchy & confusion" descending on the province, and accused the colonists of having "Perverted the necessary obligations of my duty into a voluntary attack [on] the Liberties of the People & thereby representing me . . . as an Enemy to the Province."[119] Bernard convinced himself that there was a conspiracy of "designing Men," aiming "to tumble the government, & bring it to the level of the very people."[120] He never ventured a firm opinion as to the identity of the "Gentlemen Actors" who had organized the Stamp Act riots, but left ministers and officials in little doubt as to who was responsible for inciting the crowds: James Otis and Samuel Adams, the merchant smugglers, and the Congregational pastors. (Mayhew vociferously, if not entirely convincingly, denied having inflamed the rioters with sermons about "civil and religious liberty" that scared his conservative friends such as Richard Clarke.)[121] Bernard's equally contentious comments that resistance to parliamentary taxation revealed a desire to overturn Parliament's legislative supremacy in the colonies both exaggerated the radicals' influence and misconstrued the aims of the colonial leadership.[122] And yet in trying to get the customhouse and provincial courts to ignore the provisions of the Stamp Act the Whigs had effectively subordinated imperial law to politics. These men, Bernard concluded, ought to be taught to respect Britain's "superior order" by having British troops billeted in two or three principal towns.[123]

Consumed by anxiety and stress, Bernard for once struggled to comprehend his future. "My Head is so full," he confessed to John Pownall, "that It cannot be evacuated by my pen."[124] "I have waged a most unequal War, & can hardly now procure the Liberty of remaining Neutral without pretending to exercise any real Authority."[125] Boston held little appeal for Bernard thereafter, and he moved his family five miles out of town to Jamaica Plain, Roxbury, to a fine mansion set in fifty acres near a pond, which he had purchased on 31 October. The farm was close to Dorchester Neck, from whence they could easily reach Castle William.[126]

Bernard's forthright and tactless defense of British imperialism may have been politically naive, but he was right to warn ministers in London that the spread of political radicalism in America was subjecting British-colonial relations to intense pressures. While Bernard glimpsed the nascent political and ideological divisions that in ten years' time would divide Americans into Patriots and Loyalists, his hopes of inspiring a backlash against the radical Whigs failed miserably when the friends of government for the most part remained inert. To reverse the drift to rebellion, he urged Britain to help him cultivate the support of the friends of government—men who were inimical to the radicals' position on imperial affairs though they were hostile to parliamentary taxation. Bernard hoped that the ministry might allow him to make a personal report, and conceded that Hutchinson might make a better governor. He was ready in his own mind to abdicate the governorship at the least hint of "danger," and proceeded to take a huge risk: his reports, he told Pownall, "must be used as public letter[s]" to convince Britons of the severity of the crisis in the colonies.[127]

CHAPTER FIVE

"Supporting the Authority of Government"
Bernard and the Friends of Government

*T*HE STAMP ACT crisis ushered in a period of Whig domination in Massachusetts apparently so complete that historians have barely theorized on the existence of proto-Loyalist activity before 1774.[1] Bernard was a reluctant lame duck, however, and strove where he might to create a Loyalist coalition able to compete with the radical-led Whigs. His actual successes were minor but, beginning in the autumn of 1765, he managed to project his struggle into the arena of imperial decision making. Slowly and surely he managed to convince ministers and many Members of Parliament that in Massachusetts at least the consensual foundation of royal government was breaking up.

*   *   *

Bernard's reports on the Stamp Act riots, which began arriving in London on 5 October, were a vital source of information for the Rockingham ministry, which was trying to comprehend the nature of colonial resistance to parliamentary taxation.[2] The cabinet could scarcely believe that by intimidating royal officials the colonists could defeat an imperial law with such ease. Secretary of state Henry Seymour Conway, a former general, was unenamored by Bernard's panicky reports, and on 24 October criticized Bernard for his "total Languor, and want of Energy in . . . the Suppression of Tumults, which seem to strike at the very Being of all Authority and Subordination." Why, he asked Bernard, did he not request military assistance from General Gage if the situation in Boston was as grave as he claimed?[3]

Most historians have interpreted Conway's rebuke not as evidence of the cabinet's intention to pursue a military solution to the Stamp

Act crisis but as an attempt to preempt parliamentary criticism of Rockingham's sensible decision not to enforce the stamp tax.[4] Conway, however, stopped short of making Bernard a scapegoat for the ministry's shortcomings in defending parliamentary authority. He praised the governor for trying to protect the "authority" of the "Mother Country" from the depredations of the "lower and more ignorant" colonists, and scolded the Massachusetts Council for rejecting Bernard's request for military assistance.[5] As he stated later in Parliament, Conway did not believe that the riots warranted a military response although, if Bernard was right, they cruelly exposed Britain's unpreparedness to confront any sort of insurrection in the colonies. John Pownall also communicated the ministry's disquiet, professing that he could see nothing in Bernard's accounts to warrant his preparations to abandon Boston, though he later apologized for his remarks.[6] On reflection, the cabinet thought it better to let Bernard continue with his unequal contest while it considered what to do with the Stamp Act.

The cabinet's equivocation over Bernard's reports was an indication of how divided the British were about whether or not to repeal the Stamp Act. A majority of Members of Parliament and Lords were at first in favor of continuing the stamp tax or amending it in some way, which King George wanted, to make it more palatable to the Americans.[7] Some modified their views when a second batch of Bernard's letters arrived in December. Many of Rockingham's supporters joined with the opposition factions in asking that the letters be laid before Parliament, and Grenville's motion was defeated by only thirty-five votes. The cabinet only relented after commencing discussions on whether or not to repeal the Stamp Act. On 14 January copies of Bernard's state papers were presented to the House of Commons. That same day William Pitt, no friend of the governor, convinced many of the wisdom of a repeal when he rose from the opposition benches to denounce the "erroneous principle" behind the Stamp Act—of taxing the colonists without their consent.

Bernard's reports were cited by all sides in the debates, and were praised and condemned in equal measure. Grenville's assertion that the lawless behavior of the Bostonians merited full-scale military intervention was an isolated view. The ministry's supporters used Bernard's letters to justify the refusal to enforce the Stamp Act and opponents of the Stamp Act used them to justify calls for a repeal.[8] Bernard's friend William Fitzherbert declared that he had never heard of "the Conduct of any one single person [being] so generally approved."[9] As Barrington rightly informed the governor, there were many Members of Parliament and Lords who believed that Bernard was just the sort of doughty Crown servant Britain needed to restore good relations with the colonies.[10] Benjamin Franklin concluded that Bernard had been "a little unkindly treated as if he was a favorer of the Stamp Act," when the letters he read suggested instead the governor was "warmly in favor of the province and against that Act."[11] Richard Jackson, the Massachusetts agent, who now favored repealing the Stamp Act, was more candid. There were many, he told Bernard, who complained that he ought to have "nipped the spirit of sedition in the bud." Others, however, believed that he had acted with considerable restraint when he refused to deploy troops against the colonists.[12]

Bernard's reports were of secondary importance in the cabinet's decision to introduce on 22 February a bill to repeal the Stamp Act. Pressure from British merchants and the downturn in American commerce following the colonial boycott were the most persuasive factors. However, Rockingham and Conway might have gone one step further in their attempt to pacify the colonists by recalling Bernard. That they did not is a reflection of a hardening of attitudes toward Massachusetts in light of Bernard's accounts. On 3 February Conway had presented a bill unequivocally declaring parliamentary supremacy in the colonies, which was also intended to satisfy Members of Parliament and Lords perturbed by what Bernard and other governors had revealed about the pretensions of the colonial Whigs regarding the authority to tax. It is unlikely that the Stamp Act would have been repealed had not ministers carried forward the Declaratory bill. Protests of dissent tendered by a minority of Lords on 11 and 17 March professed to reflect on "the unanimous Testimony of the Governors and other Officers of the Crown in America." In the second protest, John Pownall informed Bernard, the Lords included a quotation from the governor's letters "in one clause when they state the supposed motives for the conduct of the colonies . . . to render the authority of Parliam^t. contemptible."[13] Another condition of repeal, forced on the ministry by the earl of Bute and the king's friends on 24 February, was Bernard's idea: that Massachusetts should be asked to pay compensation to those who had suffered loss during the Stamp Act riots. In these circumstances, it was hardly politic for Rockingham to dispense with Bernard's services.

When the repeal bill and the Declaratory bill passed Parliament on 18 March, governors were left to do what they could to cool American tempers. Conway reassured Bernard that he enjoyed "the entire and hearty Approbation" of the king. The repeal of the Stamp Act, he told Bernard, was to be presented to the General Court as an act of uncommon indulgence. "A veil should be cast over the late Disturbances," but, Conway warned, the "least Coolness, or unthankfulness, the least murmuring or Dissatisfaction on any Ground . . . may fatally endanger . . . Union" between Britain and the colonies.[14] It took a while for the British to appreciate how tenuous Bernard's situation was in Massachusetts.

Bernard received confirmation of the repeal and the Declaratory Act in early May and in July welcome instructions to return the stamps to Britain, but he was bemused as to how he might "reestablish the Authority of Government" in Massachusetts when Parliament was sending conflicting messages to the colonists.[15] Unless the Declaratory Act was acted upon, the radical colonists would not think twice about resisting other legislation, given that "internal Divisions" had prompted illustrious parliamentarians such as Pitt to champion the Americans' cause.[16] Despite Conway's bark, the British never seriously expected to use the Declaratory Act to justify any future taxes, and both they and the colonists supposed that a line might be drawn under the Stamp Act crisis.[17] Bernard's pessimism, however, sprang not so much from personal bitterness or dislike of compromise so much as the manifest deterioration in his situation in Massachusetts.

Bernard was flattered that his letters had been so well received but dismayed that they were printed for Members of Parliament. It did not matter that Conway and Chief Justice Mansfield kept Bernard's authorship secret. Any intelligent observer would have deduced his identity from reports of parliamentary debates, despite the prohibition on the publication of parliamentary papers.

> *I certainly did not write them with the least Expectation of their being made so public; their own Merit is their being dictated by a Strict Regard to the Truth; but I desire no credit from them in this Country: for of late nothing has been more dangerous & obnoxious here than Truth.*[18]

Henceforth, "evrything that bears hard upon the Colonies, will be imputed to the Governors, whether they deserve it nor not: & the strictest Truth in relating the late Transactions will be most offensive."[19]

While Massachusetts's radical Whigs failed to obtain copies of Bernard's letters, they obliged the governor to engage in a propaganda war in defense of his gubernatorial record. The radicals asserted that Conway's instructions of 24 October, which Bernard presented to the General Court in May, confirmed that the ministry had contemplated sending soldiers to Boston, but the letter never progressed beyond a House committee.[20] Bernard was ruthlessly pursued by the *Boston Gazette*, however, where, amid the vitriol and satire, the radicals supposed that Bernard's reports had adversely affected British perceptions of the colonists. Bernard's prevarication in summoning the General Court during the summer of 1764 was interpreted as a deliberate attempt to deny the colonists valuable time in campaigning against the proposed stamp tax, perhaps because the governor had been promised some financial reward.[21] These and other accusations, which ranged over the familiar Whig themes of the corruption and venality of the court, were largely speculative but nonetheless damaging.

Bernard responded by showing a few Boston merchants copies of his letters to Halifax of November 1764, wherein he criticized Grenville's mercantilist reforms. He also released Richard Jackson's letters for publication in the province newspapers, for they presented a well-rounded and critical appraisal of Britons' reactions to his reports.[22] But nowhere in these letters could Samuel Adams's keen eye find any mention of what the governor thought about the principle of taxation. The Lords who dissented from repeal, Adams told his readers, only took notice of Bernard because his accounts of the riots were sensationalist. Adams was right in these respects but his assertion that ministers hurried through the repeal of the Stamp Act because they feared a rebellion cannot be upheld.[23] The Whigs soon received word from Jasper Mauduit that the weight of opinion in London was that Bernard's reports had "greatly forwarded" the repeal mainly because they convinced ministers of the strength of feeling in the colonies.[24]

Questions pertaining to Bernard's role in the Stamp Act crisis were key issues for the upcoming annual House election in early May 1766. Because of this it is wrong to suggest that the aftermath of the crisis was a "propitious time" for Bernard to repair his bridges with the Otises and establish the broad-bottom administration he de-

sired.[25] Voters were asked not only to return good Whigs but also to
review the conduct of their governor and his supporters. Was their
representative a plural officeholder like the Hutchinsons? Had he
ever tried to bribe them on Election Day? Had he actually declared
against the Stamp Act in public, or did he preach the governor's "cat-
echism" of submission?[26] The *Boston Gazette* published a blacklist of
thirty-two friends of government, preposterously decrying them as
"friends to the Stamp Act" and "Enemies to their Country,"[27] when
instead they had criticized parliamentary taxation in "moderate and
decent terms."[28]

The election results were both an indication of the Whigs' popularity and a vindication of their pursuit of Bernard. In 1765, the
Whigs comprised around one-third of the House, but from May 1766
numbered some two-thirds. Many were radicals, though it may be
inferred from Bernard's observations that the moderates comprised
between one-third and one-half of the total number of members at
any one time between 1764 and 1768. The friends of government,
however, were reduced by half to twenty-two members, just 19 percent of the House—a rate of change far higher than the average annual rate for the House (39 percent). John Adams rejoiced that
Plymouth County had made a "thorough Purgation" of its seven "tories,"[29] leaving Bernard to complain that men of "considerable property," such as Gen. John Winslow, had been replaced by "ignorant
and low men."[30] There was some consolation to be had in the fact
that more friends of government were returned than Bernard had anticipated, including "some of the ablest Men in the House," though
he did not "much expect" them to "Turn . . . the present humor."[31]
Fourteen of the ousted friends of government never returned, though
several had been members since the 1750s. Some gains were made in
1767 and 1768, but the 1766 election irrevocably altered the balance of
power in the House in favor of the Whigs. Never again would a royal
governor be able to command the support and loyalty of a majority
of Massachusetts legislators.[32]

The most distressing aspect was the failure of Thomas Hutchinson, Andrew Oliver, and Peter Oliver to win election to the Governor's Council. In response, Bernard vetoed six Whig councilors
elected by the General Court, including Col. James Otis. John
Adams thought it a "Cathartic" act of revenge; Bernard called it "a
bold Stroke . . . very well Timed," that was welcomed by Boston's
"principal people."[33] Bernard's objective was not so much to preserve

the political independence of the Council, as has been suggested,[34] but rather to prevent its radicalization, for since August 1765 the moderate Whigs had held the balance of power in that body. With Hutchinson gone, Bernard was hardly going to admit Colonel Otis. He had resolved several weeks before Election Day to reject any nominees he deemed "objectionable." This he continued to do for the remainder of his administration and with the full approval of the British government. As for the Speaker, Bernard refused the nomination of James Otis Jr., but accepted that of his fellow representative Thomas Cushing, who "had given no notorious Offence to Government."[35]

The purge of friends of government from the General Court left Governor Bernard in a weak position to defend British colonial policy thereafter. This was most evident in the dispute over the payment of compensation to the victims of the Stamp Act riots—Hutchinson, Oliver, Story, and Hallowell. This issue, which has received scant attention from historians,[36] originated in a proposal made by Bernard that had been adopted in haste by the House of Lords. Little thought was given as to how governors might persuade the provincial legislatures to make public restitution when instructions to proceed were issued to Bernard in March—two months before Parliament passed an indemnity act.

When Bernard presented these instructions on 3 June, the General Court was justified in supposing that Parliament's indulgence in repealing the Stamp Act was contradicted by Bernard's orders to procure compensation for Hutchinson, Oliver, and the others. Bernard, however, bluntly reiterated Conway's warning that any further "Offensive Conduct" would oblige the British "to draw a line to distinguish who are and who are not the proper Objects of the gracious Intention of the King and Parliament." The "justice and humanity of this requisition," Bernard insisted, was "so forcible, that it cannot be controverted," while "the authority with which it is introduced, should preclude all disputation about complying with it." By speaking so "plain[ly]," Bernard told John Pownall, he was "determined to . . . prevent all Equivocations and Subterfuges."[37]

The House was insulted by the governor's imperious use of the term "requisition," which had been used in the Lords' resolution of 24 February. Bernard's frantic search of the province records revealed that the term "requisition" was indeed commonplace when governors communicated royal instructions to the General Court.[38] But that, as the Whigs learned, was not how Conway had framed his intructions, which urged Bernard to "recommend" compensation.[39] By just one vote, the House postponed consideration of compensation until the autumn, in order for the representatives to consult with their towns.[40]

Bernard was willing to leave the matter unresolved had it not been for Hutchinson's determination to press his claim. After writing Conway (in what could be construed as a criticism of Bernard), Hutchinson had dispatched one of his sons to London.[41] The lobbying paid off when Parliament introduced an indemnity act on 30 May that obliged Bernard to seek public restitution from the General Court.

Compensation might have been granted had the General Court been allowed to decide on the method of repayment, for, as the Amory brothers observed, there was a "general Desire to have it done."[42] But there were several sticking points. First, there was the cost: the total amount subsequently sought by the injured parties was in excess of four thousand pounds currency (about two-fifths the value of the East India tea destroyed in the Boston Tea Party). Then there was the assumption that restitution ought to come from the province treasury. Compensation, the House insisted, would not be an admission of public liability or an "act of justice, but rather of Generosity."[43] Consequently, Hutchinson, Oliver, Hallowell, and Story were obliged to petition the legislature for assistance, which they did in October.

A third issue was whether the town of Boston should make compensation instead of the province. A majority of towns, according to Samuel Adams—including Salem, Braintree, Haverhill, and Concord—opposed making compensation until the Boston rioters were brought to justice. Western towns such as Hardwick, however, resolutely insisted that Boston should foot the bill.[44] Resentment against Boston threatened to shatter the unity that had warded off parliamentary taxation. Bernard was delighted at the prospect of Boston being made corporately liable. Even if the General Court refused to recommend that Boston should pay up, Parliament, he speculated, might be persuaded to take action against the town. Town government in theory could be dissolved by Parliament under English common law if the Crown could prove that the negligence of the municipal authorities abused or contravened the privileges conferred by the province charter.[45] One precedent, which Bernard discussed secretly with John Pownall, was Parliament's attempt to impugn the officials of the City of Edinburgh after the infamous Porteous riot of 7 September 1736. Prime minister Robert Walpole did not manage to persuade Parliament to arraign the corporation for failing to restrain the mobs that had hanged the captain of the city guard after he had been charged with murdering rioters, but the corporation was fined two thousand pounds.[46] If Boston's selectmen, justices, and militia officers could be brought before Parliament or the Court of the King's Bench there was always a chance that these men would buckle under cross-examination and reveal the identities of the "Abettors of Consequence" who had aided the Stamp Act rioters.

The Bostonians knew nothing of Bernard's discussions when, in August, the Boston town meeting relented in its opposition to any form of compensation and instructed its four representatives to vote in favor of payment being made from the province treasury. It was the signal Bernard had been waiting for, and he called the General Court to meet in the last week of October. "Had at that time [the moderates] joined the friends of government, it [compensation] might have been done."[47] Opposition to any form of compensation was led by the Northampton lawyer Joseph Hawley and Jerathmeel Bowers of Barnstable, whose election to the Council Bernard had vetoed. Bernard, however, was treated to the strange spectacle of James Otis and Timothy Ruggles speaking in support of public compensation, albeit for different reasons. By this stage the Whigs outside Boston were probably prepared to sacrifice Ebenezer MacIntosh and his accomplices even though a House committee quickly reported that the perpetrators of the riots could not be found. With the House so divided, Hutchinson's petition failed by seven votes and the petitions of the others by far greater margins.[48] Afterward, a committee including the Bostonians, which had been instructed to settle upon a method of repayment, reported in favor of province Treasury repayments, thus precluding any further attempt to render Boston liable. (The House also rejected a motion proposing a public lottery.)[49]

On 6 November a committee including Joseph Hawley was appointed to draft a compensation bill and the House retired to consult with the towns. When the House returned to vote on the bill on 5 and 6 December, Hawley had seized an opportunity to protect the rioters (and by extension their abettors) from prosecution by proposing a proviso to the bill making public restitution conditional on the granting of a general amnesty. Royal governors could routinely issue Crown pardons in the name of the king for anyone convicted of a

criminal offense (which would explain why so few colonists com-
mented upon the dubious legality of the amnesty).[50] Most representatives were probably pleased to get the matter out of the way in spite
of rather than because of the amnesty clause. Thirty-five representatives voted against compensation, but the revised bill passed with a
majority of eighteen votes. Its supporters defeated two motions to exclude the amnesty clause. An amendment proposing that the towns
instead of the province organize the indemnity was also defeated by
forty-five votes to twenty-seven. Hawley's bill was opposed by only
four councilors.[51]

Throughout the dispute Bernard had little leeway to coordinate a
strategy with friends of government and moderates who might have
warmed to any proposal to make Boston liable. Ten friends of government, including Timothy Ruggles, abstained from voting on
Hawley's bill, but twelve more and more than twenty other members,
reported Bernard and Hutchinson, voted according to their towns'
instructions. Such was the frustration of Thomas Hutchinson that he
remarked, "Instructions to restrain a representative from voting always appeared to me to be unconstitutional as well as absurd." While
Hutchinson and Bernard respected the towns' rights to mandate
their representatives, they entertained the British notion—developed
more fully by Edmund Burke—that, as the governor said, elected
representatives should be allowed to "act freely according to their
own judgement."[52]

The House claimed the same privilege but in a corporate sense.
Any "requisition" tended to weaken the "inherent uncontroulable
Right of the People, to dispose of their own Money to such Persons
and Purposes as they shall judge expedient." "Compliance" with
Conway's instructions "ought not hereafter to be drawn into a precedent."[53] Indeed, on 8 December, the House's message to the Council
went further in questioning the foundation of imperial law in the
province than many had yet dared. Delivered by, among others, John
Hancock and James Otis, it "inquired by what authority any acts of
the British Parliament are registered among the laws of Massachusetts."[54]

When, in his first address of the new year, Bernard protested that
there could be "no room for Disagreement or Dissatisfaction" in
"Support[ing] the Authority of Government," the House responded
with one of the most explicit assertions of colonial legislative rights
to date: sovereignty ultimately lay with the "Body of the People" by

John Hancock. By John Singleton Copley, 1765. Deposited by the City of Boston. Courtesy, Museum of Fine Arts, Boston. Reproduced with permission. Copyright 2000 Museum of Fine Arts, Boston. All Rights Reserved.

natural right.[55] An indication of how far colonial thinking had been radicalized came when the governor-in-council voted sixty pounds to pay for winter quarters for two companies of British regulars who had been bound for Quebec but were forced to take refuge in Boston because of bad weather. The House withheld approval until June, protesting that its privilege of initiating money bills had been in-fringed. Bernard was so exasperated that he justified his actions with reference to the Mutiny Act.[56] He did not exaggerate when he told Shelburne that the matter "appears to them as real a grievance as the stamp act." On reflection, Hutchinson considered that the "revolt of the colonies ought to . . . date from this time rather than the Declaration of Independence [of 1776]."[57]

While Bernard's disputes with the House entered another confrontational phase, the Board of Trade sought the advice of the king's law officers regarding the Massachusetts Indemnity Act. The cabinet might have left it to the Privy Council to disallow the measure, but instead presented the act and Massachusetts's legislative records to Parliament in order to garner support for a tougher line against the province.[58] The "word rebellion," Benjamin Franklin reported, "was used frequently" by those who denounced the provincial act as a "high Infringement of the King's prerogative" to issue pardons.[59] The Privy Council disallowed the Indemnity Act on 13 May, but the ministry's attempt to exploit Members of Parliament's anger at this latest affront to royal government nearly backfired. After criticism by the opposition, the new Chatham-Grafton ministry advised Bernard to procure another compensation act, though by then the money had already been paid to Hutchinson, Oliver, Hallowell, and Story.[60] Ministers, who feared reopening the controversy over Parliament's authority to make requisitions of the colonists, tacitly approved Bernard's negligence for more pressing concerns demanded his and Britain's attention.[61]

The colonists assumed that they had heard the last of requisitions and taxes when, in the summer of 1766, King George dismissed the weak Rockingham ministry and invited William Pitt, the darling of the Americans, to form a government. Pitt and the duke of Grafton, who led the ministry from October 1768 to 1770, were noted friends of the Americans. Between autumn of 1766 and spring of 1767, colonial policy was largely directed by the earl of Shelburne, who had replaced Conway as secretary of state for the Southern Department. He had opposed parliamentary taxation and criticized the Lords for attacking the Massachusetts Indemnity Act. The previous September he had advised Bernard to be more "temperate" in his dealings with the General Court. Shelburne was not the only minister concerned that Bernard had made a rod for his own back, but he was the only one to express his misgivings so forthrightly in official correspondence.[62] In May 1767, Shelburne drafted a letter recalling Bernard to England and appointing Hutchinson as acting governor. The proposal was shelved probably because of the opposition of Townshend and Hillsborough,[63] though it is likely that the Bostonians got wind of it.

Bernard was rightly wary of Shelburne and conscious of his friends' lack of power. Newcastle languished in opposition, and Secretary at War Barrington, though he was now meeting the king on a weekly basis,[64] was not a member of the cabinet. Bernard nevertheless proceeded to lecture Shelburne on Massachusetts politics. The "chain is very Short," he explained, that sustained the "Democratical Power" of Otis and his "gang" in the General Court.[65] "Compromise" with the radicals, he appealed to Jackson, was not an option so long as the Whigs kept winning elections. The "only way left" was "to detach" Otis's "deluded partisans from him," either by revising the electoral system or by exploiting internal divisions.[66]

Bernard's persistence never seemed so necessary as when the General Court removed Richard Jackson from the province agency on 5 February. The Whigs' motion was unanimously approved by the Council after only five members of the House dissented.[67] The House subsequently appointed its own agent, Dennis DeBerdt, a London merchant and nonconformist who also represented Delaware (1765–70). DeBerdt had none of Jackson's contacts, and frequently exaggerated his influence on public affairs,[68] but his secret correspondence with Speaker Thomas Cushing hinted at how much Shelburne distrusted Bernard. Although Bernard could do nothing to prevent DeBerdt's de facto appointment, he was able to veto two salary bills, persuade the Council to chastise the House, and, more significantly, alert the British to DeBerdt's Whig credentials.[69] The House also censured Bernard when he delayed signing the bill confirming Jackson's removal.[70]

By the spring of 1767 Bernard was facing a coherent and sustained opposition in the House. Boston representatives James Otis and Samuel Adams, and Whigs outside the chamber such as Joseph Warren and Thomas Young, never disguised their contempt for Bernard, or their determination to get him recalled. Not even the death of Bernard's fourteen-year-old son Shute on 5 April could stem the invective. Voters were warned of "wicked" plots to "enslave" them by a governor sporting "the badges of inf[am]y" and "devoid of all benevolence and patriotism."[71] With a florid sense of courtroom drama, one writer suggested that Bernard "hath maliciously perverted the

benevolent expressions of the most amiable monarch, to the vile purposes of sowing divisions among the people."[72]

Bernard might have been prepared to tolerate these tirades had not
Shelburne provided the Whigs with the ammunition they needed.
On 2 June the House confidently reviewed Shelburne's criticism of
the governor, which had been carried over from the previous session.
Thomas Cushing had already complained privately to Shelburne
about Bernard's confrontational style of government,[73] when the
House now challenged Bernard to prove that he had never maligned
the province or his opponents in his state papers.[74] Angry though he
was, Bernard did nothing. Depressed by Shute's death, he waited pa-
tiently for news from England, hoping that he was to be relocated—to the West Indies, the Carolinas, Virginia, or New
York—any place far from Boston. "Don Francisco," quipped James
Bowdoin, might find the tiny colony of Grenada more to his liking.[75]

* * *

Stunning news from London in late June silenced the trade in insults.
Between 26 May and 3 June the House of Commons introduced a
new series of colonial taxes, this time on selected articles of trade: tea,
painter's colors, lead, and glass. There was little opposition within
the government to Chancellor Townshend's taxes when Barrington
disclosed that it was costing the British seven hundred thousand
pounds a year to maintain a military presence in America and the
mercurial chancellor himself suggested that by increasing the American revenue British land taxes could be cut. The new duties were accepted demurely by Commons, Lords, and king, who were generally
convinced that the Americans would blithely tolerate such indirect
or "external" means of raising revenue even though the duties were
earmarked for paying Crown salaries to colonial governors.[76] Townshend allowed the colonial assemblies to legislate permanent salaries
for the governor and other senior officers before any parliamentary
legislation would take effect. In addition, the four surveyors-general
in charge of the customhouse were replaced by an American Board
of Customs Commissioners, while the Vice Admiralty court at Halifax was replaced by four regional courts, one of which was to sit in
Boston.

The Townshend program is a remarkable example of Britain's
shortsighted and muddled approach to colonial policymaking. First,
to the Americans taxes on paint or tea were just as offensive as stamp

duties, and prompted much the same kind of constitutional and economic arguments. One of the most influential analyses was John Dickinson's *Letters of a Pennsylvania Farmer,* which annihilated the distinction between Parliament's authority to levy trade duties (regarded as external taxes) and its questionable right to impose direct taxes. It was a "Masterly" exposition and critique, Bernard conceded, a veritable "Bill of Rights."[77]

Second, there was no better way to undermine popular confidence in the royal governors than by making them financially independent of the colonial assemblies. Bernard, of course, did not see it that way for he had learned to accept his unpopularity, and was pleased that ministers now seemed to be listening to what he said about reforming colonial government. He praised Townshend for "striking at the Root of the American Disorder," and enabling governors to use "Punishments & Rewards . . . the two Hinges of Government" in cultivating political support.[78] He asked for salaries of between five hundred and nine hundred pounds per year for the attorney general, the solicitor general, and the judges of the Vice Admiralty court. He also speculated whether Crown stipends might not be offered provincial justices of the peace.[79] Massachusetts never did enact a permanent salary bill and the subsequent controversy dissuaded the British from giving Bernard a Crown salary.

Third, by locating the Customs Board in Boston the ministry ensured that the town would remain at the center of colonial opposition for several years to come. The commissioners were vilified as the instruments of a misguided ministry and coconspirators with Bernard and Hutchinson. The insults were initially directed at the two American-born commissioners, Charles Paxton and John Robinson, whose contretemps with smugglers had brought them notoriety. Bernard was friendly with Paxton, but Robinson was enigmatic.[80] The other two Englishmen appointed to the Board, William Burch and Henry Hulton, arrived in Boston with unfortunate timing during the Pope's Day parades of 5 November. Bernard on the whole enjoyed a good relationship with these men, and Hulton in particular shared his concern about royal government.[81] The same could not be said for the fifth commissioner, his old rival the former surveyor-general John Temple, who owed his new position to the favor of William Pitt. Temple resented having to take a drop in salary, and his connections with the local Whigs soon irritated his colleagues.[82]

In Massachusetts, opposition was rather slow to gather momen-

tum, which led Bernard to suppose that the merchants were "satisfied" with the trade laws and would refrain from reinstituting a
boycott of British imports.[83] Bernard was quick to highlight the divisions within Boston's commercial community. "Midling & little
Traders" thought they might be "ruined by it [a boycott] whilst Men
of Great Property & Credit might be benefited by it by becoming
Monopolists." A second issue of concern was that many traders
feared it was "absolutely impracticable to raise such a Confederacy
without Violence."[84] That is to say, the moderates and friends of government believed that crowd action and intimidation would have to
be used by the town's radicals, albeit in a controlled fashion, to silence dissenters and to enforce the boycott. According to Bernard,
the "general Abhorrence" of "inflammatory Papers" published after
the town meeting of 14 August, the second anniversary of the first
Stamp Act riot, persuaded the majority of townspeople and merchants to vote against adopting nonimportation.[85] Bernard's observations were not ill founded, but he soon had cause to regret a
"readiness to persuade myself of the reality of what I wished & desired."[86] On 28 October Boston settled on a nonconsumption agreement, and four months later the General Court urged people to give
preference to the purchase of American manufactures over British, a
symbolic challenge to the mercantilist system.

It is difficult to determine the extent of opposition to the nonconsumption agreements, given that observance depended greatly upon
personal choices. For example, wealthy friends of government Robert
Auchmuty and Benjamin Hallowell continued to purchase British-
made apparel from shopkeepers willing to continue trading.[87] But
several politically conservative towns, such as Harwich and Salem, repudiated the capital's lead.[88] In Boston, furthermore, several "Principal Gentlemen" rejected the boycott when it was first suggested and
later consented under protest.[89] When Bernard reiterated this in the
Massachusetts Gazette a group of prominent traders were sufficiently
concerned to sign a public rejoinder.[90] The concurrence of many Boston merchants was conditional. The Amory brothers, for example,
expected the nonconsumption agreement to last only a few months
and not appreciably damage commerce in the longer term. The dis-
ruption was worth it if the British merchants could again be persuaded to clamor for a repeal. Moreover, the Amorys and other
wholesalers began to stockpile goods, which they acquired at reduced
prices, much to the irritation of importing shopkeepers. Despite

these tensions, around twenty-four towns had adopted nonconsumption agreements by the end of January 1768.[91]

Bernard awaited with trepidation the first attempt by the commissioners to enforce the Townshend Acts. A year before, when the customhouse tried to make an example of the Boston trader Daniel Malcom, a crowd of three thousand demonstrators thwarted all attempts to gain entry to his store. Instances such as these had severely damaged the confidence of the customs officers. Only six seizures were made in New England in 1766 and 1767.[92] On 21 November, the day the Townshend duties took effect, the Sons of Liberty stuck up "inflammatory" papers, and crowds paraded through the streets carrying effigies of the commissioners and signs proclaiming "Liberty & Property & no Commissioners."[93] The impetus for any direct action against the Board disappeared when James Otis urged caution in the town meeting and the Board wisely refrained from apprehending a ship carrying a cargo of glass that tried to beat the deadline.[94]

The stamp tax had been a dismal failure that exposed the weakness of royal government, whereas the Customs Board surprised everyone by its initial success.[95] Imperial laws, it seemed, were at last being rigorously enforced. Meeting in Boston four days every week from November 1767 for eight and a half months before regular meetings were disrupted, the Board condemned thirty vessels for smuggling and collected nearly three thousand pounds from seizures. Between 1767 and 1775, the average annual revenue from all trade duties was thirty thousand pounds, although the salaries of the commissioners and their thirty-two underlings ate up more than half this sum.[96]

Once established, the commissioners consulted Bernard on recruiting men whose loyalty was not compromised by their connections to the colonists. For example, the Scottish-born Thomas Irving was appointed inspector of imports and exports and the register of shipping with a salary of one hundred pounds. He was awarded a 50 percent pay raise after he "dilligently Sett himself to get Intelligence of the Party Intrigues at Boston."[97] Nathaniel Coffin, who had no previous relevant experience, owed his appointment as deputy cashier and paymaster to Bernard's preference for someone such as he "inclining to Engage in Party Matters." Coffin used his connections with the Boston Whigs and merchants to improve the Board's intelligence gathering.[98] The commissioners, often at Bernard's prompting, also got rid of officers too familiar with the Whigs such as

Timothy Folger, who was both Nantucket's collector and town representative, and owed his position to Temple.[99]

*   *   *

The unexpected success of the Customs Board prompted the Whigs
to extend their campaign against the Townshend duties by introducing an embargo on selected British imports. There was no sustained
resistance to the introduction of nonimportation, only sporadic opposition and dissent, which, as Bernard recognized, nevertheless reflected deeper ideological divisions generated by the mobs'
reappearance. The brooding menace of disciplined crowds seemed
behind most everything the Whigs attempted.

In early March 1768 the Boston merchants introduced the first of
several nonimportation agreements, which was intended to run for a
limited period in the first instance. Its adoption, Bernard claimed,
"went against the Sense of an undoubted Majority, of both Numbers,
Property and Weight."[100] Samuel Adams later derided Bernard's reports but traders were certainly anxious about joining the boycott.
One hundred and sixty-six firms were asked to subscribe—53 percent
of the town's traders; of these over 30 percent either did not subscribe
or stipulated conditions, such as promising to subscribe if the boycott
became "generall."[101] Bernard was hopeful that "there are still remaining enough of the most respectable Merchants in the Town,
Non-Subscribers, to defeat this Scheme, even if the Subscribers were
to keep their Promise."[102] After a few weeks, however, only eight still
refused to sign and thirteen others continued to insist on conditions.[103]

Bernard attributed the collapse of dissent to intimidation. When
the subscription paper was first circulated it drew a disappointing response, and "all Engines were set to Work to encrease the Subscription; some were told they would be obnoxious to the lower sort of
People; others were threatned [*sic*] with the Resentment of the
higher; some were made afraid for their Persons and Houses, others
for their Trade and Credit." The merchants' "Intercourses and Connections with the Politicians and the Fear of opposing the Stream of
the People" were powerful motives in persuading many others to acquiesce in the establishment and continuation of the boycott.[104]

Bernard's apprehension that an escalation of colonial opposition
would bring mobs back to the street seemed to be borne out. On 4
March a noisy procession of more than one hundred townspeople

passed by the Council chamber before screaming insults outside the homes of commissioners Paxton and Burch.[105] The celebrations of 17 and 18 March, jointly commemorating St. Patrick's Day and the repeal of the Stamp Act, passed off peacefully enough during the day; neither the selectmen nor the Council expected anything approaching a riot.[106] Bernard was unconvinced that violence was far from people's minds. On the night of the eighteenth, when the taverns and coffeehouses emptied, a crowd of "many hundred" and of "all Kinds Sexes and Ages," yelling and shouting, said Bernard, "shewed a great Disposition to the utmost Disorders."[107] The populace, Thomas Hutchinson recalled, never looked "more sowre and discontented." The "least hint from their Leaders," he told Richard Jackson, would surely have "encourage[d] them to any degree of violence."[108] The commissioners were not assaulted, and although the demonstrations terrified the commissioners' families, the Council refused to agree that the apprehension of danger warranted asking General Gage for troops.[109]

Of particular concern to Bernard and Hutchinson was the alacrity with which Boston's lower orders supported nonimportation. As early as the summer of 1767, laborers and journeymen spoke warmly in favor of a total boycott when many of their social superiors hesitated.[110] Laborers were "so infatuated" with the cause of liberty that they seemed prepared to forgo high wages of more than three shillings per day when commerce ceased.[111] The laborers and shipyard workers supported the merchants' decision to refuse Glasgow shipbuilders leave to sell British goods in order to raise capital to construct four ships in the Boston yards,[112] though it meant, Bernard suggested, losing contracts and trade worth some thirty thousand pounds. Salem, Newburyport, and Marblehead were poised to take advantage, but there is no evidence to suggest that these towns made significant inroads in Boston's commercial links with Scotland.[113] Resentment at the "considerable Body" of Scottish factors operating in Boston was widespread, however, for they were, "all, to a Man, importers."[114]

Over the next three years, the enforcement of nonimportation increased popular participation in local politics, giving rise to a broad-based protest movement. Successive agreements from March 1768 to October 1770, each of which extended the period of the boycott, stipulated that trading restrictions applied not only to subscribers but to all traders, and nonconsumption to all consumers. Committees of enforcement worked hard to persuade importers to return goods arriving during the boycott. The populace at large was exhorted to forgo buying anything from the importers, some of whom had their shops and stores smeared with "Hillsborough paint"—a mixture of urine and feces; those that refused to accede to the committees' demands were proscribed as "traitors" in handbills, in the records of the town, and in the press.[115]

Merchants were certainly unhappy at the prospect of what the historian Leslie Thomas called "coerced conformity" replacing "voluntary compliance" as the modus operandi of protest during the boycott.[116] Economic worries too were never far from their thoughts. The boycott forced merchants to weigh carefully the expected short-term losses arising from the suspension of trade against the unknown longer-term benefits of overturning the Townshend Acts. The participation of New York and Philadelphia, Boston's main commercial rivals, was also essential, but neither port adopted nonimportation until after Boston, in autumn 1768 and February 1769, respectively. Bernard was wrong to suppose that only wealthy merchants such as Thomas Amory and Nicholas Boylston would hold out; John and Jonathan Amory, for example, at first enthusiastically supported the boycott. By the autumn of 1769, the dissenters comprised Bernard's son John, Thomas Hutchinson's two sons, and several Scottish factors and shopkeepers.[117]

Bernard, however, was correct in surmising that simmering conflicts of interest between wholesale merchants and "midling" shopkeepers were a matter of concern to the Whigs. The resentment of wholesale merchants against importing shopkeepers, some of whom had refused to sign the agreements, was manifest when John Hancock proposed that they should be more heavily taxed and volunteered his own vessels to return goods that arrived during the boycott. Economies of scale meant that the wholesale merchants like Hancock could weather the suspension of commerce better than smaller retail traders, some of whom openly accused the Whig merchants of trying to squeeze them from the import market in dry goods.[118] Bernard encouraged such an interpretation, claiming that the quantity of goods ordered before the boycott took effect exceeded the normal amount.[119]

Failure to subscribe could be more damaging to importing shopkeepers than what might be lost because of the embargo, as John Bernard's experience testifies. He was a persistent importer, intent on

holding out "to the last extremity" or until "his person might suffer."[120] John had made investments in sixty tons of vessels, according
to the province tax list, but his business was badly affected by his defiance. When local people boycotted his shop, John was forced to call
in the debts owed by local tradesmen, and he considered making a
risky investment in a mining venture. John's business survived with a
loan of one thousand pounds from his father. The governor, however, failed to get his son appointed registrar in the Vice Admiralty
court, though John succeeded his older brother Frank as the Naval
Officer.[121]

In August 1768, when the merchants' committee resolved to introduce an embargo to run from 1 January 1769 to 1 January 1770, without
waiting for the compliance of New York and Philadelphia, resistance
was again short-lived. Thirty-five merchants refused to subscribe or
observe the new articles, whereas forty others promised observance
without signing.[122] By 10 August 1768, 211 traders had subscribed to
the agreement and only sixteen of those approached held fast against
it.[123]

However, between 1768 and 1770 John Mein's *Boston Chronicle*
published the names and cargoes of 285 traders from Boston and
fifty-six from other Massachusetts ports who imported British goods
after August 1768. Mein's source was reliable—Thomas Irving, the
inspector-general of imports and exports and the register of shipping.
The low frequency with which 80 percent of importers received
goods suggests that these violations were neither intentional nor politically motivated. Most were overlooked by the merchants' committees charged with enforcing the boycott.[124] Among the forty-seven
persistent importers were ten Whigs, who eventually complied with
the committees' instructions, and twelve friends of government with
previous records of hostility to the Whigs. Another nine were traders
with no fixed political allegiance. Antirevolutionary opinion served
gradually to unite these disparate groups.

The dissenting traders echoed much of what Bernard had been
saying about the "tyranny" of nonimportation. Whereas the Whigs
justified the suspension of their liberties in the name of an outraged
community, importers like Theophilus Lillie and the Sandemanian
Colborn Barrell denounced the boycott as an infringement of their
individual liberties.[125] Approximately seventy-nine Whigs, such as
Thomas Amory and Gilbert Deblois, defected to the friends of government during and after the nonimportation controversy, two-

thirds of whom became Loyalists.[126] It can be assumed by their membership in organizations dominated by the Whigs that they originally countenanced opposition to British colonial policies, but their disenchantment with protracted resistance involved the interplay of several personal, economic, and political factors. The common thread of experience was that in time these men came to reject the authority imposed upon them by the protest movement in regulating their lives.

For the first time since the troubles began, the province newspapers were filled with a stream of antiradical propaganda that tried to make sense of the apparent contradictions in the Whigs' motives and their methods. Attorney General Jonathan Sewall was the most prominent of the contributors, though Bernard and Peter Oliver professed ignorance of his authorship of the "Philanthrop" letters.[127] It is unlikely that Bernard or Hutchinson coordinated these publications,[128] although Bernard composed two short pieces notable only for their outdated defense of the distinction between internal and external taxes.[129] In some respects, Bernard and the friends of government were moving closer together.

A second theme addressed by the friends of government was the colonists' loyalty. Obedience to Parliament and the king, they argued, was immutable and interdependent, and did not exist from a priori acknowledgment of the colonists' constitutional rights. When the Pennsylvania Farmer denied to the king-in-Parliament "absolute jurisdiction" in taxation he logically denied legislative supremacy in all other matters concerning the colonies. For "N. P.," "The authority of the King [cannot] be denied in one respect and acknowledged in another; without destroying the whole chain of allegiance." The colonists had a "moral obligation" to respect entrenched authority.[130] The promise of political liberty, Jonathan Sewall contended later, could only be realized when people acknowledged that there were "certain rules, to which all members of the community, must conform . . . an inviolable respect for the laws, a rational submission to those in authority and Christian candour." Here Sewall anticipated Edmund Burke's conservatism, which prescribed "regulated liberty" and tradition as the foundations of civil society. "Philanthrop," however, was easily dismissed as an embittered snob, and a purveyor of the Hobbesian doctrines of "passive obedience" and "non-resistance"; by denying the colonists the right to reject parliamentary taxation, Otis responded, he was repudiating the principle of government by consent.[131]

Bernard appeared to do much the same thing when he continued the General Court by prorogation until 30 December 1767 and warned Speaker Cushing that neither Parliament nor the ministry would "bear a further Dispute of their Authority."[132] Ignoring the governor, a House committee spent eighteen days preparing a series of remonstrances asking for a repeal of the Townshend Acts on the grounds that Parliament had no authority to impose any tax on the colonists, but without challenging its legislative supremacy as Bernard feared.[133] The majority of representatives and colonists were a long way from adopting such an extreme position. When Samuel Adams presented to the House on 20 January a draft petition to the king, which implicitly denied parliamentary supremacy, it was amended paragraph by paragraph before it was approved.[134]

These debates were "very long and extremely well managed on the side of government." By "frequently canvassing" the other members the friends of government were able to get "a great part of the most offensive matter" struck out.[135] Moreover, Timothy Ruggles and Joseph Hawley both argued that the disputes over taxation could be resolved by securing colonial representation in Parliament. Otis condemned Hawley as a "madman," and a proposal to request American representation was subsequently rejected, but Hawley's about-face is a good indicator that the moderate Whigs and friends of government occupied common ground in issues pertaining to parliamentary authority.[136] Representatives who had once flinched at Adams's suggestion to annul the Stamp Act were simply unwilling to accept the radicals' proposition, which appeared regularly in the press, that Parliament did not possess supreme authority over the colonies.

Bernard was elated when, at the end of January, friends of government and moderate Whigs together defeated by a majority of two to one a motion for a circular letter to be sent to the other colonial assemblies urging them to unite against the Townshend Acts. "No one Transaction in the House has given me so great hopes that they are returning to [a] Right Sense of their Duty and their true Interest as this has done." The "Faction has never had so great a Defeat as this has been."[137] On 4 February the House appointed another Whig-dominated committee to prepare another circular letter. This time, with members leaving early to battle home through winter snows, the friends of government were unable to prevent the radicals from persuading the House to reverse its original decision, and to expunge the earlier failure from the House journals. For Bernard it was a crushing defeat even if, he admitted to Shelburne, he had been "too hasty" in his "Approbation of the Conduct of the House."[138]

The representatives were worried how Adams's circular letter would be received in London. The circular acknowledged the supremacy of Parliament, but it was wishful thinking to assume that Britain would not view it as a threat.[139] Never again, however, did the friends of government command such support in the House, though fissures within the Whig ranks would open and close with frustrating regularity. Just as the Whigs viewed the courtroom drama of the writs of assistance case as the beginning of the Revolution, so Shelburne came to view Bernard's unfortunate loss as the turning point in Britain's relations with the Massachusetts legislature.[140]

Bernard affected astonishment at the turn of events, but he was easily outmaneuvered by Adams. Prior to asking the House to reconsider the circular letter, Bernard read excerpts from one of Shelburne's letters, dated 17 September 1767, which, despite the secretary's earlier criticism, defended the governor's decision to keep the radicals out of the Council. Bernard agreed to release a copy of the letter in return for a promise that it would not be published. We might think Bernard naive were it not for the fact that Adams also promised him a copy of the circular letter, which Bernard supposed might one day be used to indict Adams.[141] Shelburne's letter was printed in the *Boston Gazette* on 7 March with an anonymous commentary by Joseph Warren claiming that it was "full proof" that the governor had led the secretary into forming "a most unfavourable opinion" about the province "in general, and some of the most respectable inhabitants in particular."[142] Bernard had ignored such insults in the past because he had no faith in colonial juries. This time, however, he wished to signify his determination to pursue the radicals by lashing out at the printers of the *Gazette*, Benjamin Edes and John Gill, who he presumed knew the identities of the authors of every piece that was even remotely seditious.

Warren's letter was debated in the House for an entire afternoon, with many members, some of them lawyers, moved to defend on principle the freedom of the press against the governor's honor. The motion accusing the printers of libel was dismissed by thirty-nine votes to thirty, a margin so narrow as to encourage Bernard to take the matter further.[143] The Council shared Bernard's outrage, declaring the insult "subversive of all order and decorum." The mood changed, however, when Otis threatened the councilors with dismissal in May. Exasperated rather than intimidated, perhaps, the councilors privately suggested to Bernard "that it would be better to leave this Matter where it stood with a continued Unanimity of the (allmost) whole Council, than by proceeding further to divide them."[144] According to Bernard, this illustrated that although councilors wished to follow the "Dictates of their own Judgments" they were wont to grow "timid & irresolute" when pressured by Otis and Adams.[145] In a parallel action, Chief Justice Hutchinson presented the libel to a grand jury of the Superior Court on 8 March, and the jury directed the attorney general to prepare an indictment. After a night's recess, during which Edes and Gill and members of their "faction visited the jurymen," the jury refused to proceed against the printers.[146] However, Samuel Adams's masterly review of the Shelburne affair was used to great effect in the May elections.[147]

Bernard blamed both Shelburne and Adams for this latest insult,[148] but was never in a position to demand anything from a colonial court let alone strike a bargain with the Whigs; shortly before 25 May he received fresh instructions about the Massachusetts circular letter from the new colonial secretary, Wills Hill, the earl of Hillsborough.

Hillsborough had been appointed American secretary in late 1767 to head a new department solely responsible for colonial affairs. Chatham's long convalescence from gout and his resignation in October 1768 exposed Grafton to an internal power struggle that marginalized Shelburne and Conway and brought Hillsborough to the fore. Unlike Shelburne, Hillsborough was a hard-liner. His "prudence firmness & temper," Barrington told Bernard, were such that he now regretted the repeal of the Stamp Act. Hillsborough was keen to reassert British authority and reestablish good links with the governors; colonial agents such as Franklin, who respected Shelburne, he kept at arm's length.[149] Hillsborough thought the Massachusetts circular more seditious in its assertion of colonial rights than it actually was, largely because he failed to discuss it or the rest of the documentation with Dennis DeBerdt, whose appointment as House agent he refused to recognize. DeBerdt too was remiss in delaying presenting the material to Hillsborough.[150]

On 21 April Hillsborough wrote the colonial governors imploring them to get their respective assemblies to ignore the Massachusetts circular. By the time they received these instructions many colonies had responded positively to the circular letter. However, encouraged by Bernard's earlier reports of how the circular letter had first been rejected, the following day Hillsborough instructed the governor to have the Speaker of the Massachusetts House propose a resolution rescinding the vote of approval. The reason was that the circular letter purported to encourage illegal combinations against the Crown.[151] When Bernard received these instructions he decided to delay presenting them to the House until 21 June, a Tuesday—a day when the chamber was usually at its fullest, and when the uproar over the *Liberty* riot of 10 June had started to subside. The affray brought its own relief.

In a rambling two-hour speech, James Otis called on the British to "rescind their Measures" and "abused all persons in Authority" in Massachusetts and Britain. He demanded also that Bernard produce copies of Hillsborough's correspondence. The filibuster might suggest that again the radicals were uncertain of majority support.[152] When Bernard released excerpts of Hillsborough's letters he knew were damaging to him, it is clear that he had abandoned all thoughts of conciliation. Although he was determined "to bring this Matter to a Crisis," Bernard had learned not to expect too much from the friends of government, even when representatives began to talk of impeaching him. The House stopped short of approving a motion to begin such a process—for it had no legal right to do anything of the sort—and instead approved a petition drafted by Samuel Adams calling for Bernard's dismissal on the grounds that he had misled the secretary into thinking that the House had acted unlawfully when it readopted the circular letter.[153]

Bernard, then, had become a prime target for the radicals' increasingly defiant stance toward the Townshend Acts. Representatives, who worried that Bernard had abandoned all "paternal regard for the welfare of the good people of this province," informed him that "if the votes of the House are to be controlled by the direction of a minister, we have left us but a vain semblance of liberty."[154] On 30 June, after a long debate from which the public was excluded, the House refused to rescind the circular letter by a vote of ninety-two to seventeen. In justification, the petition calling for Bernard's dismissal alleged that he had prevented "calm, deliberate, rational and constitutional measures from being pursued" and forced the General Court "into a state of desperation and reluctant extremity."[155]

Bernard prorogued the assembly at the end of June according to Hillsborough's instructions, and dissolved it by proclamation on 1

July. It would not meet again until May the following year. Governors elsewhere, whose colonies had accepted the Massachusetts circular (or in Virginia's case produced their own circular), dismissed their respective assemblies accordingly, North Carolina excepted. "Nothing less than a general Sacrifice of the Rights of the Sovereign state," Bernard concluded, "can make a Governor popular in this Place at this Time."[156] Bernard forwarded an extract of Otis's speech, which he hoped might lead to his expulsion from the next House,[157] and defended himself against Adams's accusations of impropriety. Hillsborough's letters and the replies of the House were printed in the newspapers, and did much to rouse the colonists against Bernard. Otis, though, disagreed vehemently with Adams over publishing Hillsborough's instructions to Bernard, probably because he was concerned about the British reaction.[158] As it was, ministers were already considering what to do in light of Bernard's reports.

The "rescinders," the most important of whom was Israel Williams, saw the dispute as a contest of wills between a powerless governor no longer concerned if he offended his charges and an assertive lower house incensed by Britain's attempt to strike down colonial legislative proceedings.[159] The rescinders included "members who were scarce ever known upon any other Occasion to vote against the Government-Side of a Question."[160] It was the end of the friends of government as a potent political force, although there was some support for their actions in a few towns.[161] Only twelve of the seventeen rescinders were returned at the 1769 elections—a "Warning," said one citizen, "to Representatives rather to act the sentiments of their Constituents than to please by a cringing conduct the greatest enemy to the Government."[162] Jonathan Sayward, who shared Williams's view of the dispute, nevertheless informed Hutchinson that henceforth he would be "with the Stream" in the House.[163] The eight friends of government who voted in opposition to Bernard now gravitated toward the Whigs, and the rescinders came to occupy a special place in popular demonology as the instruments of a British conspiracy to bring "confusion to the Whiggs and the Wiggish [sic] cause."[164] By the summer of 1769, the friends of government in the House were reduced to a rump status from which they never recovered.

*   *   *

Bernard floundered in the face of sustained opposition to the Townshend Acts. On several occasions, he claimed that the radicals aimed at independence because they contested almost every instruction he received. Full constitutional independence or even legislative independence was not the motive behind the popular protests and the legalistic and economic arguments made against the Townshend Acts, though both ideas were freely and openly discussed in Whig circles as a possible outcome to any lengthy disputes.[165] While colonial resistance escalated, the Whigs' essential aims were to restore British-colonial relations to what they had been before the Stamp Act. Bernard and Hutchinson little understood how the colonists managed to reconcile their goals with popular resistance to Britain. On the other hand, their unpopularity, together with high turnover rates in annual House membership, the mandating of representatives by their towns, and effective campaigning by the Whigs, all conspired to restrict the development of a partisan infrastructure among the friends of government. Bernard's alleged duplicity and his transparent bouts of pique at these developments disguised an urgent quest to educate policymakers in London that royal government was in need of extraordinary remedial measures.

CHAPTER SIX

"A Time of Tryals, Spies and Snares"
The Deterioration of British-Colonial Relations, 1767–1768

*B*RITAIN'S INABILITY to contain opposition to the Town-shend Acts was brutally exposed during Boston's long hot summer of 1768. The Whigs were trifling with revolutionary specters, Bernard wrote Gen. Thomas Gage on 2 July: "All real Power is in the hands of the lowest Class; Civil Authority can do nothing but what they will allow."[1] It was a self-fulfilling prophecy. Six weeks earlier, he had told the American secretary Hillsborough that "Government will not recover itself, untill these Men have received some signal Check from Great Britain, such as will open the Eyes of their deluded followers."[2] The specious checks Bernard had in mind was for the British government to dispatch British regulars to Boston and prosecute leading Whigs for sedition. The soldiers arrived in the autumn of 1768. No other measure could have been better calculated to enrage the colonists than an army of "occupation" mustering on Boston Common.

*   *   *

Following the Stamp Act crisis Bernard urged the British to move to Boston permanently one of the regular regiments stationed at Halifax or New York. He never clearly explained what the troops might be used for—whether to disperse mobs, arrest agitators, or protect Crown officers. He glibly supposed that a military "cantonment" would be a deterrent to crowd action though that had not stopped the citizens of New York from taking to the streets.[3] Bernard's thoughts were not entirely out of step with those of General Gage and Secretary at War Barrington. In an influential memorandum of May 1766, Barrington recommended concentrating British forces at strategic points on the eastern seaboard, partly to save money and also because the threat from Native tribes had receded after Pontiac's Rebellion. These measures were approved in the spring of 1767 without reference to Bernard's proposals for Boston, for the British supposed that the garrison at Nova Scotia would be able to answer any call for assistance.[4]

Barrington and Gage both knew that Bernard would never make such a request without first legally obtaining the consent of the Massachusetts Council. They also knew that the Council was never likely to sanction this course of action. Bernard's dilemma therefore was how to convince British ministers that the situation in the Massachusetts capital warranted a significant revision of colonial policy. In March, he informed the British that the Council's "assurances that no Mischief was intended at present are founded upon the Impropriety of using Violence at a Time when they were applying to the Government and Parliament of great Britain for redress." Boston was not descending into lawlessness. "The ordinary Business of the Government," he admitted, proceeded "without Interruption," except when it came to those imperial "Laws" disputed by the colonists, where he possessed "not the Shadow of Authority or Power." When the customs commissioners asked Bernard "what support" he could "afford" their officers in lieu of asking Gage for troops, "I answered none in the World."[5] The colonists, he claimed, now treated Parliament and Crown "with a Contempt . . . allmost treasonable."[6]

The probity of these perceptions and judgments was the substance of a lengthy debate between Bernard and the Council—the consequences of which were that Boston was subjected to military occupation and Bernard was eventually threatened with impeachment. At no point did Bernard seriously consider how the Bostonians might react to the presence of a British garrison. The colonists later alleged that it suited his purposes blithely to ascribe to the Whig leaders a more clearly defined revolutionary agenda than they possessed.[7] The customs commissioners did not hesitate to take advantage of Bernard's sufferance and on 28 March delivered to London a tacit request for British troops. They refrained from criticizing Bernard, and blamed the Council for leaving them to "depend on the Favour of the Leaders of the Mobs for Protection." The recent disturbances may well have been "trifling," Gage explained to Hillsborough, but the "Threats daily thrown out against Themselves, was certainly a Sufficient Reason to make them apprehensive of Danger to their own

Persons." The "Wickedness" and folly of the Bostonians, Bernard figured, must surely persuade the ministers to give him troops.[8]

The threat of violence was usually enough to discourage the most eager customs officer from prying into the affairs of Boston's merchants. Even so, the intimidation of customs men and "rescues" of cargoes impounded by the customhouse had increased following Britain's refusal in 1767 to repeal duties on imports of Madeira wine and the imposition of the Townshend Acts.[9] The illicit importation of these articles went a long way to boosting the fortunes of merchants such as John Hancock.

John Hancock was an unlikely revolutionary. Rich, handsome, vain, and loquacious, he was more at ease entertaining British and colonial dignitaries at his Beacon Hill mansion than in plotting Bernard's downfall with streetwise politicians such as Samuel Adams. Hancock and Adams made an incongruous pair, but each in his own way won the deep respect of those Bostonians who consistently elected them as their representatives. For all his gentility and munificence, Hancock was a ruthless smuggler given to boasting that he would never permit a customs officer to board one of his vessels. This was not an idle threat. In April, Hancock's men physically assaulted a tidesman, Owen Richards, when he tried to inspect the *Lydia*. The harassment of another officer a month later had more serious consequences.

On 9 May, when Hancock's sloop *Liberty* entered a cargo of twenty-five casks of wine at the Boston customhouse, an obscure customs man, Thomas Kirk, was delegated the unfortunate task of guarding the vessel before a search for contraband could be undertaken. Hancock's men detained Kirk in a locked cabin for upwards of three hours while they unloaded somewhere between sixty and one hundred pipes of wine. Curiously, Kirk did not report his maltreatment until one month had lapsed, whereupon he attributed his silence to fear of retribution. When the collector Joseph Harrison informed the commissioners of the incident on 10 June, they immediately ordered the seizure of the *Liberty*. Having thus far succeeded in enforcing the Townshend Acts, the commissioners were determined to make an example of Hancock, probably with Bernard's full knowledge.

Fearing that the *Liberty* would be rescued by a mob, Harrison and the comptroller Benjamin Hallowell boarded the sloop with a company of marines from HMS *Romney*, at anchor in the harbor since 13

May, and towed the sloop alongside the warship. The commissioners ought to have realized that the townspeople would respond angrily to sailors being used to enforce a civil law when the town authorities had been complaining about the *Romney*'s press gangs. When the officers returned ashore, Hallowell, Harrison, his eighteen-year-old son Richard, and inspector Thomas Irving were jostled and punched by a mob approaching five hundred, but were not seriously injured. The mob vented its frustration by burning Harrison's pleasure boat on Boston Common and breaking windows in the home of Inspector-General John Williams.[10]

That, in sum, was the extent of the violence, which Bernard incongruously described as a "great Riot" and a "Prelude to greater Mischiefs."[11] On the evening of Saturday, 11 June, almost the entire Customs Board, their underlings, and families—sixty-seven persons in all—retreated to the *Romney* with the revenue chest and thereafter to Castle William. Of the senior officers, only John Temple, John Williams, and the cashier Charles Steuart remained in the town. No full meetings of the Board were held for the next five months, during which time the commissioners reported nearly every instance of disorderly behavior as seditious and began compiling their own files of the Council's alleged misdemeanors.[12]

Not all of the customs men shared the commissioners' pessimism. Samuel Venner, the Board's secretary, was a middle-ranking official who was so disapproving of his superiors that he risked dismissal by leaking information to local merchants.[13] Venner had come to Boston in September 1766 and had considerable opportunity to develop friendships with the local merchants before his appointment to the Board. He was a protégé of John Temple, whose resentment toward his colleagues and Bernard had been simmering since his marriage, in January 1767, to Elizabeth Bowdoin, the daughter of the Whig merchant James Bowdoin. Temple tried unsuccessfully to interest the duke of Grafton and Lord North in his complaints about his exclusion from the Board's major decisions,[14] but was subsequently castigated as a mouthpiece of the Whigs and three years later replaced by Benjamin Hallowell.

The commissioners' retreat from Boston inevitably gave rise to suspicions that the Board and the governor had already asked the British government for soldiers. On the morning of Sunday, 12 June, a noisy crowd, between two thousand and four thousand strong according to various reports, gathered at the Liberty Pole. They were agitated by rumors of the commissioners' deceit and protested at both the seizure of the *Liberty* and impressment.[15] Hancock and his fellow Whigs tried to defuse the tension by asking Bernard to persuade Capt. John Corner to call off the *Romney*'s press gangs and for the *Liberty* to be returned. Hallowell and Harrison approved of releasing the *Liberty*, provided Hancock was still prosecuted for smuggling. After taking advice from his colleagues, however, Hancock withdrew the request, and in August his vessel was confiscated by the Vice Admiralty court. The pursuit of Hancock himself, however, became a major test of the commissioners' authority to enforce the trade laws.[16]

In the few moments of reflection his time permitted, Bernard confessed to Hillsborough, on 13 June, that "Perhaps the Commissioners retiring [to Castle William] may assist our Purpose." Their retreat was a signal that Bernard knew Hillsborough could not ignore, and which he trusted would bring a major change in British policy.[17] Bernard struggled to maintain a convincing front, however. At Jamaica Farm, on 14 June, he talked freely and civilly over wine with a delegation of twenty-one leading Bostonians, including Hancock, Samuel Adams, James Otis, and Daniel Malcom who had been "at the head" of the crowds in the last few days. If he could persuade Captain Corner to cease impressment, he hoped that he might allay the rumors that he too had already asked Britain for troops. Technically Bernard had delivered no such request, but he could not resist lecturing the colonists that a regiment or two would be just punishment for their recklessness.[18] Three days later, when the Boston town meeting instructed its representatives to procure a provincial inquiry into the *Liberty* affair, it ensured that suspicion of Bernard's motives would remain a key political issue until he left the province.[19]

The colonists did not yet realize the impact Bernard and the commissioners were having upon British policymaking. After three years as president of the Board of Trade, where he read with interest Bernard's plans for imperial reform, Hillsborough respected Bernard's judgment. He also appreciated how much damage Shelburne's strictures had caused Bernard. This may be the reason why in the spring of 1768 he authorized Barrington to let Bernard know that he was being considered for a title. Bernard's promotion would convey the Crown's displeasure, or as George III put it, "it will teach the Americans that a due obedience to the legal authority of the mother country is the means of obtaining rewards."[20] A baronetcy (which was normally reserved for political notables possessed of English estates or considerable fortunes) was an unorthodox though not unique way of rewarding colonial governors, who were more usually offered a knighthood, and Bernard did not accept his title until the following February, partly on account of the three or four hundred pounds it would cost him. He need not have worried, for, in the wake of what transpired in Massachusetts, the ministry met all the expenses attendant to creating the hereditable Baronetcy of Nettleham.[21]

Hillsborough, the most forceful hawk in the cabinet, eagerly accepted the veracity of the arguments set forth in letters emanating from Boston between mid-February and late March 1768 as to why soldiers were needed "to enforce obedience to the law" in Boston. On 8 June Hillsborough secretly ordered General Gage to send to Boston one or more regiments if he saw fit to assist in the "preservation of the public peace" and to protect customs officers. Five Royal Navy ships were also ordered to Boston. When Bernard's reports of the *Liberty* riot arrived in London on 19 July, the cabinet, on 27 July, reaffirmed its commitment to use the military in support of the "civil power" in Massachusetts. Shelburne was the only dissenter to this decision, which was fully supported by George III. On 30 July Hillsborough ordered the Sixty-fourth and Sixty-fifth Regiments based in Ireland to sail immediately for Boston.[22] A letter informing Bernard of these transactions was dispatched the same day, in which Hillsborough emphasized that Bernard's reports had been central to the cabinet's deliberations.[23]

These were not panic measures as some historians have argued, but they were ill conceived. The Massacre of St. George's Fields, on 10 May 1768 in London, was a telling example of the folly of using soldiers to police politicized crowds: six people attending a rally outside the prison where the radical John Wilkes was incarcerated were killed by a Scottish regiment sent to disperse the crowd. Hillsborough was not the most able of ministers, but he was not a "weak man" who delighted in such demonstrative actions where American affairs were concerned.[24] According to J. P. Reid, Hillsborough was probably "misled" by the "impressions" of imminent civil disorder he gleaned from Bernard's correspondence, and persuaded by Bernard's argument "that a change of measures must originate at Westminster" if royal government's manifest decline was to be reversed.[25] The cabinet, however, could not understand why Bernard had insisted on trying to obtain the Council's agreement to solicit troops, perhaps because, as Reid has pointed out, they did not appreciate Bernard's predicament and his legal obligations to consult with the Council. Hillsborough stressed that he did not consider Bernard's reluctance to act on his own authority to be worthy of a rebuke. However, he wished Bernard had been "more explicit" in identifying "any Man, or Set of Men . . . daring enough to declare openly, that they will not submit to the Authority of Parliament." Hillsborough urged Bernard to produce evidence "more satisfactory than the alarming and dark hint you give that *you dare not to repeat what you have heard till their Purposes become more apparent.*"[26]

In the meantime, Bernard was offered the incongruous advice that he should adopt more "lenient and persuasive Methods," and was given a discretionary power to call the General Court to a place outside of Boston, such as Salem or Cambridge.[27] By the autumn, the only firm instruction Hillsborough sent Bernard was to confirm that the General Court should not convene until the following May.[28] In short, after committing troops to Boston, the British decided to monitor developments in Boston before taking any further action.

Barrington was also authorized to discuss with Bernard whether he was interested in becoming lieutenant governor of Virginia in succession to Sir Francis Fauquier. Technically, this would have been a downward step, but the present governor, Sir Jefferey Amherst, had been resident in England since 1763. Bernard would have carried out more or less the same functions as he did in Massachusetts, but for more money. He accepted quickly, without realizing that he was an unwitting victim of intrigue in London. Just when it seemed that he could escape the trials of Boston, a letter arrived from Barrington apologizing for the embarrassment Hillsborough was sure to cause him: Lord Botetourt was to become lieutenant governor. As Botetourt set out for Virginia, Bernard was left to rue a lost opportunity to get out of Boston. The ministry had preferred to appoint a nobleman, Barrington explained.[29] Hillsborough was more tactful when he observed truthfully that the political situation in Virginia and London demanded a quick decision on the governorship, and without hearing from Bernard was loathe to put his name forward.[30] But the ministry rejected Bernard's request for leave when Hillsborough received even more distressing accounts of events in Boston.

*   *   *

Hillsborough's orders of 8 June did not reach General Gage until 7 September, an inexplicably long delay. However, when Gage learned of the *Liberty* riot from the customs commissioners he placed the Fourteenth Regiment at Halifax in a state of readiness to respond, as a War Office directive put it, to "an Express Requisition of the Civil Magistrate." Gage little expected he would receive any such request from the governor-in-council. Bernard supposed, rightly, that the British were considering sending soldiers direct to Boston, but instead of waiting he chose to approach the Council again, as he was obliged to do.

This was not an attempt to acquire retroactive justification for his earlier predictions of civil disorder. Bernard had no intention of presenting ministers with a fait accompli when, as he told Gage, he doubted whether he could legally ask the general for assistance without the Council's agreement.[31] Further instances of disorder in early July, including the rescue of a schooner impounded by the customhouse, and a vociferous but peaceful demonstration by more than fifteen hundred people at the Town House demanding the resignation of inspector John Williams, convinced Bernard to confront the Council.[32] His rationale was essentially political. Bernard aimed to bring into the open the latent tensions within the Council, which he believed were indicative of ideological divisions in the province.[33]

The Stamp Act crisis had radicalized the Council, although never to the extent that it was dominated by the wealthy merchant James Bowdoin, as was once supposed.[34] At forty years of age Bowdoin had retired from business and devoted his time to literature, science, and politics. He was a close ally of Samuel Adams and James Otis, and since the removal of Hutchinson and Andrew Oliver from the Council he and a radical minority of councilors had contested every controversial executive proposal. The councilors, Bowdoin once protested, "see and act for themselves: they have no leaders—no guide but law, reason, and the constitution."[35] The councilors were a mix of radical and moderate Whigs, friends of government, and personal friends of Bernard and Hutchinson. Bernard's failure to persuade the General Court to allow the lieutenant governor and the province secretary Andrew Oliver to participate fully in Council debates[36] meant that the balance of power had come to rest with moderates like Isaac Royall, William Brattle, Harrison Gray, John Erving, and Nathaniel Sparhawk. Bernard accepted their reelection most years in the hope of being able to turn them against the radicals.[37] Although the moderates campaigned for the repeal of the Townshend Acts, they were unsettled by crowd action, but they did not publicly endorse Bernard's view that it engendered widespread disrespect for imperial law. The report of a joint committee of the General Court inquiring into the causes of the *Liberty* riot refused to accept Bernard's argument that Boston's magistrates were in the thrall of the mobs. It blamed the disturbances on the manner in which the customhouse impounded the *Liberty,* and asked Bernard for assurances that neither he nor the commissioners had asked the British for soldiers.[38] The report was never considered, for Bernard prorogued the General Court indefinitely in accordance with Hillsborough's instructions. Bernard dismissed these proceedings as the "Voice of a Faction" pretending to be the "voice of the People," but councilors who had refused to believe that their governor had misrepresented the province soon found reason to change their mind.[39]

Petitions to the king or Parliament normally were drawn up when the General Court was in session, sometimes by the House or Council alone, but more often together—and always with the governor's approval. In early July, the moderate William Brattle and friends of government Thomas Flucker and James Russell joined Bowdoin and Tyler in drafting a series of petitions to the king and Parliament. Their intention was to counter whatever information Bernard and the commissioners had already communicated to Whitehall, for which purpose it was necessary to exclude not only Bernard from the proceedings but also those councilors who were still close to him, especially Nathaniel Ropes and Timothy Paine. The petitions did not challenge Parliament's legislative supremacy and contested the propriety of the Townshend Acts on economic grounds, which the moderates could accept without hesitation.[40] Even then differences of opinion were manifest, Bernard later reported, among the minority of councilors who actually subscribed to the petitions (Royall, Tyler, Erving, Bowdoin, Danforth, Thomas Hubbard, Samuel Dexter, and James Pitts). Two regretted subscribing, and Bernard could "fix upon another who I dare say acquiesced rather than concurred." This last councilor may have been John Erving, who later confessed to Hutchinson that he felt "obliged to sign every thing that was voted by the Board" until he learned that Bernard had not slandered particular councilors.[41]

Despite all this, the Council emphatically and unanimously rejected, on 27 and 29 July, Bernard's proposal to ask Gage for troops. It cannot be determined whether those friends of government who were present—Nathaniel Ropes, Thomas Flucker, Timothy Paine,

James Bowdoin II. By Robert Feke. Bowdoin College Museum of Art, Brunswick, Maine, bequest of Mrs. Sarah Bowdoin Dearborn.

and James Russell—helped to draft the Council's reply of 29 July, but Bernard was taken aback by "the high Strain of the present Popularity with which this Question was treated." The Council accused the commissioners of having a "preconcerted" plan to provoke a riot by seizing the *Liberty* in order to justify making an appeal for soldiers. Anyone making such a request, Bernard was warned, would be held "in the highest degree unfriendly to the Peace and good Order of this

Government."⁴² After this latest rebuke, Bernard supposed he could "no longer . . . depend upon the Council for the Support of the small Remains of royal & parliamentary Power now left."⁴³ It was several months before the Council explicitly accused the governor of treachery, and in return for the Council's agreeing not to publish its July proceedings, Bernard agreed to send the Council's petitions to Hillsborough; they came before Parliament in November.⁴⁴

"Now all the Burthen is to be laid upon me," Bernard complained, but he told Gage he had resolved "to wait till orders shall come from England" respecting the soldiers.⁴⁵ "Neither by the due Consideration of my Instructions & the Rules of other Governments," Bernard explained to Hillsborough, "nor by the Terms of this Government where the Governor is more connected with & restrained by the Council than in the Governments which are merely royal, did I think myself Authorised to introduce Troops into a Town not used to them upon my own Opinion only & contrary to that of the Council."⁴⁶

In the first week of September, General Gage informed Bernard that he had received Hillsborough's instructions of 8 June authorizing him to send the regulars to Boston. Bernard dreaded having to tell the councilors privately. By 8 September at the latest, Bostonians knew that the Fourteenth and Twenty-ninth Regiments were on their way from Halifax. One week later they learned that two more regiments would be arriving from Ireland.⁴⁷

The extraordinary scenes at the Boston town meeting of 12 September weakened Bernard's resolve to make preparations for the troops or to decide, as Gage reminded him, how many regiments he wanted quartered in the town.⁴⁸ Bernard's informants reported how speaker after speaker—Samuel Adams and James Otis Jr. among them—cursed the governor, demanded to see his latest orders from London, and pledged to defend themselves "at the utmost peril of their lives and fortunes." Chests containing four hundred muskets were thrown open for all to see, and citizens were reminded of their obligation to bear arms in times of danger.⁴⁹ These were angry gestures and nothing more, for the arms were not distributed, but there were rumors that Bernard was the target of an assassination plot. Consequently, Bernard, Hutchinson, Sewall, and the Anglican clergy began to fear that the Bostonians would attempt to prevent the regiments from disembarking.⁵⁰ Bernard, as one American remarked, had been "caught in a snare" of his own devising.⁵¹

For the next two weeks, Bernard remained at the Province House nervously awaiting the arrival of the regiments. He refused Boston's request to summon the General Court and lied when he denied having received any official notification that the regulars were on their way. Boston responded by calling a "convention" of the Massachusetts towns, which met at Faneuil Hall between 22 and 29 September with Samuel Adams in the chair. There was some opposition to participating in a body that Bernard denounced as an "illegal combination," and certainly no enthusiasm among the delegates for confronting the soldiers. One issue on which they agreed, however, was that their governor had failed them.[52]

The province was obliged by the Mutiny Act of 1765 to provide accommodation and victuals for the soldiers when they arrived, but the nefarious practice of billeting soldiers in private houses had been outlawed. The Council's strict interpretation of the act proposed cramming all the soldiers into the barracks at Castle William before hiring any private premises or requisitioning public buildings in the town. This would effectively defeat the purpose of Gage's orders. On Sunday, 16 September, Bernard received a copy of Hillsborough's orders of 30 July indicating that two more regiments—the Sixty-fourth and Sixty-fifth—were on their way from Ireland. It would be impossible to fit all the soldiers into the castle barracks, but three days later the Council refused to fit out the Manufactory House, a large public building in the heart of Boston, even though Bernard had suggested this might forestall putting troops in private buildings. It was questionable whether Bernard or Gage could have done this without first filling the barracks, but they were entitled to commandeer private and public property if the civilian authorities refused to cooperate. Protracted obstruction by the Council, however, risked parliamentary censure, as had happened recently to the New York assembly for a similar infraction.[53] Consequently, councilors Gray, Bowdoin, and Tyler began compiling their own records lest they ever needed to defend themselves in a court of law.[54]

British officers were puzzled by Bernard's indecisiveness in not requisitioning quarters without fully appreciating the political reasons for his forbearance. The divisions within the Council had been subsumed in a concerted campaign that justified colonial opposition by undermining Bernard's gubernatorial authority. As Thomas Cushing put it, ministers would soon see how "Egregiously" Bernard had "misrepresented" the province.[55] Bernard gave Hillsborough a list of names of those who, on 24 September, unanimously refused to procure quarters and questioned the legality of Gage's orders to billet any soldiers in the town. It suggests that the radicals (Bowdoin and Tyler), the moderates (Danforth, Erving, Gray, and Brattle), and two friends of government (Flucker and Russell) had just managed to maintain a united front since the *Liberty* affair.[56] The internal dynamics of the Council were such that there were "4 principal Managers, 2 Aides & Abettors, 3 Acquiescers overawed, [and] 1 opposer and Protestor [against the Whig majority] through the whole [dispute]."[57]

These stresses came to the fore when James Bowdoin sought to publicize details of the Council's proceedings. Bernard insisted that the whole Council should retract several offensive passages in an address drafted by Bowdoin protesting the quartering of the soldiers, because it criticized him directly. Bernard was ignored, and the document entered into the Council records states that the councilors "are fully persuaded his Majesty's Ministers could never have judged it either necessary or expedient to go into such extraordinary measures [as sending troops to Boston] unless in the representations made from here by some ill minded Persons, the . . . Riots had been greatly magnified & exaggerated." Seven councilors voted in favor of adopting this clause and only three against. One other, who Bernard said "rather acquiesced than approved," signed the document when a colleague warned of retribution by the Sons of Liberty.[58]

Gen. Thomas Gage, meanwhile, waited impatiently in New York for the "Day of Tryal" when his regiments stepped ashore in Boston. He was the younger son of an Irish peer and a career soldier who had succeeded Amherst as commander in chief of British forces in North America in 1764 when he was forty-five years old. His marriage to a wealthy American was to prove as unhappy an experience as his short stint as Massachusetts's last royal governor. Gage had learned to be tolerant of royal governors, whom he outranked in all military affairs, but his patience was sorely tried by Bernard's plodding negotiations with the Council to find billets for his men. A trusted engineer, Capt. John Montresor, was sent ahead to prepare Castle William's defenses, and with clear orders for the regimental commander Lt. Col. William Dalrymple to put one of the Halifax regiments in the Manufactory House and establish a temporary camp on Boston Common for the other. Gage had also secretly arranged for two more regiments to be brought up from Florida, though he canceled the orders when

Boston under Siege, 1768. A Perspective View of the Blockade of Boston. *By Christian Remick. Courtesy of the Massachusetts Historical Society.*

he learned that the regiments from Ireland were on their way, though they did not arrive until mid-November.[59]

The troop transports from Halifax dropped anchor in the harbor on 28 September. When the Council refused Dalrymple's entreaty to turn the Manufactory House into a barracks, Bernard requisitioned it, together with Faneuil Hall and the Town House, as temporary accommodation.[60] Dalrymple's relief turned to dismay when Bernard took off for the castle and only returned to Jamaica Farm when the troops had landed. The Fourteenth and Twenty-ninth Regiments entered Boston on the morning of 1 October in full "Battle Array" and with "the same precaution," observed Thomas Cushing, of an army approaching an enemy city.[61] The landings were completed by noon, and at 4 P.M. the regiments paraded on the Common without incident. Sheriff Greenleaf, who had welcomed Bernard to the province so many years before, was sent to meet Dalrymple, but there was no grand reception this time. It was a moment symbolic of Bernard's "time of tryals"—when the governed lost all confidence in the gover-

nor and the governor seemed to abdicate responsibility for his actions.

With the troops at his back, Bernard regained his composure, but efforts to get the Council and the magistracy to comply with the Mutiny Act were ultimately unsuccessful. A compromise of sorts, brokered privately by two councilors (we know not who) on 5 October, was for the Council to approve funds for supplies for the soldiers and for Bernard to persuade Gage to remove one of the regiments. At least eight councilors approved the plan, but that was not enough to convince Bernard to approach Gage, who arrived in Boston on 12 October. The governor was soon at loggerheads with the Council when, on 14 October, the councilors reneged on the gentleman's agreement not to publish an account of the proceedings of 27 and 29 July. With the redcoats now settling in, the councilors saw no reason to keep these matters secret, and the proceedings were published in the *Boston Gazette* two days later—to curry favor with the "Tavern Politicians" and Whig magistrates, Bernard scoffed, who had organized an occupation of the Manufactory House. Bernard responded by taking a careful record of what each councilor now said at meetings.[62]

While Gage appreciated Bernard's problems, he needed a "decisive answer" as to where the troops would be billeted before the cold weather set in—that was not going to be easy. After long and acrimonious debates the Council eventually agreed, six votes to five, to issue province funds to refurbish the Manufactory House. However, "modulated popular violence," as Hiller Zobel put it, coupled with the refusal of the town's justices of the peace and constables to enforce the Riot Act, frustrated all attempts by Hutchinson and Greenleaf to clear the squatters. Whig justices also threatened to prosecute any British officer or commissary who failed to follow the letter of the law in obtaining quarters. On 26 October Bernard appointed civilian quartermasters to oversee the operations, and the next day the soldiers began moving into hired warehouses and stores.[63] Only then did Bernard dare think that the town might become accustomed to the soldiers, and on 8 November the Customs Board returned to the town.

The councilors' capitulation might have signaled their end as a vanguard of the Whig protest movement had Bernard been able to exploit the internal tensions arising from his question whether the Council thought it safe for the customs commissioners to return to Boston. "If they said no, they would Contradict all their Assertions that there was no Occasion for Troops to support the Civil power." A positive answer, however, would elicit the condemnation of the town's radicals. Nineteen councilors were present to hear the question, which they considered for over two hours. A majority of thirteen councilors, including Bowdoin, answered positively, while the other six refused to give an answer.[64] Bernard, though, was sorely disappointed if he supposed that Bowdoin and his colleagues had neglected to consider how the townspeople might react to the Council's denouement. On 27 October fifteen (out of twenty-two) councilors of various political views signed an address to General Gage calling for the immediate removal of the regiments.[65]

That same day, Bowdoin drafted a petition to the king asking that Bernard be dismissed forthwith. It was never presented to the Council, however, probably because Bowdoin was uncertain of obtaining a majority without the requisite documentary evidence.[66] Most councilors probably suspected Bernard of misrepresenting the state of the province to ministers, but the evidence against him still had to be as-

British troops landing in Boston, 1768. By Paul Revere. Courtesy of the American Antiquarian Society.

sembled. Two further petitions to Parliament were drafted in December, again without the sanction of the General Court, but this time without any pretense of asking Bernard for his blessing. The petitions, produced by the self-styled "major part" of the Council under the presidency of Samuel Danforth, the eldest of the group, were sent direct to the Council's agent in London, Dennis DeBerdt. The Council claimed that Bernard had once improperly suggested that the province was prepared to "acquiesce" in the introduction of the Townshend Acts, when in fact the Council had firmly advocated their repeal.[67] It seems a tame complaint from a people who were reproaching Bernard for their current problems. But Bowdoin and the radicals were unsure how far they could carry the others in their unconstitutional proceedings.

The Council said nothing more in public about Bernard's character or his motivation until the publication of the governor's letters in April 1769. Eleven councilors, who had been named by Bernard in dispatches, subscribed to a series of public vindications accusing him of treachery and of misleading ministers as to their motivation in refusing Bernard's offer of troops and in obstructing the quartering of the soldiers. With the exception of Thomas Flucker, who, noted Hutchinson, was now left "out of their Secrets,"[68] this was the coalition that had come into being after the *Liberty* riot: radicals Tyler, Pitts, Bowdoin, and Dexter; and moderates Danforth, Royall, Erving, Brattle, Hubbard, Gray, plus James Russell. To this list should be added Benjamin Lincoln and Nathaniel Sparhawk, who later protested to Hillsborough about the way in which they had been slandered in the journals and correspondence of the customs commissioner (their source was probably John Temple).[69] Still, eight others took no part in these transactions: of these Nathaniel Ropes, John Worthington, Timothy Paine (and Flucker too) were ejected from the Council by large majorities in 1769.

*   *   *

There was another sting in the tail when the British recommended that *in personam* prosecutions for smuggling were to be brought against John Hancock and four others involved in the *Liberty* affair. Hancock's trial, which got under way on 7 November, was sensationalized early on by the realization that Bernard, as governor, stood to profit to the tune of three thousand pounds if Hancock was found guilty of smuggling. The libel against Hancock set a penalty of nine thousand pounds, one-third of which would go to the governor as of right.[70] It was wholly proper therefore that Hancock's counsel tried to destroy the credibility of the prosecution by exposing Bernard as a profiteer. The jury, which had been picked by local constables and included Daniel Malcom, would have drawn much the same conclusion. Attorney General Jonathan Sewall abandoned the case the following March after Crown witnesses, who had been examined in secret, refused to testify against Hancock.

Collecting evidence was not Sewall's forte. The attorney general was a "litigator not an investigator" and he had never been asked to prepare a case of this scale.[71] Sewall's morale was already low after criticism by the customs commissioners that he was "very unfit" to hold such an office. Sewall considered resigning and suing for libel, until dissuaded by Bernard. The source of the rumor was not the commissioners but Samuel Venner, the pro-Whig secretary, who was soon dismissed. Bernard left Hutchinson and the injured parties to resolve the issue, but never once doubted Sewall's ability or loyalty.[72]

When Sewall resigned his other more profitable position as advocate-general of Vice Admiralty to become a judge in the same court, he made an extraordinary offer to his old friend, the Whig lawyer John Adams, that he could succeed him as advocate-general. Sewall was acting with Bernard's blessing, although the recommendation may have originated with Sewall. Bernard, it seems, saw little amiss in supposing that Adams could be bought, and was said to have promised that the lawyer "should be at full Liberty to entertain [his] own [political] Opinions." Adams professed no ill will to the governor, but refused the offer "on Account of the unsettled State of the Country, and my Scruples about laying myself under any restraints, or Obligations of Gratitude to the Government for any of their favours." Thomas Hutchinson wrongly supposed that at this point in his career Adams was "at a loss which side to take."[73] Even if Adams experienced a *crise de conscience* in the mid-1760s, he was not for turning. He subsequently distinguished himself as a defense counsel for the British soldiers accused of murder in the Boston Massacre trial. Sewall's absence from the biggest criminal trial in Massachusetts's history is puzzling, but may be an indication of a profound lack of confidence among royal officials.[74] The solicitor general, Samuel Quincy, who equated the "Encreasing Zeal for Liberty" with "Mobbism,"[75] handled the prosecution. Bernard has left no record of what he thought about the professionalism of the Massachusetts bar; one-third of Massachusetts's lawyers, including Sewall, Quincy, and Auchmuty, were to become Loyalists, but Bernard came too readily to the conclusion that restricted career opportunities and modest incomes had been the making of rebels such as James Otis and John Adams. He could not admit, even to himself, that when both men spurned his offers of government office they were motivated by anything other than personal resentment.

Bernard's problem in finding resolute and loyal officers was most pronounced in his problems with the Boston magistracy. As with so many issues, Bernard's room for maneuver was very limited: he could neither renew nor annul the commission (as King George wished), nor make new appointments without the Council's approbation. Hillsborough wanted "men of considerable Weight" and "others of different Sentiments," but did not suggest how Bernard might achieve this.[76] Bernard's "reforming plan" entailed offering commissions to twelve prominent friends of government including Andrew Oliver, Thomas Flucker, Rev. Jonathan Ashley, Oliver Partridge, and Jonathan Bliss. They all refused, for none welcomed the prospect of having to work alongside the radical justices, and insisted that Britain would have to revoke the entire commission before they would reconsider. Bernard appointed a total of twenty-one new justices of the peace in the next ten months, of whom only six were friends of government (though Ashley and Bliss later accepted the commission from Hutchinson).[77]

James Murray was the first of the justices appointed under Bernard's "reforming plan," but was not the kind of man anyone listened to. A Scots-born sugar merchant, Murray had made his money in North Carolina before coming to Boston in 1765, where his support of the Stamp Act won him few friends. He was an outspoken and tactless man, ridiculed as a drunkard in the press, but he knew how to turn a quick profit when he hired out his sugarhouse as an army barracks. The Council approved his commission for he "was allowed to be in every other respect a most unexceptionable Man." Within a few months he was being taunted in the streets, and once had to be rescued by his friends from a baying mob. Murray refused to resign, but he resolved to take no further part in local politics lest he be "Seized" again.[78] A despondency, born of Britain's indecisiveness and Bernard's recklessness, which historians once wrongly described as timidity, now deeply affected the friends of government.

*   *   *

British ministers were slow to develop a coherent response to Bernard's startling accounts of events in Boston. The cabinet panicked upon receiving, on 4 November, Bernard's accounts of the Boston town meeting of 12 September. They assumed that royal government had been toppled in a "bloodless coup" before the troops landed unopposed.[79] Hillsborough and John Pownall spent several days sifting through the morass of information forwarded by Bernard, trying to make sense of what had happened in Boston. Pownall was moved to praise the governor's "uniformly wise prudent & firm" conduct.[80] Hillsborough was pleased at the sense of outrage that characterized Parliament's debates on the king's speech of 8 November, which had proclaimed Boston to be "in a state of disobedience to all law and government." When the long-serving Hans Stanley, a placeman and Chathamite, seconded the address, probably at Hillsborough's instigation, he also challenged the opposition to consider what else might be done to redress the "insurmountable difficulties" Bernard faced. Hillsborough, however, did not intend to goad the opposition into calling for the revision of the Massachusetts Charter, for the cabinet had yet to formulate a measured response to Bernard's reports.[81]

For the first time in nearly two years, as P. D. G. Thomas notes, ministers were forced to justify American policy to Parliament. The decision to dispatch the regulars to Boston was roundly criticized by the opposition. The Rockingham Whigs—William Dowdeswell, Sir George Savile, and Edmund Burke—called for a full parliamentary inquiry into affairs in Massachusetts, at that moment an unwelcome scenario for Hillsborough, and published Bernard's letters in their mouthpiece, the *Annual Register*.[82] The empathy these men displayed for Bernard in having to cope with Hillsborough's alleged lack of judgment over Massachusetts's circular letter was no more than a foil with which to strike the ministry; they lamented Bernard's "love of controversy" for having incited popular opposition. When George Onslow asked the House of Commons to consider whether Hillsborough or Bernard "was to blame" for the "threats" contained in the king's speech, Hillsborough might be forgiven for thinking it was time to deliver Bernard as a scapegoat for the ministry's heavy-handed approach to the situation in Boston.[83]

Hillsborough's concern to protect Bernard was compromised not only by the exigencies of parliamentary politics but also by the flaws in Bernard's reporting of events. Hillsborough was acutely aware of the vulnerability of colonial governors to intrigue in London, but equally, he was having to justify his own actions, by proving either that Bernard was right or that he had been misled by the governor. The "Facts," Hillsborough told Bernard, were "so interwoven" with the governor's "own observations & opinions that it [was] altogether impracticable to seperate [*sic*] them." Hillsborough needed to be sure that Bernard's talk of insurrection could be proven in a court of law, and asked the government's law officers for an opinion.[84] Attorney General William De Grey could find nothing in Bernard's reports about the *Liberty* riot or the September town meeting to warrant immediate proceedings. De Grey did, however, propose that there was a prima facie case to be answered, and advised that under an archaic and feared statute (35 Henry 8) Parliament could form itself into a special commission to hear cases of treason or misprision of treason arising in the colonies. De Grey's opinion was not a vindication of Bernard. He insisted that the governor should supply corroborating documentation relating, for example, to what had been said by Otis and Adams on 12 September and evidence of "any design laid or persons Names, or times appointed, or other measures taken, for Seizing Castle William."[85] On 15 November Hillsborough instructed Bernard to inquire into "illegal and unconstitutional Acts" committed in the province during and after the *Liberty* riot and to bring the perpetrators to justice. In a separate missive, he promised Bernard that he would do what he could to keep secret some of the most sensitive material in his letters.[86]

Hillsborough's credibility probably would not have survived any public disparagement of the governor. That is perhaps why he presented such an extensive portfolio of Bernard's correspondence to Parliament on 28 November—some sixty documents plus enclosures, including Bernard's correspondence with the secretaries of state. Another batch of letters written mainly by Commodore Hood and Colonel Dalrymple, which appeared to confirm Bernard's apprehensions of insurrection, was presented on 7 December. All this information did not materially change the nature of the debates concerning Massachusetts and colonial policy, but it certainly drew attention to the question of how far Bernard's perceptions and preconceptions were influencing Hillsborough. "I can't see where the fault lies by reading the papers before the House [of Commons]," observed William Beckford, though Hillsborough "does find fault" with Bernard; the governor, said another, had clearly "aggravated matters" in Boston. As it was, Beckford continued, Bostonians would be justified in calling for Bernard's impeachment.[87]

Hillsborough's reputation survived the debates, and on 15 December he moved a series of eight resolutions in the House of Lords. Regardless of the textual evidence, it was resolved that the petitions and remonstrances issued by the Massachusetts legislature in January and February 1768 purported to impugn parliamentary sovereignty. The proceedings of the Boston town meeting on 14 June and 12 September were also deemed to be "illegal and Unconstitutional [and] subversive," while the Convention of Towns was declared an "unlawful combination." The third, fourth, and fifth resolutions asked the Lords to endorse Bernard's conclusion that the return of crowd action to Boston in the spring and summer of 1768 produced a "State of great disorder and Confusion," which both the Council and the magistracy neglected to address, and which justified the deployment of British regulars. While suggesting that rebels might be tried in England, Hillsborough did not propose to amend, revise, or revoke the Massachusetts Charter, as Bernard favored. The resolutions were approved in the Lords without a division, though several Lords doubted whether Hillsborough could rely on Bernard's testimony in the event of any colonists being impeached or tried. When the duke of Richmond suggested that Bernard had "misconstrue[d] that to be treason which was not," Hillsborough and Shelburne engaged in "some sparring about the conduct of Governor Bernard."[88]

The resolutions passed the Commons in the last week of January 1769, where the ministry's American policy was subjected to much greater scrutiny. An address was adopted asking the king to obtain further information about treasonable activities in Massachusetts and to establish a commission of inquiry.[89] Beckford and Burke continued their tirade against Bernard on 25 January, when the government contested the legitimacy of the petition submitted by the Massachusetts Council, before Beckford was allowed to present it to the lobby. The next day a succession of speakers accused Bernard of bullying the Council and treating the colonists with contempt.[90] Had he been present, Bernard would have winced at how Attorney General De Grey defended him. For sure, Bernard had not supplied incontrovertible evidence of overt acts of treason, De Grey admitted, but "Look into the papers," he urged, "see how well these men understand the Crown law. I doubt whether they have been guilty of an overt act of treason, but they came within an ace of it. I think Governor Bernard . . . stopp[ed] . . . a traitorous convention." On the other hand, if Bernard's accusations proved to be groundless, then he, not the leading Whigs, should be impeached. Any proceedings under the Henrician treason laws, De Grey continued, were also justifiable if they might "stop and awe" the colonists "from entering into rebellion." Thus it was that De Grey and not Hillsborough ventured to make Bernard a scapegoat for what the opposition was calling the "folly" of ministers.

A few Members of Parliament came to Bernard's defense, but most speakers assailed the governor. Barlow Trecothick, Burke, Dowdeswell, Beckford, and others deplored the governor's "dark insinuations" and his patent failure to name those colonists who he claimed were intent on insurrection. Thomas Pownall, the former governor, knew more about Massachusetts's affairs than anyone in London, including Franklin, and urged that Bernard be recalled forthwith. George Grenville—who would have been able to recount in detail the internal divisions of the Massachusetts Council—by contrast criticized the resolutions for doing nothing to tackle the deficiencies in the Massachusetts magistracy that Bernard had brought to light.[91] The colonists had able advocates aplenty outside Parliament, who were also able to counteract Bernard's impressionistic reports. It was with the "deepest concern" that the Massachusetts Whigs learned from William Bollan and Thomas Pownall that ministers were formulating policy on the basis of information supplied by the governor.[92] Colonial agents such as Franklin and British merchants worried that everyone was losing sight of the fundamental constitutional and economic issues raised by American taxation.[93]

The Lords' resolutions, on the other hand, were dismissed by Barrington as a futile gesture because they were not accompanied by a set of prescriptive measures such as Bernard had been urging.[94] On 13 February, however, Hillsborough presented the cabinet with several proposals that went some way to address that problem: that the province charter should be forfeited if the House of Representatives continued to deny parliamentary supremacy; that the Council should hereafter be appointed directly by the Crown; and that the governor be given a discretionary power to move the General Court from Boston. Bernard was finally recalled to England to make a personal report and to receive his baronetcy. No mention was made of bringing rebels to trial in England.[95] John Pownall and Barrington may have been privy to the preliminary discussions. Pownall, despite his brother's growing enmity toward Bernard, criticized the "Spirit of procrastination" that dogged American policymaking,[96] and drafted a nine-point paper summarizing his and Bernard's draconian thinking on Massachusetts and the American Question.[97] Barrington drafted a paper proposing that the Quartering Act be amended to allow army commanders to override the civil government if they faced again the obstruction they encountered in Boston and New York, but this was shot down in flames by both "Court & Opposition," he noted.[98]

The cabinet was simply unable to agree how far they should go in punishing Massachusetts, and (with the king's blessing) rejected Hillsborough's proposals to revoke the province charter and institute a mandamus Council. Ministers also preferred to wait and see if the Massachusetts General Court would comply with Townshend's provision for a colonial civil list before giving Bernard a Crown salary, partly because of growing concern about the size of the civil list itself. (It was not until 1771 that Parliament legislated Crown salaries for the Massachusetts governor, lieutenant governor, the Superior Court justices, and senior law officers.)[99] Bernard's hopes for condign punishment began to fade, however, when American affairs took second place to the John Wilkes saga (Wilkes was expelled from Parliament on 3 February).[100] The prevailing view that emerged was in favor of conciliation, not confrontation. In April 1769, when Thomas Pownall moved unsuccessfully that Parliament repeal the Townshend Acts, he attracted support not only from the Rockinghamites Sir George Savile and Barlow Trecothick but from two men already implicated in Bernard's "conspiracy"—Richard Jackson and Henry Seymour Conway. Within a few weeks the cabinet had resolved to repeal the Townshend duties, except that on tea, which Parliament agreed to do on 5 March 1770.[101]

*   *   *

While he waited further directions from London, Bernard secretly compiled evidence that might be used against the leading colonists in any trial for sedition or treason. The necessity of answering the colonists' claims of duplicity or any subsequent charge by the British concerning a "Want of Spirit" prompted Bernard to prepare a defense. "I write as I speak," he confessed to Hillsborough,

> *from my Heart, & with a Strict Regard to Truth, so far as it is discernible by means in my Power. . . . The Inaccuracies which occur in [my letters] are Proofs that they are wrote freely. Freedom of Writing like Freedom of Speech is more conducive to Truth than Accuracy [and] attentive more to Forms than Matter. In my Situation a Suppression or Perversion of Truth would*

have been highly criminal; & . . . keeping good Terms with the
Sons of Liberty might have led me into Misprision of treason.[102]

It was just possible that by portraying himself as the victim, Bernard
might excuse the many gaps in the evidence that purported to show
that the colonists' treasonable and seditious talk had resulted in treasonable and seditious actions.

If we can believe Bernard's spies, Samuel Adams and several other
Whigs in 1768 publicly declared for colonial legislative independence.
Such a view did not become Whig orthodoxy until several years later
when it was clear that Britain had no intention of making any concessions on parliamentary supremacy. However, when the House debated calls for Bernard's dismissal in the summer of 1769, Adams and
his fellow Boston representatives did propose a resolution that
amounted to a denial of Parliament's legislative supremacy, though it
was rejected. Adams's early advocacy of nonimportation also reflected
his enthusiasm for encouraging the colonies to become more eco-
nomically self-sufficient, a proposal not only Bernard but many of
Adams's supporters dismissed as a pipe dream.[103] Be that as it may,
Bernard accused Adams and his henchmen of fomenting treason and
plotting an armed rebellion. The evidence for this, to say the least, is
sketchy.

On 23 December Bernard delivered a startling claim: among those
who spoke at the Boston town meeting and the Convention of
Towns were some who "undoubtedly intended . . . to bring about a
Revolt." He spoke of plans to "seize" both himself and Hutchinson,
and to invest Castle William, which he claimed were only aborted
when he learned the names of the five hundred people "enrolled for
that Service."[104] Bernard never identified the participants or the leaders of this insurrection, and we will never know fully what the radicals
discussed on the eve of the troops' arrival. However, Bernard collected accounts about related events, from which he alleged that treason, sedition, and other felonies may have been committed. He
considered leading colonists to have been principals in these crimes,
including having actually committed such offenses or having encouraged others to commit them.

From the testimony of several informers, Bernard tried to piece together what had been said at the tempestuous town meeting of 12
September. It was easy to expose the pretext of a French invasion as
a sham, but far more difficult to show that the radicals were planning

to resist the troops. Otis was attributed with a rambling, seditious speech in which he announced that the "Inhabitants had nothing more to do, but gird the Sword to the [t]high and shoulder to the Musquet."[105] Bernard's précis of Otis's advocacy of natural rights was subtler, inasmuch as it suggested that in carrying "these Arguments so far . . . his own Party was obliged to silence him." Samuel Adams was equally animated, and supposedly told one informer, the innkeeper Richard Silvester, to expect "thirty thousand men from the Country with their Knapsacks and bayonets fixed" if British regulars landed in Boston.[106]

Furthermore, at the time of the *Liberty* riot, the physician Benjamin Church and the distiller Thomas Chase were said to have joined Adams in calling for Bostonians to rise against the customhouse. Prosecutions for inciting disorder were normally brought under the infamous Riot Act, although under English law riots with political objectives could also be interpreted as "constructive treasons." Church and Chase were both prominent Whigs, the former as a satirist and orator, the latter as a member of the Loyal Nine.[107] Also warranting investigation, Bernard claimed, were the printers Benjamin Edes and John Gill for publishing the proceedings of the Convention of Towns in the *Boston Gazette*.[108] He was pleased to learn later that Doctors Joseph Warren and Benjamin Church had panicked when they heard of his interest in the printers. Warren burned his personal papers, while Church managed to recover from the printers the manuscript of one incriminating piece he had written. Within a few years, however, Church was spying for Hutchinson.

The problem for any prosecuting Crown lawyer was the absence of legal "fact." There had been no armed insurrection, of course, and it was extremely doubtful whether hearsay evidence would be enough to indict Otis, Adams, Church, and Chase either as principal felons or as accessories before the fact. Misprisions of treason—where the colonists failed to report seditious and treasonable talk—were also punishable. Bernard himself could be included in this category if he failed to inform the king of any such behavior. Bernard fully appreciated these problems and the procedural difficulties involved in any attempt to prosecute civilians for sedition. (It was not until the 1790s that the deplorable Treasonable Practices Act and Seditious Meetings Act gave the British government wide powers to prosecute persons for seducing or inciting Crown servants and others to commit sedition.)[109]

Securing evidence of treasonable behavior was equally problem-

atic. Utterances that were disrespectful of the king or threatening to
his person did not in themselves amount to treason unless they were
connected to a specific act. Thomas Chase, for example, made no secret of what he thought of George III—a "fool and a rascal" he called
him—but this did not amount to high treason. One of the depositions sent to London accused the Sons of Liberty of being antimon-
archists after one praised the "glorious" Cromwell and mused "That
it would be no Sin to murder Govr Bernard" or the customs commissioners.[110]

The only firm piece of evidence Bernard tendered was the precept
issued by the Boston selectmen on 14 September inviting the Massachusetts towns to the Convention of Towns. Bernard argued that the
selectmen had acted *ultra vires* and claimed the precept was libelous,
though not in itself seditious or treasonable. The selectmen had accused Bernard of "aggravating" the "concern and perplexity" of the
townspeople when he let it be known that the regulars were on their
way to Boston. Bernard named nine local politicians. Otis, in his capacity as moderator of the Boston town meeting, headed the list; the
name of Samuel Adams, the clerk of the convention, came at the bottom, along with William Cooper, the town clerk who had drawn up
the precept. Bernard had long-standing grievances with three of the
other signatories: Col. Joseph Jackson of the militia, John Ruddock,
the irascible magistrate, and John Hancock. The willingness of
wealthy merchants and moderates John Rowe and Samuel Pemberton to cooperate with the other selectmen was more unexpected.[111]

The inclusion on Bernard's lists of rebels of Thomas Cushing, the
speaker of the convention, is the most intriguing for what it reveals
about moderate Whigs' deep antipathy toward their governor. Bernard never attempted to block Cushing's election as Speaker of the
House—as he had that of James Otis—ever hopeful that his public
deportment did not wholly reflect his own views. In the summer of
1767 Cushing had raised discreetly in a supposedly private capacity
the subject of Bernard's disposition toward the colonists,[112] and his
participation at the Convention of Towns ruled out any future conciliation of Bernard. When Cushing was interviewed by Nathaniel Coffin, shortly after the town meeting had decided to summon the
convention, Coffin "expostulated . . . upon the misery which he and
his party were bringing upon the Town by opposition which they
were meditating." Cushing replied, to Coffin's horror, "that for his
part he had always been for moderate measures and [yet] had proposed among them to drive off the Governor and Lieutenant Gover-

nor" so that "they should have the Council in their own hands and could oblige them to call an assembly."

Coffin was surprised by Cushing's spontaneity, given that the Speaker in the same breath declared that he was considered "obnoxious to his own party." "[James] Otis had said to him, that he was so great an Enemy to his Country as Frank Bernard, Thom Hutchinson, and the commissioners." Hitherto, Cushing insisted, "he had always behaved with decency towards the Governor and he was dissatisfied with the load of Calumny and scurrility which was flung upon his Excellency." He had supported the convention in the (well-founded) expectation that "it would bring together some prudent People who would be able to check the violent designs of Others." Cushing adamantly opposed armed resistance, claiming "he should make no scruple to shoot the man who should by such means bring misery upon him and his family." When the townspeople "came to feel the effects of it" they would direct their "resentment" at the likes of Adams and Otis. Yet he had "mentioned the driving off the Governor and Lieutenant Governor . . . as a desirable act, . . . only to prevent more violent measures."[113]

Coffin's testimony was no less inherently biased than the others Bernard sent to Britain in January and February 1769, but his intelligent appraisal of the Whigs' dilemmas contrasts with other depositions that hysterically accuse the Sons of Liberty of treason. If Coffin's account is accurate, then clearly, although divisions had appeared in Whig ranks over calls for arming the townspeople, the moderates would not consider cooperating with the provincial administration in doing anything to allay their fears of a possible bloodbath.[114]

In the event of a trial in England, the prosecution would require, in addition to documentary evidence, at least two witnesses to testify against the accused. Men like Coffin and Silvester—"who abhor the Proceedings of the Faction and yet have been let into their Secrets"— were hard to find, observed Bernard.[115] But there is nothing to suggest that these men were ready to bring down the Whigs. Bernard's approaches to friends of government were invariably brushed aside with a skill, he said, reminiscent of John Wilkes's facile evasiveness: "You have leave to ask as many Questions as you please, but *I beg leave* to give no Answer to any of them."[116]

There was little enthusiasm among Massachusetts's senior officials when, on 20 April 1769, Bernard received fresh instructions from

Hillsborough to continue with his investigations into "treasonable proceedings" committed since 30 December 1767. Bernard asked Chief Justice Hutchinson and Attorney General Sewall to collect more depositions, but they found nothing that might prove that "treasonable consultations" among the radical Whigs had incited treasonable behavior.[117] Having collected as much evidence as he could, Bernard was appalled to learn that Parliament's resolutions against Massachusetts did not propose any form of remedial action. Bernard was not alone in his criticism. James Murray, for example, concluded, "if these Resolves are not attended with some more effectual Cure, it is not imagined here that our Disorders will be removed."[118]

Bernard and Hutchinson did not dare apprehend any of the radicals. If Bernard's allegation of sedition is accurate, royal government in Massachusetts would probably not have survived the arraignment of Otis, Adams, or any other leading Whigs. One indication of the governor's uncertainty is that he (and Hutchinson) remained naively optimistic that British-colonial relations would be unscathed by a trial in England. That, of course, would have depended upon the nature of the charges, the decision of the Court of the King's Bench (where any trial would probably have taken place), and, if found guilty, the nature of the punishment meted out. No one, not even Bernard, dared mention in correspondence that it might involve an act of attainder, by which the Whigs would forfeit their lives and property.[119]

Bernard's preferred method of proceeding was an impeachment before the House of Commons, a no-less-controversial method used sparingly in criminal proceedings. To that end, he urged the British government to establish a special parliamentary commission to investigate not only the activities of James Otis and Samuel Adams but those of others who had lately come to prominence: the writer and physician Thomas Young, Boston's town clerk William Cooper, the merchant William Molineux, and councilor James Pitts.[120] Parliament, Bernard hoped, could bar these men from holding local or provincial office (in much the same way as the government tried to oust John Wilkes from the House of Commons). Similarly, the Boston magistrates' refusal to find quarters for the regulars warranted the dissolution of the entire commission. Altogether, Bernard's proposals invoked Parliament's contested authority to overturn acts of incorporation, in this case the Massachusetts Charter.[121]

Compromise with the colonists, Thomas Hutchinson warned Bernard, would never be possible if the British ever acted upon his suggestion to give the Crown the right to choose the Massachusetts Council. (This indeed was the case when the Massachusetts Government Act of 1774 provoked massive resistance.) Instead, Hutchinson suggested limiting Council elections to every two or three years. Hutchinson had often suffered Bernard's imprudence, although never in silence. But this was one of the most tense moments in their long relationship. Bernard was annoyed by the Crown grant of two hundred pounds Hutchinson had recently received (after the General Court cut his chief justice's salary) when his own labors and sacrifices had yet to be recognized by a Crown salary. A frank discussion of both issues prevented any acrimony.[122] Bernard's revised proposal for the reform of the Council—that the charter be amended to allow the governor a discretionary power of appointing at least half the board—was as contentious as his earlier ideas. This would enable him to restore the executive officers and friends of government such as Paine and Ropes, and with places reserved for the attorney general and customs commissioners he would be able to isolate opponents without too much difficulty. Bernard did not rule out appointing moderates such as Isaac Royall and John Erving, if they took "Steps to reconcile themselves to Government."[123] Any such reforms, as Hutchinson well knew, would incense the General Court, but neither man realized that what they were offering Americans was a paradox, not a solution.

*　　*　　*

Bernard failed at a basic level to empathize with the colonists over the Townshend Acts, let alone rationalize the resurgence of the colonial protest movement within the wider context of how the colonists viewed imperial relations. All he could see around him were symptoms of malaise—an empire waiting for the barbarians. The fall began when the accusations of disloyalty and treachery Bernard and the New Englanders flung at each other intruded in the formulation and execution of British colonial policy, on occasions when sensitive diplomacy was necessary to prevent further deterioration in relations. The collective folly of British ministers and officials was to accept, largely uncritically, Bernard's grim warnings that respect for royal government was crumbling so fast as to require British soldiers to restore it.

CHAPTER SEVEN

"Unmasked"

Bernard and the Imperial Crisis, 1769–1774

A PAUCITY OF EVIDENCE rather than a lack of conviction had hampered the efforts of Samuel Adams and James Bowdoin to have Bernard called to account for misleading government ministers. All that changed on Saturday, 5 April 1769, when the brig *Last Attempt* arrived in Boston with a package for Bowdoin. The package contained six letters written by Bernard to the earl of Hillsborough between 1 November and 5 December 1768, recounting the governor's struggle with the Council in finding quarters for the British regiments. They had already been laid before Parliament, and the pro-American Member of Parliament William Beckford was only too happy to let the Council's agent William Bollan make copies. Bollan was responding to the Council's request to find documentary proof of the governor's perfidy, but he was also motivated by the desire to exact revenge for having lost the province agency in 1762 and with it a principal source of income; lately Bernard had withheld approval of the salary for Bollan's new post.[1] The trickle became a flood when there arrived in Boston copies of twenty-seven other letters composed by Bernard between January and October 1768, in which he talked freely about his controversial proposals for reforming colonial government and of punishing the province by revoking the charter. Other documents authored by General Gage and the customs commissioners seemed to confirm suspicions that the governor and the imperial elite had exploited the *Liberty* riot to obtain British regulars. Cheap imprints of these state papers were published within a few weeks together with an official version issued by the General Court containing a lengthy riposte by the Governor's Council. Excerpts were also printed in the *Boston Gazette*.[2]

Bernard's "unmasking" was a brilliant piece of propaganda. Hitherto the radicals had failed to carry the majority of representatives and councilors in their calls for Bernard's dismissal and impeachment. Even though the radicals did not acquire copies of Hillsborough's orders to Bernard and Gage with respect to the troops, ordinary colonists such as the shopkeeper Harbottle Dorr could read at their leisure how their once respected governor had perpetrated a "vile slander" against the province and "poisoned" the king's ear. John Speed, deputy clerk to Samuel Adams, underscored the sections of one such letter where Bernard had accused the "faction" and its leaders of planning an insurrection. For others like John Temple, Bernard's embarrassment was an opportunity to open old wounds,[3] but any idea that the governor was the victim of a conspiracy received short shrift. Not one newspaper, including the *Boston Chronicle,* defended Bernard when Boston again instructed its representatives to procure a provincial inquiry into the governor's conduct and urged that Bernard be indicted for libel.[4] A series of resolutions calling for Bernard's removal and castigating General Gage, Commodore Hood, and the customs commissioners were adopted, and copies of Bernard's letters sent to the colonists' friends in England: agents Bollan, DeBerdt, and Franklin, and Members of Parliament Isaac Barré, Barlow Trecothick, and Thomas Pownall.[5] The most comprehensive analysis of Bernard's letters was by Samuel Adams in *An Appeal to the World,* published under the auspices of the Boston town meeting. It was his version of recent events that began the patriotic process of demonizing Bernard. The governor, it seemed, harbored "an aversion to free assemblies"—the "scourge of tyrants"—where men "think as they please and speak as they think."[6] Reaction in the Massachusetts towns was more muted, but friends of government who deigned to defend Bernard were generally not reelected in May. More surprising, reported Bernard, was that "Officers of the Crown" discreetly avoided commenting on the affair.[7]

Thomas Hutchinson, who would suffer a similar indignity four years later, rightly pointed out that generally there was nothing in the letters Bernard had not been saying in public.[8] But Hutchinson was profoundly disturbed by the sense of revelation that greeted the governor's exposure as a conspirator against the charter. Unpopular as he was, Hutchinson was inevitably implicated in the conspiracy. He feared that his chances of succeeding Bernard were slipping away, and again remonstrated vehemently with the governor over his proposal for a mandamus Council. "I am not desirous of a change in the Constitution," Hutchinson told an old friend, for "I have attachments to old modes and customs, civil and religious which are not to be expected in" Bernard.[9]

Bernard's reaction to the affair was uncharacteristically muted, though he rightly suspected that the Whigs would use it to justify their opposition to the Townshend program and later persuade the House of Representatives to withhold his salary grant.[10] Bernard was already preparing his defense when, in early May, he received confirmation of his baronetcy and permission to return home.[11] The publication of the letters, he informed Richard Jackson, would "effectually prevent all confidential Writing to Ministers of State for the future," for they were written "in Confidence & in Obedience of strict Orders."[12]

> It is impossible for a Governor who has been engaged in such Contests as I have been, & as well by special Orders as by his own Sense of His Duty, given free & full Information of the Proceedings of the factious Party, to think of staying in the Province, after his most confidential Letters are put in the Hands of the Faction and printed & dispersed among the People. For tho the Letters may be very justifiable with indifferent & impartial Persons, yet it cannot be expected that they will be treated with any Degree of Candour by those whom they affect.[13]

Bernard gave some thought to publishing a rejoinder, which he did in 1774, but for the moment he held fire lest he damage his defense that he had faithfully executed his instructions and "for having declared against the Policy of the Constitution of the Government after it had been rendered impracticable by the Successful Machinations of the wickedest Men in it."[14]

With few supporters left in the General Court, there was nothing to be gained from a protracted argument over the publication of the letters, let alone their contents. Nevertheless, Bernard rejected eleven of the councilors elected that year, including James Bowdoin and William Brattle, leaving him with an upper chamber of just sixteen members out of a possible twenty-eight. Bernard had probably intended proroguing the General Court, but because General Gage had presented him with his regiments' accounts in mid-May he was obliged to continue the session.[15]

*   *   *

Bernard's last-ever session as governor was dominated by the House's demand to know whether or not the governor had the authority to withdraw the regulars from Boston. The bravado of 12 September had given way to sullen resentment by the spring of 1769, but Boston was never the same again. The British soldiers who were deployed on guard duty encountered "daily hostility" from the townspeople in the form of verbal abuse, robbery, and random acts of violence; soldiers were hauled before the provincial courts for seemingly petty offenses, while their officers complained that civilians were rarely punished for the same crimes; desertion, too, was a major problem.[16] Bernard was ridiculed in the *Journal of the Times,* a radical newssheet published in New York as well as in Boston, which cataloged, with considerable embellishment, the disputes between the townspeople and the British troops and propagated a simple message: the troops were only in Boston because of what Bernard had told British ministers. As Bernard explained to the House, he could not overrule Gage's orders from London by withdrawing all four regiments,[17] but, as the Whigs suspected, he did have the authority to advise Gage on how many regiments should be quartered in town.

This would have been a sterile debate had not Bernard received on 10 June a letter from Gage informing him that because Boston had been so quiet of late he had ordered to Halifax two of the four regiments stationed in the town and castle—the Sixty-fourth and Sixty-fifth. Bernard was asked to decide whether he wanted the other two regiments—the Fourteenth and Twenty-ninth—to be withdrawn also.[18] Bernard could not bring himself to admit to Gage what he now accepted: that the troops he had desired were no longer needed because there "was no Prospect at present of a forceable Opposition to Government."[19] He flatly refused to give any answer so long as the friends of government wanted the troops to remain,[20] and on 14 June exercised his new discretionary power by removing the General Court to Cambridge. Gage and Commodore Hood commenced the withdrawal of the Sixty-fourth and Sixty-fifth Regiments anyway, only to suspend the operation when the Whigs mounted their most vitriolic attack yet on the governor.

The main business transacted in Cambridge concerned Bernard's conspiracy to "overthrow the present constitution of government in this colony, and to have the people deprived of their invaluable charter rights." When, on 27 June, the 109 members of the House unanimously voted to send a petition to the king requesting Bernard's dismissal from office, friends like Timothy Ruggles were conspicuous by their absence.[21] Four principal accusations were made. First, that Bernard had always treated the House with undisguised contempt. Second, there were listed several instances of Bernard's inciting quarrels (the offense of barratry under English law) or acting unconstitutionally (as when he obstructed the House from choosing DeBerdt as its own agent, or when he granted a charter to Queen's College without consulting the Council). Third, Bernard had regularly abused several "gentlemen of character." Finally, he had misled ministers into thinking that the people of Massachusetts and the General Court were "disaffected" to the Crown and Parliament. The next day, when Bernard informed the members that he was returning home, his salary grant was refused for the first time ever. The same committee that drafted the petition—it included the Otises, Cushing, and Hancock—issued a set of resolves composed by Samuel Adams on 29 June that firmly placed Bernard's infamy within the context of the colonists' struggles against British "tyranny." The resolves were published on 3 July, before the Council could debate them, but the Council subsequently amended the committee's second resolution, which had denied Parliament's legislative supremacy, to read that the "sole right" of taxation lay with the colonial legislatures. All parties agreed, however, that Bernard should be punished for introducing "military government" to Boston and conspiring to "violate" the charter.[22] In sum, the specific charge was that Bernard exceeded the terms of his royal commission, an offense punishable by parliamentary impeachment if the Privy Council decided there was a case to answer.[23]

Bernard did not dismiss the General Court until 15 July, after the House voted the annual supply bill for the provincial administration but refused to meet its legal obligation to pay for the upkeep of the British soldiers quartered in Boston.[24] Never had he witnessed "assertions, declarations, and resolutions" so contemptible of parliamentary sovereignty and "entirely inconsistent with the idea of this province being a part of the British empire."[25] The account he forwarded to Hillsborough was equally direct: "in denying the Power of the Parliament, arraigning and condemning its Acts, abusing the Kings Ministers at home & his principal Officers in America, reproaching the whole British Nation," the colonists were "decring [*sic*] in plain, if not direct Terms their right & Intention to separate themselves from its Government."[26] Another aspect of Bernard's defense was taking

shape: by impugning the reputation of the governor and other imperial officials the colonists were vividly demonstrating a contempt for
royal authority.

Bernard's parting shot was to ensure that an army of "occupation"
remained in Boston to quell the radicals. When Gage resumed the
withdrawal of the Sixty-fourth and Sixty-fifth Regiments, Bernard
finally asked that the Fourteenth and Twenty-ninth Regiments be retained. Radicals such as Thomas Young, as well as the House of Representatives and the Boston town meeting, were certain that Gage
would have withdrawn all four regiments if Bernard had asked.
Gage's orders did not allow this, but the governor's hesitancy gave
credence to the fallacy that both he and Gage had arbitrarily interpreted royal instructions. Nine months later, on a wintry March evening, the town and the British came to rue the consequences of the
governor's caution.[27]

Bernard's last public appearance was at the Harvard College commencement, which passed without incident or insult, though an "air
of indecency," Hutchinson observed, pervaded most other "publick
proceedings."[28] At 10 A.M. on 1 August, Bernard boarded HMS *Rip-
pon* with a fifteen-gun salute ringing in his ears and a copy of the
House's petition for his dismissal in his pocket, nine years to the day
since he first entered Massachusetts. After he bade farewell to his
wife and children, incoming winds delayed the sailing by one day.
With Bernard ensconced in his cabin, the good citizens of the town
celebrated his departure, trusting, as William Palfrey put it, that it
was a "favorable omen" for improved relations with Britain.[29]
Thomas Young was less sanguine, thinking that only a change of
ministry could restore Americans' confidence in Britain.[30] Other colonies were more concerned to protest their grievances with British
policy than they were with Bernard's conduct,[31] yet, as one colonist
remarked, there was some comfort to be had in the "hope the Baronet will in the end meet with his just Deserts, and that you may
never more see his face in Boston."[32]

As it was, Bernard's "expulsion" stoked resentment toward royal
officials in Boston. In early September, commissioner John Robinson
became embroiled in a coffeehouse brawl with James Otis, in which
the latter came off worse, when Otis learned that he had been maligned in the commissioners' letters that had been published along
with Bernard's letters. William Palfrey outrageously claimed that the
incident was a botched attempt to assassinate Otis. Robinson found

redress in the provincial law courts, but Bernard was soon to find himself indicted. When Attorney General Jonathan Sewall refused Boston's request to prepare a bill of indictment in the Suffolk County Court against Bernard, Gage, Hood (whose name was subsequently removed from the list), the customs commissioners, and customsmen Joseph Harrison and Benjamin Hallowell, the jury chairman Thomas Brattle, William Brattle's son, found his own lawyer easily enough. The bill accused these imperial officials of engaging in a conspiracy to "maliciously, wilfully and falsely, misrepresent and libel, slander, and defame the Council, the town of Boston, and the people of the province." Bernard's motive was said to be "an earnest desire to procure the dissolution of the present form of civil government in this Province and to introduce into it an arbitrary Government and a military Tyranny." Palfrey mischievously sent a copy of the bill to John Wilkes for his "amusement." The proceedings ended when Chief Justice Hutchinson was instructed by the Crown to enter pleas of *nolle prosequi* for Bernard and his coaccused, but this did not mean that the governor had been pardoned of any offense alleged to have been committed.[33]

The Whigs, then, justified the escalation of colonial opposition to the Townshend Acts by pointing to the provocation offered by Bernard, Gage, and the customs commissioners. The only problem with such an approach was that British ministers and officials—though not the opposition—viewed events in Massachusetts through the lens of Bernard's hostile reports. No matter how hard the General Court strove to present a counterinterpretation, first Grafton's administration then Lord North's was presented with more powerfully distressing images: the defiance of the House over the circular letter, the Council's unconstitutional proceedings, the Convention of Towns, the bravado of the Boston town meeting, the magistrates' dereliction of duty, and the arraignment of Bernard himself. The radicals' error was to suppose that after insulting a royal governor, the British government would listen any more sympathetically to complaints. Indeed, despite everything that had transpired Bernard's "reception" in London, observed Hutchinson, was "beyond" all expectations.[34]

*   *   *

Bernard arrived in England in early September and took lodgings at Chidley Court in Pall Mall. He did not see his wife for another seventeen months, the first time they had been apart in many years. It was a worrying time, for Amelia had remained behind not only to tend to family affairs but to nurse her ailing son Frank. She did not leave Boston until Christmas Day, 1770, and arrived at the Spithead on 1 February. The long winter crossing on board the *Tweed* did nothing for her frail constitution. The *Tweed* ran into dreadful storms in the English Channel; the cabin windows were stove in and the family's luggage swept overboard. For four days the younger children huddled together in their wet clothes with nothing to eat but chocolate, only for the vessel to be grounded for nineteen hours on a sandbar as it passed the Needles at the Isle of Wight.[35] Bernard, meanwhile, was reunited with his daughter Jane whom he had not seen for eleven years, and visited old friends in Buckinghamshire, Oxford, Berkshire, and Hampshire in preparation for the impending inquiry.

He was shocked to find that Dennis DeBerdt had already presented Massachusetts's petition to the king, which he later published. Moreover, Bernard's misdemeanors were quickly seized upon by the Whigs' allies in London, including the Virginian Arthur Lee, author (probably) of the *Junius Americanus Letters*, and Franklin, who published regularly in the *London Chronicle*. John Wilkes promised Palfrey that he would find the New Englanders the "best" lawyers in town.[36] In October, Bernard submitted his own memorial to the Privy Council, which, as might be expected from a lawyer, was prepared with great care. Bernard was confident that with the support of Hillsborough, Welbore Ellis, Lord Chief Justice Mansfield, and Lord Sandys he would be vindicated by the Privy Council, despite several matters of concern.[37]

First were the penalties for maladministration: immediate dismissal, a *sine die* ban on holding Crown office, and a fine of one thousand pounds.[38] Bernard was also subject to the full penalty of law for any criminal act, and learned from Andrew Oliver that DeBerdt had offered his services as an attorney to Adams and Cushing in case they wished to initiate a civil prosecution for "acts of Oppression."[39] Bernard also knew DeBerdt was waiting anxiously for further documentation. No royal governor had ever been fined or punished on such allegations as those made against Bernard, but the possibility remained that the weak Grafton ministry could sacrifice Bernard, and Hillsborough too, for the failure of its American policy. Bernard's predicament was excellent partisan fodder for the Rockingham Whigs, even though Edmund Burke empathized with Bernard when he remarked that America seemed "more wild and absurd than ever."[40] Hillsborough, however, survived the formation of a new administration under Lord North in January 1770 and remained American secretary for another two years.

In these circumstances, Bernard was anxious to secure an early hearing before the Privy Council's committee on plantation affairs, where decisions affecting the colonies were taken. But after a preliminary hearing on 25 October 1769, DeBerdt was given until 27 January, then 28 February, to collect the evidence he needed. Whatever it was that DeBerdt expected—perhaps a fuller statement by the General Court as well as a power of attorney—never came, leaving him only with the petition and the resolves of the House with which to substantiate the allegations against Bernard.[41] DeBerdt floundered before the committee when asked whether he was acting as an attorney for Massachusetts or if he had fed information to Junius Americanus. Master of the Rolls Richard Rigby, Mansfield, Hillsborough, Lord Marchmont, and others pursued a bullish line of inquiry friendly to the governor. Bernard had little difficulty in casting himself as the victim of a conspiracy in which DeBerdt was implicated.[42]

The Massachusetts petition, Bernard claimed, merely repeated articles "with a few Additions & Alterations" that the colonists (he did not identify Bowdoin as the author) had prepared in July 1768 but that never passed the General Court. This was a clever argument, for it rationalized the claims Bernard had made at the time that "civil authority" in Boston was at the mercy of the mobs and the radicals, and that justified his part in bringing the regulars to Boston.[43] Bernard presented a mass of documentation, including letters to and from the secretaries of state for the colonies, parliamentary papers, newspaper cuttings, and the journals of the assembly—all of which appeared to confirm that whatever he had done in Boston, whatever he had said about the colonists, was undertaken with due attention to preserving the authority of Parliament and the prerogatives of the Crown.[44] The province's allegation that Bernard had exceeded the terms of his commission was dismissed on 7 March as "groundless, vexatious and scandalous."[45]

More relieved than contented, in May 1770 Bernard rented a house in the quiet London suburb of Hampstead, where he remained for about a year attending to official business. He spent much of his time observing Parliament's proceedings and advising ministers on Massachusetts. Bernard's bitterness toward the New Englanders had mellowed somewhat after his day of reckoning. He favored North's plan to repeal the Townshend duties as a concession to the Americans, bar that on tea, which was retained on principle—unlike Welbore Ellis and Lord Barrington, who opposed making any concessions. (Bernard's critics, meanwhile—Conway, Beckford, Trecothick, and Thomas Pownall—wanted all the duties repealed.)[46] But Bernard's basic views on colonial policy remained the same. In conversations with Hillsborough, North, and other officials he proposed that repeal should be made conditional on the cessation of the boycott, and raised again the possibility of reforming and reorganizing the colonial governments.[47]

Bernard's intimacy with ministers did not spare him from the opposition. On 8 May the House of Commons debated American affairs at length with several speakers commenting upon Bernard's administration as an adjunct to discussions on the Boston Massacre of 5 March, in which five civilians were shot and killed by British soldiers. The debate arose from a motion proposed by Thomas Pownall to address the king about the apparent confusion over the demarcation of authority between colonial governments and the commander in chief, General Gage. After the Massacre, the Fourteenth and Twenty-ninth Regiments were withdrawn from Boston to Castle William by their commanding officer, Lt. Col. William Dalrymple, at the request of acting governor Thomas Hutchinson and without express clearance from Gage, who vainly tried to halt the evacuation.[48] Why, Pownall asked, couldn't Bernard have done earlier what Hutchinson did? The Massacre itself might have been averted, Pownall implied, if Bernard had shown the courage to trust the colonists who beseeched him to withdraw the troops. Pownall also spoke at length on the deteriorating relations between the colonists and their governors, with support from Barré, Beckford, and Burke.[49] North, Pownall reassured the colonists, was fooling himself if he followed Bernard's advice in supposing, for example, that governors and colonial officials could be made financially independent of the assemblies without inciting further opposition.[50] When Edmund Burke proposed censuring the North administration—a motion that failed—he cited some choice items from the Hillsborough-Bernard correspondence that illustrated well the Rockinghamites' contention that the "disorders" in America had been brought on by the incompetence of Hillsborough.[51] New Yorkers were so impressed that they made

Burke their agent at the end of the year; thereafter, he voted against virtually every measure North proposed for America.[52]

Bernard was an easy target for North's critics, but ministers listened to what he had to say during the Privy Council inquiry into the state of the province held between 26 June and 4 July. The inquiry began with the committee on plantation affairs mulling over a lengthy report prepared by Undersecretary John Pownall concerning the "State of the Disorders" in Massachusetts, which was based largely on the information contained in Bernard's state papers.[53] Bernard and five other witnesses were called to give evidence: Capt. James Scott, Hancock's valued employee; Ebenezer Bridgeham, a loyal Boston merchant; commissioner John Robinson; and customsmen Benjamin Hallowell and Joseph Harrison. In asking Bernard to give "an account of the Disturbances in general from the beginning," the committee allowed him to reiterate his hostile interpretation of Massachusetts politics. "No Governor lived better with the people" until the Stamp Act crisis threw up a determined "faction" of ne'er-do-wells and thwarted office-seekers like the Otises. Bernard said nothing of his own role during the crisis, and claimed Rockingham's repeal of the Stamp Act was a gross error in judgment. "From that time the Doctrine that the Colonies were not Subject to Taxation here began to be publicly avowed," and the radicals in America found common cause with the Wilkesite radicals in Britain. This somewhat telescopic account of revolutionary ideology may have endeared him to North, who was eager to quell doubts about the wisdom of retaining the tea duty. Bernard was less comfortable in fielding the one question he had never been able to answer: whether the Bostonians actually intended to mount an insurrection in the autumn of 1768. However, he deftly avoided the imputation of scaremongering by highlighting the inadequacies of the militia as a police force and the decline of the friends of government in the General Court as a principal reason why he had had such a troublesome administration. All the witnesses save Scott corroborated Bernard's view that with the advent of nonimportation and return of crowd action the trade laws could not be enforced effectively, and that parliamentary intervention was required to compensate for the failure of Massachusetts's legislature and magistracy to tackle law-and-order problems.[54]

Bernard's evidence was the most detailed and the most damaging to the colonists—a "very cruel and unjust" litany of accusations, Thomas Cushing later recalled.[55] The Privy Council cautiously accepted Bernard's comments about sedition in Boston, and more fully accepted the allegations he made against the Council, the House, and the Boston town meeting.[56] It passed a series of resolutions asking Parliament to undertake a full investigation of the situation in Massachusetts, which was not acted upon until after the Boston Tea Party, and made two recommendations that were immediately adopted by North: the Royal Navy station was moved from Halifax to Boston and British regulars were sent to garrison Castle William.

American policy had undoubtedly suffered from the vacillation of previous governments, and historians have suggested that in adopting these measures North was mainly trying to deflect criticism from his own supporters, particularly, one suspects, Hillsborough himself.[57] Barrington, for example, took up Hillsborough's proposal for reforming the provincial magistracy, while Shelburne uncharacteristically called for retribution against the crowds that had provoked the Boston Massacre.[58] Be that as it may, Bernard had a more significant role in policy discussions than has hitherto been thought.

With Hillsborough's approval, Bernard began to collect information that might be used in a parliamentary inquiry. Particularly valuable was Andrew Oliver's suggestion that on the day after the Boston Massacre councilor Royal Tyler knew of a plan hatched by men of the "best characters . . . of estates and . . . of religion" to drive the redcoats and the customs commissioners from the town. Tyler vehemently denied knowledge of any such plan, but Bernard supposed that the rumors may well have been the crucial factor in persuading Hutchinson and Dalrymple to withdraw the troops from the town.[59] Oliver was a firm advocate of Bernard's proposal for a mandamus Council,[60] but Bernard showed surprisingly little regard for his reputation when a copy of Oliver's memorial, which Bernard had presented to the Privy Council, was leaked to the press. Bernard was not callous and accepted that his carelessness had jeopardized Oliver's already tenuous position in the colony. Oliver was censured by the Massachusetts Council for doctoring its minutes and breaching confidentiality, although after pressure from Britain the censure was withdrawn.[61] Meanwhile, Bernard was sure that a murder conviction, which carried the death penalty, would be returned in the Boston Massacre trial. Capt. Thomas Preston was acquitted although two of his men were found guilty of manslaughter.[62] Had that not been the case, Bernard was sure, Britain would have been obliged to act against the colonial juries and courts.

Over the summer Bernard joined Hillsborough, John Pownall, and William Knox in discussions about amending the Massachusetts Charter in order to establish a mandamus Council. Despite Knox's reservations, they drafted a bill for that purpose. The ministry, Bernard observed however, was "cooler rather than averse" to reform,[63] although in 1771 the Crown issued a new instruction to Hutchinson forbidding irregular meetings of the Council at which he was not present.[64] The threat of war with Spain over the Falkland Islands and Hillsborough's resignation put an end to these discussions. But in 1774 Bernard's central ideas formed the basis of the Massachusetts Government Act. Until then Bernard's advice to his erstwhile colleagues in Massachusetts was to endure "the Despotism of . . . Adams Cooper Molineux & Young."[65]

*   *   *

It was several years before the full consequences of Bernard's influence on British colonial policymaking would be evident, for early in 1771 Bernard resigned the Massachusetts governorship. Nine years in the province had placed enormous strains on his family, and the death of his eldest son Frank in Boston on 20 November 1770 probably hastened his decision to relinquish office and leave London. He had little to gain by returning to Massachusetts, although Hutchinson kept him informed of events in the province.[66] In 1771, the Bernards returned to Lincoln, probably to attend to Francis's elderly cousin Jane Beresford, who was living at Nettleham Hall. The Bernards leased the College House from the diocese, a sixteenth-century building near the junction of Eastgate and Priorygate long since demolished,[67] and when Jane died in November of that year they returned to Nettleham Hall. (In 1776, Bernard acquired proprietary rights to over four hundred acres in the parish when he joined and advised a local movement to enclose the land.)[68] While he lobbied Hillsborough to get him a handsome pension of one thousand pounds per year, a sinecure with the Irish Revenue Board, which Bernard held for little more than a year, provided some incidental relief.[69] The government instead settled on six hundred pounds because of growing public concern at the size of the civil list.[70] Bernard pressed Hillsborough for additional "compensation" and was rewarded by confirmation of his title to Mount Desert.

Having been an energetic man all his life, Bernard shuddered at the prospect of having "to eat the bread of Idleness."[71] His third son

Sir Thomas Bernard (1750–1818), the governor's third son and biographer, a prominent philanthropist and social reformer. Artist unknown. By permission of Robert Spencer Bernard, Nether Winchendon House. Photograph by Charles Crisp, A.B.I.P.P.

and amanuensis, Thomas, now twenty-one years old, bore the brunt of his father's broody existence. Bernard was reluctant to encourage Thomas to become a lawyer, seeing more opportunities for him in government service. But he relented when he found him a sinecure as Commissary of Musters in the War Department under Barrington, which left Thomas plenty of time to study.[72] Bernard, however, objected strenuously when Thomas proposed undertaking a grand tour of France in the company of a Harvard classmate, Isaac Smith Jr. Smith was not the problem, nor Bernard's Francophobia—Why, he protested, did Thomas have to go to Paris to learn French?—so much as his overprotectiveness. Having already lost three sons, and with John still in Boston, he could not bear to let Thomas go when the young man came down with a fever—a "little feveret," Thomas insisted. Thomas resolved to abscond to Dover when his father returned to Lincoln, but he eventually received his father's blessing and enjoyed the tour.[73]

Bernard suffered a stroke sometime between May 1771 and January 1772, before his sixtieth birthday, which for a while restricted his mobility. It also caused epilepsy. A period of recuperation at the spas of Bath, followed by a "strict Regimen" of medication and daily exercise, including riding, aided his recovery if not his spirits. The whole experience, he wrote, "quite frightened me & I cannot in my own mind realize the expectation every body gives me that I shall not be the worse for it."[74] The demise of his dear cousin Jane, however, offered Bernard some prospect that at last he would find the "Ease, affluence and Health" he had long desired.[75]

Jane had bequeathed Francis and his heirs Nether Winchendon manor, the most valuable piece of real estate Bernard ever acquired. On hearing of Jane's death, Barrington—with characteristic insensitivity—could not "help rejoicing at the considerable addition made to your Fortune."[76] Nether Winchendon was a farming community of some fifty families, a few miles southeast of Aylesbury.[77] The drafty manor house was in need of considerable repair, but there were two other houses on the estate, plus a farm, meadows, and an orchard. It was valued at five thousand pounds, whereas additional lands at nearby Cuddington were worth £272.[78] The Bernards moved to a near town, Aylesbury, while Francis considered how best to develop the estate. For the most part they lived at the Prebendal House, which in September 1772 Bernard leased from Sir William Lee of Hartwell, the son of the former chief justice. (A previous occupant was John Wilkes, when he was the local Member of Parliament.) The Lees and the Bernards became close friends, and Sir William encouraged Bernard to take an interest in local issues: Bernard designed and paid for the construction of a bridge and causeway, and participated in the affairs of the local church.[79] When Bernard's health began to deteriorate in early 1773, it was clear that he would never be able to test his architectural skills in improving Nether Winchendon House, which was later undertaken by Scrope Bernard.

*   *   *

The most celebrated American of his day was certain that the colonists had not heard the last of Sir Francis Bernard. Benjamin Franklin never met Bernard in the colonies, having spent most of the 1760s living in London. From the little that he knew of the governor from their brief correspondence, Franklin initially respected Bernard and was interested in his plans to develop Mount Desert and Nova Scotia. He also empathized with the governor's predicament during the Stamp Act crisis. After Bernard's "unmasking," Franklin quickly shed what little respect he retained, and like the governor's adversaries held him personally responsible for exacerbating the imperial crisis. He viewed with grave concern Bernard's proposal to introduce Crown salaries for royal governors, for it would remove forever the one lever colonial assemblies had on the "Wrangling Proctors" and "pettyfogging Lawyers" like Bernard who owed their positions to friendly ministers.[80] He suspected too that Bernard's reports on the divisions among the Boston merchants had been influential in North's decision to retain the tea duty in the expectation that the nonimportation agreements would peter out (as they did).[81]

Bernard's gratitude for the help Franklin provided in finding his eldest son in Virginia had long since cooled following rumors that Franklin had been earmarked to replace Bernard as Massachusetts governor.[82] On arriving in England, however, Bernard was taken aback by Franklin's criticism in the *London Chronicle*, and surprised how radical the agent had become. Franklin "seems . . . to have no fixed Principles at all. . . . It . . . seems to be his Intention to avoid all Declarations which may set Bounds to the American Pretensions; and that he may be at Liberty to go as far as his Constituents [in Pennsylvania] shall please."[83]

When, in the summer of 1770, Franklin was appointed agent of the Massachusetts assembly in succession to DeBerdt, who had died, he was already agent for three other colonies and inching his way toward a more radical position on imperial affairs, which conceived the British empire as a conglomeration of "autonomous" states united only by their loyalty to the sovereign.[84] He moved too slowly for Samuel Adams, who insisted that Arthur Lee should shadow him as a deputy. It was an unsatisfactory arrangement that irritated both men.[85]

Franklin's brief was to counteract the influence of Bernard and Hutchinson, who had "constantly represented" the province in "the most disagreeable and odious Light."[86] In January 1771, when Franklin called on Hillsborough to present his credentials, he was shocked to find Bernard waiting in an antechamber. When Hillsborough refused to acknowledge his status as House agent, Franklin knew whom to blame.[87] Hillsborough, Rev. Dr. Samuel Cooper ventured, was "a Tool to St Francis."[88] Franklin never went that far, and was delighted when Hillsborough resigned in August 1772 after a dispute with the Privy Council over an American land grant. However, he knew that the cabinet was discussing plans to extend the colonial civil list, as Bernard had long recommended,[89] and later that year Hutchinson was awarded a Crown salary of fifteen hundred pounds per year. Hillsborough's replacement as colonial secretary was the earl of Dartmouth, a stepbrother of Lord North, who nonetheless was more sympathetic to the Americans, and promptly snubbed Bernard and Hutchinson by receiving from Franklin a colonial petition protesting the award.

In December 1772 Franklin took the most outrageous gamble of his entire career when he sent Thomas Cushing a cache of letters written by Hutchinson and others as sensational as those that had destroyed Bernard's reputation in America five years before. How Franklin obtained the letters is unclear; neither is his intention. Perhaps he aimed to placate his radical critics in Massachusetts by undermining Hutchinson, with whom he had had no personal quarrel. More likely he was providing Dartmouth with a scapegoat in his endeavors to improve relations with Massachusetts; that supposition, however, worked both ways: with both Bernard and Hutchinson out of the way, the radicals should be less strident in their demands.[90] The Massachusetts General Court certainly preferred the second interpretation, when, in protesting Hutchinson's desire to see an "abridgement" of colonial liberties, it explained that "The original causes of the interruption of that union and harmony may probably be found in the letters sent from hence to administration . . . since the appointment of Sir Francis Bernard to the government of this province." There was little opposition to the General Court's decision to ask Dartmouth to dismiss Hutchinson.[91]

Franklin was fêted by colonists such as John Adams for humbling another "tyrant,"[92] and continued the attack on Hutchinson and Bernard in his several publications.[93] Excoriating the governors for the enthusiasm of the radical colonists, however, was an ultimately un-sustainable proposition when Franklin had sacrificed his own credibility with the British. Bernard relished his moment of *schadenfreude*. Franklin's dismissal from the office of deputy postmaster general in February 1774 for his part in stealing the Hutchinson letters, wrote Thomas Bernard, was condign punishment. His treachery in part accounted for the "general Indignation" that characterized British reactions to the Boston Tea Party. "Perhaps," Bernard informed an American friend, the ministry will "make you drink Tea till it acts as an Emetic."[94]

*   *   *

On the eve of the most serious crisis in imperial relations since 1765, there was no obvious intermediary of stature who had the confidence of both Britain and the Massachusetts colonists to help resolve their mutual disagreements. The colonists deigned to suppose that Dartmouth was a calming influence on North and the cabinet, but like so many other British politicians of his day he lacked verve and a good measure of acumen. Franklin was now in his middle sixties but was far from being a spent force. But he and other Americans in London were kept at arm's length by ministers, even with the onset of war in 1775. With Bernard lurking on the fringes after Hillsborough's departure, the history of his troubled administration cast a shadow on virtually every American measure regarding Massachusetts that North pursued between 1770 and 1774. Equally important was the legacy of hostility and mistrust that pervaded Hutchinson's relationship with the friends of government after Bernard's departure. Hutchinson's failure to arrest the political decline of royal government in Massachusetts before the Tea Party owed as much to Bernard's legacy as it did to the radicalization of colonial politics. When an upsurge in support for compromise occurred in Massachusetts in the spring and summer of 1774, royal government was already teetering on the brink.

To friends of government such as Nathaniel Coffin, the deputy cashier of the Board of Customs, the nonimportation controversy of 1768 to 1770 was the key development that explained both the radical ascendancy and the alienation of the friends of government from the Whigs. The boycott, Coffin argued, provided opportunities for political extremists such as Samuel Adams and James Otis Jr., as the Stamp Act riots had done briefly for the cordwainer Ebenezer Mac-Intosh, to create in Boston the eighteenth century's archetypal political monster—a "sheer Democracy." It was "true," Coffin admitted, surprised by a political unity that transcended social boundaries, that "this Power frequently shifts hands. One While a McIntosh, at another time Otis & Adams, at another the Body of Merchants are our demagogues."[95] Although Coffin overplayed the extent to which political power was being devolved to artisans and tradesmen, these groups did have a higher profile in the committees of enforcement and also in the merchants' deliberations through their participation in an inclusive association, the "Body of Trade." As John W. Tyler has shown, merchants, townspeople, and Whigs acted in conjunction with the town meeting and merchants' committees through this association. More than a thousand inhabitants regularly attended its meetings, which were akin to a protest rally rather than an ordered town meeting,[96] with "every master of a Sloop and broker Shopkeeper or Huckster" allowed to vote regardless of property qualifications.[97]

While the radicals and Whig merchants succeeded in mobilizing popular opinion in a corporatist movement to enforce the boycott, the inability of the provincial administration to provide protection for importers and customs officers was exposed within a few months of Bernard's departure. Nathaniel Coffin in particular provided his superiors in Britain with reports of a series of attacks on importers and customs officers that appeared to vindicate much of what Bernard had been saying about the feebleness of the province's law enforcement agencies. The scale of crowd action against importers stunned Crown officials, beginning with the "drubbing" of John Mein, the Edinburgh-born bookseller and proprietor of the anti-Whig *Boston Chronicle*. Mein and his partner John Fleeming had endeavored to expose the boycott as a sham by the Whig wholesale merchants to drive out competitor shopkeepers. A chance encounter with some of the Whigs they had lampooned led to the printers being pursued through King Street by a mob; according to some observers Mein only escaped being lynched when he found refuge in the British army guardhouse.[98]

As the level of political violence increased, there was little prospect of importers gaining legal redress. In John Mein's case the law became a political weapon used against him. First, Samuel Adams and William Molineux indicted Mein for unlawfully discharging a firearm during the scuffles in King Street. Then, having fled Boston, Mein was pursued for a debt of sixteen hundred pounds by the English publisher Thomas Longman, acting through John Hancock, which succeeded in closing the *Chronicle*. Despite his friends organizing a subscription for the debt, the printer was incarcerated in the King's Bench prison until February 1771.[99]

In January 1770 crowds numbering a thousand or more, led by William Molineux and the merchants' committees, took to calling on persistent importers at their homes and stores, though not actually assaulting them. Chief Justice Hutchinson warned against "such unlawful assemblies," advising the Whig merchants that "it may be out of your Power" to restrain artisans and tradesmen. However, lacking the support of the Council, the town's selectmen, the justices of the peace, the militias, and the confidence of juries, Hutchinson, like Bernard, was effectively deprived of legal means by which to suppress the crowds or committees—or to offer victims of tarring and feathering such as the tidesman Owen Richards, who was nearly blinded by one assault, any form of redress. Moreover, from the moment they arrived, British troops were deployed to protect buildings and officials, not importers faced with hostile crowds, whose predicament was the responsibility of the provincial law officers and courts. The Boston Massacre fatally exposed the limitations of using British regulars to disperse angry mobs, but at no point were they used against the crowds and committees enforcing the boycott, who, in May for example, brutally assaulted the Scottish factor Patrick McMasters.[100]

It is difficult to say whether a majority of traders were silenced by the mobs or wholeheartedly supported nonimportation. The merchants had incurred substantial financial losses and were said to resent "the weight of this oppressive Power." Discontent, though not outright opposition, had grown since August 1769, when the merchants first proposed to extend the embargo to 1 January 1770 and then to continue it indefinitely until the tea duty was repealed. Coffin claimed there were "many dissenters from this new agreement, & some very principal Merchants amongst them who look upon it as a piece of Quixotism." The merchants' nemesis arrived, he said, when they "foolishly called into their assistance all the Rabble of the Town," in order "to intimidate the Discontents & bring them into their Measures."[101]

Although the nonimportation controversy exposed divisions among the merchants, it is difficult to see what Hutchinson could have done to exploit them. Hutchinson was in "high hopes to have formed a party among the Merchants" in the spring of 1770. But those whom he approached, including Nicholas Boylston, rejected his overtures until the British did something to halt crowd action.[102] As Hutchinson told Hillsborough, there was no overriding political reason why friends of government such as Boylston should assist his administration when the North ministry seemed reluctant to enforce the House of Lords' resolution against "unlawful combinations."[103] They scoffed at Hutchinson's suggestion that they might sue their fellow merchants for the losses they incurred during the boycott. Hutchinson responded by asking Britain to enact "express penalties" against merchants such as John Rowe and John Hancock, such as confiscating the property of all persons concerned with enforcing the boycott. What had originated as a scheme to compensate the importers financially now purported to treat the Whigs as rebels.[104] The success of John and Jonathan Amory in persuading the majority of merchants to abandon in October 1770 the general boycott of British goods (the exception being the duted tea) owed nothing to Hutchinson. It followed from the decision of the Bostonians' commercial rivals in New York and Philadelphia to end general nonimportation after the partial repeal of the Townshend Acts.[105]

Hutchinson achieved no more success than Bernard in trying "to reconcile to each other the friends of government and those moderate opposers" of his administration who desired "an end" to the imperial crisis "upon reasonable terms."[106] Bernard's decision to hold the General Court outside of Boston presented Hutchinson with a major constitutional crisis, which dogged provincial politics and government for three years when the House of Representatives refused to proceed to business in protest of the British troops stationed in the town and the guns positioned outside the Town House.[107] Bernard wanted Hutchinson to be given a "peremptory order" to keep the General Court at Cambridge, but Hillsborough allowed Hutchinson discretion in this matter.[108] Hutchinson refused to be bullied by either Bernard or the Whigs but his reluctance to compromise won him few friends; that he persisted until June 1772 was perhaps due to the growing anxiety of moderates such as John Erving (and even perhaps staunch Whigs such as John Hancock) that the House's stubbornness boded ill for the future.[109]

Hutchinson made some progress during the period of uneasy calm that followed the Boston Massacre. At the request of Ruggles and Worthington, he offered an olive branch of sorts by accepting nine councilors who had been vetoed by Bernard at one time or another, though he still refused John Hancock and Jerathmeel Bowers.[110] Moderates like Gray, Royall, Brattle, and Hubbard were impatient with the House, and Hutchinson tried to make "good use of the divisions" that were emerging between them and Bowdoin. By September 1770 Hutchinson counted twelve councilors as friends, still three short of a majority.[111] His wooing of moderates was compromised by their desire to remain free of what "Mrs" Harrison Gray (as he was dubbed by the *Boston Gazette*) called the "quarrel[s] of hot headed politicians" on both sides.[112]

Hutchinson had little time for Bernard's plans to reform the Council, and his responses to Bernard were evasive and noncommittal—"like a lawyer's Opinion."[113] The future of the Council remained moot, however, though it was three years before Britain was prepared to act upon Bernard's suggestions.[114]

Disillusionment with Britain was behind Hutchinson's failure to make any inroads in the General Court. When the "rescinder" Jonathan Sayward refused the offer of a position, he bluntly told Hutchinson that he had no desire to be a "publick Mark" for the Sons of Liberty "to Shoot bitter Arrows" at (though he later accepted an appointment as a judge of the Inferior Court of York County).[115] Both John Murray and Timothy Ruggles appeared to have "lost . . . interest" in provincial affairs because of the Whigs' dominance. Not a "single person," Hutchinson moaned, was willing to join him "in supporting Government."[116] Ruggles, however, had reprimanded Parliament for failing to come up with any concrete measures to protect customs officers or to apprehend the Boston radicals who controlled the crowds.[117] John Worthington promised to do what he could to rally the friends of government and the moderates, but his expectations were very low now that his countrymen "conceived" of him "as an Enemy to my Country."[118] Some gains were made in House elections, including the return of five "rescinders," among them the able physician John Calef of Ipswich and Col. Josiah Edson, but the friends of government had little sense of an *esprit de corps*. Hutchinson was once forced to remind even Israel Williams, Jonathan Bliss, and Josiah Strong of "their duty" to attend the General Court regularly.[119]

With some justification, the colonists complained of cronyism when Britain's plans for filling royal offices were revealed in the spring of 1771, but the principal aim of Bernard and Hillsborough was to give "all possible Proofs of . . . Attention to the Service of the

Friends of Government."[120] Hillsborough never doubted that Hutchinson should succeed Bernard as governor, despite Hutchinson's ill health and bouts of depression that at one stage led him to decline the offer, to Bernard's embarrassment. On taking up the governorship in March, Hutchinson relinquished the chief justiceship that had been the source of so much antagonism. He was succeeded by the knowledgeable Benjamin Lynde (who himself was replaced by Peter Oliver in 1772) and his place on the Superior Court taken by his brother Foster. Andrew Oliver was promoted to lieutenant governor, with a Crown allowance of three hundred pounds. The post of province secretary Oliver vacated was originally promised to Hutchinson's sickly nephew Nathaniel Rogers, but was given instead to Thomas Flucker, whose previous indiscretions were forgiven.

Hutchinson could be just as bullish as Bernard—as during his famed debates with Samuel Adams—but was equally ineffective in defending the doctrine of parliamentary supremacy. Leading Whigs were moving toward a more radical interpretation of the imperial relationship, one that located legislative sovereignty with the colonial assemblies instead of Parliament, wherein the "ligaments" or ties that bound them to Britain were loyalty and fealty to the Crown. Adams cleverly forced Hutchinson to acknowledge that in theory there were no limits to what Parliament might do. Inexplicably, Hutchinson expected a landslide victory in 1772 when the House of Representatives debated Britain's attempt to institute Crown salaries for senior law officers; only nineteen representatives supported his position, with the majority apprehensive of any attempt to make the judiciary or the executive "independent" of the legislature. Hutchinson, like Bernard, failed to appreciate the depth of feeling on this issue, and persisted in the fiction that the threat of intimidation had removed majority support for him on this issue.[121] His address to the General Court of 14 July 1772, shortly after the legislature had returned to Boston, echoed the conservative Whiggism of Bernard's speeches. Although his constitutional arguments were presented with more coherent Lockean themes, they rested on the myopic premise that conceding legislative supremacy to the colonists would create an abomination—an *imperium in imperio*.[122]

The Hutchinson-Adams debates were a formative episode in determining the subsequent loyalties of moderate Whigs. Some became friends of government, but the majority now accepted the leadership of the radicals. James Otis, however, was now a shambling, sorry figure, racked by dementia and succumbing to alcoholism. Hutchinson's overtures to other Whig leaders such as John Hancock and James Bowdoin, who had become weary of Samuel Adams, came to naught.[123] The few political gains Hutchinson had made counted for nothing when the radicals published the letters obtained from Franklin. On 16 June the House of Representatives, with only twelve dissenters, voted to petition the king for the removal of both Hutchinson and Andrew Oliver. Only five councilors refused to concur.[124]

Hutchinson might have done a better job as governor if he had been appointed in 1760 instead of Bernard. But in spite of his strong ties to Massachusetts and his undoubted political talents and intellect, Hutchinson's fate had been sealed by his loyalty to Bernard. Hutchinson could do little to allay the fallacy that in following dictates from London he was gleefully exploiting and betraying fellow Yankees.

*   *   *

Lords North and Dartmouth had never been more in favor of conciliating the Americans over the Tea Act and tea duty when news of the Boston Tea Party arrived in January. They were convinced by Hutchinson's reports that the destruction of nine thousand pounds worth of East India Company tea on 16 December was the work of a rebellious faction. Such a view was inadvertently encouraged by the pleas of moderates such as Isaac Royall for "Lenitive, Pacific Measures, rather than warm coercive ones," for he held the governors culpable for a crisis springing from their "Insatiable Thirst after Power and Gain." He urged that Hutchinson be immediately replaced by Thomas Pownall.[125] Parliament's sense of outrage and desire to see Boston held corporately liable offered ministers little room for maneuver. The tragedy was that with a clear majority in both houses of Parliament, there was little chance for pro-Americans such as Pownall to water down the controversial measures that were proposed.[126]

Bernard's analyses of colonial affairs and his proposals for action proved instructive when the British began in earnest to counteract resistance in Boston. His *Select Letters on Trade and Government* was published in London in 1774, though it contributed nothing new to the debates on the American Question apart from condemning in stronger terms than before parliamentary taxation and any possibility of making concessions on the principle of Parliament's supremacy.[127]

A few of his letters were cited in parliamentary debates, but it was through undersecretary John Pownall that Bernard had some influence on ministers. Pownall's report on the "State of the Disorders, Confusion and Mis-government" in Massachusetts was presented by the government to the House of Lords on 28 January 1774. It was an updated version of the paper he presented to the inquiry into Massachusetts held four years before. Pownall presented Bernard's state papers and legislative records as supporting evidence, and reiterated much of what Bernard had been saying about how "illegal, violent & unwarrantable" proceedings had challenged the very basis of royal government in the province after the repeal of the Stamp Act.[128] After a cabinet meeting on 29 January, when ministers resolved to punish Boston for the Tea Party, Pownall produced another paper with, *inter alia,* specific recommendations to close the port of Boston and strengthen military and naval forces in Massachusetts. Each proposal was subsequently adopted and acted upon, while in April the British dispatched reinforcements to Massachusetts and sent out Gen. Thomas Gage as the new governor.[129]

At the same time, ministers looking for another modus operandi were attracted to some of Bernard's proposals regarding colonial government. As an alternative to blockading Boston port, Dartmouth, Knox, and Mansfield again expressed interest in Bernard's ideas for a mandamus Council and curtailments on town meetings. Dartmouth, North, and the rest of the cabinet had earlier rejected these measures, rightly supposing that any attempt to revise the Massachusetts Charter would inflame the colonists. So too had George III, who now regretted that the "fatal compliance in 1766" had led the colonists "annually to encrease their pretentions."[130] But ministers were in no mood to compromise after the Tea Party, when to a man—Dartmouth included—they subscribed to Bernard's view that only by reforming the Massachusetts government could they ever roll back the Whig dominance.

The Boston Port bill, which passed the Commons without a division on its third reading and received royal assent at the end of March, owed nothing directly to Bernard. It pronounced the closure of Boston harbor to incoming vessels on 1 June and outgoing traffic on 15 June. It was to remain in force until such time as the king and Privy Council decided "that peace and obedience to the laws" were restored in Boston. Members of Parliament and Lords accepted the principle of Boston's corporate liability without any qualms, but they had no intention of holding an inquiry that might give the town's magistrates and officials the chance to defend themselves. Rose Fuller's motion to fine Boston fell flat because men of all sides had come to the conclusion that the colonists' affronts could only be halted by draconian action.[131] The men who voted for the bill were not only exacting restitution for the East India Company but retribution for a decade of slights and provocations, some real and others imaginary, all of which had been cataloged in Pownall's report. No one seriously thought that it would push the Americans to the brink of war. (In this triumphant mood the Commons, with forty dissenters, refused to accept a petition from William Bollan on behalf of the Massachusetts Council blaming Hutchinson for the crisis. It also ignored the petition of Americans residing in London, who warned of a "shocking and unnatural" contest ahead.)[132]

However, on 19 April Rose Fuller and Burke proposed repealing the tea duty as one means of placating the Americans. Burke's famous speech on American taxation was a masterly exposé of the "folly" of successive ministries that, despite several factual inaccuracies, showed some understanding of both colonial ideology and Bernard's predicament. Bernard's advice to Grenville not to tax the colonists until he had strengthened royal government or at least until the colonial economies had been allowed time to recover from the French Wars, Burke recalled, seemed like a missed opportunity to have averted ten years of disputation. Consistency was never Burke's strong point where Bernard was concerned.[133] Others who spoke against the port bill and taxation, such as Richard Jackson, reluctantly accepted that the British ought to make examples of Samuel Adams and John Hancock, as Bernard had suggested. For hawks like Captain Phipps, who rejoiced at the prospect of the military governor Gage being given leave to seize the Americans, Bernard's indiscretions and tribulations seemed a distant irrelevance.[134]

The second Coercive Act, the Massachusetts Government Act, more clearly encompassed much of what Bernard had been proposing. It centralized power in the governor's office by establishing a mandamus Council and by giving the governor new powers to appoint sheriffs and judges without the consent of the Council; jurors too were henceforth to be selected by the county sheriffs instead of by local constables, and were to hold office at the discretion of the governor. Town meetings, the power base of the popular party, were to be restricted to one per year for the election of officials, the permission of the governor being required for all other extraordinary meetings. The Administration of Justice Act also allowed British officials to be tried in England or in other colonies.

*   *   *

When Thomas Hutchinson, who had sailed for Britain in May, called on Bernard he was shocked to find him much "altered by a paralitick shock" though his "intellectual powers" were not "sensibly impaired." The pair dined regularly together, talking of British politics and American affairs.[135] Bernard little appreciated how much his own failings had contributed to the imperial controversies. He liked to think that his disputes with the General Court had never been "personal" and that "no Governor could stand his ground after [the popular] party had opened the trenches against him," or when he became a "victim to the bad policy and irresolution of the supreme Government."[136] Bernard and Hutchinson were appalled by the venomous tirades delivered against the Americans by Sir William Lee, a Grenvillite, but when the war began and they were again much "abused" by the opposition,[137] Bernard became as "hot" as any patriotic Englishman, and "talked much about what ought to have been done four years ago."[138] On reviewing the Bernard years, the former Lord Chancellor, Camden, wrote: "An American Governor is not so big as a King; he don't wear a crown, nor bear a scepter, nor sit on a throne, nor is he worshipped on the knee, nor has a navy, nor an army, nor makes Bishops, nor judges, nor is his civil list perhaps above a thousand pounds a year. He seems to be much more responsible and more removeable, than a King."[139]

"In one sense," P. D. G. Thomas has written, "what was occurring in America was a clarification rather than a change of attitude. A state of confrontation became apparent because the behavior of men like Bernard and Hutchinson in America and [the earl of] Hillsborough and [Lord] North in Britain obliged the colonists to devise logical and explicit expressions of hitherto unformulated assumptions."[140] Be that as it may, the extraordinary attempts to have Bernard and Hutchinson dismissed are less important for what they tell us about the conduct of royal governors than for what they reveal about the radicalization of colonial politics. These were grand, public demonstrations of unity, as meticulously organized as the Boston Tea Party, but they concealed a bitter truth that Samuel Adams and James Bowdoin found difficult to stomach: the colonists were not and never had been united in their responses to British colonial policy.

Revolution and Counterrevolution

THE AMERICAN PATRIOTS were perplexed by how quickly British-colonial relations deteriorated when Francis Bernard became governor of Massachusetts. Americans may have railed at Bernard's Anglicanism and imperialism, but the governor was at first much impressed by life in the colonies. His exemplary mediation in New Jersey's disputes with Britain was altogether too fleeting a lesson. Bernard's ambitious plans to establish a nonpartisan administration in Massachusetts were quickly undermined, partly by his hubristic English nationalism but also because of his failure to smooth-talk the Congregational clergy and the merchants. His subsequent estrangement from the colonial elite also owed much to the personal frustrations he encountered in trying to accumulate a decent income by means fair and foul.

Thwarted and frustrated at every turn, it seemed, Bernard rationalized his own problems within the wider context of imperial relations. He reinvented himself as an imperial reformer, but made the fatal error of demanding unconditional loyalty from the American fringe and supposing that their aspirations were reconcilable with an unprecedented extension of royal authority in colonial government. Bernard's attempts to persuade successive British administrations to reverse decades of neglect in attending to colonial government, however, were so ill-timed as to leave him open to accusations of conspiracy. When the momentous controversy over parliamentary taxation broke, Bernard's natural ebullience had been severely dented by factional strife and criticism from leading colonists.

Had it not been for Grenville's revision of the mercantilist system, colonial aspirations to enjoy greater commercial freedom and de facto self-government would have received scant attention from the imperial elite. Latent tensions in the imperial relationship can only partly explain why the Stamp Act crisis of 1765–66 was such a turning point. The imperial crisis began as a crisis of confidence in the virtue of Britain's imperial servants, but with the alienation of the colonial elites became the most serious crisis of authority the British imperial state had yet faced. Bernard struggled to comprehend why colonial ideologues professed to be reclaiming and restoring colonial liberties yet propagated new doctrines of colonial rights. His feeling of isolation was compounded by the emergence of a pluralist protest movement that began to unravel the fabric of royal government. Political pluralism, from which in time grew America's first party system, confounded Bernard's elitist view of the world.

Bernard aimed to convince the friends of government, a hitherto silent but substantial body of political opinion, that the spread of political radicalism and the upsurge in crowd action were subjecting royal government to intense strain. Thereafter, he argued consistently that to reverse the drift to rebellion, Britain needed to help him cultivate the political support of the friends of government. Bernard's "open & communicative" approach to public affairs disturbed both friend and foe, however. The well-informed customs commissioner, Henry Hulton, supposed that someone of "less abilities and merit than himself with more address art and intrigue might have succeeded better" as a colonial governor. "Choleric and sanguine, obstinate and designing" was how Mercy Otis Warren, the sister of James Otis, described him.[1] In another time and place, colonists might have appreciated Bernard's assertive gubernatorial style and welcomed his influence with the British political elite, despite the suspicions of corruption first raised by John Temple. Bernard wallowed not in power, however, but in the illusion of power.

Like all beleaguered conservatives, Bernard resolutely defended that which he knew best, but he was never able to convince the colonists that he had done much to aid their complaints about the Revenue Act and the Stamp Act. His second major error was to proscribe as rebels colonists who dared to challenge Parliament's legislative authority or exploit the weakness of royal power for political gain. The emergence of a popular protest movement in 1765 confirmed what Bernard already suspected: a revolution of sorts was already under way—in the colonists' minds and in their attitudes toward their so-called betters, if not yet in their basic loyalties. His efforts to confront the dangerous "mobocracy" unleashed by the Stamp Act riots polarized political opinion in Massachusetts without any tangible benefits.

While friends of government and moderate Whigs were troubled by fears of social conflict, they were as yet reluctant to do anything that might actually ease the imperial crisis. The friends of government at least offered Bernard the prospect of creating a royal faction, and the proto-Loyalism of these men marks them out as early counterrevolutionaries. It is wrong to presume that when Bernard lost influence with the Council, his natural political ally, and the House of Representatives—or indeed with the province merchants, the magistracy, and towns—that he accepted defeat meekly. On the contrary, Bernard aimed to exploit internal divisions within these institutions and groups for the benefit of British colonial policy. As he became the object of partisan criticism, his star shone brightest in London, where hawks like Hillsborough and John Pownall found in his voluminous reports reason enough to justify sending British troops to Boston in 1768.

Bernard's fractured relationship with the friends of government can help explain why the Whigs were in the dominant position by 1774 and why Britain had little chance—had it wished to—of negotiating an end to the imperial crisis. Even at that late stage, British policy was being formulated on the basis of old information tendered by Francis Bernard, and the consequences were catastrophic.

A tragedy was already unfolding when Bernard left Massachusetts in the summer of 1769. Despite the deep-rooted desire for compromise among the colonists, the demonization of Bernard and Hutchinson delayed the rise of an antiradical political group dedicated to resolving the imperial controversy. The radical Whigs succeeded in mobilizing popular opinion against British policies and discouraging active support for the royal governors. Although the friends of government in the legislature found common cause with the governors on several occasions, they lacked the organization and common purpose of the Whigs and were unable to sustain an antiradical coalition; similarly, the friends of government in the town meetings throughout the colony were minority factions bereft of popular support. The friends of government functioned neither as a court faction—similar to the King's Friends in George III's Parliament—nor later as a militant Loyalist group akin to the "Church and King" mobs that were so effective in stifling popular radicalism in Britain after the French Revolution.

The emergence of the friends of government after the Boston Tea Party, however, was a momentary opportunity for Britain to repair the bridges that had been so badly damaged by the controversies over taxation during Bernard's administration. They represented the center ground in Massachusetts politics, inasmuch as they urged the British to be more sympathetic to American concerns and condemned the radicalism of the leading Whigs. Between December 1773 and October 1775, more than five hundred colonists subscribed to antiradical protests in towns such as Marshfield, Plymouth, Petersham, Worcester, and Deerfield, whose representatives had once been courted by Bernard,[2] or, as in Salem, Boston, and Marblehead, signed addresses to governors Hutchinson and Gage.[3]

When news of the Port Act arrived in Boston on 10 May, it precipitated an attempt by the conservative and moderate merchants, led by George Erving and John Amory, to realize what many merchants and townspeople were hitherto reluctant to say publicly: that the town should compensate the East India Company for the destruction of its property. When the proposal was rejected by the town meeting, the friends of government asked the new governor, General Gage, to intervene with the ministry. The Port Act did not include an indemnity clause specifying precise conditions by which it might be repealed; neither could Gage treat the friends of government as if they formally represented the town meeting. But the general lacked initiative and failed to promote the Erving-Amory compromise during the critical period of late May to early June, when the dispute over the Port Act escalated and before reports of the other Coercive Acts arrived. Any prospect of compromise evaporated when the Massachusetts Government Act tore up the province's constitution.[4]

The friends of government were not a small core of embittered officeholders like Nathaniel Coffin, but, as he notes, represented a broader spectrum of opinion drawn mainly from the town's merchants and shopkeepers. A full meeting of the merchants on 24 May had refused to deliver the customary address to the departing governor, Thomas Hutchinson. One reason, given later in a Whig source, was that

> It was reported by Hutchinson's bosom Friends, that he had told them that if the Tea could be paid for, which would be stated at the lowest Rate by the East India Company, he should upon his Arrival [in Britain] be able to set aside the Port-Bill, and remove every other Difficulty—this accounts for the Names of some honest tho' weak Men in the late Address.[5]

More than one hundred "Persons of respectable Character, many of them of the first fortune & understanding in the province," were emboldened by the presence of nine British warships in the harbor to subscribe to a farewell address to Hutchinson on 30 May and another welcoming General Gage. The 123 signatories to Hutchinson's address formed a significant minority intent on resolving the political crisis, including disaffected moderates Province Treasurer Harrison Gray and John Erving Jr. The addressers "greatly deplore[d]" the "Calamities" that were "impending" with the closure of the port. They wished its implementation delayed until the town had sufficient time to reimburse the East India Company "as Testimony against such lawless proceedings." Hutchinson was urged to present this case to the ministry when he reached England, and this he did.[6]

The lines of internal conflict were more sharply defined when the Boston committee of correspondence took the "extraordinary step" in the first week of June of bypassing the town meeting and circulating throughout the province a "Solemn League and Covenant" calling for the suspension of "all commercial intercourse" with Britain from 31 August until the Port Act was repealed. In one swoop, the Covenant resurrected the threat of proscription: signatures were sought not only from shopkeepers and merchants but from "all adult persons of both sexes," while nonsubscribers were reviled as "enemies" to their country.[7] The title of the agreement and its communitarian vision echoed the crusading zeal of the Scottish Presbyterians of the 1640s whose own "Solemn League and Covenant" was a vehicle to eradicate Catholicism and Episcopalianism; in 1774 the targets of Whig Protestant orthodoxy were "Toryism" and the friends of government.

On 17 June, when the town again refused to consider compensating the East India Company, the only option for the friends of government was to wrest control from the radical leadership by destroying the committee of correspondence. On the twenty-seventh at the Old South Meeting House, where more than five thousand people had gathered on the night of the Tea Party, a crowd estimated by Nathaniel Coffin to have been "perhaps the largest assembly ever conven'd here" heard a motion to censure the committee for exceeding its authority. On the following day "when the Question was put the Hands held up for the motion were ab^t one fifth of those against." The radicals' victory "occasion'd a general Hissing," which "determined the minority to quit the Ground. They all went off in a Body." Coffin thought this

> an unfortunate maneuvre as it prevented a motion that was in-
> tended to be made for a Committee to fall on ways & means to
> pay for the Tea. In this they would have been probably as success-
> full as in their other motion, but it would have given the opposi-
> tion an opportunity of protesting against their proceedings in this
> important particular as they have done against their proceedings
> relative to the Committee.[8]

The friends of government probably constituted between one-fifth and one-sixth of voters (rather than the 10 percent John W. Tyler has proffered) though it is difficult to be exact.[9]

The efforts of the friends of government to defuse the imperial crisis occurred at the same time as ministers in London were compiling a list of mandamus councilors. The councilors were a mixture of experienced officeholders such as Thomas Flucker and Chief Justice Peter Oliver; dissident Whigs such as Harrison Gray, Daniel Leonard, John Erving Sr., and his son John Jr.; a few Boston merchants; and friends of government from the country towns (Israel Williams, John Worthington, Timothy Ruggles, John Murray, Josiah Edson, and Nathaniel Ray Thomas of Plymouth). Dartmouth once remarked that the ministry could have done a better job of selecting the councilors had he had "more perfect and satisfactory information both of the character and connections of the principal persons in the colony."[10] This disingenuous piece of face-saving ignores the fact that in the reports of governors Bernard and Hutchinson, on which the selection process was based, he had sufficient information to judge how these men would respond to the commission and also how the colonists might react. When Gage summoned the Council to meet on 8 August the councilors were "exposed to every species of Indignity & affront [and] their families kept in continual alarm."[11] Only twenty-five out of thirty-six nominees took the oath of office, which forever broke their bonds with their countrymen. Several councilors living outside Boston were subject to crowd action forcing them to issue public resignations and recantations. The most serious losses were John Worthington and Israel Williams.[12] Gage was full of praise for the "sensible," imperious manner in which William Pepperrell, Daniel Leonard, and Timothy Ruggles had refused to bow to intimidation but unfairly accused moderates such as Isaac Royall of "Timidity."[13] Only John Erving Sr., who had "connections with all sides, and would keep well with all," managed to avoid committing himself to the Crown until the last possible moment; his son John, however, accepted his vacant seat on the Council. Like everyone else, the Ervings had much to lose if war should come, including, if the rebels were victorious, some £18,648 in loans they had made to the provincial government.[14]

As autumn approached, the collapse of the Council and the upsurge in crowd action in the Massachusetts countryside led Gage to concentrate his small force of three thousand British troops in Boston. He effectively abandoned the friends of government, despite a brief foray into Marshfield, cutting them off from their last means of support. Provincial officials, judges, magistrates, and civilians alike had little option but to submit to the dictates of local Patriot committees to disavow the Massachusetts Government Act. The Revolution began with a "revolutionary assumption of authority" when the colonists collected a military force to lay siege to Boston and established a Provincial Congress and local committees to assume temporarily the functions of government.[15]

To Patriot pamphleteers such as John Adams, the origins of the imperial crisis owed as much to the intransigence of imperial officials such as Bernard as it did to the colonists' forbearance in pressing their grievances upon a series of weak and ignorant ministries. When Adams, as "Novanglus," and Daniel Leonard, as the mysterious "Massachusettensis" (whom Adams mistook for Jonathan Sewall), reviewed Bernard's controversial administration in 1775 they did not put the blame on British tyranny but, respectively, the treachery of an English governor and the revolutionary ardor that he had in some measure provoked. Adams wrongly claimed that Bernard's 1764 essay "Principles of Law and Polity" had inspired Grenville's reforms, but he was right to suggest that in general Bernard's antagonistic reports had helped to turn ministers and a good many Members of Parliament and Lords against the colonists in the years that followed.[16] Massachusettensis's criticism of Bernard was never so prescriptive, but he imbibed much of the conservative rhetoric with which Bernard had tried to browbeat the General Court; Parliament may have made a mistake with the Stamp Act, but "an argument drawn from the actual abuse of power, will not conclude to the illegality of such a power; much less will an argument drawn from the capability of its being abused."[17] This line of reasoning placed other Loyalist propagandists, such as Rev. Thomas Bradbury Chandler, in the incongruous position of having to justify the Coercive Acts as a moderate exercise of power.[18] Leonard countered this by suggesting, as Bernard did in 1765, that resistance to parliamentary authority ultimately "dissolves the social bond, annihilates the security resulting from law and government, introduces fraud, violence, rapine, murder, sacrilege, and the long train of evils that riot uncontrouled in a state of nature. . . . I once thought it chimerical."[19] After nine years of debate over the nature and extent of Parliament's authority the Loyalist pamphleteers had arguably nothing new to offer Americans: parliamentary sovereignty was inviolable and indivisible.

The onset of military conflict in any civil dispute inevitably narrows the range of options available to people, and between August 1774 and the first few months of 1775 the distinctions afforded by the labels "friend of government" and "Loyalist" are blurred. The friends of government were those colonists who actively supported governors Bernard and Hutchinson at one time or another between 1765 and 1775 or broke with the Whig protest movement during this period. The Loyalists, on the other hand, were those colonists, including many friends of government, who sided with the British against the colonial "Patriots" when the fighting began in April 1775.[20]

The composition of Massachusetts's 727 friends of government did not reflect a cross section of provincial society. Merchants, shopkeepers, professionals from Boston and the eastern ports, and farmers from commercial-farming communities in the east comprised the bulk of the various occupational groups that can be determined; very few were artisans. No significant disparities in status or property-based wealth divided the friends of government and the Whigs. The median annual rental value of estates belonging to Boston friends of government, based on the province tax list of 1771, is £33.38, whereas that for the Whigs is £32.69: both are significantly higher than the median value for the total number of Boston rentiers, £18.26, and reflect the middling to upper social status of the political elite. In smaller towns, such as Marshfield and Worcester, differences in wealth between the friends of government, who were wealthier, and the Whigs may have magnified political divisions.[21]

Several subgroups deserve mention. The Sandemanians, who included the importer Colborn Barrell, were a pacifist Calvinist sect of no more than thirty Boston families. They had little influence on town politics but often refused to enlist in the provincial militia. Scottish-born traders, factors, and officials, as well as other immigrants, were also conspicuous among the friends of government and Loyalists. Cultural, commercial, personal, and professional ties to Britain compelled many immigrants to oppose the Revolution; so too in Massachusetts, as in the Chesapeake and the Carolinas, did the intimidation they suffered during the nonimportation controversy. Officeholders were the most likely of all colonists to be found in opposition to the Whigs and Patriots, who condemned the plural officeholding by which many had advanced their careers. Some 23 percent of the friends of government were officeholders, nearly two-thirds of whom became Loyalists, but they were not politically predisposed toward Loyalism; Loyalist officeholders comprised just 2 percent more of appointments than the Patriots between 1761 and 1774.[22]

Bernard drew some satisfaction from the knowledge that the Church of England had been "distinguished by not joining in the diabolical Spirit of Calumny" that had long prevailed.[23] That was certainly true of fifteen Anglican clergymen, for whom loyalty to the king as head of state and head of the Church was indivisible. An embittered Henry Caner tried to blame the war on Britain's failure to introduce an episcopate, which had allowed "levelling principles" to flourish in the civil and religious domains.[24] The elderly Caner left Boston with the British in 1776, but several churchmen remained behind to preach Loyalist doctrines, and it often took threats of violence to stop them from conducting prayers for the king and the royal family. The allegiances of Anglican laity were everywhere much less certain, but secular politics rather than ecclesiastical affairs can account for the loyalty of the Ervings, the Amorys, and the Debloises.[25] The American Anglicans did not get their bishop until after the war. Even then the cabinet and government were wary of offending the Americans, and Bishop Samuel Seabury was consecrated in the Scottish Episcopal Church in 1784 to avoid taking the requisite oath of allegiance to the king.

The political defeat of the friends of government in Boston and elsewhere can ultimately explain why, after the commencement of military hostilities at Lexington and Concord in April 1775, the Loyalist counterrevolution in Massachusetts was so short-lived. Generally, friends of government outside Boston did not seek to use force to win political power until the end of 1774, when some organized defensive units and requested General Gage to send out troops. By then, the Patriots had effectively rendered royal government inoperative everywhere but in Boston itself. Most communities were indeed divided in their responses to the beginning of the Revolutionary War, but Patriots dominated local offices and ran the militia while their countrymen flocked to fight the British.

The principal dilemma faced by most friends of government from 1775 onward was not so much which side to support but whether or not to become actively involved in Britain's war effort. Only 391 friends of government became Loyalists with 322 remaining neutral for the duration of the conflict; only 14 were Patriots. Military service in either the Loyalist or British regiments was not an attractive option for at least 44 percent. Conversely, less than one-third of Massachusetts's Loyalists were active friends of government before the outbreak of war. Those friends of government who were in opposition to the colonial protest movement during Bernard's administration were more inclined to become neutrals than Loyalists, in comparison to those whose political activity first dates from 1773.[26]

The Loyalists formed around 16 percent of the American population (or 513,000 of 3,210,000 based on figures for 1783).[27] Massachusetts's 1,427 Loyalists included colonists who were proscribed for their political views after the outbreak of war in April 1775—by which they suffered arrest, banishment, or forfeiture of property; those who fled the province; those who joined the Loyalist or the regular regiments; and those who assisted the British war effort in some other way. The diaspora brought tens of thousands of Loyalists to Canada, Great Britain, and distant imperial outposts from Massachusetts and other colonies. The Loyalists were numerically much weaker in Massachusetts than in other colonies: in New York, for example, the Loyalists made up 15 percent of the population, and in Georgia and South Carolina they numbered between 20 and 40 percent of combatants during the war.[28] The Massachusetts Loyalists comprised just 1.89 percent of white adult males. They were scattered throughout 157 of the province's 260 towns and districts, but nowhere did they constitute a majority of the local population. Sixty-six percent of towns in which Loyalists were active contained less than five Loyalists; only in Boston and in the frontier town of Jericho (renamed Hancock in 1776) did they comprise significant proportions of adult males, around one-fifth and one-third respectively.[29]

Loyalist counterrevolutionary activity played a major part in British military strategy throughout the war, but to the despair of the British the Loyalists never seemed to materialize in great numbers when required.[30] Counterrevolutionary activity was virtually nonexistent in Massachusetts and limited to sporadic uprisings against the Patriot authorities; only in Boston between 1774 and 1776 was there a broad-based counterrevolutionary "party," based on the newly formed Loyalist regiments and Timothy Ruggles's militant Boston Association. When the British evacuated Boston in March 1776, they took with them to Nova Scotia some four hundred Loyalists plus their families—more than one thousand civilians in all. Some westerners fought alongside the British forces that were defeated at Bennington and Saratoga in the autumn of 1777, but the Loyalists were generally a silent minority. The Patriot authorities were free to proscribe intractable opponents at will, to confiscate the property of absentee proprietors, and to discourage dissenters from taking a more active role in politics until the War of Independence drew to a close.[31] Elsewhere in America, the presence of British regulars was a powerful stimulus for those wanting to settle old scores.

Massachusetts's Loyalists were, on the whole, treated leniently by the new state government—with the notable exception of Bernard, Hutchinson, and the mandamus councilors.[32] Bernard's treatment by the Americans constituted an exemplary lesson to all those who denied the maxims of popular sovereignty enshrined in the Declaration of Independence. Some six months before the Declaration, the Massachusetts legislature proclaimed that

> When Kings, Ministers, Governors, or Legislators . . . instead of exercising the Powers entrusted with them, according to the Principles, Forms, and Proportions stated by the Constitution, and established by the original Compact [of government], prostitute those Powers to the Purposes of Oppression;—to subvert, instead of supporting a free Constitution;—to destroy, instead of preserving the Lives, Liberties and Properties of the People; —they are no longer to be deemed Magistrates vested with a sacred Character, but become public Enemies, and ought to be resisted.[33]

Bernard's name was placed at the head of the state's list of "certain notorious conspirators against the government and liberties of the inhabitants of the late province."[34] His Massachusetts property, with the exception of Mount Desert, was confiscated on 30 April 1779 and sold at public auction. The proceeds were used to defray claims from Patriot creditors, many of which were probably false.[35]

Bernard's contact with the Loyalist exiles, who began arriving in Britain in 1775, was limited by illness and residence at Lincoln and Aylesbury. The more moderate Loyalists, such as Isaac Royall, were wary of being associated with Bernard for fear of damaging their chances of recovering their American estates.[36] Bernard remained a useful contact for others who required assistance in submitting memorials to the Loyalist Claims Commission, or, like Thomas Flucker, who sought a commission in the British army for his son.[37] Bernard helped to pay for the education of the son of William Logan, the Scots-born comptroller of customs at Perth Amboy who was captured by the Americans when he fled in 1775 and obliged to eke out a sparse living on his Loyalist pension of twenty-five pounds a year.[38] William Story too found Bernard a sympathetic patron when he tried to get some compensation from the Crown in recognition of his sufferings during the Stamp Act riots.[39]

*   *   *

The war with America brought tragedy to the Bernard family as it did to thousands of others. William Bernard, Francis's fourth son, drowned in 1776 at the age of twenty-one when the Royal Navy ship on which he was serving sank in the English Channel. John Bernard and his partner William Gale had tried resolutely to preserve their business interests in Boston. Because of the British blockade of the harbor, John was unable—or unwilling—to pay his debts to a Patriot merchant and thought it "expedient" to leave with the evacuation fleet. He lost a house, land, wharves, and flats in Boston's Leverett and Brighton streets worth six hundred pounds, and some five hundred pounds' worth of goods.[40]

Bernard's last years were blighted by his wife's ill health. Amelia died at Aylesbury on 26 May 1778 while their old friend Charles Paxton was visiting.[41] The following year, Bernard suffered prolonged ill health and epileptic seizures. One seizure, on the night of Wednesday, 16 June 1779, was so intense that he had to be pinned to the bed by his sons; thinking he was at sea, he exclaimed, "Never fear; if you will have but patience I don't doubt we shall get safe through; but take care how you ever get into such a scrape again." Racked by "frightfull Convulsions" he died bewildered and confused later that night. He was sixty-seven years old.[42]

By then, however, Sir Francis Bernard had firmly reestablished his family's membership in the English country gentry. He died a wealthy man. In spite of claims against his estate from mortgagees and the confiscation of his property in Suffolk County, Massachusetts, Bernard was possessed of real estate worth some £8,771 sterling, a sum that does not include the estimated value of the undeveloped island, Mount Desert, that he had bequeathed to John. He was able too to honor and make legacies, maturities, and annuities totaling £11,510.[43] Through service in America and a fortuitous inheritance his children were able to contemplate a secure future within the English elite. John Bernard had returned to America in 1776 to recover Mount Desert, but lived a lonely existence at Passamaquoddy in Maine. In 1785 he was given title to one-half the island, which he later sold to land speculators. He was appointed governor of Barbados, dying unmarried at the age of sixty-three in Dominica on 25 August 1809.[44] Thomas, who inherited the title (which did not expire until 1883),[45] made his name as a philanthropist, social reformer, and treasurer of the London Foundling Hospital. His pious sister Frances Elizabeth, the author of the popular *Female Scripture Characters*, was also a social reformer, particularly concerned with women's issues. Both Thomas and Frances attributed their interest in poverty to their parents' influence.[46] Scrope, with Thomas's help and blessing, managed to consolidate the family estates in Buckinghamshire and Lincolnshire in the 1780s and 1790s, and refurbished and improved Nether Winchendon House in a grand neo-Gothic style.[47] His career in government began in 1782 when the marquis of Buckingham took him to Ireland as private secretary during his tenure as lord lieutenant; a succession of prominent offices followed his patronage by Buckingham and the Grenville family.[48] The intellectualism of Sir Francis and Amelia certainly impressed their daughters. Julia, Jane, and Frances were strong-willed and intelligent young women who all married much older, scholarly men, although young Amelia, known as Emily, never married.[49]

The former colonists never forgot Francis Bernard. When the Reverend William Gordon congratulated James Bowdoin on his election as Massachusetts governor in 1786 he had one important message: do not antagonize the House of Representatives, for in flouting representative government Bernard had been the agent of his own destruction.[50] In the coming years, Americans ignored the bitter internal conflicts that existed in the colonies prior to the Revolution, preferring a more comfortable myth—that Bernard and others like him were the embodiment of British tyranny.

In Nathaniel Hawthorne's *True Stories*—a prepossessing children's book of New England's "eminent characters and remarkable events"—the narrator, a sagacious grandfather, was a disciple of the nationalist historian George Bancroft, and captivated his young audience with tales of what happened to the keepers of an old oaken chair. With Hawthorne's world beset by sectional tensions over slavery and states' rights, the chair was a powerful symbol of continuity in America's inexorable rise from colony to nation-state: its early custodians were his Puritan forebears who had vanquished the tyrant Andros; by comparison Bernard's administration was a confusing interregnum, best forgotten. Bernard "looked at the old chair, and thought it quite too shabby to keep company with a new set of mahogany chairs, and an aristocratic sofa, which has just arrived from London [and] ordered it to be put away in the garret." While the children "were loud in their exclamations against this irreverent conduct," Hawthorne's alter ego "defended the governor as well as he could," for when Bernard succeeded to the chair it was already well worn, the wood scoured, and the upholstery misshapen and tattered.[51]

Abbreviations

AHR *American Historical Review*

APC W. L. Grant and James Munro, eds., *Acts of the Privy Council of England: Colonial Series, 1613–1783*, 6 vols. (London: HMSO, 1909–12)

BC *Boston Chronicle*

BEP *Boston Evening Post*

BGCJ *Boston Gazette and Country Journal*

BGHU John L. Sibley and Clifford K. Shipton, eds., *Biographical Sketches of Graduates of Harvard University*, 17 vols. (Cambridge and Boston: Harvard University Press and Massachusetts Historical Society, 1873–1975)

BNL *Boston Newsletter*

BP Bernard Papers, 13 vols. Sparks Papers, Houghton Library, Harvard University

BRO Buckinghamshire Record Office

BTR *Reports of the Record Commissioners of the City of Boston*, 38 vols. (Boston: Rockwell and Churchill, 1876–1909)

CCT Commissioners of Customs in America, typescripts, 1755–77, Bowdoin-Temple Papers, Massachusetts Historical Society

CO	Colonial Office Papers, Public Record Office, London
DAB	*Dictionary of American Biography*, 22 vols. (London: Oxford University Press, 1928–58)
DAJA	Lyman H. Butterfield et al., eds., *The Diary and Autobiography of John Adams*, 4 vols. (Cambridge: Harvard University Press, Belknap Press, 1961)
DLTH	Peter Orlando Hutchinson, ed., *The Diary and Letters of His Excellency Thomas Hutchinson*, 2 vols. (London: Sampson, Low Marston, Searle & Rivington, 1883)
DNB	Sir Leslie Stephen and Sir Sidney Lee, eds., *Dictionary of National Biography*, 63 vols. (London: Smith, Elder, & Co., Humphrey Milford, 1885–)
HMSO	Her (His) Majesty's Stationery Office
HUO	L. S. Sutherland and L. G. Mitchell, eds., *The History of the Univ. of Oxford.* Vol. 5, *The Eighteenth Century*, ed. T. H. Aston (Oxford: Clarendon Press, 1986)
JBT	*Journals of the Commissioners for Trade and Plantations*, 14 vols. (London: HMSO, 1920–38)
JHRM	*The Journals of the House of Representatives of Massachusetts, 1715–1776*, 53 vols. (Boston: Massachusetts Historical Society, 1919–85)
Lincs. Arch.	Lincolnshire Archives
Mass. Council Records	Massachusetts Governor's Council, Executive Records, series 327, vol. 16, 1765–74
MG	*Massachusetts Gazette*
MHS	Massachusetts Historical Society

NEHGR — *New England Historic and Genealogical Register*

PDBP — P. D. G. Thomas and R. C. Simmons, eds., *Proceedings and Debates of the British Parliament respecting North America, 1754–1783*, 5 vols. (Millwood, N.Y.: Kraus International Publications, 1982–86)

PHE — *The Parliamentary History of England from the earliest period to the year 1803*, 36 vols. (London: Hansard, 1806–20)

Procs. MHS — *Proceedings of the Massachusetts Historical Society*

Select Letters — [Francis Bernard], *Select Letters on the Trade and Government of America; and the Principles of Law and Polity, applied to the American Colonies. Written by Governor Bernard in the years 1763,4,5,6,7, and 8* (London: W. Bowyer and J. Nichols, 1774)

THLB — [Thomas Hutchinson Letterbooks]. Transcripts of Thomas Hutchinson Correspondence, Massachusetts Historical Society (originals in the Massachusetts Archives Collection, vols. 25–27)

WMQ — *William and Mary Quarterly*, 3d ser.

Notes

INTRODUCTION

1. *BNL*, 10 February 1763; *JHRM*, 39: 245.

2. *BNL*, 24 March 1763; Oxenbridge Thacher to Benjamin Prat, n.d. [1762], *Procs. MHS*, 1st ser., 20 (1883): 46.

3. Bernard Bailyn, *The Ideological Origins of the American Revolution* (Cambridge: Harvard Univ. Press, Belknap Press, 1967), 122–23.

4. *DAJA*, 2: 93.

5. [Benjamin Church], *An Elegy to the Infamous Memory of Sr F-B-* ([Boston], 1769).

6. Museum artifact 0170, MHS.

7. Andrew S. Walmsley, *Thomas Hutchinson and the Origins of the American Revolution* (New York: New York Univ. Press, 1999); Michael C. Batinski, *Jonathan Belcher, Colonial Governor* (Lexington, Ky.: Univ. Press of Kentucky, 1996); Paul W. Wilderson, *Governor John Wentworth and the American Revolution: The English Connection* (Hanover, Mass.: Univ. Press of New England, 1994). See also the impressive Bernard Bailyn, *The Ordeal of Thomas Hutchinson* (Cambridge: Harvard Univ. Press, Belknap Press, 1974).

8. See Patricia U. Bonomi, *The Lord Cornbury Scandal: The Politics of Reputation in British America* (Chapel Hill: University of North Carolina Press, 1998).

9. On revolutionary theory see Jack Goldstone, *Revolution and Rebellion in the Early Modern World* (Berkeley: University of California Press, 1991), 1–62.

10. For example, see Guy Carleton Lee, ed., *The History of North America*, vol. 4, ed. C. W. Veditz and B. B. James (Philadelphia: George Barrie & Sons, 1904), 120–21; W. E. Chancellor and F. W. Hewes, *The United States: A History of Three Centuries, 1607–1904* (New York: G. P. Putnam & Sons, 1905), 207, 220–21; James Grant Wilson and John Fiske, eds., *Appleton's Cyclopedia of American Biography*, 4 vols. (New York: D. Appleton & Co., 1887), 1: 247–48.

11. George Minot, *Continuation of the History of the Province of Massachusetts Bay, from . . . 1748, with an introductory Sketch of events from the original settlement*, 2 vols. (Boston: Manning & Loring, 1798–1803), 1: preface; 2: 73–74, 78–80.

12. See Stephen T. Riley, "Some Aspects of the Society's Manuscript Collection," *Procs. MHS*, 3d ser., 70 (1950–53), 243; and the minutes of the Massachusetts Historical Society's monthly meetings listed in the Bibliography.

13. George Bancroft, *History of the United States of America from the Discovery of the Continent*, 6 vols. (London: Macmillan, 1876), 3: 347, 505; 4: 8, 101–22, 162–76.

14. James K. Hosmer, *Samuel Adams* (1885; Boston: Houghton Mifflin, 1898), 124–27.

15. George Otto Trevelyan, *History of the American Revolution*, 4 vols. (New York: Longmans, Green & Co., 1921), 1: 14–18.

16. Douglass Adair and John A. Schutz, eds., *Peter Oliver's Origin & Progress of the American Rebellion: A Tory View* (Stanford: Stanford Univ. Press, 1961), 57–58.

17. Thomas Hutchinson, *The History of the Colony and Province of Massachusetts Bay*, 3 vols., ed. Lawrence S. Mayo (1936; New York: Da Capo Press, 1971), 3: 229. See also *DAB*, 1:221–22.

18. Thomas Bernard, *Life of Sir Francis Bernard* (London: n.p., 1790); Mrs. Napier [Sophie Elizabeth] Higgins, *The Bernards of Abington and Nether Winchendon: A Family History*, 4 vols. (London: Longmans, Green & Co., 1903–4).

19. Jordan D. Fiore, "Francis Bernard, Colonial Governor" (Ph.D. diss., Boston Univ., 1950). Fiore was on stronger ground when he argued that Bernard's unwillingness to "modify his devotion to English manners, customs, and political ideals" meant he could not "appreciate the American point of view." But he lapsed into romantic nationalism when he contended that the success of the revolutionaries attested to their superior strength of character. *Ibid.*, vi, 452–53, 465.

20. Bailyn, *Hutchinson*, 46. See Edmund S. Morgan and Helen M. Morgan, *The Stamp Act Crisis: Prologue to Revolution* (Chapel Hill: University of North Carolina Press; New York: Collier Books, 1963), 6–7; John R. Galvin, *Three Men of Boston: Leadership and Conflict at the Start of the American Revolution* (Washington & London: Brasseys, 1976), 13; William M. Fowler Jr., *Samuel Adams: Radical Puritan* (New York: Longman, 1997), 67, 86.

21. The most important studies are Marc Egnal, *A Mighty Empire: The Origins of the American Revolution* (Ithaca, N.Y.: Cornell Univ. Press, 1988), 38–50, 150–67; William Pencak, *War, Politics & Revolution in Provincial Massachusetts* (Boston: Northeastern Univ. Press, 1981); Stephen E. Patterson, *Political Parties in Revolutionary Massachusetts* (Madison: University of Wisconsin Press, 1973); Pauline Maier, *From Resistance to Revolution: Colonial Radicals and the Development of American Opposition to Britain, 1765–1776* (London: Routledge & Kegan Paul, 1973), 51–53, 73–74, 151–57, 198–227; Leslie J. Thomas, "Partisan Politics in Massachusetts during Governor Bernard's Administration, 1760–1770," 2 vols. (Ph.D. diss., University of Wisconsin, 1960); Robert E. Brown, *Middle-Class Democracy and the Revolution in Massachusetts, 1691–1780* (Ithaca, N.Y.: Cornell Univ. Press, 1955), 176–77, 182–89, 221–32.

22. Colin Nicolson, "Governor Francis Bernard, the Massachusetts Friends of Government, and the Advent of the Revolution," *Procs. MHS*, 3d ser., 101 (1991): 24–113; Colin Nicolson, " 'McIntosh, Otis & Adams are our demagogues': Nathaniel Coffin and the Loyalist Interpretation of the Origins of the American Revolution," *Procs. MHS*, 3d ser., 108 (1996–97): 73–114. See also *idem*, "The Friends of Government: Loyalism, Ideology and Politics in Revolutionary Massachusetts, 1765–1776," 2 vols. (Ph.D. diss., University of Edinburgh, 1988).

23. See T. H. Breen, *Puritans and Adventurers: Change and Persistence in Early America* (Oxford: Oxford Univ. Press, 1980), 82–105.

24. Bernard to Richard Jackson, Boston, 1 March 1766, BP, 5: 80.

25. Massachusetts had seven principal executive officers, excluding the Council: the governor, the lieutenant governor, the province secretary, the treasurer, the attorney general, the solicitor general, and the commissioner of impost and excise. They were all supported by clerks and underlings, and worked closely with county officers such as the sheriffs.

26. Royal Instructions to Governor Francis Bernard, 27 May 1761, Spencer Bernard Family Papers, Nether Winchendon House, Aylesbury. See Leonard Woods Labaree, ed., *Royal Instructions to British Colonial Governors, 1670–1776*, 2 vols. (New

York: D. Appleton–Century Company, 1935). A useful summary is Evarts B. Greene, *The Provincial Governor in the English Colonies of North America*, Harvard Historical Studies Series, vol. 8 (New York: Longmans, Green & Co., 1889), 64–65, 91–95. There is a copy of Bernard's instructions as governor of New Jersey at 226–60. A total of 135 royal governors were appointed to the North American colonies and West Indies between 1670 and 1776, of whom 44 were titled. Labaree, ed., appendix A to *Royal Instructions*, 2: 799–808.

27. Richard L. Bushman, *King and People in Provincial Massachusetts* (Chapel Hill: University of North Carolina Press, 1985), 22–54, 112–14.

28. Stanley Katz, *Newcastle's New York: Anglo-American Politics, 1732–1753* (Cambridge: Harvard Univ. Press, Belknap Press, 1968), esp. 12–20, 39–58; James A. Henretta, *"Salutary Neglect": Colonial Administration under the Duke of Newcastle* (Princeton: Princeton Univ. Press, 1972), esp. 285–87, 297, 313, 319, 333, 342; Jack P. Greene, *Peripheries and Center: Constitutional Development in the Extended Polities of the British Empire and the United States, 1607–1788* (New York: W. W. Norton, 1986), 79–81.

29. Hannah Arendt, *On Revolution* (1963; London: Penguin, 1990), 28, 44, 47.

30. Jack P. Greene, "An Uneasy Connection: An Analysis of the Preconditions of the American Revolution," *Essays on the American Revolution*, ed. Stephen G. Kurtz and James H. Hutson (Chapel Hill: University of North Carolina Press, 1973; New York: W. W. Norton, 1973), 32–80, at 41–42.

31. Bernard to the earl of Shelburne, Jamaica Farm, 21 September 1767, BP, 6: 243.

32. Bernard to Shelburne, Boston, 24 January 1767, BP, 4: 297–98.

33. Arendt, *On Revolution*, 177.

34. Nicolson, "Governor Francis Bernard," 24–113; Nicolson, " 'McIntosh, Otis & Adams are our demagogues,' " 73–114. The author's work has aimed to carry forward Janice Potter's systematic study of Loyalist ideology. Potter concentrated mainly upon the ideas formulated in pamphlets and political writing between 1774 and 1776, and made little reference to the prewar views and activities of rank-and-file Loyalists. *The Liberty We Seek: Loyalist Ideology in Colonial New York and Massachusetts* (Cambridge: Harvard Univ. Press, 1983), 15–38, 80–101. Like other historians of prerevolutionary America, I have applied Poulantzas's definition of ideology—a cogent though not necessarily a systematic "ensemble" of "values, representations, and beliefs." Nicos Poulantzas, *Political Power and Social Classes*, trans. Timothy O'Hagan (London: Verso, 1978), 206.

35. John Philip Reid, *In a Rebellious Spirit: The Argument of Facts, The Liberty Riot and the Coming of the Revolution* (University Park, Penn.: Pennsylvania State Univ. Press, 1979), 121–26.

36. James H. Stark, *The Loyalists of Massachusetts and the Other Side of the American Revolution* (Boston: n.p., 1910); Edward A. Jones, *The Loyalists of Massachusetts: Their Memorials, Petitions and Claims* (London: St. Catherine's Press, 1930); Wallace Brown, *The King's Friends: The Composition and Motives of the American Loyalist Claimants* (Providence, R.I.: Brown Univ. Press, 1965), 294–98; Pencak, *War, Politics & Revolution*, 213–29.

CHAPTER ONE

1. "John Hampden" [James Otis Jr.], *BGCJ*, 14 November 1766; Otis to Jasper Mauduit, 28 October 1762, "Jasper Mauduit, Agent in London, 1762–1765," ed. Worthington C. Ford, *Collections of the Massachusetts Historical Society* 74 (Boston, 1918), 77–78.

2. Quoted in Higgins, *The Bernards*, 1: 283; 2: 301.

3. Lawrence Stone and Jeanne C. Fawtier Stone, *An Open Elite? England, 1540–1880* (Oxford: Clarendon Press, 1984), 409.

4. Bernard's date of birth is unknown, but babies were usually baptized about three days after birth.

5. Alan Dell, Buckinghamshire Family History Society, letter to the author, 20 September 1996.

6. [Benjamin Church], *The Tom-Cod Catcher: On the Departure of an Infamous B–r–t* ([Boston, 1769]).

7. Joseph Foster, comp., *Alumni Oxoniensis: The Members of the University of Oxford, 1500–1714* . . . (London: Parker & Co., 1891–92), 1: 20; G. V. Bennett, "University, Society, and Church, 1688–1714," *HUO*, 5: 362.

8. The father of Rev. Bernard (1660–1715), Francis Bernard (d. 1679 or 1680), was the eldest son of Thomas Bernard (d. 1628), who possessed a house and small plot in St. Mary's Parish. Thomas Bernard was the fourth son of Francis Bernard (c. 1509–1602) of Abington, a substantial landowner, who sired twelve children. Abington's eldest son inherited the Abington estate and lands in Yorkshire, while his grandson Robert Bernard was created a baronet in 1662. Bernard, *Life of Bernard*, 1; Higgins, *The Bernards*, 1: 95–104, 109–15; G. E. Cockayne, *The Complete Baronetage*, 6 vols. (Exeter, Eng.: William Pollard, 1906), 5: 150–52. The family history of the Bernards of Reading would appear to confirm the Stones' observation that the landed elite was mainly "open in the sense that there was little to prevent most of the male children sliding out of it." Stone and Stone, *An Open Elite*, 5.

9. Peter Ditchfield and William Page, eds., *The Victoria History of Berkshire*, 4 vols. (London: [Institute of Historical Research], 1906–27), 3: 464–71. Brightwell is in the modern-day county of Oxford. In 1844, when the first reliable list of Anglican clergy and their livings was published, Brightwell (population 611) was valued at £674 per annum, more than twice the value of Codford, St. Mary's (pop. 338). *The Clergy List for 1844* (London: C. Cox, 1844), 29, 47, 146.

10. Alsop, B.A. (1695), M.A. (1696 or '97), B.D., had been prebendary of Winchester in 1706; rector at Nursling, Hampshire, in 1712; and at Alverstoke, in the same county, in 1714. Both rectories were in Trelawney's patronage. Higgins, *The Bernards*, 1: 174–80; Foster, *Alumni Oxoniensis*, 1: 20.

11. [Francis Bernard, ed.], *Antonii Alsopi Ôdarum libri duo* (London, 1752); Leicester Bradner, *Musae Anglicanae: A History of Anglo-Latin Poetry, 1500–1925* (New York: Oxford Univ. Press, 1940), 233–36.

12. Bradner, *Musae Anglicanae*, 230–37; E. G. W. Bill, *Education at Christ Church, Oxford, 1660–1800* (Oxford: Clarendon Press, 1988), 44; M. L. Clark, "Classical Studies," *HUO*, 5: 526.

13. Higgins, *The Bernards*, 1: 115, 170–82.

14. The card index to the records of the dean and chapter of Lincoln in Lincolnshire Archives notes that Moses Terry was a clerk in the chapter from 1716, though Higgins suggests that he did not move to the close until 1720, in *The Bernards*, 1: 188–89.

15. Bernard to Lord Barrington, Castle William, 21 May 1763, BP, 3: 62.

16. Bernard, *Life of Bernard*, 1–5. See also Higgins, *The Bernards*, 1: 175, 182.

17. Bernard to the earl of Halifax, Perth Amboy, 23 May 1759, BP, 1: 174–77.

18. Bernard to Barrington, Boston, 27 August 1768, BP, 6: 142.

19. See V. H. H. Green, "The University and Social Life," *HOU*, 5: 310–11, 328; I. G. Doolittle, "College Administration," *HOU*, 5: 256–58; John Cannon, *The Aristocratic Century: The Peerage of Eighteenth Century England* (Cambridge: Cambridge Univ. Press, 1984), 47–48, 54, 58. Thirty-four students matriculated at Christ Church

in 1729: Bernard and three other Westminster "students"; one nobleman and eight "gentlemen commoners"; seventeen "commoners," a generic term applied virtually to all other students; and four "servitors" who were usually poor students. A total of 429 Westminster students were elected in the eighteenth century. Bill, *Christ Church*, 91–103, 125, 168.

20. Green, "The University and Social Life," 323–26, 340–45, 445–51.

21. Bernard's "collections" are in Bill, *Christ Church*, 327–40.

22. John Conybeare, *A Defence of Reveal'd Religion against the exceptions of a late writer: in his book, intituled, Christianity as old as the creation, &c.*, 3d ed. (London: S. Wilmot, 1732).

23. Dorothy Marshall, *English People in the Eighteenth Century* (London: Longmans, Green & Co., 1957), 52, 119; John Rule, *Albion's People: English Society, 1714–1815* (New York: Longman, 1992), 9–13, 60–64; Robert Robson, *The Attorney in Eighteenth-Century England* (Cambridge: Cambridge Univ. Press, 1959), 134–37, 141; Harold Perkin, *The Origins of Modern English Society, 1780–1880* (London: Routledge & Kegan Paul, 1969), 252–70, 319–23.

24. Robson, *The Attorney*, 144–47; Paul Lucas, "A Collective Biography of Students and Barristers of Lincoln's Inn, 1680–1804: A Study in the 'Aristocratic Resurgence' of the Eighteenth Century," *Journal of Modern History* 46 (1974): 227–61; C. E. A. Bedwell, "The Inns of Court," *London Society Journal* 213 (1939): 165–71.

25. H. A. C. Sturgess et al., comps., *Register of Admissions to the Honourable Society of the Middle Temple, from the Fifteenth Century to 1975*, 5 vols. ([London]: Society of the Middle Temple, 1949–78), 1: 315.

26. Terry is mentioned in Lincs. Arch., Lincoln Diocesan Records: Accounts from the Registrar's Office, R/Ac. 13/1/7; the Court Records, the Assignation Book of the Consistory Court, 1741–43, Cj/40. He was appointed rector of Leadenham, Lincs., in 1742, and also held the vicarage of Willingbore.

27. Sidney and Beatrice Webb, *English Local Government*, 11 vols. ([London]: Frank Cass & Co., 1963) 1: 321–23; 2: 405.

28. See Sir Francis Hill, *Georgian Lincoln* (Cambridge: Cambridge Univ. Press, 1966), 1–7, 146, 148, 183, quotation at 8.

29. There are no law lists for this period, but by 1790 Lincoln had 12 lawyers, which was normal for county towns; cities like Birmingham had 40, Bristol 61, and London, the seat of the king's courts, 1,755. Robson, *The Attorney*, 68–83, 111, 166–67.

30. The Midlands Assize met twice yearly, once in the summer and once in the winter, to administer justice in the counties of Lincoln, York, Nottingham, Leicester, and Derby. On the assizes see Norma Landau, *The Justices of the Peace, 1679–1760* (Berkeley: University of California Press, 1984), 38–39, 64, 82; J. M. Beattie, *Crime and the Courts in England, 1660–1800* (Oxford: Clarendon Univ. Press, 1986).

31. Lewis B. Namier, *The Structure of Politics at the Accession of George III*, 2d ed. (1929; London: Macmillan, 1958), 107; John Beresford Owen, *The Rise of the Pelhams* (London: Methuen, 1957), 51–52 and passim; Romney Sedgwick, *The House of Commons, 1715–1754* . . . (London: HMSO, 1970), 2: 265.

32. Bernard to [Charles Monson], Lincoln, 19 December 1741, Monson Papers 25/2/97, Lincs. Arch.

33. Vivian had attended Lincoln's Inn and was also a resident of the close. His mother Ann belonged to the Hyde family, who held manors and lordships at Langcroft and Boston. His father-in-law was Gervase Scrope, a prominent Lincolnian. Ancaster Papers, 3 Anc 1/11/9–10, 11–12, Lincs. Arch.

34. Hill, *Georgian Lincoln*, 82–83.

35. Lincoln City Records: Apprentices Register, L1/5/2, 357, Lincs. Arch.; Hill, *Georgian Lincoln*, 149. Bernard, however, is not mentioned in the Monson papers

and accounts concerning local elections, either as an agent or as a campaign donor. Mon 22A/1/2A.

36. There are no extant records to confirm Higgins's suggestion that Bernard became steward of Lincoln in 1744. It is unlikely that this post was connected with the affairs of the Common Council or the diocese and may have been an honorarium—steward of the Bail—held under the duchy of Lancaster. Mr. C. Johnson, letter to the author, Lincs. Arch., 28 January 1997; Church Commissioners records: Court Rolls, CC 85/313735, Lincs. Arch.

37. Jonathan Mitchell to Bernard, Bath, 8 July 1759, BP, 9: 53-59; Betty Coy et al., eds., *Transcription of the Minutes of the Corporation of Boston* (Boston, Lincs.: History of Boston Project, 1993), 659, 664, 666, 689.

38. G[eorge] Reynolds to Mr. [Moses?] Terry, Buckden, 7 May 1739, Dean and Chapter of Lincoln muniments, Dij/50/1/3, Lincs. Arch.; Bernard to Anholm Jenner, Perth Amboy, 4 July 1758, BP, 1: 27-28.

39. Judith Curthoys, letter to the author, Christ Church Library, Oxford, 6 May 1997.

40. Patent appointing Francis Bernard of the close of Lincoln to the office of receiver-general of the church of Lincoln, 16 September 1745, Spencer Bernard Papers, BRO.

41. Lincs. Arch., Registrar's Office: [Accounts of Francis Bernard, deputy to registrar and archdeacon of Lincoln, and clerk to Common Chamber of the dean and chapter, from 1745], R/Ac. 3/1; Account of fees received by Francis Bernard, Esq., deputy registrar, for the use of the registrars of the bishop and archdeacon of Lincoln, from the 10th day of October 1749, till the 9th day of October, 1750, R/Ac. 13/1/14.

42. Lincoln Diocesan Records: Account of Business Done at Visitations, R/Ac. 7/5-9; Court Books, Instruments of Procuration, XII, Proxies, Box 71, 1717-59; Visitation Records, L.C./XX/C.: 83; Foster Library Collection: FL King Deeds 5/3-4.

43. Bernard, *Life of Bernard*, 3.

44. The proprietors and subscribers raised a total of £2,007 17s 11d, which was used to reimburse Bernard for the quite substantial sums he had to pay out to tradesmen and fitters. Where Bernard obtained this money in the first place is unclear, but he would have used the creditworthiness of his illustrious clients. The Accounts of the Assembly Room at Lincoln, 2 Anc. 10/6/1 and 5.

45. Bernard to the duke of Ancaster, Lincoln, 4 September 1756, 2 Anc. 10/6/3.

46. Bernard to the bishop of Bristol, Perth Amboy, 7 January 1760, BP, 1: 192.

47. Barrington to Bernard, 9 May 1768, BP, 11: 183-85.

48. Sir Lewis Namier and John Brooke, *The House of Commons, 1754-1790* (London: HMSO, 1964) 3: 637; *HOU*, 5: 199n1, 202.

49. Bernard to William Fitzherbert, Boston, 16 November 1765, BP, 5: 35; John R. G. Tomlinson, ed., *Additional Grenville Papers, 1763-1765* (Manchester, Eng.: Manchester Univ. Press, 1962), 190n.

50. Welbore Ellis (1713-1802) probably met Bernard at Westminster School, for he entered Christ Church somewhat later than Bernard in 1732. An ally of Newcastle, Ellis (B.A. 1736) was an M.P. for several safe constituencies (1741-94), a lord of the Admiralty (1747-53), secretary at war (1762-65), and American secretary (1782). *DNB*, 6: 710-11.

51. Adair and Schutz, ed., *Peter Oliver's Origin & Progress*, 25.

52. [William Warburton], *Letters from a Late Eminent Prelate to One of his Friends*, 2d ed. (London: T. Cadell and W. Davies, 1809), 124.

53. *Procs. MHS*, 2d ser., 10 (1885–96): 546; Probate of the Will of Sir Francis Bernard, 12 July 1779, Spencer Bernard Papers.

54. Catalogue of Printed Books, UAIII 50.27.64.2. PF VT, Harvard Archives, Pusey Library.

55. Higgins, *The Bernards*, 1: 194–204.

56. Francis Bernard to ?, Lincoln, 31 October 1741, in Higgins, *The Bernards*, 1: 194.

57. When Joseph Offley died in 1751, Norton Hall passed to his unstable eighteen-year-old son Edmund. Having been "sent" to Edinburgh to complete his education, Edmund created a scandal by bequeathing the estate to an Episcopalian clergyman with whom he had taken lodgings. Norton Hall was recovered for Edmund's two younger sisters after protracted negotiations, in which the Bernards assisted. Higgins, *The Bernards*, 1: 210–12.

58. Bernard to Frank Bernard, Boston, 4 January 1766, BP, 4: 95.

59. Bernard to Thomas Pownall, Boston, 2 March 1766, BP, 5: 85–86.

60. *The Book of Common Prayers and Administration of the Sacraments and other Rites and Ceremonies of the Church* . . . (London: John Baskett, 1713), Spencer Bernard Family Papers.

61. Roy Porter, *English Society in the Eighteenth Century* (London: Allen Lane, 1982), 21, 64–66, 86.

62. Bradner, *Musae Anglicanae*, 233–36.

63. Higgins, *The Bernards*, 1: 174–80; Atterbury, *DNB*, 1: 705–10. Robert Friend, *DNB*, 7: 681–83. On Toryism and Oxford University see Bill, *Christ Church*, 17–90; G. V. Bennett, "The Era of Party Zeal, 1702–1714," *HOU*, 61–98; Paul Langford, "Tories and Jacobites, 1714–1751," *HOU*, 5: 99–128; Christopher Wordsworth, *Scholae Academicae: Some Account of Studies at the English Universities in the Eighteenth Century* (1877; Cambridge Univ. Press, 1968), 11–17, 42–43.

64. Liber Subscriptionum, SUB VIII: 70, Lincs. Arch.

65. Linda Colley, *Britons: Forging the Nation, 1707–1837* (New Haven: Yale Univ. Press, 1992), 11–54.

66. Bernard to Richard Jackson, Boston, 23 January 1763, BP, 2: 248–50.

67. William Page, ed., *The Victoria History of the County of Lincoln*, vol. 2 (London: J. Street, 1906), 283–87.

68. F. J. McLynn, *The Jacobite Army in England, 1745: The Final Campaign* (Edinburgh: John Donald, 1983), 107, 130–31; Colley, *Britons*, 81–85, 376–77; Hill, *Georgian Lincoln*, 83–85. Joseph Offley also raised a Loyalist company. Higgins, *The Bernards*, 1: 207; Bernard, *Life of Bernard*, 4.

69. There are two copies of the subscription: List of Voluntary Subscribers to pay the forces raised in Lincolnshire for the defence of the realm, begun at Lincoln Castle, October 1, 1745, Mon 7/10/18; Historical Manuscripts Commission, *Report on the Manuscripts of the Earl of Ancaster Preserved at Grimsthorpe* (Dublin: HMSO, 1907), 445–46. The HMC copy contains names not entered in the first list. Records relating to the duke of Ancaster's regiment are in MISC DEP 89/1–7, Lincs. Arch.

70. Copy of the Lincoln Address presented to His Majesty 28 September 1745, 25 September 1745, Mon 7/10/17; Coy et al., eds., *Minutes of the Corporation of Boston*, 693–94.

71. J. R. Western, *The English Militia in the Eighteenth Century* (London: Routledge & Kegan Paul, 1965), 123–25, 290–302; John Stevenson, *Popular Disturbances in England, 1700–1870* (London: Longman, 1979), 35–37; Hill, *Georgian Lincoln*, 149; R. Wells, "Counting Riots in Eighteenth-Century England," *Society for the Study of Labour History* 37 (1978): 68–72.

72. On conservative Whiggism see H. T. Dickinson, *Liberty and Property: Politi-*

cal Ideology in Eighteenth Century Britain (London: Wiedenfield and Nicolson, 1977), 121–62; Geoffrey Holmes and Daniel Szechi, *The Age of Oligarchy: Pre-Industrial Britain, 1722–1783* (London: Longman, 1993), 269.

73. See Colley, *Britons*, 68–69, 102–4; J. C. D. Clark, *The Language of Liberty, 1660–1832: Political Discourse and Social Dynamics in the Anglo-American World* (Cambridge: Cambridge Univ. Press, 1994), 62–140.

74. Bernard to Thomas Hutchinson, Pall Mall, 21 March 1770, BP, 8: 77.

75. Bernard to the earl of Hillsborough, Boston, 16 June 1768, BP, 6: 320.

76. Bernard to Hillsborough, Boston, 16 September 1768, BP, 7: 41–42.

77. Bernard, *Life of Bernard*, 1–5.

78. Greene, *Provincial Governor*, 54; Katz, *Newcastle's New York*, 28–31; Stephen S. Webb, *The Governors-General: The English Army and the Definition of the Empire, 1569–1681* (Chapel Hill: University of North Carolina Press, c. 1979).

79. Richard Archer, "A New England Mosaic: A Demographic Analysis for the Seventeenth Century," *WMQ* 47 (1990): 477–502, at 483.

80. I am indebted to Robert Spencer Bernard for bringing to my attention the memorial in Boston, Lincs., which commemorates the town's roll call of governors. The recorders (with the corrected dates of service as governor) were Richard Bellingham, M.P. for Boston 1625, and Massachusetts governor 1644–45, 1649–65; Thomas Dudley, steward to the earl of Lincoln, governor 1635–36; Simon Bradstreet, Dudley's son-in-law and governor 1686 and 1702–15; John Leverett, governor 1679–86, 1689–92.

81. John A. Schutz, *Thomas Pownall: British Defender of American Liberty* . . . (Glendale, Calif.: Arthur H. Clark, 1951), 17, 20–21.

82. Thomas Pownall to Charles Monson, Philadelphia, 20 June 1755, Mon 25/1/47.

83. See also R. A. Humphreys, "Two Colonial Governors: Thomas Pownall and Francis Bernard," *Lincolnshire Magazine* 1, no. 7 (1932–34): 209–14.

84. See Franklin B. Wickwire, "King's Friends, Civil Servants, or Politicians," *AHR* 71 (1965): 18–42.

85. Franklin B. Wickwire, *British Subministers and Colonial America, 1763–1783* (Princeton: Princeton Univ. Press, 1966), 71. William Fitzherbert could also have promoted Bernard's interests though he did not enter Parliament until 1761 and joined the Board of Trade much later. Fitzherbert and Bernard were both acquainted with one "Mr. Roberts," possibly John Roberts, a member of the Board of Trade, whose high opinion of Bernard is noted in the duke of Newcastle to Henry Seymour Conway, 1765, Newcastle Papers, Add. MS. 32,971: 69, British Library. Another such "acquaintance" from the "early part" of Bernard's life was Claudius Amyand, an undersecretary of state between 1750 and 1756. Bernard to Claudius Amyand, Boston, 8 December 1764, BP, 3: 269–70.

86. Henretta, *"Salutary Neglect,"* 333; Katz, *Newcastle's New York*, 25–26.

87. Barrington succeeded his father John Shute as Viscount Barrington in 1734 and as M.P. for Berwick-upon-Tweed in the 1740s. He was appointed one of the Lords of the Admiralty in 1748, and served on the committee that condemned the Jacobite Simon, Lord Lovat for high treason. He was M.P. for Plymouth in 1754 and secretary at war from 1755 to 1761, and 19 July 1765 to 1778. His brother Samuel Barrington (1729–1800) was an admiral, while the youngest of the three, Shute Barrington (1734–1826), was consecrated bishop of Llandaff in 1769. *DNB*, 1: 1215; Tony Hayter, ed., *An Eighteenth Century Secretary at War: The Papers of William, Viscount Barrington* ([London]: Bodley Head for the Army Records Society, 1988), 3–18; Higgins, *The Bernards*, 1: 202.

88. Reed Browning, *The Duke of Newcastle* (New Haven and London: Yale Univ.

Press, 1975), 185–88; Ray A. Kelch, *Newcastle: A Duke without Money: Thomas Pelham-Holles, 1693–1768* (London: Routledge & Kegan Paul, 1974), 38–41. Newcastle was parliamentary leader of the Whigs, a secretary of state since 1724, and prime minister between 1754 and 1756 and July 1757 to May 1762. For his impact on imperial administration see Richard Middleton, "The Duke of Newcastle and the Conduct of Patronage during the Seven Years War, 1757–1762," *British Journal for Eighteenth Century Studies* 12 (1989): 175–86; Katz, *Newcastle's New York*; Henretta, *"Salutary Neglect,"* esp. 133, 223–25.

89. Browning, *Newcastle*, 5, 9–10, 13, 20–21, 124; Bill, *Christ Church*, 122, 124; Kelch, *A Duke without Money*, 71; Henretta, *"Salutary Neglect,"* 216–17.

90. Bernard to Dr. Bearcroft, Perth Amboy, 26 July 1759, BP, 1: 180.

91. Quoted in P. D. G. Thomas, *British Politics and the Stamp Act Crisis: The First Phase of the American Revolution, 1763–1767* (Oxford: Oxford Univ. Press, 1975), 137.

92. Bernard to Barrington, Boston, 17 January 1761, BP, 1: 292–94; Greene, *Provincial Governor*, 60–63. His salary of £1,200 in New Jersey currency was worth about £800 sterling. Mon 25/1/47.

93. Bernard to Richard Nichols, Perth Amboy, 29 August 1758, BP, 1: 42.

94. Bernard to the bishop of Bristol, Perth Amboy, 24 March 1759, BP, 1: 169–70.

95. Bernard to Thomas Boone, Perth Amboy, 18 February 1760, BP, 1: 216–17.

96. Bernard to the bishop of Bristol, Perth Amboy, 24 March 1759, 171.

97. Thomas L. Purvis, *Proprietors, Patronage, and Paper Money: Legislative Politics in New Jersey, 1703–1776* (New Brunswick, N.J.: Rutgers Univ. Press, 1986), 4, 64–69, 72–73, 113–17.

98. Colin Nicolson, "Francis Bernard, Governor of Colonial New Jersey, 1758–1760" (forthcoming).

99. Fiore, "Francis Bernard," 27–63, 454–58; Donald L. Kemmerer, *Path to Freedom: The Struggle for Self-Government in Colonial New Jersey, 1703–1776* (Cos Cob, Conn.: John E. Edwards, 1968), 256–66.

100. Bernard to Halifax, Perth Amboy, 7 January 1760, BP, 1: 191.

101. Bernard to Halifax, Perth Amboy, 18 July 1760, BP, 1: 267.

102. Bernard to Barrington, Perth Amboy, 18 February 1760, BP, 1: 194. News of his appointment came in Halifax to Bernard, London, 13 November 1759, BP, 9: 71–72.

103. Bernard to Barrington, New York, 19 April 1760, BP, 1: 202–3.

104. Bernard is rarely mentioned, but never disparagingly, in his children's correspondence, which mainly postdates his decease, in Spencer Bernard Papers.

105. Quoted in Higgins, *The Bernards*, 1: 281; 2: 70–71, 238–40.

106. Bernard to Barrington, 3 March 1761, BP, 1: 302–3; Bernard to Benjamin Franklin, Boston, 13 December 1763, BP, 3: 11–14; *MG*, 19 July 1770.

107. Bernard to Franklin, Boston, 13 December 1763, 11–14.

108. Bernard to Barrington, Boston, 31 March 1764, BP, 3: 134–35; Bernard to [Lord Barrington], Castle William, 24 May 1762, BP, 2: 191.

109. Bernard to Franklin, Boston, 13 December 1763, 13.

110. Bernard to [Lord Barrington], Castle William, 24 May 1762, BP, 2: 191.

111. Bernard to J[ohn] Stevens, Castle William, 8 November 1762, BP, 2: 285–86; Bernard to J[ohn] Stevens, Boston, 27 December 1762, BP, 2: 291–92.

112. Bernard to Lords Commissioners for Trade and Plantations, Boston, 16 August 1764, BP, 3: 165–68; Barrington to Bernard, Beckett, 7 September 1764, BP, 10: 187. The Naval Officer kept records pertaining to the entry and clearance of vessels,

and though paid a small salary (£30 p.a.) could profit from the prosecution of smugglers.

113. Bernard to George Lewis, Boston, 5 January 1765 [1766], BP, 4: 90.

114. Bernard to Franklin, Boston, 13 December 1763, 11–14; Bernard to Franklin, Boston, 27 December 1763, BP, 3: 15; Bernard to Franklin, Boston, 23 January 1764, BP, 3: 19–20; Bernard to Franklin, Boston, 13 February 1764, BP, 3: 25.

115. Bernard to James Gilpin, Boston, 4 January 1766, Boston, BP, 4: 97.

116. [Bernard], Instructions to his son Frank upon his return to College, [Boston], February or March, n.d., 1764, BP, 10: 151–58; Bernard to Frank Bernard, Boston, 4 January 1766, BP, 4: 95.

117. Bernard to James Gilpin, Boston, 4 January 1766.

118. Bernard to George Lewis, Boston, 5 January 1765 [1766].

119. Bernard to Frank Bernard, Boston, 15 January 1766, BP, 4: 101.

120. Barrington to Bernard, London, 8 June 1766, BP, 11: 14.

CHAPTER TWO

1. Bernard to Andrew Oliver, New London, 14 April 1760, [draft], BP, 1: 246.

2. Bernard to Oliver, Perth Amboy, 15 June 1760, BP, 1: 262.

3. BNL, 7 and 11 August 1760; BGCJ, 11, 18, and 25 August 1760; Thomas Hutchinson to Israel Williams, Boston, 4 March 1760, Israel Williams Papers, MHS; Bernard to Barrington, Boston, 7 August 1760, BP, 1: 272.

4. Bernard to Barrington, Boston, 23 August 1760, BP, 1: 275.

5. Batinski, Belcher, 2.

6. JHRM, 37, pt. 1: 84–85, 89–90.

7. See Bushman, King and People, 14–15; Simon P. Newman, Parades and the Politics of the Street: Festive Culture in the Early American Republic (Philadelphia: University of Pennsylvania Press, 1997), 12–19.

8. Higgins, The Bernards, 1: 282.

9. Bernard to Col. Fullerton?, Boston, 2 November 1762, BP, 2: 245–46; Bernard to Lt. Col. Pringle, Boston, 3 October 1765, BP, 4: 73.

10. Higgins, The Bernards, 287–88; BGCJ, 3 September 1770.

11. Procs. MHS, 2d ser., 1 (1884–85): 224–25.

12. Quoted in Higgins, The Bernards, 1: 282; Bernard to Barrington, New York, 19 April, 1760, BP, 1:203.

13. Bernard to Barrington, Boston, 7 February 1768, BP, 6: 83.

14. Letters of a Loyalist Lady: Ann Hulton, Sister of Henry Hulton, Commissioner of Customs at Boston, 1767–1770 (Cambridge, Mass.: n.p., 1927), 45.

15. Cookbook of Jane Beresford, 1722–92, Spencer Bernard Family Papers.

16. Franklin to Bernard, Philadelphia, 21 February 1764, The Papers of Benjamin Franklin, 28 vols., ed. Leonard W. Labaree et al. (New Haven: Yale Univ. Press, [1959]–) 11: 87–88; Franklin to Bernard, Philadelphia, 28 March 1764, ibid., 11; Bernard to Franklin, Boston, 23 January 1764, BP, 3: 19–20, 133.

17. Bernard to Messrs. Etty, Offley and Co., Boston, 9 January 1768, BP, 6: 61.

18. Randall [sic] Wilbraham to Bernard, Lincoln's Inn, 21 February 1761, BP, 9: 167.

19. Adair and Schutz, eds. Peter Oliver's Origin & Progress, 97.

20. Bernard to the governor of Newfoundland, [May], 1761, BP, 2: 111; Bernard to Gen. Jefferey Amherst, Boston, 19 June 1763, BP, 3: 1; JHRM, 37, pt. 2: 362.

21. E. L. Pierce, ed., "Extracts from the Diary of John Rowe," Procs. MHS, 2d ser., 10 (1895–96): 33; William Fowler Jr., The Baron of Beacon Hill: A Biography of John Hancock (Boston: Houghton Mifflin, 1980), 51.

22. Bernard to Dr. Burton, Boston, 18 August 1764, BP, 3: 248. Bernard probably spoke with syntactical precision if his letters are anything to go by. Examples of phonetic spelling in his papers, such as "haply" (BP, 5: 51) and "listning" (BP, 7: 221), which are associated with east Midlands dialects, are very rare no doubt because Bernard was educated in London and Oxford.

23. Thomas Hutchinson to Israel Williams, Boston, 25 August 1760, Israel Williams Papers.

24. Bernard to Barrington, New York, 19 April 1760, BP, 1: 201.

25. Bernard to Lords Commissioners for Trade and Plantations, Boston, 18 August 1761, BP, 2: 37.

26. See Gerald Newman, *The Rise of English Nationalism: A Cultural History, 1740–1830* (London: Macmillan, 1997), 192; Colley, *Britons,* 11–54; T. H. Breen, "Ideology and Nationalism on the Eve of the American Revolution: Revisions *Once More* in Need of Revising," *Journal of American History* 84 (1997): 13–39.

27. Bernard to Halifax, Boston, 29 September 1760, BP, 1: 282.

28. *JHRM,* 37, pt. 1: 100–101.

29. *JHRM,* 37, pt. 1: 115–17.

30. *DAJA,* 1: 185–86.

31. Bernard to Amherst, Boston, 5 May 1762, BP, 2: 143.

32. Bernard to the earl of Egremont, Boston, 7 June 1762, CO 5/755: 9–11.

33. Accounts of the negotiations at Paris were printed in the province newspapers from January 1762. The articles of peace were printed in *BNL,* 11 January 1763.

34. Bernard to Amherst, Boston, 4 April 1761, BP, 2: 103; *JHRM,* 37, pt. 2: 293–94; 38, pt. 2: 288, 302–3, 308–9.

35. Bernard to [Amherst?], Boston, 18 April 1761, BP, 2: 106–7.

36. See John Shy, *Toward Lexington: The Role of the British Army in the Coming of the American Revolution* (Princeton: Princeton Univ. Press, 1965), 89–93.

37. Bernard to [Amherst?], Boston, 18 April 1761.

38. Amherst to Bernard, New York, 9 April 1761, BP, 9: 183.

39. Bernard to Amherst, Castle William, 19 June 1762, BP, 2: 160.

40. Bernard to Lt. Gov. Belcher, Boston, 5 August 1762, BP, 2: 172.

41. *JHRM,* 39: 119–21; James Otis, *A Vindication of the Conduct of the House of Representatives of the province of the Massachusetts-Bay: more particularly, in the last session of the General Assembly* (Boston: Edes & Gill, 1762).

42. Bernard to John Pownall, Castle William, 20 October 1762, BP, 2: 209–10; Shy, *Toward Lexington,* 107.

43. Bernard to the earl of Shelburne, Boston, 21 March 1768, BP 6: 293–94. See Pencak, *War, Politics & Revolution,* 153–55, 162–64.

44. John McCusker and Russell R. Menard, *The Economy of British America, 1607–1789* (Chapel Hill: University of North Carolina Press, 1985), 79–81, 222–92.

45. Lawrence Henry Gipson, *The British Empire before the American Revolution,* 14 vols. (Caldwell, Idaho: 1936; rev. ed., New York: Knopf, 1958–71), 10: 53–61.

46. Hugh F. Bell, " 'A Personal Challenge': The Otis-Hutchinson Controversy, 1761–1762," *Historical Collections of the Essex Institute* 106 (1970): 297–323; John J. Waters Jr., *The Otis Family in Provincial and Revolutionary Massachusetts* (Chapel Hill: University of North Carolina Press, 1968), 139–40.

47. Bernard to Shelburne, Boston, 27 August 1767, BP, 6: 231–35.

48. *JHRM,* 40: 9–10, 29–31; Pencak, *War, Politics & Revolution,* 153–55, 162–64; Gipson, *The British Empire,* 10: 61.

49. Bernard to Thomas Pownall, Boston, 20 April 1768, BP, 6: 108.

50. Jerome Reich, *Colonial America,* 4th ed. (Upper Saddle River, N.J.: Prentice Hall, 1998), 112.

51. Bernard to Lords Commissioners for Trade and Plantations, Boston, 17 May 1762, BP, 2: 59.

52. Bernard to Shelburne, Boston, 28 March 1767, BP, 6: 199–200; Bushman, *King and People* , 112–14.

53. Zuckerman, *Peaceable Kingdoms*, 192–98, 200–209; Alison G. Olson, "Eighteenth-Century Colonial Legislatures and Their Constituents," *Journal of American History* 79 (1992): 543–67.

54. Bernard accepted the colonists' contention that the original province charter, held in London, enfranchised those possessing forty pounds of freehold property instead of fifty pounds as the Board of Trade maintained. See J. R. Pole, *Political Representation in England and the Origins of the American Revolution* (London: Oxford Univ. Press, 1966), 47–48.

55. Bernard to Barrington, Boston, 18 March 1769, BP, 7: 265.

56. For recent discussions see "Deference or Defiance in Eighteenth-Century America? A Round Table," *Journal of American History* 85 (1998): 13–97; Richard R. Beeman, "Deference, Republicanism, and the Emergence of Popular Politics in Eighteenth-Century America," *WMQ* 49 (1992): 403–30.

57. Edward M. Cook Jr., *Fathers of the Towns: Leadership Structure in Eighteenth-Century New England* (Baltimore: Johns Hopkins Univ. Press, 1976), 10–37, 80–84.

58. Gregory H. Nobles, *Divisions throughout the Whole: Politics and Society in Hampshire County, Massachusetts, 1740–1775* (Cambridge: Harvard Univ. Press, 1983).

59. William Bentick-Smith, "Nicholas Boylston and His Harvard Chair," *WMQ* 93 (1981): 17–39; Norman E. Saul, "The Beginnings of the American-Russian Trade, 1763–1766," *WMQ* 26 (1969): 596–600.

60. Bernard to Gov. DeLancey, [Perth] Amboy, 31 March 1760, BP 1: 240–42. See G. B. Warden, *Boston, 1689–1776* (Boston: Little, Brown, 1970), 149; Gary B. Nash, *The Urban Crucible: Social Change, Political Consciousness, and the Origins of the American Revolution* (Cambridge: Harvard Univ. Press, 1979), 245.

61. See Pencak, *War, Politics & Revolution*, 150–67; Patterson, *Political Parties*, 30–48; Bushman, *King and People*, 76–175; Robert M. Zemsky, *Merchants, Farmers and River Gods: An Essay on Eighteenth-Century American Politics* (Boston: Gambit, 1971), 12–13, 22–38.

62. Nash, *Urban Crucible*, 271–82; Warden, *Boston*, 128–58.

63. Marc Egnal identifies two elite groups of opinion, discernible by their discursive thoughts on the prospects of the American colonies: the "expansionists" were mainly country leaders who became Patriots, while "nonexpansionists" tended to be "court" men and future Loyalists. *A Mighty Empire*, 6–7.

64. See Ian R. Christie, ed., *Myth and Reality in Late Eighteenth-Century British Politics* (London: Macmillan, 1970), 300; Holmes and Szechi, *The Age of Oligarchy*, 280–81.

65. Egnal, *A Mighty Empire*, 38–46.

66. See Ellen E. Brennan, *Plural Office-Holding in Massachusetts, 1760–1780: Its Relation to the 'Separation' of Departments of Government* (Chapel Hill: University of North Carolina Press, 1945).

67. See Waters Jr., *The Otis Family*, 116–18; Bailyn, *Hutchinson*, 47–50; Hiller Zobel, *The Boston Massacre* (New York: W. W. Norton, 1970), 10, 47; *DLTH*, 1: 65, 195; William Pencak, *America's Burke: The Mind of Thomas Hutchinson* (Lanham, Md.: Univ. Press of America, 1982), 3; *DAJA*, 1: 167–68.

68. Bailyn, *Hutchinson*, 45.

69. Bailyn, *Hutchinson*, 17, 47; Bernard to Richard Jackson, Boston, 6 February 1765, BP, 3: 274–75.

70. Quoted in Bailyn, *Hutchinson*, 47.

71. Merrill Jensen, *The Founding of a Nation: A History of the American Revolution, 1763–1776* (New York: Oxford Univ. Press, 1968), 46; Gipson, *The British Empire*, 10: 113n5; Bernard to Governor Palliser, Boston, 22 July 1765, BP, 4: 53.

72. See John W. Tyler, *Smugglers & Patriots: Boston Merchants and the Advent of the Revolution* (Boston: Northwestern Univ. Press, 1986), 30–32, 41–49, 53; Gipson, *The British Empire*, 10: 114, 228–29; Thomas, "Partisan Politics," 1: 40–44; Bernard to Lords Commissioners for Trade and Plantations, Boston, 6 August 1761, BP, 2: 49.

73. Bernard to William Pitt, Boston, 9 May 1761, BP, 1: 311–13; Bernard to Pitt, Boston, 5 May 1761, BP, 1: 310–11.

74. Bernard to John Pownall, Boston, 15 June 1761, BP, 1: 318; Bernard to John Pownall, Boston, 13 July 1761, BP, 1: 324.

75. Bernard to [Thomas Pownall?], Boston, 12 July 1761, BP, 2: 7.

76. Waters Jr., *The Otis Family*, 132–38; Gipson, *The British Empire*, 10: 113, 120, 126–28; Thomas, "Partisan Politics," 1: 22–24, 38–39.

77. Bernard to the earl of Shelburne, Boston, 21 December 1766, BP, 4: 275–76.

78. *JHRM*, 38, pt. 1: 11–12.

79. Bernard to Jackson, Boston, 1 February 1763, BP, 2: 253.

80. Bernard to Barrington, Boston, 12 January 1762, BP, 2: 26; Bernard to John Pownall, Boston, 2 August 1764, BP, 3: 244.

81. Peter Shaw, *American Patriots and the Rituals of Revolution* (Cambridge: Harvard Univ. Press, 1981), 86–107.

82. Bernard to Lords Commissioners for Trade and Plantations, Boston, 20 and 22 February 1762, BP, 2: 27–28.

83. *BNL*, 6 May 1762.

84. Bernard to Barrington, Castle William, 1 May 1762, BP, 2: 189.

85. *JHRM*, 38, pt. 1: 11–12.

86. See P. D. G. Thomas, "George III and the American Revolution," *History* 70 (1985): 16–31.

87. Bolingbroke's *Idea of a Patriot King* (1738) envisaged a politically independent monarch, whose powers were limited by the constitution, being able to rule wisely "in balance" with the Commons and Lords. Bolingbroke repudiated the idea that competition between factions was a source of stability, though he did not reject the legitimacy of a loyal opposition, provided the raison d'être of opposition was to ensure good government. H. T. Dickinson, *Bolingbroke* (London: Constable, 1970), 247–76, 307.

88. John Brewer, *Party Ideology and Popular Politics at the Accession of George III* (London: Oxford Univ. Press, 1976), 13–14, 42, 45–46.

89. William D. Liddle, "A Patriot King or None: Lord Bolingbroke and the American Renunciation of George III," *Journal of American History* 65 (1979): 951–70, at 955.

90. William H. Whitmore, ed., *The Massachusetts Civil List for the Colonial and Provincial Periods* (Albany, N.Y.: J. Munsell, 1870), 130–53; Egnal, *A Mighty Empire*, 48–49; Fiore, "Francis Bernard," 100, 117–23; Nicolson, "Governor Francis Bernard," 68–108; appendix B: 109–14. Figures for the commissions in England and Wales are in appendix A, Landau, *Justices of the Peace*, 366–72.

91. John M. Murrin, "Review Essay," *History and Theory* 11 (1972): 226–75, at 266–70.

92. Cushing to Thomas Hutchinson, [Scituate], 10 February 1767, THLB, 25: 159; Cushing to Thomas Hutchinson, Scituate, 6 January 1767, THLB, 25: 192–93.

93. Nicolson, "Governor Francis Bernard," 41.

94. Waters Jr., *The Otis Family*, 147.

95. *JHRM*, 38, pt. 2: 299.

96. Bernard to John Pownall, Boston, 4 March 1762, BP, 2: 34; Bernard to Jackson, Castle William, 29 October 1762, BP, 2: 216; [Bernard], Memorial to the Lords Commissioners for Trade and Plantations, n.d., October 1764, BP, 10: 199–200.

97. Bernard to Lords Commissioners for Trade and Plantations, Boston, 13 April 1762, BP, 2: 58.

98. The Townshend Acts of 1767 permitted the writs to be issued by colonial courts, despite continued objections. Thomas C. Barrow, *Trade and Empire: The British Customs Service in Colonial America, 1660–1775* (Cambridge: Harvard Univ. Press, 1967), 202–3; George G. Wolkins, "Daniel Malcom and the Writs of Assistance," *Procs. MHS*, 3d ser., 58 (1924–25): 5–11, 23–25.

99. Ruth Owen Jones, "Governor Francis Bernard and His Land Acquisitions," *Historical Journal of Massachusetts* 16 (1988): 121–39, at 130–31; William O. Sawtelle, "Sir Francis Bernard and His Grant of Mount Desert," *Publications of the Colonial Society of Massachusetts* 24 (1920–22): 197–254, at 203; *JHRM*, 38, pt. 2: 282; 39: 277–79. The Kennebeck Company had already established a settlement at Fort Frankfort on the Kennebeck River, some eighty miles to the south. Gordon Kershaw, *The Kennebeck Proprietors, 1749–1775* (Somersworth, N.H.: New Hampshire Publishing Co., 1975), xv.

100. Bernard to William Bollan, Boston, 2 March 1762, BP, 2: 32.

101. *JHRM*, 38, pt. 2: 319–20.

102. Carl Bridenbaugh, *Mitre and Sceptre: Transatlantic Faiths, Ideas, Personalities and Politics* (New York: Oxford Univ. Press, 1962), 100–150.

103. See Clark, *The Language of Liberty*.

104. See Bridenbaugh, *Mitre and Sceptre*, 99–112, 207–29, 239–42; Jack M. Sosin, "Proposal for Establishing Anglican Bishops in the Colonies," *Journal of Ecclesiastical History* 13 (1962): 76–84, at 80–81.

105. Labaree, ed., *Royal Instructions*, 2: 482.

106. *BNL*, 24 December 1761.

107. Bernard to Mr. [the Rev. Edward] Bass, Boston, 21 September 1761, BP, 2: 123.

108. Bridenbaugh, *Mitre and Sceptre*, 211.

109. John E. Sexton, "Massachusetts Religious Policy with the Indians under Governor Bernard, 1760–1769," *Catholic Historical Review* 24 (1938–39): 310–28.

110. Bernard to Lords Commissioners for Trade and Plantations, Boston, 12 April 1762, BP, 2: 53; *APC*, 4: 559–60.

111. He complained of not receiving copies of the SPG's annual sermon for the first six years he was in America. Bernard to Dr. Burton, Boston, 18 August 1764, BP, 3: 248. His letter to the Archbishop of Canterbury dated Boston, 18 August 1764, was probably the first he sent Secker, BP, 3: 247.

112. The Rev. Samuel Johnson, for example, had proposed taxation to give one or two bishops annual salaries of between £300 and £500. Bridenbaugh, *Mitre and Sceptre*, 76.

113. This was typical of other proponents of the episcopate after 1750, including Secker and Joseph Butler, the Bishop of Durham. *Ibid.*, 97–98.

114. A plan for appointing a bishop to reside in America for the purposes of Ordination, and for the support of such a Bishop, n.d., BP, 12: 261–64.

115. Quoted in Bridenbaugh, *Mitre and Sceptre*, 218.

116. Mayhew to Bernard, [Boston], 18 December 1761, in Alden Bradford, *Memoirs of the Life and Writings of Rev. Jonathan Mayhew* (Boston: C. C. Little, 1838), 217–24.

117. Bernard to John Pownall, Boston, 25 April 1762, BP, 2: 183.

118. Bernard to Richard Jackson, Boston, 23 January 1763, BP, 2: 248–50.

119. Carl Van Doren, ed., *Letters and Papers of Benjamin Franklin and Richard Jackson, 1753–1785* (Philadelphia: American Philosophical Society, 1947), 1–3; *DNB*, 10: 541; Bernard to Thomas Pownall, Boston, 15 March 1766, BP, 5: 91.

120. Bernard to Jackson, Castle William, 6 July 1762, BP, 2: 194.

121. Bailyn, *Hutchinson*, 58–60.

122. Bernard to John Pownall, Boston, 25 April 1762, BP, 2: 183; Bernard to Jackson, Castle William, 6 July 1762, BP, 2: 194.

123. Bernard to Halifax, Boston, 9 January 1764, CO 5/755: 77.

124. Bernard to Amherst, Castle William, 26 September 1762, BP, 2: 280.

125. Bernard to Jackson, 7 February 1762, BP, 2: 260–61.

126. Bernard to Governor Popple, Boston, 26 March 1763, BP, 2: 296; *Pietas et Gratulatio Collegii Cantabrigiensis Apud Novanglos Bostoni, Massachusettensium* (1761; London: J. Green and J. Russell, 1762); Justin Winsor, "Pietas et Gratulatio. An Inquiry into the Authorship of the Several Pieces," Harvard Univ. Library, *Bulletin* 1 (1879), 305–8.

127. William L. Welch, "Israel Williams and the Hampshire College Project of 1761–1764," *Historical Journal of Massachusetts* 13 (1985): 53–62, esp. 58.

128. Henry Lefavour, "The Proposed College in Hampshire County in 1762," *Procs. MHS*, 3d ser., 66 (1936–41): 53–79.

129. Nicolson, "Friends of Government," 1: 153.

130. Bernard to Jackson, Boston, 2 February 1764, BP, 3: 123–24; *Procs. MHS*, 2d ser., 4 (1887–88): 61; Bernard to the archbishop of Canterbury, Boston, 18 August 1764, BP, 3: 247.

131. Bernard to Lords Commissioners for Trade and Plantations, Boston, 21 October 1762, BP, 2: 60; Apthorp Foster, "The Burning of Harvard Hall, 1764, and Its Consequences," *Publications of the Colonial Society of Massachusetts* 14 (1911–13): 2–43, at 15–16.

132. Albert Matthews, *The Portraits of Sir Francis Bernard* (Boston: Club of Odd Volumes, 1922); *Procs. MHS*, 2d ser., 4 (1887–88): 61. On student loyalties see Louis Leonard Tucker, "Centers of Sedition: Colonial Colleges and the American Revolution," *Procs. MHS*, 3d ser., 91 (1979): 16–34.

133. Bernard to Barrington, Boston, 7 June 1762, BP, 2: 193.

134. Bernard to ?, Boston, 19 January 1760, BP, 1: 296.

135. Bernard to Jackson, Boston, 21 February 1763, BP, 2: 262–63.

CHAPTER THREE

1. [Francis Bernard], *Select Letters on the Trade and Government of America; and the Principles of Law and Polity, applied to the American Colonies* (London: W. Bowyer and J. Nichols, 1774).

2. The best analyses of Bernard's reform plans are Aeilt E. Sents, "Francis Bernard and English Imperial Reconstruction" (Ph.D. diss., Columbia Univ., 1973); Jordan D. Fiore, "Governor Bernard for an American Nobility," *The Boston Public Library Quarterly* 4 (1952): 125–36; Morgan and Morgan, *Stamp Act Crisis*, 25–35.

3. Bernard to John Pownall, Boston, 11 July 1764, BP, 3: 239–40.

4. Bernard to Barrington, Boston, 17 January 1761, BP, 1: 293.

5. Bernard to John Pownall, Boston, 13 January 1760, BP, 1: 288.

6. Bernard to Jackson, Castle William, 29 October 1762, BP, 2: 216.

7. *Ibid.*; Bernard to Barrington, Boston, 17 January 1761, 293–95; Bernard to Barrington, Boston, 23 August 1760, BP, 1: 275.

8. Bernard to Jackson, Castle William, 21 May 1763, BP, 3: 66; Bernard to Bar-

rington, Boston, 15 November 1765, BP, 5: 38. It is probable, however, that Bernard profited from investments made in "consolidated Annuities" by his financial agent, the London lawyer Leverett Blackbourne. Bernard to William Bollan, Boston, 12 January 1761, BP, 1: 28.

9. Welbore Ellis to Bernard, Tulney Hall, 24 July 1760, BP, 9: 115–18.

10. Bernard to Richard Jackson, 22 October 1764, BP, 3: 258; *APC*, 4: 816–17.

11. Kershaw, *Kennebeck Proprietors*, 176–93.

12. Herbert Denio, "Massachusetts Land Grants in Vermont," *Publications of the Colonial Society of Massachusetts* 24 (1920–22): 35–59, at 38; Jones, "Bernard and His Land Acquisitions," 128–34.

13. Bernard to Lt. Gov. Colden, Boston, 1 June 1765, BP, 4: 49; Bernard to John Pownall, Boston, 6 September 1766, BP, 5: 154.

14. [Bernard], Journal of a Voyage to the Island of Mount Desert, 28 September–15 October 1762, BP, 10: 21–27; [Bernard], Proposals for a Fishery at Mount Desert, 5 October 1764, BP, 10: 207–15; [Bernard], Proposals for Settling a Town in Mount Desert, October 1764, BP, 10: 220–21; [Bernard], Proposals for Settling Mount Desert, October 1764, BP, 10: 222–23; [Bernard], Proposals for Settling a Colony of Germans at a Town in the Island of Mount Desert made to John Martin Shaffer and John Mort, 8 September 1764, BP, 10: 228.

15. Bernard to Thomas Pownall, Castle William, 28 August 1767, BP, 6: 38.

16. Bernard to William Fitzherbert, Boston, 13 August 1763, BP, 3: 97–98; Bernard to Lords Commissioners for Trade and Plantations, Boston, 13 August 1763, [draft] BP, 3: 85–87; Bernard to Thomas Pownall, Castle William, 28 August 1767, BP, 6: 37; Bernard to Peter Templeman, Castle William, 28 August 1767, BP, 6: 38–40.

17. A State[ment] of the Grant of the Island of Mount Desert to Francis Bernard, n.p., [October 1764?], BP, 10: 216–19.

18. Bernard to John Pownall, Boston, 4 March 1762, BP, 2: 33; Bernard to John Pownall, Castle William, 31 October 1762, BP, 2: 214–15; Bernard to John Pownall, Boston, 8 April 1763, BP, 2: 265–66.

19. Lords Commissioners for Trade and Plantations to Bernard, Whitehall, 24 December 1762, BP, 10: 41; Extract from the Minutes of Proceedings from the Lords Commissioners for Trade, 2 December 1762, BP, 10: 37–39; Bernard to John Pownall, Boston, 17 April 1763, BP, 3: 49–50.

20. Bernard to Jackson, Castle William, 6 July 1762, BP, 2: 194; Michael Kammen, *A Rope of Sand: The Colonial Agents, British Politics and the American Revolution* (Ithaca, N.Y.: Cornell Univ. Press, 1968), 32–33.

21. Bernard to Jackson, Boston, 23 January 1763, BP, 2: 248–53.

22. [Bernard], A State of the Facts upon which the Massachusetts Title to the Lands between the Penobscot and St Croix depends, April 1763, [draft], BP, 10: 83–88; [Bernard], Description & Boundaries of six townships in Sagadahock, February 1763, BP, 10: 97; [Bernard], The Boundary Lines of seven townships East of Mount Desert or Union River, February 1763, BP, 10: 109; [Bernard], An Enquiry into the Origin of the Terms Acadia & Nova Scotia and the use thereof, April 1763, [draft], BP, 10: 91–94; Copy of the Records of the Establishing Possession by Gov. Pownall in behalf of the Province of Massachusetts Bay, to the lands east of the Penobscot, 23 May 1759, BP, 10: 89–90.

23. "A Brief State of the Title of the Province of Massachusetts Bay to the Country between the Rivers Kennebeck and St. Croix," [1763], appendix to *JHRM*, 39: i–xix.

24. The Lords Commissioners for Trade and Plantations to Bernard Whitehall,

11 March 1763, BP, 10: 63–65; Sawtelle, "Bernard and Mount Desert," 230–31; *JBT*, 12: 57.

25. Sawtelle, "Bernard and Mount Desert," 236–37.

26. Bernard to Barrington, Boston, 20 October 1764, BP, 3: 254–56.

27. Bernard to John Pownall, Boston, 19 October 1764, BP, 3: 250; Sawtelle, "Bernard and Mount Desert," 244–45.

28. Bernard to Halifax, Perth Amboy, 24 August 1758, BP, 1: 143.

29. Lords Commissioners for Trade and Plantations to Bernard, Whitehall, 28 April 1761, BP, 9: 194–95.

30. Bernard named twenty-six of them, some of them after places and people important in his own life, such as Great Barrington, Tyringham, Shutesbury, and Winchendon. *Procs. MHS*, 1st ser., 12 (1871–73): 271, and 2d ser., 5 (1889–90): 167.

31. Bernard to Lords Commissioners for Trade and Plantations, Boston, 3 August 1761, BP, 2: 41–43. The Privy Council doubted whether the Crown had any right to suspend the incorporation of new towns, and by February 1762 the clause in his instructions reserving to the king the right to forbid new towns from electing a representative had been withdrawn. *APC*, 4: 475–76; *JHRM*, 38, pt. 2: 272.

32. Bernard to John Pownall, Boston, 5 December 1762, BP, 2: 234; Bernard to Richard Jackson, Boston, 6 December 1762, BP, 2: 238; Bernard to Jackson, Castle William, 21 May 1763, BP, 3: 68; Bernard to Halifax, Boston, 15 June 1763, BP, 3: 81; Morgan and Morgan, *Stamp Act Crisis*, 26, 364.

33. See, for example, Bernard to John Pownall, Boston, 16 December 1766, BP, 5: 178; Bernard to Lords Commissioners for Trade and Plantations, Boston, 7 July 1766, BP, 4: 236.

34. Henretta, *"Salutary Neglect,"* 241.

35. Bernard to Jackson, Boston, 6 January 1763, BP, 2: 245.

36. Bernard to John Pownall, Boston, 12 September 1763, BP, 3: 98.

37. See Anthony Bruce, *The Purchase System in the British Army, 1660–1871* (London: Royal Historical Society, 1980), 32–40.

38. Barrington to Bernard, London, 23 February 1764, BP, 10: 163.

39. Bernard to Shelburne, Boston, 25 July 1763, BP, 3: 84–85; L. J. Bellot, *William Knox: The Life and Thought of an Eighteenth-Century Imperialist* (Austin: University of Texas Press, 1977), 46–47.

40. Bernard to Welbore Ellis, Boston, 25 November 1763, BP, 3: 108.

41. Franklin B. Wickwire, "John Pownall and British Colonial Policy," *WMQ* 20 (1963): 543–54.

42. Hutchinson to Nathaniel Rogers, Milton, 31 May 1768, THLB, 25: 259.

43. Tyler, *Smugglers & Patriots*, 15–17, 69–71; Ian R. Christie and Benjamin W. Labaree, *Empire or Independence, 1760–1776: A British-American Dialogue on the Coming of the American Revolution* (Oxford: Phaidon Press, 1976), 27–28; Morgan and Morgan, *Stamp Act Crisis*, 36.

44. Bernard to Barrington, Boston, 10 August 1761, BP, 2: 4. On the trade laws see Barrow, *Trade and Empire*, 178–80, 186; Oliver M. Dickerson, *The Navigation Acts and the American Revolution* (New York: Octagon Books, 1974), 84–85.

45. Lords Commissioners for Trade and Plantations to Bernard, Whitehall, 11 October 1763, BP, 10: 131–32.

46. *BEP*, 26 September 1768 and 4 December 1769; House of Lords Record Office, Main Papers, 3 February 1766: Henry Hulton, Plantation Clerk, A List of the Officers of the Customs in North America, [London], 28 January 1766; A List of Civil Officers employed in North America whose Appointment arises at the Treasury, Treasury Chambers, 31 January 1766.

47. *APC*, 4: 560–61; Egremont to Bernard, Whitehall, 9 July 1763, BP, 10, 119–23;

Dora Mae Clark, *The Rise of the British Treasury: Colonial Administration of the Eighteenth Century* (Newton Abbot, Devon: David & Charles, 1960), 134.

48. Bernard to Jackson, Castle William, 26 July 1763, BP, 3: 82–84.

49. Tyler, *Smugglers & Patriots*, 64–74; Gipson, *The British Empire*, 10: 212, 217–19, 225; Jack M. Sosin, *Agents and Merchants: British Colonial Policy and the Origins of the American Revolution, 1763–1775* (Lincoln, Nebr.: University of Nebraska Press, 1965), 45.

50. Bernard to Jackson, Boston, 3 August 1763, BP, 3: 93–94.

51. Bernard, "Answers to Queries," 5 September 1763, BP, 13: 18.

52. Bernard to Lords Commissioners for Trade and Plantations, Boston, 26 November 1763, BP, 2: 90.

53. Bernard to Jackson, Boston, 7 January 1764, BP, 3: 120.

54. Gipson, *The British Empire*, 10: 217–30; Tyler, *Smugglers & Patriots*, 65–107; Barrow, *Trade and Empire*, 180–85; Carl Ubbelohde, *The Vice-Admiralty Courts and the American Revolution* (Chapel Hill: University of North Carolina Press, 1960), 5, 15, 48–50.

55. Bernard to Jackson, Boston, 3 August 1763, BP, 3: 93–94.

56. Bernard to Lord Colville, Boston, 21 February 1764, BP, 3: 27–29; Bernard to Colville, Boston, 25 April 1764, BP, 3: 39–40.

57. Bernard to John Pownall, 29 December 1763, BP, 3: 119–20; Bernard to Jackson, Boston, 13 February 1764, BP, 3: 131.

58. Bernard to Halifax, Boston, 18 February 1764, BP, 3: 141–43; Bernard to Halifax, Boston, 10 April 1763, BP, 3: 148–51; Bernard to Halifax, Boston, 9 July 1764, BP, 3: 159–61.

59. Lords Commissioners for Trade and Plantations to Bernard, Whitehall, 13 July 1764, BP, 10: 179; Temple to Lords Commissioners for Trade and Plantations, Boston, 14 June 1769, John Temple to Commissioners of Customs, CCT, MHS.

60. Tyler, *Smugglers & Patriots*, 36.

61. Bernard to John Pownall, Boston, 10 February 1764, BP, 3: 129.

62. During the Barons affair he was said to have amassed the improbably large sum of £20,000 from his alliance with Paxton. Bernard to Thomas Lechmere, Province House, 2 June 1761, BP, 2: 113.

63. Hutchinson, *History of Massachusetts*, 3: 117–18; Hutchinson to Jackson, Boston, 5 May 1765, THLB, 26: 138.

64. Bernard to Barrington, Boston, 15 November 1765, BP, 5: 38.

65. Bernard, Memorial to the earl of Shelburne, n.d., CO 5/756: 65–70.

66. [Henry Hulton], Some Account of the Proceedings of the People of New England from the Establishment of the Board of Customs in America to the breaking out of the Rebellion in 1775, [post 1783], Andre de Coppet Collection, Manuscript Division, Department of Rare Books & Special Collections, Princeton University Library, 116.

67. Temple to the Board of Customs, Boston, 1 January 1762, Establishment of the Northern District, 1: 10–12, CCT. Merchants convicted of illicit trading could forfeit both their vessel and cargo, and be fined up to three times the total value of the property seized. Prosecutions could be brought against their property (*in rem*) or their person (*in personam*). Shipowners would usually try to "compound" with the Crown, by which they reached a financial settlement before the case came to trial: the vessel would normally be returned and the owner asked to pay a much smaller fine of around one-third the value of the property seized, together with a nominal sum to cover trade duties. Zobel, *Boston Massacre*, 21.

68. Thomas, "Partisan Politics," 1: 125–31, 135–42.

69. Morgan and Morgan, *Stamp Act Crisis*, 135.

70. Bernard to John Pownall, Boston, 2 August 1764, BP, 3: 244.

71. The final copy of Mauduit's instructions are not extant, but a draft letter is in *JHRM*, 41: 54, 72–77. See Morgan and Morgan, *Stamp Act Crisis*, 53, 140; Bernhard Knollenberg, *Origin of the American Revolution, 1759–1766* (1960; New York: Free Press, 1961), 173–74, 184; Thomas "Partisan Politics," 1: 143–45.

72. Bernard to Barrington, Castle William, 23 June 1764, BP, 3: 235–36; Bernard to Barrington, Castle William, 22? July 1764, BP, 3: 236–37.

73. Anthony Pagden, *Lords of All the World: Ideologies of Empire in Spain, Britain, and France, c.1500–c.1800* (New Haven and London: Yale University Press, 1997), 13, 131–32, 137.

74. See Edward Channing and Archibald Cary Coolidge, eds., *The Barrington-Bernard Correspondence and Illustrative Matter, 1760–1770*, Harvard Historical Studies Series, vol. 17, 1912 (Reprint, New York: DaCapo Press, 1970), 95–102; Bernard, *Life of Bernard*, 44–48; Sents, "Bernard and Imperial Reconstruction," 73, 75, 88–89, 96, 109–11, 119–201.

75. For example, Boston to Dennis DeBerdt, Boston, 21 December 1765, Massachusetts Papers, MHS; Samuel White, Speaker, to Dennis DeBerdt, Boston, 7 November 1765, *ibid*.

76. Bailyn, *Hutchinson*, 62–63; Edmund S. Morgan, "Thomas Hutchinson and the Stamp Act," *New England Quarterly* 21 (1948): 459–92, at 463–67; Waters Jr., *The Otis Family*, 152–53.

77. See also Bernard to John Pownall, Boston, 11 July 1764, BP, 3: 239–40.

78. Bernard to [Barrington], Boston, 23 December 1768, BP, 7: 257–58.

79. For an overview see Charles F. Mullet, "English Imperial Thinking, 1764–1783," *Political Science Quarterly* 55 (1930): 548–79.

80. Bernard to Thomas Pownall, Boston, 15 March 1766, BP, 5: 93.

81. [Joseph Galloway], *A Candid Examination of the Mutual Claims of Great-Britain and the Colonies: with a Plan of Accommodation on Constitutional Principles* (1775; London, 1780), 65–70. Galloway's subsequent plans, which he submitted to British ministers, were less sympathetic to the Americans and included a proposal for a bicameral legislature with an upper chamber appointed by the Crown. Julian P. Boyd, *Anglo-American Union: Joseph Galloway's Plans to Preserve the British Empire, 1774–1788* (Philadelphia: University of Pennsylvania Press, 1941), 158–77.

82. Bernard to Barrington, Boston, 23 November 1765, BP, 5: 47–51; Bernard to John Pownall, Boston, 11 December 1765, BP, 5: 57.

83. Greene, *Peripheries and Center*, 14, 33, 64, 207; J. P. Reid, *In a Defiant Stance: The Conditions of Law in Massachusetts Bay, the Irish Comparison, and the Coming of the American Revolution* (University Park, Penn.: Pennsylvania State Univ. Press, 1977), 2, 15–16.

84. Thomas Pownall, *The Administration of the Colonies*, 4th ed. (London: J. Walter, 1768), vi, 85.

85. Pownall to Cooper, 25 February 1769, quoted in Mullet, "English Imperial Thinking," at 552n17.

86. Bernard to John Pownall, Boston, 30 October 1768, BP, 6: 153; Bernard to Barrington, Boston, 22 October 1768, BP, 6: 161; Hillsborough to Bernard, Whitehall, 15 November 1768, BP, 12: 16; Barrington to Bernard, London, 2 January 1769, BP, 12: 33.

87. Barrington to Bernard, Beckett, 7 September 1764, BP, 10: 187.

88. Bernard to Jackson, Boston, 9 July 1764, BP, 3: 237; Bernard to John Pownall, Boston, 11 July 1764, BP, 3: 239–40.

89. Bernard to John Pownall, Boston, 11 July 1764, 239–40.

90. Bernard to Jackson, Boston, 22 October 1764, BP, 3: 257; Bernard to Jackson, 24 November 1764, BP, 3: 264–65.

91. John L. Bullion, *A Great and Necessary Measure: George Grenville and the Genesis of the Stamp Act, 1763–1765* (Columbia, Mo.: University of Missouri Press, 1982), 180, 205; Morgan and Morgan, *Stamp Act Crisis*, 79–80, 84.

92. Bernard to Richard Jackson, Boston, 16 August 1764, BP, 3: 248–49.

93. Morgan and Morgan, *Stamp Act Crisis*, 83–84; Bernard to Lords Commissioners for Trade and Plantations, Boston, 16 August 1764, BP, 3: 165–68; Bernard to Lords Commissioners for Trade and Plantations, Boston, 27 October 1764, BP, 3: 179. See Gipson, *The British Empire*, 10: 265; Morgan and Morgan, *Stamp Act Crisis*, 83.

94. Bernard to Jackson, Boston, 17 November 1764, BP, 3: 260.

95. Temple to the Board of Customs Commissioners, Boston, 10 September 1764, Establishment of the Northern District, 1: 52.

96. Bernard to Temple, Castle William, 29 September 1764, BP, 3: 43.

97. John Temple to the Board of Customs Commissioners, Boston, 3 October 1764, in folder containing typescripts of original manuscripts. "Mr. Cockle's Suspension, with the whole of his, and Governor Bernard's proceedings relating to the Anguilla Forgeries . . . Copied from the Original Letters and Depositions; now in the Possession of Mr. Temple the Surveyor General, 1764," 1–4, CCT.

98. In May, Cockle had demanded payment of £150 in duties for a cargo of sugar that the *Gloucester* had imported from Guadeloupe. He probably did not know that when Britain returned the island to France, in accordance with the Treaty of Paris, the British merchants who remained were allowed to export sugar to American ports duty-free. Although he realized his error, Cockle threatened to prosecute the merchants if they complained about his retention of £50 from the sum of money he was obliged to return to them.

99. Pierce, "Extracts from the Diary of John Rowe," 60.

100. Board of Customs Commissioners to Temple, London, 30 October 1764, Commissioners of Customs to the Surveyor-General, 4, CCT.

101. "Mr. Cockle's Suspension," 37.

102. John Temple to the Board of Customs Commissioners, Boston, 3 October 1764, "Mr. Cockle's Suspension," 1–4. See also Temple to the Board of Customs Commissioners, Boston, 3 October 1764, Establishment of the Northern District, 1: 60; Temple to Jackson, Boston, 5 December 1764, Establishment of the Northern District, 2: 88.

103. Temple to Jackson, Boston, 3 October 1764, Establishment of the Northern District, 1: 70; Temple to Jackson, Boston, 5 December 1764, Establishment of the Northern District, 2: 89.

104. Jordan D. Fiore, "The Temple-Bernard Affair," *Historical Collections of the Essex Institute* 90 (1954): 58–83.

105. Hutchinson, *History of Massachusetts*, 3: 117–18; Hutchinson to Jackson, Boston, 5 May 1765, THLB, 26: 138.

106. The Answer of James Cockle to the Surveyor-General John Temple, Boston, 24 November 1764, "Mr. Cockle's Suspension," 31–34.

107. Case, with the Opinion of the Advocate-General and the Attorney General thereon, [Boston], 8 December 1764, CO 5/755: 195–99.

108. Board of Customs Commissioners to John Temple, London, 4 September 1764, Commissioners of Customs to the Surveyor-General, 1; John Temple to the Judge of the [Vice] Admiralty [court], Boston, 14 September 1764, CO 5/755: 191.

109. Temple to Grenville, Boston, 9 December 1764, Establishment of the Northern District, 2: 92.

110. Bernard to Jackson, Boston, 27 July 1767, BP, 6: 32; Bernard to Jackson, Boston, 30 November 1764, BP, 3: 267.

111. James Cockle, Deposition, 3 September 1764, "Mr. Cockle's Suspension," 5.

112. Temple to the Board of Customs Commissioners, Boston, 1 January 1762, Establishment of the Northern District, 1: 10–12.

113. Bernard to Jackson, Boston, 30 November 1764, BP, 3: 267; Bernard to Jackson, Boston, 18 January 1766, BP, 5: 75–76.

114. Bernard to James Cockle, Boston, 8 July 1769, BP, 8: 2.

115. Board of Customs Commissioners to Temple, London, 9 March 1765, Commissioners of Customs to the Surveyor-General, 5.

116. John Temple to Thomas Whately, Boston, 17 May 1765, quoted in "The Missing Temple-Whately Letters," ed. Neil R. Stout, *Procs. MHS*, 3d ser., 104 (1992): 124–39, at 141.

117. Bernard to John Pownall, Boston, 11 July 1764, BP, 3: 239–40.

118. *JHRM*, 41: 11; Bernard to Halifax, Boston, 10 November 1764, BP, 3: 189.

119. Bernard to Richard Jackson, 17 November 1764, BP, 3: 262.

120. Tyler, *Smugglers & Patriots*, 85–86; Bailyn, *Hutchinson*, 64–65. A copy of the petition is in Alden Bradford, ed., *Speeches of the Governors of Massachusetts 1765–1775* (1818; New York: Da Capo Press, 1971), 21–23.

121. Bernard to Jackson, 17 November 1764, 261–63; Bernard to Halifax, Boston, 10 November 1764, BP, 3: 178–79; Bernard to the earl of Halifax, Boston, 17 November 1764, BP, 3: 263; Bernard to Halifax, Boston, 12 November 1764, CO 5/755: 143.

122. *BNL*, 17 January 1765.

123. Bernard to Thomas Pownall, 15 March 1765, BP, 5: 91–92; Knollenberg, *Origin of the American Revolution*, 187.

124. Bernard to Jackson, Boston, 25 January 1765, BP, 3: 279–81; Bernard to John Pownall, Boston, 26 January 1765, BP, 3: 273.

125. Bernard to Jackson, Boston, 6 February 1765, BP, 3: 274; Bernard to Thomas Pownall, Boston, 15 March 1766, BP, 5: 91–93; *JHRM*, 41: 203, 216–25, 293.

126. Bernard to Richard Jackson, Boston, 25 January 1765, 279–81; *JHRM*, 41: 293.

127. Sosin, *Agents and Merchants*, 58–59.

128. Arthur Savage to Samuel P. Savage, London, 12 January 1765, Samuel P. Savage II Collection, MHS.

129. *APC*, 4: 692–93; *JBT*, 12: 122.

130. Clark, *Rise of British Treasury*, 116, 121, 137; Ubbelohde, *Vice-Admiralty Courts*, 57–60.

131. Bernard to John Pownall, Boston, 6 May 1765, BP, 3: 289; *JHRM*, 41: 54, 72–77. On Otis see Morgan and Morgan, *Stamp Act Crisis*, 53, 140; Ellen E. Brennan, "James Otis: Recreant and Patriot," *New England Quarterly* 12 (1939): 691–725.

132. James Otis Jr., *The Rights of the British Colonies Asserted and Proved* (Boston, 1764), 13, quoted in Waters Jr., *The Otis Family*, 111.

CHAPTER FOUR

1. Bernard never received a copy of the Stamp Act, though he was fully aware of its provisions from reports in the province newspapers. *MG*, 8 April 1765; Morgan and Morgan, *Stamp Act Crisis*, 136.

2. "The Colonists' Advocate," *Public Advertiser*, 12 February 1770, *Papers of Benjamin Franklin*, 17: 68.

3. *DAJA*, 1: 271.

4. Fowler Jr., *Samuel Adams*, xi, 53.

5. John Philip Reid, *Constitutional History of the American Revolution*, vol. 3, *The*

Authority to Legislate (Madison, Wisc.: University of Wisconsin Press, 1991), 12, Bernard at 35. See also Maier, *From Resistance to Revolution*, 198–227.

6. Nash, *Urban Crucible*, 271–82; Warden, *Boston*, 128–58; Richard D. Brown, *Revolutionary Politics in Massachusetts: The Boston Committee of Correspondence and the Towns, 1772–1774* (Cambridge: Harvard Univ. Press, 1970), 26–28, 158–218.

7. "Tacitus" [James Otis Jr.], *BGCJ*, 16 November 1767; "Philalethes," *BGCJ*, 11 May 1767. On political orthodoxy see Patterson, *Political Parties*, 55, and Zuckerman, *Peaceable Kingdoms*, 247.

8. *DAJA*, 1: 294–95, 299, 309; the Rev. Henry Caner to Archbishop Thomas Secker, Boston, 15 May 1766, *Letterbook of the Rev. Henry Caner*, ed. Kenneth Cameron (Hartford, Conn.: Transcendental Books, 1972), 126; James Murray to John Murray, Boston, 13 November 1765, *Letters of James Murray*, ed. Nina M. Tiffany and Susan I. Lesley (Boston: n.p., 1901), 154.

9. Extracts of [Thomas Whately], *The Regulations lately Made concerning the colonies and the Taxations imposed upon them* (London: J. Wilkie, 1765), were printed in *MG, Supplement*, 11 April 1765, on the authority of Bernard and the Council.

10. Nicolson, "Governor Francis Bernard," 33, 62; Nicolson, "The Friends of Government," 1: 42–44, 52–70, 89–91.

11. Saltonstall in *BGHU*, 13: 125–30, and Robert Moody, ed., "The Saltonstall Papers, 1607–1815," *Collections of the Massachusetts Historical Society* 80 (1912): 87–89; Williams in *BGHU*, 8: 301–33; Murray in Jones, *Loyalists of Massachusetts*, 216–17.

12. *DAJA*, 1: 83, 107; Ruggles in *BGHU*, 9: 199–200.

13. Thomas, "Partisan Politics in Massachusetts," 1: 170–72; Copy of the Votes & Resolutions, from 5–25 June 1765 of the House of Representatives of the Province of Massachusetts Bay with respect to the Act for levying a Stamp duty and to other Acts of the Parliament of Great Britain, BP, 10: 312–15.

14. Thomas, *British Politics and the Stamp Act Crisis*, 134.

15. Bernard to Conway, Boston, 19 December 1765, BP, 4: 181–82.

16. Fewer than thirty Bostonians who held municipal office between 1758 and 1775 became Loyalists, and of these only three had any real influence as friends of government. Nicolson, "The Friends of Government," 1: 55–57.

17. "A Puritan" [Samuel Adams], *BGCJ*, 18 April 1768.

18. Caner to [Bishop Richard Terrick], Boston, 15 May 1766, Fulham Papers, American Colonial Section 6 (Massachusetts), Lambeth Palace Library: 60.

19. Adair and Schutz, eds., *Peter Oliver's Origin & Progress*, 42–44, 51.

20. Appendix 1 to Nicolson, "Governor Francis Bernard," 63–107.

21. Bruce E. Steiner, "New England Anglicanism: A Genteel Faith?" *WMQ* 27 (1970): 122–35.

22. Arthur Savage to Samuel P. Savage, London, 1 March 1765, S. P. Savage II Collections.

23. Henry Barnes to Bishop Richard Terrick, Marlborough, 25 September 1769, Fulham Papers, American Colonial Section 6: 72–73; Nicolson, " 'McIntosh, Otis & Adams are our demagogues,' " 90–91.

24. Pencak, *War, Politics & Revolution*, 214–15.

25. Nicolson, "Governor Francis Bernard," 37; Nicolson, " 'McIntosh, Otis & Adams are our demagogues,' " 79.

26. Bernard to Richard Jackson, Boston, 5 June 1765, BP, 4: 5.

27. Bernard to Halifax, Castle William, 15 August 1765, BP, 4: 137.

28. Accounts of the Stamp Act riots are in Dirk Hoerder, *Crowd Action in Revolutionary Massachusetts, 1765–1780* (London: Academic Press, 1977), 40–84, 97–105, 117, 185–206; Nash, *Urban Crucible*, 293–97; Morgan and Morgan, *Stamp Act Crisis*, 163–67; *BGCJ*, Supplement, 19 August 1765. In addition to the sources cited below,

Bernard's accounts of the riots can also be found in his letters to the Lords Commissioners for Trade and Plantations of 15–31 August 1765, which were later presented to Parliament, *PHE*, 16: 126–31.

29. Bernard to Halifax, Castle William, 15 August 1765, BP, 4: 137.

30. *Ibid.*, 137–40; Malcolm Freiberg, "An Unknown Stamp Act Letter," *Procs. MHS*, 3d ser., 78 (1966): 138–42, at 141.

31. Bernard to Halifax, Castle William, 16 August 1765, BP, 4: 142–43.

32. Bernard to Halifax, Castle William, 15 August 1765, 137.

33. Hoerder, *Crowd Action*, 110; Hutchinson, *History of Massachusetts*, 3: 125.

34. Bernard to Halifax, Castle William, 31 August 1765, BP, 4: 149–52; Bailyn, *Hutchinson*, 35–36.

35. Bernard to Halifax, Castle William, 16 August 1765.

36. Bernard to Halifax, Castle William, 31 August 1765; Kershaw, *Kennebeck Proprietors*, 261–62; Tyler, *Smugglers & Patriots*, 61–62.

37. Zobel, *Boston Massacre*, 37.

38. *DAJA*, 1: 260–61; Hoerder, *Crowd Action*, 102; Thomas, "Partisan Politics," 1: 194–95.

39. Pencak, *War, Politics & Revolution*, 191.

40. Nash, *Urban Crucible*, 296–97.

41. Bernard to Halifax, Boston, 31 August 1765, 152.

42. Bernard to Halifax, Castle William, 16 August 1765.

43. *Ibid.*

44. Bernard to John Pownall, Castle William, 18 August 1765, BP, 4: 12–13; Reid, *In a Rebellious Spirit*.

45. Mass. Council Records, 16: 39.

46. Bernard to Halifax, Castle William, 31 August 1765, 156.

47. Bernard to the Lords Commissioners for Trade and Plantations, Boston, 17 October 1765, BP, 5: 166.

48. Mass. Council Records, 16: 38; Bernard to Halifax, Castle William, 31 August 1765, 149–52; Thomas, "Partisan Politics," 1: 190–91; Nicolson, "Friends of Government," 1: 63–70.

49. Bernard to General Thomas Gage, Castle William, 27 August 1765, BP, 4: 62; Bernard to Lord Colville, Castle William, 27 August 1765, BP, 4: 64–65.

50. Gage to Conway, New York, 23 September 1765, *The Correspondence of General Thomas Gage and the Secretaries of State, 1763–1775*, 2 vols. ed. Clarence E. Carter (New Haven: Yale University Press, 1931–33), 1: 68.

51. Gage to Bernard, New York, 6 September 1765, BP, 10: 285.

52. Mass. Council Records, 16: 32–33, 50–51.

53. Bernard to Saltonstall, Castle William, 26 August 1765, BP, 4: 67; Bernard to Halifax, Castle William, 7 September 1765, BP, 4: 158–61; Bernard to Conway, Boston, 28 September 1765, BP, 4: 162; Mass. Council Records, 16: 40–43, 46–51; Jones, *Loyalists of Massachusetts*, 254; Moody, "The Saltonstall Papers, 1607–1815," 87–89.

54. Bernard to Halifax, Castle William, 7 September 1765, 159; Bernard to Saltonstall, Province House, 11 September 1765, BP, 4: 68.

55. John Stevenson, *Popular Disturbances in England, 1700–1870* (London and New York: Longman, 1979), 5–6, 9, 13, 76–90; F. W. Maitland, *The Constitutional History of England* (Cambridge: Cambridge Univ. Press, 1909), 228–29.

56. CO 5/755: 275.

57. CO 5/755: 305.

58. *DLTH*, 1: 71.

59. Nicolson, " 'McIntosh, Otis & Adams are our demagogues,' " 80–81.

60. Hoerder, *Crowd Action*, 107–13; Bernard to the Lords Commissioners for

Trade and Plantations, Boston, 12 October 1765, BP, 4: 10; Reid, *In a Rebellious Spirit*, 18–19; Bernard to John Pownall, Boston, 19 October 1765, BP, 5: 10.

61. Bernard to Halifax, Castle William, 31 August 1765, 157–58.

62. Bernard, Commission to Major Jeremiah Green, n.p., 2 September 1765, Samuel A. Green Papers, MHS.

63. Bernard to Halifax, 7 September 1765, Castle William, 158.

64. Bernard to Halifax, Castle William, 31 August 1765, 156.

65. Bernard to Halifax, Castle William, 7 September 1765, 160.

66. Bernard to General Gage, Boston, 12 September 1765, BP, 4: 69–70.

67. Bernard to Halifax, Castle William, 31 August 1765, 155–56.

68. Bernard to Halifax, Castle William, 7 September 1765, 161; *BTR*, 16: 155–56.

69. Bernard to Halifax, Castle William, 7 September 1765, 161; Bernard to Conway, Boston, 28 September 1765, 163.

70. Bernard to Halifax, Castle William, 7 September 1765, 161; Bernard to Jackson, Boston, 10 September 1765, BP, 5: 2.

71. A copy of Bernard's speech and other documentation concerning the General Court that ministers received are in CO 5/755: 335–80.

72. *JHRM*, 42: 118–23.

73. Bernard to Conway, Boston, 28 September 1765, BP, 4: 163.

74. Bernard to Conway, Boston, 28 September 1765, 163–64; *BEP*, 30 September 1765 in CO 5/755: 349–52; "The Book of America," Albert Matthews ed. *Procs. MHS*, 3d. ser., 62 (1928–29): 171–97, Bernard at 189–91; Bruce Ingham Granger, *Political Satire in the American Revolution, 1763–1783* (Ithaca, N.Y.: Cornell Univ. Press, 1960), 34–36.

75. Mayhew quoted in Bradford, *Memoir of Mayhew*, 419; "Humphrey Ploughjogger" [John Adams], *BGCJ*, 14 October 1765.

76. *JHRM*, 42: 138–39.

77. See Nicolson, "The Friends of Government," 1: 69–70.

78. *JHRM*, 42: 143–59.

79. Bernard to the Lords Commissioners for Trade and Plantations, Boston, 30 November 1765, BP, 4: 179; *BEP*, 28 October 1765; *BGCJ*, 14 October 1765; *BGCJ Supplement*, 4 November 1765; Hoerder, *Crowd Action*, 91.

80. *JHRM*, 42: 131–39.

81. Bernard to John Pownall, Castle William, 1 November 1765, BP, 5: 17.

82. Bernard to Lord Colville, Boston, 30 October 1765, BP, 4: 78–79.

83. Bernard to Ruggles, Boston, 28 September 1765, BP, 4: 72; C. A. Weslager, *The Stamp Act Congress: with an Exact Copy of the Complete Journal* (Newark: University of Delaware Press, [1976]), 144, 148–52, 204–14; *JHRM*, 42: 254, 271–72, 294; Ruggles in *BGCJ*, 5 May 1766; "Remarks on Brigadier Ruggles's reasons for his dissent from the resolution of the Congress at New York," *BGCJ*, 12 May 1766.

84. Hutchinson, *History of Massachusetts*, 3: 325.

85. William Franklin to Benjamin Franklin, Burlington, 7 September 1765, *Papers of Benjamin Franklin*, 12: 367–69; Morgan and Morgan, *Stamp Act Crisis*, ch. 8.

86. Thomas, "Partisan Politics," 1: 219–22; Shaw, *American Patriots*, 184–85.

87. Francis D. Cogliano, *No King, No Popery: Anti-Catholicism in Revolutionary New England* (Westport, Conn.: Greenwood Press, 1995), 24–39.

88. Bernard to John Pownall, Castle William, 1 November 1765, BP, 5: 18–20.

89. Ibid., 21.

90. Bernard to John Pownall, Castle William, 5 November 1765, BP, 5: 21.

91. Kershaw, *The Kennebeck Proprietors*, 50–51.

92. Bernard to Lords Commissioners for Trade and Plantations, Boston, 17 October 1765, BP, 4: 167–69; *BNL*, 17 October 1765.

93. Bernard to John Pownall, Castle William, 5 November 1765, 21.

94. See Thomas Hutchinson to Francis Bernard, Boston, 27 October 1769, THLB, 26: 395–96; Thomas Hutchinson to Francis Bernard, Boston, 4 August 1770, THLB, 25: 530–31.

95. *DAJA*, 1: 271; Jones, *Loyalists of Massachusetts*, 151–52; Louis L. Tucker, ed., "Memoir of Dr. Jonathan Mayhew by Harrison Gray," *Proceedings of the Bostonian Society* 80 (1961): 28–48; "Letters of Harrison Gray and Harrison Gray Jr., of Massachusetts," *Virginia Magazine of History and Biography* 8 (1901): 225–36; Tyler, *Smugglers & Patriots*, 215.

96. Mass. Council Records, 16: 39, 50–51.

97. Bernard to John Pownall, Boston, 26 November 1765, BP, 5: 43–44.

98. Bernard to John Pownall, Castle William, 5 November 1765, 21.

99. *JHRM*, 42: 170.

100. Mass. Council Records, 16: 76–79; Bernard to Conway, Boston, 21 December 1765, BP, 5: 66–68.

101. Thomas Hutchinson to Thomas Pownall, n.p., 8 March 1766, THLB, 26: 207–14.

102. Bernard to Messrs. Sheaffe, Hallowell and Waldo, Province House, 31 October and 16 November 1765, BP, 4:80.

103. *JHRM*, 42: 186–89.

104. *DAJA*, 1: 266–69; 3: 284; Mass. Council Records, 16: 76–79; Bernard to Conway, Boston, 21 December 1765, 66–68; *BTR*, 16: 159.

105. *BGCJ*, 6 January 1766. Also "Freeborn Armstrong" [James Otis Jr.], *BGCJ*, 3 February 1766.

106. Grey Cooper to Bernard, London, 8 October 1765, BP, 10: 304.

107. Morgan and Morgan, *Stamp Act Crisis*, 180–81.

108. Bernard to Conway, 18 December 1765, BP, 4: 183; Andrew Oliver to Bernard, Boston, 17 December 1765, CO 5/755: 415–20; Oliver to Bernard, Boston, 19 December 1765, CO 5/755: 421.

109. Twenty-nine future friends of government belonged to the BSETC and no evidence exists for 1764 and 1765 that they were in conflict with Whig members. The Boston Society for Encouraging Trade and Commerce, Membership List, [Boston, c. 1763], Ezekiel Price Papers, 293–94, MHS. It is logical to assume that friends of government were among the 250 subscribers to the agreement (around three-quarters of Boston's traders). The names of the signatories are unknown. Appendix A in Nicolson, "Governor Francis Bernard," 63–107; Tyler, *Smugglers & Patriots*, 66, 71–73.

110. *DAJA*, 1: 290.

111. Priscilla Lord Sawyer and Virginia Clegg Gamage, *Marblehead: The Spirit of '76 Lives Here* (Philadelphia: Chilton Book Co, [1971, c. 1972]), 104–5.

112. Gertrude E. Meredith, *The Descendants of Hugh Amory, 1605–1805* (London: n.p., 1901), 120–54.

113. *DAJA*, 1: 294–95, 309; Thomas Boylston, Petition to the General Court and Governor, [Boston], 29 May 1765, Massachusetts Papers, 1; Thomas Boylston, Petition to the General Court and Governor, [Boston], 3 November 1766, *JHRM*, 42: 21–22, 60, 70; 43, pt. 1: 183; Bradford, ed., *Speeches of the Governors*, 31–32; Bernard to Lord Colville, Boston, 30 September 1765, BP, 4: 73; Samuel Adams to Dennis DeBerdt, n.p., 15 November 1766, *The Writings of Samuel Adams*, 4 vols. ed. Harry Alonzo Cushing (New York: G. P. Putnam, 1904–1908), 1: 99; *BTR*, 16: 261–63.

114. Bernard to Lord Colville, Boston, 11 December 1765, BP, 4: 85; Thomas, "Partisan Politics," 1: 241–42; Gipson, *The British Empire*, 10: 344–45.

115. *JHRM*, 42: 214–15; John Cushing to Thomas Hutchinson, Scituate, 2 Febru-

ary 1766, THLB, 25: 52–55; Bernard to Lords Commissioners for Trade and Plantations, Boston, 10 March 1766, BP, 4: 209, 212.

116. Bernard to Conway, Boston, 21 January 1766, BP, 4: 192; Bernard to Conway, Boston, 25 January 1766, BP, 4:199; Bradford, ed., *Speeches of the Governors*, 65–67.

117. Quotation from Galvin, *Three Men of Boston*, 124; Bailyn, *Hutchinson*, 110–11; Gipson, *The British Empire*, 10: 353–57; Bernard to the Lords Commissioners for Trade and Plantations, Boston, 10 March 1766, 210; Peter Oliver to Thomas Hutchinson, Middleborough, 16 December 1765, Photostat, MHS; *DAJA*, 1: 259–60, 305; John Cushing to Thomas Hutchinson, Scituate, 2 February 1766, 52–54; John Cushing to Thomas Hutchinson, n.p., 9 February 1766, THLB, 25: 55–56.

118. Morgan and Morgan, *Stamp Act Crisis*, 184–86; Thomas, "Partisan Politics," 1: 267–69.

119. Bernard to Conway, Boston, 25 November 1765, BP, 4: 172.

120. Bernard to Shelburne, Boston, 22 December 1765, BP, 4: 274–75.

121. See Bernard to Jackson, Boston, 1 March 1766, 5: 80; the Rev. Jonathan Mayhew to Richard Clarke, Boston, 3 September 1765, *NEHGR*, 46 (1892): 16–20; Bradford, *Memoir of Mayhew*, 420–21.

122. Bernard to Conway, Boston, 25 January 1766, BP, 4: 200.

123. Bernard to Conway, Boston, 23 January 1766, BP, 4: 195–96.

124. Bernard to John Pownall, Castle William, 15 November 1765, BP, 5: 31.

125. Bernard to Barrington, Boston, 23 November 1765, [draft], BP, 5: 54.

126. Bernard to [Philip] Kearney, Boston, 4 May 1766, BP, 4: 122; Suffolk County Registry of Deeds, Boston, Record Book, 98: 113; 102: 39; 108: 89; 123: 114.

127. Bernard to John Pownall, Castle William, 5 November 1765, 24–25.

CHAPTER FIVE

1. Two exceptions are Pencak, *War, Politics & Revolution*, 172–74, 185–206; James Kirby Martin, *Men in Rebellion: Higher Governmental Leaders and the Coming of the American Revolution* (New Brunswick, N.J.: Rutgers Univ. Press, 1973).

2. The marquis of Rockingham, the first lord of the Treasury, received Bernard's account of the first Stamp Act riot on 12 October, and news of the riot of 26 August shortly thereafter. Sheffield Archives: John Pownall to Lord Rockingham, Kensington, 12 October 1765, Wentworth Woodhouse Muniments, R24/16, enclosing Bernard's letter to John Pownall of 18 August 1765, WWM, R24/17; Bernard to John Pownall, Castle William, 1 September 1765, WWM, R24/18. Bernard's letters to John Pownall of 31 August and 7 September 1765 were presented to the Board of Trade on 17 October. *JBT*, 12: 214.

3. Conway to Bernard, St. James's [London], 24 October 1765, BP, 10: 318–20.

4. See John L. Bullion, "British Ministers and American Resistance to the Stamp Act, October–December, 1765," *WMQ* 49 (1992): 89–107.

5. Conway to Bernard, St. James's [London], 24 October 1765.

6. Pownall to Bernard, London, 13 December 1765, BP, 10: 324–25; Pownall to Bernard, London, 29 March 1766, BP, 10: 354–56.

7. See John Derry, *English Politics and the American Revolution* (London: J. M. Dent & Sons, 1976), 74–85; Sosin, *Agents and Merchants*, 66–80; Thomas, *British Politics and the Stamp Act Crisis*, 150–52, 158–59, 160–73, 178–84; Gipson, *The British Empire*, 10: 375; Thomas, "George III and the American Revolution," 22–24. Bernard's letters to John Pownall of 12 and 17 October 1765 were discussed by the Board of Trade on 17 December and copied to the king. *JBT*, 12: 235.

8. *PHE*, 16: 121–31, 161–62.

9. William Fitzherbert to Bernard, London, 30 March 1766, BP, 10: 358.

10. Barrington to Bernard, London, 6 February 1766, BP, 10: 332; Barrington to Bernard, London, 25 March 1766, BP, 10: 344.

11. Franklin to Jane Mecom, London, 1 March 1766, *Papers of Benjamin Franklin*, 13: 188.

12. Quoted in Bradford, ed., *Speeches of the Governors*, 70–73.

13. Pownall to Bernard, London, 29 March 1766, BP, 10: 354–56; *PHE*, 16: 182, 191.

14. Conway to Bernard, St. James's [London], 31 March 1766, CO 5/755: 507–14.

15. Bernard to Jackson, Boston, 28 April 1766, BP, 5: 108.

16. Bernard to Lord Barrington, Boston, 1 September 1766, *Barrington-Bernard Correspondence*, 113.

17. *PHE*, 16: 161–206; Reid, *Authority to Legislate*, 36–37, 54–55; Derry, *English Politics and the American Revolution*, 57–59.

18. Bernard to Jackson, Boston, 17 April 1766, BP, 5: 107.

19. Bernard to Jackson, Boston, 29 March 1766, BP, 5: 98.

20. Thomas, "Partisan Politics," 1: 266.

21. See for example, "B. F.," "A Speech," *BGCJ*, 25 November 1765; "Paskalos" [Joseph Warren], *BGCJ*, 6 and 16 June 1766.

22. Bernard to Jackson, Boston, 28 April 1766, BP, 5: 109; Bernard to Pownall, Boston, 30 May 1766, BP, 5: 114.

23. "A" [Samuel Adams], *BGCJ*, 22 and 29 December 1766; "Veritas" [Samuel Adams], *BGCJ*, 5 May 1766.

24. *MG*, 19 May 1766.

25. Waters Jr., *The Otis Family*, 159.

26. "B. W.," *BGCJ*, 14 April 1766; *BGCJ*, 31 March 1766; *DAJA*, 1: 277. See also the instructions to the Boston Representatives of 10 May 1766, *BTR*, 16: 182–84.

27. *BGCJ*, 31 March 1766; Bernard to the Lords Commissioners for Trade and Plantations, 7 July 1766, BP, 6: 230; Bernard to John Pownall, Boston, 30 May 1766, BP, 5: 115.

28. Bernard to Lords Commissioners for Trade and Plantations, Boston, 10 April 1766, BP, 4: 220.

29. *DAJA*, 1: 312.

30. Bernard to Pownall, Boston, 30 May 1766, BP, 5: 114.

31. *Ibid.*, 115–16; Bernard to Jackson, Boston, 7 June 1766, *ibid.*, 126–27.

32. Nicolson, "Governor Francis Bernard," 52.

33. *DAJA*, 1: 327; Bernard to Jackson, Boston, 31 May 1766, BP, 5: 121. The six nominees were Thomas Saunders, Joseph Gerris, Col. James Otis, Jerathmeel Bowers, Nathaniel Sparhawk, and Samuel Dexter. *JHRM*, 43, pt. 1: 8–10.

34. Leonard W. Labaree, *Conservatism in Early American History* (New York: Oxford Univ. Press, 1948), 25; Thomas, "Partisan Politics," 1: 313–16.

35. Bernard to Pownall, Boston, 30 May 1766, BP, 5: 116; Nicolson, "Friends of Government," 1: 160–62.

36. Thomas, "Partisan Politics," 1: 326–37; Jensen, *Founding of a Nation*, 210–11.

37. *JHRM*, 43, pt. 1: 29–31; Bernard to John Pownall, Boston, 6 June 1766, BP, 5: 125.

38. Bernard to Lords Commissioners for Trade and Plantations, Boston, 30 November 1765, BP, 4: 174; Bernard to Jackson, Jamaica Farm, 17 November 1766, BP, 5: 167; CO 5/756: 16–19.

39. "T. S.," *BGCJ*, 21 July 1766. According to the Amory brothers, "had he delivered himself in the mild . . . terms used by Secretary Conway whose letter he had

before him it would have tended much to have restor'd the Harmony & Quiet he [Bernard] seems so much to desire." Meredith, *Descendants of Hugh Amory*, 140.

40. Bernard to Jackson, Boston, 18 June 1766, BP, 5: 131.

41. Hutchinson to Conway, Boston, 1 October 1765, CO 5/755: 353–54; Hutchinson to Conway, Boston, 27 October 1765, CO 5/755: 361–64; Walmsley, *Thomas Hutchinson*, 81.

42. John and Jonathan Amory to Messrs. Devonshier and Reeve, Boston, 16 June 1766, Meredith, *Descendants of Hugh Amory*, 140.

43. *JHRM*, 43, pt. 1: 67, 78, 125.

44. Bernard to Shelburne, Boston, 14 November 1766, *A Collection of Papers Relative to the Dispute Between Great Britain and America, 1764–1775* [ed. Thomas Hutchinson] (London: J. T. Almon, 1777), 113–15; *BTR*, 16: 188; Hutchinson to ?, Milton, 7 November 1766, THLB, 26: 249; Samuel A. Bates, ed., *Records of the Town of Braintree, 1640–1793* (Randolph, Mass.: D. H. Huxford, 1886), 412–13; John C. Miller, *Sam Adams: Pioneer in Propaganda* (1936; Stanford, Calif.: Stanford Univ. Press, 1960) 109; Samuel Adams to Dennis DeBerdt, n.p., 15 November 1766, *Writings of Samuel Adams*, 1: 102; Robert J. Taylor, *Western Massachusetts in the Revolution* (Providence, R.I.: Brown Univ. Press, 1954), 56; Lucius R. Paige, *History of Hardwick, Massachusetts* (Boston: Houghton Mifflin, 1883), 63.

45. Sir William Blackstone, *Commentaries on the Laws of England*, 4 vols. (London: William Reed, 1811), 1: 468, 472, 480, 484.

46. [Bernard], Observations on the Proceedings for the Indemnification of the Sufferers in the Riots at Boston, [1766], CO 5/755: 573–88, enclosed in Bernard to Lords Commissioners for Trade and Plantations, Boston, 19 July 1766, CO 5/755: 569–70. On the Porteous riot see H. T. Dickinson and Kenneth Logue, "The Porteous Riot: A Study of the Breakdown of Law and Order in Edinburgh, 1736–1737," *Journal of the Scottish Labour History Society* 10 (June 1976): 21–40; W. Roughead, ed., *The Trial of Captain Porteous* (Glasgow: William Hodge & Co., 1909). One likely source for the Edinburgh precedent was William Murray, the earl of Mansfield, who was the corporation's counsel during Parliament's inquiry. He was successful in persuading Parliament not to introduce the Bill of Disenfranchisement, for which he received the freedom of the city. C. H. S. Fifoot, *Lord Mansfield* (Oxford: Clarendon Press, 1963), 35–36. Another precedent discussed by Pownall and Bernard concerned the Glasgow Malt Tax riots of 1725, when mobs demolished the houses of the city's M.P. and other persons of authority; the victims were compensated by the town. This case was cited by Hugh Baillie, a former judge of the Admiralty Court in Ireland, in his discussion of the Coercive Acts of 1774. *A Letter to Dr. Shebear: Containing a Refutation of his Arguments Concerning the Boston and Quebec Acts of Parliament* (London: J. Donaldson, 1774), 23.

47. Bernard to Shelburne, Boston, 14 November 1766, *Collection of Papers*, 116.

48. *JHRM*, 43, pt. 1: 153–59.

49. *JHRM*, 43, pt. 1: 166, 170–71, 209–10; Bernard to Shelburne, 14 November 1766, CO 5/755: 841–48.

50. Israel Williams to Thomas Hutchinson, Hatfield, 5 January 1767, THLB, 25: 140–41; *DAJA*, 1: 273–75.

51. *JHRM*, 43, pt. 1: 180, 192, 203.

52. Hutchinson to ?, Milton, 7 November 1766, THLB, 26: 249; Bernard to Jackson, Jamaica Farm, 17 November 1766, BP, 5: 168–69. Also Bernard to Shelburne, Boston, 6 December 1766, BP, 4: 271.

53. *JHRM*, 43, pt. 1: 206–11.

54. *JHRM*, 43, pt. 1, 216.

55. *JRHM*, 43, pt. 2: 232–33.

56. *Ibid.*, 299–300.

57. Bernard to the earl of Shelburne, Boston, 30 May 1767, BP, 6: 187–88; Hutchinson, *History of Massachusetts*, 3: 123–28. The incident encouraged the New York assembly to defy the Mutiny Act. John C. Miller, *Origins of the American Revolution* (Stanford, Calif.: Stanford Univ. Press, 1957: revised repr. [1959]), 238–39.

58. *JBT*, 12: 373, 375, 384.

59. *Papers of Benjamin Franklin*, 14: 108–9.

60. Thomas Hutchinson received £3,168 17s 9d in provincial currency (worth £2,736 13s 4d, sterling); Andrew Oliver, £172 4s (£129 3s); Benjamin Hallowell, £542 12s 4d (£412 19s 1d); William Story, £136 2s (£102 1s 6d). CO 5/755: 535–51, 555, 559–63.

61. Shelburne to Bernard, Whitehall, 7 August 1767, BP, 11: 75. For British reactions see Hutchinson, *Collection of Papers*, 137–41; *Journals of the House of Commons, 1715–1774*, 34 vols. (London: 1715–74), (hereafter *Commons Journals*), 31: 369; Gipson, *The British Empire*, 10: 26; Christie and Labaree, *Empire or Independence*, 102.

62. R. A. Humphreys, "Lord Shelburne and British Colonial Policy, 1766–1768," *English Historical Review* 50 (1935): 257–77; Shelburne to Bernard, Whitehall, 13 September 1766, CO 5/755: 593–96. One of Shelburne's advisers accused the governor of wanting "wisdom and management"—of retiring "to his closet to vent his chagrin in womanish complaints, instead of combining men and forming bold plans of administration as the exigencies of affairs . . . require[d]." Lord Edmond Fitzmaurice, *Life of William, Earl of Shelburne, afterwards First Marquis of Lansdowne, with extracts from his Papers and Correspondence*, 2 vols. (London: Macmillan, 1912), 1: 317–19.

63. R. A. Humphreys, "Lord Shelburne and a Projected Recall of Colonial Governors in 1767," *AHR* 37 (1931–32): 269–72.

64. Hayter, *An Eighteenth-Century Secretary at War*, 3–14, 29.

65. Bernard to Shelburne, Boston, 22 December 1766, BP, 4: 274–92; Bernard to Shelburne, Boston, 28 March 1767, BP, 6: 199–208.

66. Bernard to Jackson, Jamaica Farm, 30 August 1767, BP, 6: 42.

67. Bernard to Jackson, n.p., 20 June 1767, BP, 6: 25–26.

68. Kammen, *A Rope of Sand*, 128–30.

69. "Letters of Thomas Cushing from 1767 to 1775," *Collections of the Massachusetts Historical Society*, 4th ser., 4 (1858): 347–66, at 347–49, 351; *JBT*, 12: 417.

70. Bernard to Jackson, n.p., 20 June 1767; *JHRM*, 43, pt. 2: 250, 313.

71. *BGCJ*, 27 April 1767; "Freeborn American" [James Otis Jr.], *BGCJ*, 9 March 1767; "Philalethes," *BGCJ*, 9 March 1767; "Populus," *BGCJ*, 4 May 1767.

72. "Philalethes," *BGCJ*, 11 May 1767.

73. Cushing to Shelburne, Boston, 6 December 1766, Massachusetts Papers, MHS.

74. The House's reply was produced by a committee that included friends of government William Browne and Oliver Partridge as well as Otis and Adams. Bradford, ed., *Speeches of the Governors*, 110–11.

75. Quoted in Kershaw, *Kennebeck Proprietors*, 267.

76. Sir Lewis Namier and John Brooke, *Charles Townshend* (London: Macmillan, 1964), 173–75, 179; J. Steven Watson, *The Reign of George III, 1760–1815* (Oxford: Clarendon Press, 1960), 189–90; Derry, *English Politics and the American Revolution*, 87.

77. Bernard to John Pownall, Boston, 9 January 1768, BP, 6: 59–60; Bernard to Richard Jackson, Boston, 20 February 1768, BP, 6: 92.

78. Bernard to John Pownall, Boston, 23 April 1769, BP, 7: 283.

79. Bernard to Barrington, Boston, 22 October 1768, BP, 6: 158–59.

80. Paxton was appointed after a recent visit to England, and was accused of persuading Townshend to embark on his reform program. "Candidus," *BEP*, 21 No-

vember and 2 December 1768; Barrow, *Trade and Empire*, 120. For Robinson see Morgan and Morgan, *Stamp Act Crisis*, 59–74; Ubbelohde, *Vice-Admiralty Courts*, 67–69.

81. Nothing is known of Burch's early career. Hulton, however, had been a customs comptroller in Antigua, an inspector in London, and a clerk to the Board of Trade before being dispatched to North America. Henry Hulton to ?, n.p., 12 April 1772, Letterbooks of Henry Hulton, 2 vols., Houghton Library, 1: 44; Christie and Labaree, *Empire or Independence*, 108; Gipson, *The British Empire*, 11: 119; Hutchinson to Israel Mauduit, Boston, 13 November 1767, THLB, 25: 223–24.

82. Hulton, Account of the People of New England, 113–16.

83. Bernard to Shelburne, Boston, 27 July 1767, BP, 6: 222.

84. Bernard to Shelburne, Boston, 7 September 1767, BP, 6: 238.

85. Bernard to Jackson, Jamaica Farm, 14 September 1767, BP, 6: 46.

86. Bernard to Shelburne, Jamaica Farm, 14 September 1767, BP, 6: 240.

87. Robert Auchmuty to David Watson & Co., n.p., 29 December 1769, Boylston Papers, MHS; Account of Benjamin Hallowell with Thomas Finney, n.p., 5 November [1768] to 2 September 1769, *ibid.*

88. Josiah Paine, *A History of Harwich, Barnstable County, Massachusetts, 1620–1800* (Rutland, Vt.: Tuttle, 1937), 307; *BEP*, 11 January 1768.

89. Bernard to Shelburne, Boston, 14 November 1767, BP, 6: 252.

90. Joseph Jackson, Samuel Sewall, John Ruddock, John Hancock, William Phillips, Timothy Newall, John Rowe. *MG*, 24 November 1767.

91. Meredith, *Descendants of Hugh Amory*, 148; Jensen, *Founding of a Nation*, 270.

92. Barrow, *Trade and Empire*, 202–3; Gipson, *The British Empire*, 10: 36; Ubbelohde, *Vice-Admiralty Courts*, 93, 117–18; Bernard to the Lords Commissioners for Trade and Plantations, Boston, 18 August 1766, BP, 6: 246–47; Commissioners of Customs to Lords Commissioners for Trade and Plantations, Boston, 18 February 1768, CO 5/757: 60–62.

93. Mass. Council Records, 16: 263; Bernard to Shelburne, Boston, 21 November 1767, BP, 6: 254–55; *Letters of a Loyalist Lady*, 8.

94. Hutchinson to Jackson, Boston, 19 November 1767, THLB, 25: 226–27; Thomas, "Partisan Politics," 1: 412–16.

95. See Joseph R. Frese, "Some Observations on the American Board of Customs Commissioners," *Procs. MHS*, 3d ser., 81 (1969): 3–30.

96. See Edward Channing, "The American Board of Commissioners of the Customs," *Procs. MHS*, 3d ser., 43 (1909–10): 477–91; Edward Channing, *A History of the United States* (New York: Macmillan, 1920), 3: 90–91; Ubbelohde, *Vice-Admiralty Courts*, 105–14; Barrow, *Trade and Empire*, 206–9, 240.

97. Samuel Venner, Memorial to the Duke Grafton and Lords Commissioners for Trade and Plantations, London, 1 May 1769, CCT, 10: 14–15.

98. Venner, Memorial, 13. See Nicolson, " 'McIntosh, Otis & Adams are our demagogues,' " 82.

99. Venner, Memorial, 1–19; Minutes of the Commissioners of Customs, Boston, 1769–70, CCT, 6: 115.

100. Bernard to Hillsborough, Boston, 21 March 1768, BP, 6: 291.

101. "Alfred" [Samuel Adams], *BGCJ*, 2 October 1769; [Samuel P. Savage], "A List of Subscribers to the Non Importation Agreement of March 1768, reported March 9, 1768," Samuel P. Savage II Collection.

102. Bernard to Hillsborough, Boston, 21 March 1768, 291.

103. Tyler, *Smugglers & Patriots*, 113.

104. Bernard to Hillsborough, Boston, 21 March 1768, 291.

105. Bernard to Barrington, Boston, 4 March 1768, BP, 6: 96–99; Bernard to Shelburne, Boston, 19 March 1768, BP, 6: 281.

106. See Thomas, "Partisan Politics," 2: 496–97; Hulton, Account of the People of New England, 84; Anne R. Cunningham, *Letters and Diary of John Rowe* (Boston: n.p., 1903), 70.

107. Bernard to Shelburne, Boston, 19 March 1768, BP, 6: 282–84.

108. Hutchinson to Nathaniel Rogers, n.p., 26 March 1768, THLB, 26: 297; Hutchinson to Jackson, Boston, 23 March 1768, THLB, 26: 295–96.

109. Mass. Council Records, 16: 299.

110. Hutchinson to ?, Boston, 18 July 1767, THLB, 26: 281–83.

111. Hutchinson to Hillsborough, Boston, 24 January 1770, *Documents of the American Revolution, 1770–1783*, 21 vols., ed. K. G. Davies (Shannon: Irish Univ. Press, 1972–81), 2: 34; Bernard to Hillsborough, Boston, 21 May 1768, BP, 6: 298–300.

112. *BEP*, 2 October 1769; "Bostonian," *BC*, 1–5 February 1770.

113. Bernard to Hillsborough, Boston, 21 May 1768, BP, 6: 298–300.

114. Hutchinson to Hillsborough, Boston, 29 April 1769, BP, 7: 162.

115. *BTR*, 16: 298; 18: 16.

116. Leslie J. Thomas, "The Nonconsumption and Nonimportation Movement Against the Townshend Acts, 1767–1770," in Walter H. Conser Jr., Ronald M. Mc-Carthy, and D. J. Toscano, eds., *Resistance, Politics, and the American Struggle for Independence, 1765–1775* (Boulder, Colo.: Lynne Rienner Publishers, 1986), 156–57. See also Jensen, *Founding of a Nation*, 266–67.

117. Tyler, *Smugglers & Patriots*, 109–38.

118. Tyler, *Smugglers & Patriots*, 109–38; Hoerder, *Crowd Action*, 206.

119. Bernard to Hillsborough, [Boston], 30 July 1768, Massachusetts Papers, MHS.

120. Hutchinson to Bernard, Boston, 4 October 1769, THLB, 26: 383.

121. Bettye Hobbs Pruitt, ed., *The Massachusetts Tax Evaluation List of 1771* (Boston: G. K. Hall, 1978), 28–29; Suffolk Deeds 122: 189, 6 February 1771; Hutchinson to Bernard, Boston, 29 January 1772, THLB, 27: 287; Bernard to Edmund Quincy Jr., Jamaica Farm, 11 August 1768, BP, 5: 278; Bernard to Sir Edward Hawke, Boston, 28 February 1768, BP, 7: 150–52.

122. Bernard to Hillsborough, Boston, 9 August 1768, BP, 7: 23.

123. *BEP*, 8 May 1769; Tyler, *Smugglers & Patriots*, 114.

124. Tyler, *Smugglers & Patriots*, 190–206; McCusker, "Colonial Civil Servant," 328–34.

125. Lillie, *BC*, 11–15 January 1770; Colborn Barrell, *BC*, 7–11 December 1769.

126. The phenomenon of colonial Whig-Loyalism is explored in William A. Benton, *Whig-Loyalism: An Aspect of Political Ideology in the American Revolutionary Era* (Rutherford, N.J.: Fairleigh Dickinson Univ. Press, 1969).

127. Bernard to Charles Paxton, Boston, 21 January 1767, BP, 6: 4; Peter Oliver to Thomas Hutchinson, Middleborough, 3 August 1767, THLB, 25: 189–90. The "Philanthrop" letters were printed in *BEP* between 1 December 1766 and 10 August 1767, and occasionally thereafter.

128. John Mein's *Boston Chronicle*, which first appeared on 21 December 1767, was denounced as an instrument of the "Jacobite party" (*BGCJ*, 18 January 1768), although it was not until the summer of 1769 that the *Chronicle* adopted a clear pro-government stance, after Mein's appointment as stationer to the American Board of Customs Commissioners. The first paper established by and for the government was *The Censor*, which was printed in Boston between November 1771 and May 1772.

129. "A True Patriot," *MG*, 24 September 1767; "Tacitus" [James Otis Jr.], *BGCJ*,

16 November 1767. See also "Remarks Attributed to A True Patriot," *BGCJ*, 21 December 1767. Bernard may have also authored a piece in the *BEP* of 2 January 1769, signed "Z. T.," which justified parliamentary taxation and drew a vehement response from "T. Z." in *BGCJ*, 9 January 1769. "Z. T." produced another piece reviewing some of the arguments made against taxation by Daniel Dulany in *Considerations on the Propriety of Taxing the Colonists* in 1766. *BEP*, 3 July 1769.

130. "N. P.," *BEP*, 20 and 27 March 1769. "N. P." wrote a series of rejoinders to the "Farmers Letters." *BEP*, 6 February–5 July 1769. For a fuller discussion see Nicolson, "The Friends of Government," 1: 71–73.

131. "Philanthrop," *BEP*, 14 January 1771; "Freeborn American" [James Otis Jr.], *BGCJ, Supplement*, 9 February 1767.

132. Bernard to Shelburne, Boston, 21 January 1768, BP, 6: 256–57.

133. Gipson, *The British Empire*, 11: 149.

134. House of Representatives to the King, Massachusetts Bay, 20 January 1768, *Writings of Samuel Adams*, 1: 162–65.

135. Bernard to Jackson, Boston, 1 February 1768, BP, 6: 79–80.

136. Bernard to Shelburne, Boston, 21 January 1768; Bernard to Jackson, Boston, 1 February 1768; Bernard to John Pownall, Boston, 16 January 1768, BP, 6: 62–65; Bernard to Barrington, Boston, 28 January 1768, *Barrington-Bernard Correspondence*, 137–39. On Hawley see Shaw, *American Patriots*, 146–47.

137. Bernard to Jackson, Boston, 1 February 1768, 81; Bernard to Shelburne, Boston, 30 January 1768, BP, 6: 263.

138. Bernard to Shelburne, Boston, 16 February 1768, BP, 6: 265–66; Bradford, ed., *Speeches of the Governors*, 134–36; *JHRM*, 44: 134; "Z. T.," *BEP*, 17 October 1768.

139. The House of Representatives to the Speakers of Other Houses of Representatives, Massachusetts Bay, 11 February 1768, *Writings of Samuel Adams*, 1: 184–85; Gipson, *The British Empire*, 11: 149; Miller, *Sam Adams*, 123.

140. Shelburne to the earl of Chatham, London, 3 February 1774, *Correspondence of William Pitt, Earl of Chatham*, 4 vols., eds. William Stanhope Taylor and Capt. John Henry Pringle (London: John Murray, 1849), 4: 352.

141. Bernard to Shelburne, Boston, 20 February 1768, BP, 6:269–71; *JHRM*, 44: 188. Shelburne's letter was also printed in *JHRM*, 44: 250–51.

142. "A True Patriot" [Joseph Warren], *BGCJ*, 29 February 1768.

143. *Collection of Papers*, 199; Bernard to Shelburne, 5 March 1768, BP, 6: 274; *JHRM*, 44: 214–15; Granger, *Political Satire*, 5.

144. Mass. Council Records, 16: 293–94; Bernard to Shelburne, 5 March 1768, 276.

145. Bernard to Shelburne, 12 March 1768, BP, 6: 278–80; Bernard to John Pownall, Boston, 14 March 1768, BP, 6: 102–3; Bernard to Jackson, Boston, 14 March 1768, BP, 6: 103.

146. Thomas, "Partisan Politics," 2: 445.

147. "A Puritan" [Samuel Adams], *BGCJ*, 11 April 1768; Nicolson, "The Friends of Government," 1: 137–38.

148. Bernard to Hillsborough, Boston, 12 May 1768, BP, 6: 295–97.

149. Barrington to Bernard, 16 April 1768, BP, 11: 168. See John Brooke, *The Chatham Administration, 1766–1768* (London: Macmillan, 1956), 241–47, 282–83, 314; "On the Conduct of Lord Hillsborough," [August? 1772], *Papers of Benjamin Franklin*, 19: 216–26.

150. Hillsborough to Bernard, 15 November 1768, BP, 12: 11–13; Benjamin Franklin to Dennis DeBerdt, *The Public Advertiser*, 31 August 1768, *Papers of Benjamin Franklin*, 13: 196–98.

151. Hillsborough to Bernard, Whitehall, 4 April 1768, BP, 11: 163–65; Hillsborough to Bernard, Whitehall, 22 April 1768, CO 5/757: 55–57.

152. Bernard to Hillsborough, Boston, 17 June 1768, BP, 6: 325; *JHRM*, 45: 68.

153. Bernard to Hillsborough, 1 July 1768, BP, 6: 322.

154. *JHRM*, 45: 91–94.

155. Province of Massachusetts Bay to Hillsborough, 30 June 1768, CO 5/757: 312–14.

156. Bernard to Hillsborough, Boston, 18 July 1768, BP, 7: 11–12.

157. Bernard to Hillsborough, 1 July 1768, BP, 6: 329.

158. Galvin, *Three Men of Boston*, 164–65.

159. Israel Williams to Thomas Hutchinson, Hatfield, 28 December 1767 [1768], THLB, 25: 234–35.

160. Bernard to Hillsborough, Boston, 1 July 1768, 331.

161. Timothy Ruggles of Hardwick was the only rescinder who was not formally rebuked by his town. The friends of government of Salem, including the wealthy merchants the Pickmans and several officeholders, staged a counterprotest at the proscription of their two representatives, the rescinders William Browne and Peter Frye. See *BGCJ*, 25 July 1768 and 1 August 1768; Nicolson, "The Friends of Government," 1: 141.

162. "A Bridgewaterian," *BEP*, 29 May 1769.

163. Hutchinson to ?, n.p., 29 May 1769, THLB, 26: 352–53.

164. *BGCJ*, 11 July 1768, 1–3; *BGCJ, Supplement*, 15 August 1768.

165. For example, "Pelopidas," *BGCJ*, 26 October 1767; "Benevolus," *BGCJ*, 9 November 1767; Boston town meeting, *BGCJ*, 28 March 1768; "Caius Memmius" [Aaron Bancroft], *BGCJ*, 7 November 1768; "Vindex" [Samuel Adams], *BGCJ*, 19 December 1768.

CHAPTER SIX

1. Bernard to Gage, Roxbury, 2 July 1768, BP, 5: 266.

2. Bernard to Hillsborough, Boston, 19 May 1768, BP, 6: 302.

3. Bernard to Barrington, Boston, 20 July 1768, BP, 6: 136–39.

4. Don Cook, *The Long Fuse: How England Lost the American Colonies, 1760–1785* (New York: Atlantic Monthly Press, 1995), 109, 121.

5. Bernard to Shelburne, Boston, 19 March 1768, BP, 6: 280–88, at 285; Bernard to Hillsborough, Boston, 19 March 1768, CO 5/757: 66–70. See also Bernard to Hillsborough, Boston, 21 March 1768, CO 5/755: 74–77. Duplicate letters were sent to the outgoing and incoming secretaries.

6. Bernard to Hillsborough, Boston, 19 May 1768, BP, 6: 303.

7. *An Appeal to the World; or a Vindication of the Town of Boston from many false and malicious Aspersions* (1769; London: J. Almon, 1770).

8. Memorial of the Commissioners of Customs to Lords Commissioners for Trade and Plantations, Boston, 28 March 1768, CO 5/757: 82–94; Gage to Hillsborough, Boston, 31 October 1768, *Correspondence of Gage*, 1: 204; Bernard to Barrington, Boston, 4 March 1768, BP, 6: 96–99.

9. Commissioners of Customs to Lords Commissioners for Trade and Plantations, Boston, 18 February 1768, CO 5/757: 60–62.

10. Hoerder, *Crowd Action*, 165–68; Thomas, "Partisan Politics," 2: 505–8; Fowler Jr., *Baron of Beacon Hill*, 84–86.

11. Bernard to Hillsborough, Boston, 11 June 1768, BP, 6: 311.

12. Commissioners of Customs to Lords Commissioners for Trade and Plantations, HMS *Romney*, 12 June 1768, CO 5/757: 205–6; Proceedings of the Governor

and Council of Massachusetts Bay, 16 March 1768–11 January 1769, CCT. Hulton eventually retreated to his thirty-acre estate at Brookline, while Paxton went to Cambridge and Burch to Portsmouth, New Hampshire.

13. Samuel Venner, Memorial, to the duke of Grafton, and Lords Commissioners for Trade and Plantations, 1–19.

14. Temple's correspondence with North is in CCT, 2; Temple to the duke of Grafton, Boston, 14 May 1768, CCT, 1; Temple to the duke of Grafton, Boston, 25 October 1769, CCT, 2.

15. Bernard to Hillsborough, Boston, 16 June 1768, BP, 6: 320.

16. Joseph Harrison and Benjamin Hallowell to John Robinson, Boston, 12 June 1768, CO 5/757: 197; Minutes of the Treasury, 21 July 1768, CO 5/757: 165–66; John Cary, *Joseph Warren: Physician, Politician, Patriot* (Urbana, Ill.: University of Illinois Press, 1961), 76.

17. Bernard to Hillsborough, Boston, 13 June 1768, CO 5/757: 315.

18. Bernard to Hillsborough, Boston, 16 June 1768, BP, 6: 320.

19. Bernard to Hillsborough, HMS *Romney*, 13 June 1768, CO 5/757: 205.

20. Barrington to Bernard, London, 9 May 1768, BP, 11: 183–85; George III quoted in Thomas, "George III," 26–27.

21. Bernard to Hillsborough, Boston, 26 January 1769, BP, 7: 128–29. Twenty-one baronets were constituted or reconstituted between 1766 and 1770, to add to the 138 of the previous sixty years. J. V. Beckett, *The Aristocracy in England, 1660–1914* (Oxford: Basil Blackwell, 1986), 116–17, 489.

22. P. D. G. Thomas, *The Townshend Duties Crisis: The Second Phase of the American Revolution, 1767–1773* (Oxford: Clarendon Press, 1987), 82–83, 86, 91; Hillsborough to King George III, Hanover Square [London], 19 July 1768, *The Correspondence of King George III from 1760 to December 1783*, 6 vols., ed. Sir John Fortescue (London: Macmillan, 1927–28), 2: 35–36.

23. Hillsborough to Bernard, Whitehall, 30 July 1768, CO 5/757: 241–47. The letters to which Hillsborough referred were Bernard to Hillsborough, Boston, 11 June 1768, CO 5/757: 115–17; Bernard to Hillsborough, Boston, 14 June 1768, *ibid.*, 118–20, enclosing depositions from the American Board of Customs Commissioners, *ibid.*, 121–37; Bernard to Hillsborough, Boston, 16 and 18 June 1768, *ibid.*, 138–42, enclosing a petition of the Boston Town Meeting to Bernard, 14 June 1768, *ibid.*, 142–45; Bernard to Hillsborough, Boston, 17 June 1768, *ibid.*, 146–47. The reports of the Commissioners and other supporting documentation are in CO 5/757: 150–86. Another significant source of information was the Boston comptroller Benjamin Hallowell, who arrived in London on 18 July in time to make a personal report to the Treasury. Minutes of the Treasury, 21 July 1768, CO 5/757: 165–66.

24. Brooke, *Chatham Administration*, 365.

25. Reid, *In a Rebellious Spirit*, 84–85, 127.

26. Hillsborough to Bernard, Whitehall, 11 June 1768, "Secret," BP, 11: 190.

27. Hillsborough to Bernard, Whitehall, 30 July 1768, CO 5/757: 241–47.

28. Hillsborough to Bernard, 12 October 1768, BP, 12: 1–2.

29. Barrington to Bernard, 11 August 1768, BP, 11: 277–78.

30. Hillsborough to Bernard, 19 November 1768, BP, 12: 17–20. Hillsborough created a minor controversy by appointing Botetourt without consulting the cabinet when General Amherst refused to return to Virginia. See Thomas, *Townshend Duties Crisis*, 89–91; Brooke, *Chatham Administration*, 366–68.

31. Bernard to Gage, Roxbury, 12 July 1768, BP, 5: 267; Bernard to Gage, Roxbury, 18 July 1768, BP, 5: 273–74; Bernard to Hillsborough, Boston, 30 July 1768, BP, 7: 14.

32. Zobel, *The Boston Massacre*, 80–81; Gage to Hillsborough, New York, 28 June 1768, *Correspondence of Gage*, 1: 183.

33. Bernard to John Pownall, Boston, 11 July 1768, BP, 6: 130–31.

34. Internal divisions are largely ignored in Francis G. Walett, "The Massachusetts Council: The Transformation of a Conservative Institution," *WMQ* 6 (1949): 605–62; Thomas, "Partisan Politics," 1: passim; Walmsley, *Thomas Hutchinson*, 78–79; Miller, *Origins of the American Revolution*, 238–39.

35. Bowdoin to Hillsborough, Boston, 5 April 1769, *BC*, 3–7 August 1769.

36. *JHRM*, 44: 7, 23; Bernard to Shelburne, Boston, 30 May 1767, BP, 6: 211–12.

37. Nicolson, "The Friends of Government," 1: 162; 2: 535n44; Bernard to Jackson, Boston, 6 May 1767, BP, 6: 19–20.

38. Report of the Resolves [of the joint committee of the House and Council] Relative to the Riot of 10 June, [Boston], 14–16 June 1768 [draft], Bowdoin-Temple Papers.

39. Bernard to Hillsborough, Boston, 9 July 1768, BP, 6: 338.

40. [James Bowdoin], Petition of the Massachusetts Council to the King, [Boston], 7 July 1768, Bowdoin-Temple Papers; *Letters to the Right Honourable The Earl of Hillsborough from Governor Bernard, General Gage, And the Honourable His Majesty's Council for the Province of Massachusetts Bay with an Appendix containing divers proceedings referred to in the said letters* (1769; London: J. Almon, 1769), 105–20.

41. Bernard to Hillsborough, Boston, 5 December 1768, BP, 7: 114–15; Hutchinson to Bernard, 11 and 17 August 1769, THLB, 26: 363.

42. Bernard to Barrington, Boston, 30 July 1768, BP, 6: 139; Mass. Council Records, 16: 336–37.

43. Bernard to Barrington, Boston, 30 July 1768.

44. Bernard to Hillsborough, Boston, 16 October 1768, BP, 7: 77; Mass. Council Records, 16: 330–31.

45. Bernard to Barrington, Boston, 30 July 1768; Bernard to Gage, Boston, 30 July 1768, BP, 5: 276.

46. Bernard to Hillsborough, Boston, 30 July 1768, 13.

47. Bernard to Hillsborough , Boston, 18 September 1768, BP, 7: 45.

48. Gage to Bernard, 12 September 1768, BP, 11: 297.

49. Resolves of the Boston Town Meeting, 12 September 1768, *Rebellion in America: A Contemporary British Viewpoint, 1765–1783*, ed. David Murdoch (Santa Barbara, Calif.: Clio Books, 1979), 73–75; Minutes of the Town Meeting of Boston, New England, 12 September 1768, New England Papers, 2, Sparks MSS 10, Houghton Library; Bernard to Hillsborough, Boston, 16 September 1768, BP, 7: 41–43.

50. Thomas, "Partisan Politics," 2: 577, 582; Miller, *Sam Adams*, 141–47; The Clergy of New England to [the bishop of London], Boston, 22 September 1768, Fulham Papers, 6: 68.

51. Lachlan McIntosh to Henry Laurens, [Charleston, S.C.], 15 October 1768, George C. Rogers et al., eds., *The Papers of Henry Laurens* (Columbia: University of South Carolina Press, 1976), 6: 127–28.

52. *BTR*, 16: 260–64; Richard D. Brown, "The Massachusetts Convention of Towns, 1768," *WMQ* 26 (1969): 95–104; The Proceedings of the Convention of Towns, enclosed in Bernard to Hillsborough, Boston, 3 October 1768, CO 5/757: 441.

53. Mass. Council Records, 16: 353–55; Bernard to Hillsborough, Boston, 23 September 1768, BP, 7: 48–49; Shy, *Toward Lexington*, 163–67; Gipson, *The British Empire*, 11: 39–69, 160.

54. Bernard to Barrington, Boston, 20 February 1769, *Barrington-Bernard Correspondence*, 190.

55. Thomas Cushing to Stephen Sayre, Boston, 7 October 1768, Massachusetts Papers.

56. Bernard to Hillsborough, Boston, 26 September 1768, BP, 7: 53–57; "List of Councillors who passed upon the Answer," [26 September 1768], CO 5/757: 429; Mass. Council Records, 16: 356–57.

57. Bernard to Hillsborough, Boston, 30 September 1768, "Supplement," BP, 7: 65.

58. James Bowdoin to John Erving, Minutes of the Massachusetts Council, 22 September–5 October [1768], n.p., Bowdoin-Temple Papers; Mass. Council Records, 16: 360–61; Bernard to Hillsborough, Boston, 26 September 1768, CO 5/757: 419–22.

59. David Hackett Fischer, *Paul Revere's Ride* (New York: Oxford Univ. Press, 1994), 31–40; Shy, *Toward Lexington*, 125–26, 134–36; Gage to Bernard, New York, 25 September 1768, BP, 11: 307–8; John R. Alden, *General Gage in America: Being Principally His Role in the American Revolution* (New York: Greenwood Press, 1948), 161.

60. Bernard to Hillsborough, Boston, 1 October 1768, BP, 7: 67–70; Mass. Council Records, 16: 361–62.

61. Cushing to Stephen Sayre, Boston, 7 October 1768.

62. Bernard to Hillsborough, Boston, 5 October 1768, BP, 7: 74–75, 77; Mass. Council Records, 16: 364–65; *BGCJ*, 16 October 1768.

63. Gage to Hillsborough, Boston, 31 October 1768, *Correspondence of Gage*, 1: 202–4; Mass. Council Records, 16: 368–70; Bernard to Hillsborough, Boston, 1 November 1768, BP, 7: 3–93; Zobel, *Boston Massacre*, 99–104.

64. Bernard to Hillsborough, Boston, 5 November 1768, BP, 7: 95–99; On the Question relative to the Commissioners return to Boston, CO 5/757: 517–18, enclosed in Bernard to Hillsborough, Boston, 5 November 1768, CO 5/757: 513–17.

65. Mass. Council Records, 16: 369–70; Gage to the Council, [Boston], 28 October 1768, Bowdoin-Temple Papers.

66. [James Bowdoin], Petition to the King to remove Governor Bernard, [Boston], 27 October 1768, [draft], Bowdoin-Temple Papers.

67. Samuel Danforth to William Bollan, Boston, 5 December 1768, "Bowdoin-Temple Papers," *Collections of the Massachusetts Historical Society*, 6th ser., 9 (1897): 113–15; Petition of the Major Part of the Council to the House of Lords, [Boston], 5 December 1768, Bowdoin-Temple Papers; Petition of the Major Part of the Council to the House of Commons, [Boston], December 1768, *PHE*, 16: 480–81. To Bollan's relief, the Council's petitions avoided any "positive Assertions of [legislative] Right," which he supposed would strengthen the case for "repeal on the grounds of inexpediency." Bernard, however, spied "several Intimations" of colonial rights "too plain to be unnoticed." William Bollan to Samuel Danforth, [London], 8 March 1769, Bowdoin-Temple Papers; Bernard to Hillsborough, Boston, 5 December 1768, BP, 7: 114–15.

68. The Massachusetts Council to Hillsborough, Boston, 15 April 1769, *BC*, 27–31 July 1769; Hutchinson to Thomas Pownall, Boston, 17 April 1769, THLB, 26: 351.

69. *JHRM*, 45: 117–38, 168–72, 191–99; The Massachusetts Council to Hillsborough, Boston, 15 April 1769, *BC*, 27–31 July 1769, and CO 5/758: 90–104; The Massachusetts Council to Hillsborough, Boston, 12 June 1769, *BC*, 3–7 August 1769.

70. William De Grey, Attorney-General, Case [of the *Liberty*], 25 July 1768, CO 5/757: 229–32; Fowler Jr., *Baron of Beacon Hill*, 99–101; Barrow, *Trade and Empire*, 233–36; Ubbelohde, *Vice-Admiralty Courts*, 123–27.

71. Zobel, *Boston Massacre*, 106.

72. See Hutchinson to the Commissioners of Customs, Milton, 17 September 1768, THLB, 25: 277–78; Hutchinson to ?, Boston, 8 and 10 August 1768, THLB, 26: 320–21; Hutchinson to the Commissioners of Customs, Boston, 29 October 1768, THLB, 25: 275; John Robinson to Charles Steuart, Boston, 11 August 1769, MS. 5025: 73–174, Charles Steuart Papers; Bernard to the Commissioners of Customs, Province House, 6 January 1769, CCT, 7: 6–7; Robert Auchmuty to the Commissioners of Customs, Boston, 16 September 1768, CCT, 7: 1.

73. *DAJA*, 3: 287–98; Hutchinson, *History of Massachusetts*, 3: 213–14; Bernard to Philip Stephens, Boston, 15 March 1769, BP, 7: 153–55.

74. See Zobel, *Boston Massacre*, 218–19.

75. Samuel Quincy to [Josiah Quincy], Boston, 26 August 1768, Samuel Quincy Papers, MHS.

76. Hillsborough to Bernard, Whitehall, 30 July 1768, 241–47; *Correspondence of King George III*, 2: 85.

77. Bernard to Hillsborough, Boston, 14 November 1768, BP, 7: 103–8; Bernard to Hillsborough, Boston, 26 December 1768, BP, 7: 118–20; Israel Williams to Thomas Hutchinson, Hatfield, 9 January 1769, THLB, 25: 287; Israel Williams to Thomas Hutchinson, Hatfield, 23 January 1770, THLB, 25: 352–53.

78. Bernard to Hillsborough, Boston, 14 November 1768; *Letters of James Murray*, 159–61; *Boston Under Military Rule, 1768–1769, as Revealed in a "Journal of the Times,"* ed. Oliver M. Dickerson (1936; New York: Da Capo Press, 1970), 106; Murray in *BEP*, 29 May 1769.

79. Thomas, *Townshend Duties Crisis*, 93; Barrington to Bernard, 1 November 1768, BP, 12: 6; Barrington to Bernard, 9 November 1768, BP, 12: 9.

80. John Pownall to Bernard, London, 19 November 1768, BP, 12: 21.

81. On Stanley (1721–1780) see Namier and Brooke, *House of Commons*, 3: 468–72; Thomas, *Townshend Duties Crisis*, 104–5.

82. Murdoch, ed., *Rebellion in America*, 5, 7–8, 41, 51–56.

83. *PDBP*, 3: 7–8, 12; Thomas, *Townshend Duties Crisis*, 104–5; Hillsborough to Bernard, Whitehall, 20 February 1769, BP, 12: 5.

84. Hillsborough to Bernard, Whitehall, 19 November 1768, BP, 12: 17–18; Hillsborough to the Attorney General and Solicitor General, Whitehall, 6 November 1768, CO 5/757: 452.

85. William De Grey to Hillsborough, n.p., 25 November 1768, CO 5/757: 464–66.

86. Hillsborough to Bernard, Whitehall, 15 November 1768, BP, 12: 11; Hillsborough to Bernard, Whitehall, 19 November 1768, BP, 12: 17–18.

87. *PDBP*, 3: 12, 22–27, 29–30.

88. *PDBP*, 3: 35, 38, 49; Resolutions of both Houses of Parliament, relative to the Public Transactions in His Majesty's Province of Massachusetts Bay, BP, 12: 275–78.

89. Christie and Labaree, *Empire or Independence*, 122, 236–41; Gipson, *The British Empire*, 11: 235; Bernard to John Pownall, Boston, 13 January 1769, BP, 7: 253; Hutchinson to [Thomas Whately], n.p., 20 January 1769, *Copy of Letters Sent to Great-Britain by His Excellency Thomas Hutchinson, the Hon. Andrew Oliver, and Several Other Persons, Born and Educated Among Us . . .* (Boston: Edes and Gill, 1773); Hutchinson to Jackson, Boston, 28 January 1769, THLB, 26: 349.

90. Lord North managed to persuade the House to admit the petition of the "major part" of the Council as if coming from Bollan himself. Bernard to Hutchinson, Pall Mall, 10 March 1770, BP, 8: 75; *PDBP*, 3: 59–60; *Commons Journals*, 32: 136–37; *PHE*, 16: 480–84.

91. *PDBP*, 3: 67–69, 72–74, 79, 81–82, 90–91; George Grenville to William Knox,

Wotton, 19 September 1768, Historical Manuscripts Commission, *Report on Manu-scripts in Various Collections . . .* 6 (Dublin: HMSO, 1909), 100–101.

92. Samuel Danforth (for the Council) to Hillsborough, Boston, 12 June 1769, *Speeches of the Governors,* ed. Bradford, 162–65; William Bollan to Samuel Danforth, [London], 30 January 1769, Bowdoin-Temple Papers; Thomas Pownall to Dr. Samuel Cooper, London, 1 January and 6 February 1769, Franklin Letters, Sparks MSS 16: 94, Houghton Library.

93. Thomas, *Townshend Duties Crisis,* 123–26; [Franklin], "Queries recommended to the Consideration of those Gentlemen who are for vigorous Measures with the Americans," *Papers of Benjamin Franklin,* 13: 187–88.

94. Barrington to Bernard, London, 12 February 1769, BP, 12: 49–50.

95. *Correspondence of King George III,* 1: 82–84.

96. Pownall to Bernard, London, 24 December 1768, BP, 12: 29.

97. From Pownall came the proposals relating to New York, the reform of the Quartering Act, the repeal of the act prescribing colonial civil lists, and the partial withdrawal of the British regulars. We cannot be certain of Bernard's views on these points but both men were agreed that Parliament should disqualify rebels from office and begin reforming the Council. The remaining suggestions were entirely reflective of Bernard's personal agenda: a baronetcy, leave to come to England, and confirmation of the Mount Desert grant. Pownall to Bernard, 19 February 1769, BP, 12: 53–55.

98. Barrington to Bernard, London, 21 March 1769, BP, 12: 65–67.

99. Thomas, *Townshend Duties Crisis,* 131; Memorandum by the King, [February 1769], *Correspondence of King George III,* 1: 84–85; E. Reitan, "The Civil List, 1761–1777: Problems of Finance and Administration," *Institute of Historical Research Bulletin* 47 (1974): 186–201.

100. Bernard's friends, Welbore Ellis and Lord Barrington, supported Wilkes's expulsion from the Commons, whereas his critics on the opposition benches—William Beckford, Col. Isaac Barré, Edmund Burke, and William Dowdeswell—voted against. *Correspondence of King George III* 2: 80.

101. Bernard to Hillsborough, Boston, 25 May 1769, BP, 7: 157–59; Christie and Labaree, *Empire or Independence,* 122–29; Charles R. Ritcheson, *British Politics and the American Revolution* (Norman, Okla.: University of Oklahoma Press, 1954), 142–43; Thomas, *Townshend Duties Crisis,* 130, 154–55; Benjamin Franklin to Samuel Cooper, London, 24 February 1769, *Papers of Benjamin Franklin,* 16: 52–53; Franklin to Cooper, London, 24 April 1769, *ibid.,* 119.

102. Bernard to Hillsborough, Boston, 26 January 1769, BP, 7: 130.

103. Fowler Jr., *Samuel Adams,* 94–95.

104. Bernard to Hillsborough, Boston, 16 September 1768, BP, 7: 41–43.

105. Minutes of the Town Meeting of Boston, New England, 12 September 1768, New England Papers, 2: 81.

106. Bernard to Hillsborough, Boston, 16 September 1768, 40; Information of Richard Silvester of Boston, Innholder, taken on 23 January 1769, New England Papers, 3: 12.

107. Information of Richard Silvester; Sentiments of the Sons of Liberty, [1769], New England Papers, 3.

108. Bernard to Hillsborough, Boston, 25 January 1769, BP, 7: 127; Bernard to John Pownall, Boston, 8 April 1769, BP, 7: 277.

109. See *The Commentaries on the Laws of England of Sir William Blackstone adapted to the present state of the Law,* ed. Robert Malcolm Kerr, 4th ed., 4 vols. (London: John Murray, 1876), 4: 64–66, 73, 80–81, 106–8.

110. Sentiments of the Sons of Liberty.

111. Bernard to Barrington, Boston, 23 December 1768, BP, 7: 239–49, at 242–43; *Procs. MHS*, 1st ser., 4 (1856–60): 385–88.

112. Thomas Cushing to Dennis DeBerdt, Boston, 9 May 1767, "Letters of Thomas Cushing from 1767 to 1775," 347–49.

113. Deposition of Nathaniel Coffin, 6 February 1769, CO 5/759: 52. An earlier version was enclosed in Bernard to Hillsborough, 24 January 1769, CO 5/758: 50–52, and BP, 7: 124. According to George Chalmers's notation on the copy in New England Papers, vol. 3, Coffin's deposition was read at the Board of Trade on 6 December 1769.

114. For a fuller discussion see Nicolson, " 'McIntosh, Otis & Adams are our demagogues,' " 91–94. The Cushing-Coffin exchange, however, is interpreted differently by Thomas in "Partisan Politics," 573–74, as confirmation of the governor's view that Adams, Otis, and others were planning an insurrection.

115. Bernard to Hillsborough, 24 January 1769, BP, 7: 124.

116. Bernard to Hillsborough, Boston, 21 December 1768, BP, 7: 115; quotation from Bernard to Lord Barrington, n.p., 18 March 1769, *Barrington-Bernard Correspondence*, 197; Ubbelohde, *Vice-Admiralty Courts*, 123–27.

117. Bernard to Hillsborough, Boston, 25 May 1769, BP, 7: 157–59.

118. Bernard to John Pownall, Boston, 25 March 1769, "private," BP, 7: 270–73; James Murray to Charles Steuart, Boston, 18 March 1769, MS. 5025: 111–12, Charles Steuart Papers.

119. Maitland, *Constitutional History of England*, 318.

120. Hutchinson to Bernard, Boston, 26 June 1770, THLB, 26: 514, 516.

121. Bernard to [Barrington], Boston, 23 December 1768, BP, 7: 256–57; Hutchinson to ?, n.p., 16 February 1769, THLB, 26: 345; Hutchinson to Jackson, Boston, 18 August 1769, THLB, 26: 366; Hutchinson to Hillsborough, Boston, n.d., October 1770, THLB, 27: 22–23.

122. Bailyn, *Hutchinson*, 143–44, 146–48; *BGHU*, 7: 406–7; Bernard to Barrington, Boston, 20 October 1768, *Barrington-Bernard Correspondence*, 177–78.

123. Bernard to Hillsborough, Boston, 4 February 1769, BP, 8: 132–37. The councilors were named in an appendix, *ibid.*, 140.

CHAPTER SEVEN

1. Francis G. Walett, "Governor Bernard's Undoing: An Earlier Hutchinson Letters Affair," *New England Quarterly* 38 (1965): 217–26; Malcolm Freiberg, "William Bollan, Agent of Massachusetts," part 4, *Boston Public Library, More Books* 23 (1948): 168–82, at 179–80. Bollan's antipathy toward Bernard is downplayed in Joel D. Myerson, "The Private Revolution of William Bollan," *New England Quarterly* 41 (1968): 536–50.

2. *Letters to the Right Honourable The Earl of Hillsborough from Governor Bernard, General Gage, and the Honourable His Majesty's Council for the Province of Massachusetts Bay with an Appendix containing divers proceedings referred to in the said letters* (1769; London: J. Almon, 1769); *Letters to the Ministry from Governor Bernard, General Gage, and Commodore Hood, and also Memorials to the Lords of the Treasury, from the Commissioners of Customs with sundry Letters and Papers annexed to the said Memorials* (1769; London: J. Almon, 1769); *BGCJ*, 11 December 1769. For bibliographic details see Thomas R. Adams, *American Independence. The Growth of an Idea: A Bibliographical Study of the American Political Pamphlets Printed Between 1764 and 1776 Dealing with the Dispute Between Great Britain and Her Colonies* (Providence, R.I.: Brown Univ. Press, 1965), 51–52.

3. Harbottle Dorr's annotated copy of *Letters to the Ministry from Governor Ber-*

nard is in the MHS; John Speed, Extract of Bernard to the earl of Hillsborough, Boston, 16 September 1768, Massachusetts Papers. On Temple see Bernard to John Pownall, Boston, 8 April 1769, BP, 7: 276–77.

4. *BTR*, 16: 286–87.

5. *BTR*, 16: 299–301.

6. *An Appeal to the World; or a Vindication of the Town of Boston from Many False And Malicious Aspersions* (1769; London: J. Almon, 1770) and *BTR*, 16: 303–25. William Bollan arranged for the reprinting by Almon, *Papers of Benjamin Franklin*, 16: 222–23, 278. Adams's authorship is confirmed by William Palfrey to John Wilkes, Boston, 11 October 1769, "John Wilkes and Boston," ed. Worthington C. Ford, *Procs. MHS*, 3d ser., 47 (1913–14): 191–200, at 211.

7. Bernard to Hillsborough, Boston, 1 June 1769, BP, 7: 167; Nicolson, "Governor Francis Bernard," 54–55.

8. Walmsley, *Hutchinson*, 98.

9. Hutchinson to Israel Williams, Boston, 6 May 1769, Israel Williams Papers.

10. Bernard to John Pownall, Boston, 9 May 1769, BP, 7: 282–83; Bernard to John Pownall, Boston, 23 April 1769, "private," BP, 7: 282–83.

11. Bernard to Hillsborough, Boston, 1 May 1769, BP, 7: 156.

12. Bernard to Jackson, Boston, 12 April 1769, "private," BP, 7: 286; Bernard to Jackson, Boston, 18 April 1769, "private," BP, 7: 274–76.

13. Bernard to Barrington, Boston, 12 April 1769, "private," BP, 7: 278.

14. Bernard to Thomas Hutchinson, Pall Mall, 16 December 1769, BP, 8: 27–28.

15. Gage to Bernard, New York, 15 May 1769, BP, 12: 91–92.

16. See Zobel, *Boston Massacre*, 113–44.

17. *JHRM*, 45: 123, 130–31.

18. Gage to Bernard, New York, 5 June 1769, BP, 12: 103–6.

19. Bernard to Hillsborough, Boston, 1–13 July 1769, BP 7:182.

20. Bernard to Gage, Boston, 12 June 1769, BP, 7: 226; Maj. Gen. Alexander Mackay to Bernard, 10 June 1769, BP, 12: 107–8; Bernard to Gage, Boston, 19 June 1769, BP, 7: 227–29; Bernard to Hillsborough, Boston, 25 June 1769, BP, 7: 175–77.

21. Andrew Oliver to Jasper Mauduit, [Boston], 10 July 1769, Andrew Oliver Letterbooks, 1: 106, MHS.

22. *JHRM*, 45: 137–38, 151, 168–72, 197–99; Bernard to Hillsborough, Boston, 1–13 July 1769, 177; Bernard to Barrington, Boston, 8 July 1769, BP, 8: 1–2.

23. Kerr, *Commentaries on the Laws of England of Sir William Blackstone*, 108; William Renwick Riddell, "Impeachment in England and English Colonies," *New York University Law Quarterly Review* 7 (1930): 702–8.

24. *JHRM*, 45: 164, 180.

25. *JHRM*, 45: 196–97.

26. Bernard to Hillsborough, Boston, 17 July 1769, BP, 7: 185–90, at 186.

27. Gage to Hillsborough, New York, 22 July 1769, *Correspondence of Gage*, 1: 229; Thomas Young to John Wilkes, Boston, 6 July 1769, "John Wilkes and Boston," 203; *BTR*, 16: 296; Hutchinson, *History of Massachusetts*, 3: 251.

28. Hutchinson to Benjamin Franklin, Boston, 29 July 1769, *Papers of Benjamin Franklin*, 16: 181–82.

29. Palfrey to John Wilkes, Boston, 13 June 1769, Ford, "John Wilkes and Boston," 201.

30. Thomas Young to John Wilkes, Boston, 3 August 1769, *ibid.*, 207.

31. *Copies of Proceedings in the Several Assemblies, in Consequence of the Resolutions of Parliament in the Last Session* ([London], 1769).

32. Benjamin Smith to [Isaac Smith], Charlestown [Charleston, S.C.], 12 December 1769, Smith-Carter Papers, MHS.

33. Suffolk County, Superior Court of Judicature, [draft] Indictment of Sir Francis Bernard, Boston, 21 November 1769, bMS Am 1704.18 (16), Houghton Library; William Palfrey to John Wilkes, Boston, 21 October 1769, "John Wilkes and Boston," 211; Thomas, "Partisan Politics," 2: 657–58.

34. Hutchinson to Israel Williams, Boston, 25 November 1769, Israel Williams Papers.

35. Bernard to Hutchinson, Hampstead, 9 February 1771, BP, 8: 157–58.

36. *London Chronicle*, 6–8 February 1770, Labaree, *Papers of Benjamin Franklin*, 17: 61; J. G. Palfrey, *The Life of William Palfrey*, vol. 7, *Library of American Biography*, ed. Jared Sparks (Boston: Little, Brown, 1848), 364–65.

37. Bernard to Hutchinson, Pall Mall, 4 October 1769, BP, 8: 11; Bernard, Petition to the King, October 1769, BP, 12: 147–48, 167; *Copy of the Complaint of the House of Representatives of Massachuset's-Bay against Sir Francis Bernard: With Sir Francis Bernard's Answer. Now Depending before His Majesty's Council* [London, 1770]. Other imprints were issued at Boston. See Adams, *American Independence*, 62–63.

38. The Act for Punishing Governors for Crimes Committed in the Plantations, 11 and 12 Will. 3. A parliamentary bill intended to make this act "more effectual" was debated in 1757 but never brought in. Charles M. Andrews, *The Colonial Period of American History* (New Haven: Yale Univ. Press, 1938), 4: 162.

39. Andrew Oliver to Bernard, Boston, 3 December 1769, BP, 12: 161–62.

40. Thomas W. Copeland, ed., *The Correspondence of Edmund Burke*, 9 vols. (Cambridge: Cambridge Univ. Press and Chicago: University of Chicago Press, 1958–70), 2: 77.

41. Dennis DeBerdt, Petition to the King in Council, London, 13 November 1769, "copy," Massachusetts Papers; John Pownall to Dennis DeBerdt, Whitehall, 10 November 1769, Massachusetts Papers; Dennis DeBerdt, [Memorial to the King's Council], n.p., [1770], bMS Am 811(59), Houghton Library; Order of the Lords of the Committee of the Council, [London], 20 January 1770, BP, 12: 203; Petition on behalf of the Massachusetts House of Representatives to the Lords of the Committee of the Privy Council [on Plantation affairs], 15 February 1770, BP, 12: 207–9.

42. Thomas Bernard, Some Account of the hearing before the [Privy] Council, February 28, 1770, BP, 12: 211–18; The Answer of Sir Francis Bernard . . . to the Complaint preferred against him by the House of Representatives, Bernard, *Select Letters*, 94–117.

43. Bernard, Petition to the Lords of the Committee of [the Privy] Council, February 24, 1770, 12: 175–77; Some Account of the hearing, 211.

44. References of Evidence for the hearing before the [Privy] Council, [February], 1770, BP, 12: 179–80; A List of Gentlemen of the Council of Massachusetts Bay, who have been turned out of the Council since the Repeal of the Stamp Act, 1766 to 1769, [February], 1770, BP, 12: 183; Extracts of Letters from the Secretaries of State to Gov. Bernard [February], 1770, BP, 12: 187–98, 281; Extracts of Letters from Gov. Bernard [February], 1770, BP, 12: 199–201. See also Bernard, *Select Letters*, 117–23.

45. *APC*, 5: 211–14.

46. Bernard to Hutchinson, Pall Mall, 7 March 1770, BP, 8: 70–71; *Commons Journals*, 32: 750.

47. Bernard to Hutchinson, Pall Mall, 19 September 1769, BP, 8: 9–10; Bernard to Hutchinson, Pall Mall, 16 November 1769, BP, 8: 17–18; Bernard to Hutchinson, Pall Mall, 16 December 1769, BP, 8: 27; Bernard to Hutchinson, Pall Mall, 14 February 1770, BP, 8: 62–64; Bernard to Lord North, Pall Mall, 22 February 1770, BP, 8: 67–69; Bernard to Andrew Oliver, Pall Mall, 8 March 1770, BP, 8: 74.

48. See Zobel, *Boston Massacre*, 206–10.

49. *PHE*, 16: 982–95.

50. Thomas Pownall to Dr. Samuel Cooper, London, 4 July 1770, Franklin Letters, 113–20.

51. *PDBP*, 3: 299; *Correspondence of King George III*, 2: 146; *Commons Journals*, 32: 970.

52. Kammen, *A Rope of Sand*, 140–41; Sosin, *Agents and Merchants*, 146–47.

53. [John Pownall], State of the Disorders, Confusions and Misgovernment which have lately prevailed and still continue to prevail, in the province of the Massachusetts Bay, CO 5/754: 41–69.

54. *APC*, 5: 246–65.

55. Cushing to Stephen Sayer, Boston, 6 November 1770, "Letters of Thomas Cushing," 356–57.

56. *APC*, 5: 262–65.

57. Ritcheson, *British Politics and the American Revolution*, 142–43; Thomas, *Townshend Duties Crisis*, 192–93.

58. Bernard to Hutchinson, Pall Mall, 28 April 1770, BP, 8: 89; Bernard to Hutchinson, Pall Mall, 13 May 1770, BP, 8: 93.

59. *JHRM*, 47: 257–89; Hutchinson, *History of Massachusetts*, 3: 319–21; *BGHU*, 7: 405; Nicolson, "The Friends of Government," 1: 175–99.

60. Bernard to Hutchinson, Hampstead, 7 July 1770, BP, 8: 106; Thomas, *Townshend Duties Crisis*, 207.

61. Bernard to Hutchinson, Hampstead, 13 November 1770, BP, 8: 144–45; Bernard to Andrew Oliver, Hampstead, 6 and 13 November 1770, BP, 8: 148–49.

62. Bernard to Hutchinson, Hampstead, 25 July 1770, BP, 8: 109.

63. Thomas, *Townshend Duties Crisis*, 207–8.

64. Labaree, ed., *Royal Instructions*, 1: 48–49.

65. Bernard to Hutchinson, Hampstead, 9 October 1770, BP, 8: 133–34.

66. Hutchinson wrote him regularly and sent him copies of the Boston newspapers. File of American Newspapers, 1770, Spencer Bernard Family Papers.

67. Hill, *Georgian Lincoln*, 11.

68. Higgins, *The Bernards*, 1: 209; Florence Baker, *Nettleham: A Short History of the Village* (Lincoln: n.p., 1938), 43–44; Enclosure Act, Manor and Parish of Nettleham, 1777, Church Commissioners records: Court Rolls, CC 85/313734.

69. John Pownall to Bernard, London, 3 December 1771, BP, 12: 239; Barrington to Bernard, London, 10 March 1772, BP, 12: 247–51.

70. Bernard to Hutchinson, Pall Mall, 13 January 1771, BP, 8: 44–47.

71. Bernard to North, Hampstead, 29 September 1770, [draft?], BP, 12: 227.

72. Higgins, *The Bernards*, 2: 272; Barrington to Bernard, London, 7 January 1772, BP, 12: 243.

73. Thomas Bernard to [Isaac Smith Jr.] n.p., n.d. [1771?], Smith-Carter Papers, MHS; Thomas Bernard to [Isaac Smith Jr.], Hampstead, 28 February [1771?], *ibid.*

74. Bernard to [Hillsborough], Bath, 1 February 1772, BP, 8: 180–81.

75. Barrington to Bernard, London, 10 March 1772, BP, 12: 247.

76. Barrington to Bernard, London, 30 November 1771, BP, 12: 235.

77. List of Inhabitants of Nether Winchendon, D/X 525, BRO.

78. Probate of the Will of Sir Francis Bernard, 12 July 1779.

79. Hugh Hanley, *The Prebendal, Aylesbury, A History* ([Aylesbury, Bucks.]: Ginn & Co., 1986); Higgins, *The Bernards*, 2: 236–38; [Amelia] Bernard to Scrope Bernard, Aylesbury, Saturday, n.d., Spencer Bernard Papers; Hutchinson to Bernard, Boston, 10 March 1773, THLB, 27: 465.

80. *Papers of Benjamin Franklin*, 20: 393.

81. Franklin to [Charles Thomson], London, 18 March 1770, *ibid.*, 17: 111.

82. Benjamin Kent to Franklin, [c. September 1766], *ibid.*, 13: 431.

83. Bernard to Hutchinson, Pall Mall, 17 November 1769, BP, 8: 21–24.

84. See *Papers of Benjamin Franklin*, 17: 310–13; 18: xxv–xxvi, 26–30, 102–4, 120–27, 147–53.

85. *Ibid.*, 17: 257–58. For Franklin's role as Massachusetts's agent see Cecil B. Currey, *Road to Revolution: Benjamin Franklin in England, 1765–1775* (Garden City, N.Y.: Anchor Books, Doubleday & Co., 1968), 303–50.

86. House of Representatives of Massachusetts to Benjamin Franklin, n.p., 6 November 1770, *Papers of Benjamin Franklin*, 17: 275–83.

87. See *ibid.*, 18: 9–16, and Franklin's unpublished essay, "On the Conduct of Lord Hillsborough," [August 1772?], *ibid.*, 19: 216–26.

88. Cooper to Franklin, Boston, 10 July 1771, *ibid.*, 18: 173.

89. Franklin to Samuel Mather, London, 7 July 1773, *ibid.*, 20: 286.

90. See *ibid.*, 19: 399–408; 20: xxxi–xxxiii; Bailyn, *Hutchinson*, 221–44.

91. *JHRM*, 50: 26–35.

92. *DAJA*, 2: 93.

93. "Rules by which a Great Empire may be reduced to a Small One," *Papers of Benjamin Franklin*, 20: 391–93. His *Causes of the Present Distractions in America* (1774) was a sustained attack on colonial governors. Franklin believed Bernard was "D. E. Q.," the author of a "long [and] laboured" riposte in the *Public Advertiser*, 29–30 October 1773, which he sent to Thomas Cushing. See "On Governor Bernard's Testimony to the Loyalty of Massachusetts," in *Papers of Benjamin Franklin*, 20: 405–6, and 454–55, and Higgins, *The Bernards*, 2: 215, 248.

94. Thomas Bernard to Isaac Smith Jr., London, 12 February 1774, Smith-Carter Papers.

95. Coffin to Charles Steuart, Boston, 30 October 1769, MS. 5025: 222–25, Charles Steuart Papers.

96. Tyler, *Smugglers & Patriots*, 114, 143–44; Warden, *Boston*, 219.

97. Hutchinson to Bernard, Boston, 8 August 1769, THLB, 26: 362.

98. Mein's offending piece appeared in *BC*, 23–26 October 1770 [publication delayed to October 28]. On the mobbing see John E. Alden, "John Mein: Scourge of Patriots," *PCSM* 34 (1937–42): 571–99, at 586–89; Nicolson, " 'McIntosh, Otis & Adams are our demagogues,' " 86–87.

99. Alden, "John Mein," 586–89; James Murray to Charles Steuart, Boston, 12 November 1769, MS. 5025: 232–33, Charles Steuart Papers. Longman's involvement may be followed in the Hancock Family Papers, MHS, and Hiller B. Zobel, "Law Under Pressure: Boston, 1769–1771," George A. Billias, ed., *Law and Authority in Colonial America* (Barre, Mass.: Barre Publishers, 1965), at 194–96.

100. Mass. Council Records, 16: 448–50; *BGCJ*, 29 January 1770; Hutchinson to Bernard, Boston, 27 January 1770, THLB, 26: 434–35; Nicolson, " 'McIntosh, Otis & Adams are our demagogues,' " 86–95.

101. Nicolson, "Governor Francis Bernard," 50; Coffin to Charles Steuart, Boston, 22 May 1770, MS. 5026: 56–59, Charles Steuart Papers; Coffin to Steuart, Boston, 30 October 1769.

102. Hutchinson to Hillsborough, Boston, 27 April 1770, THLB, 25: 391–94; Hutchinson to Bernard, Boston, 28 April 1770, 25: 396; Hutchinson to John Pownall, Boston, 18 May 1770, 25: 84.

103. Hutchinson to Hillsborough, Boston, 27 April 1770, 391.

104. Hutchinson to Whately, Boston, 24 August 1769, THLB, 26: 367–68; Hutchinson to Bernard, Boston, 28 April 1770, 396; Hutchinson to John Pownall, Boston, 16 May 1770, THLB, 26: 484.

105. Tyler, *Smugglers & Patriots*, 159–69; Nicolson, "Governor Francis Bernard," 59.

106. Hutchinson to the earl of Dartmouth, Boston, [16] September 1773, *Documents of the American Revolution*, 6: 221. For an overview see Nicolson, "The Friends of Government," 1: 280–98.

107. See Donald C. Lord and Robert M. Calhoon, "The Removal of the Massachusetts General Court from Boston, 1769–1772," *Journal of American History* 55 (1969): 735–55.

108. Hillsborough to Bernard, 24 March 1769, BP, 12: 77–80.

109. Hutchinson to Bernard, Boston, 4 August 1770, THLB, 25: 530–31; Tyler, *Smugglers & Patriots*, 74; Nicolson, "Friends of Government," 1: 256.

110. Hutchinson to Bernard, Boston, 1 June 1770, THLB, 26: 496; Whitmore, *Massachusetts Civil List*, 63.

111. Hutchinson to John Pownall, n.p., 30 September 1770, THLB, 27: 9–10; Hutchinson to Bernard, n.p., 28 September 1770, THLB, 27: 6; Nicolson, "The Friends of Government," 1: 202.

112. Gray to John Boylston, Boston, 15 February 1772, Boylston Papers, MHS; *BGCJ*, 31 August 1772.

113. Bernard to Hutchinson, Hampstead, 10 November 1770, BP, 8: 139–42.

114. Bernard to Hutchinson, Hampstead, 3 December 1770, BP, 8: 152; Bernard to Hutchinson, Hampstead, 22 December 1770, BP, 8: 152; Bernard to Hutchinson, Hampstead, 11 February 1770, BP, 8: 160.

115. Sayward to Hutchinson, York, 22 August 1769, THLB, 25: 328.

116. Hutchinson to Bernard, Boston, 18 March 1770, THLB, 26: 456.

117. "Extract of Brigadier Timothy Ruggles to Joseph Harrison," n.p., 18 November 1769, New England Papers, 3.

118. John Worthington to Hutchinson, Springfield, 5 September 1770, THLB, 25: 427–28.

119. Hutchinson to Israel Williams, 25 November 1769, Israel Williams Papers; Nicolson, "The Friends of Government," 1: 275–76.

120. Bernard to Hutchinson, Hampstead, 8 October 1770, BP, 8: 132.

121. Hutchinson to John Pownall?, n.p., [1772], THLB, 27: 360–61; Hutchinson to ?, Boston, 21 July 1772, THLB, 27: 365–68. For a fuller discussion see Nicolson, "The Friends of Government," 1: 284–87.

122. *JHRM*, 49: 72–73, 127–32.

123. On Hutchinson's decision to accept Hancock's election to the Council and Hancock's subsequent refusal, see Samuel Adams to James Warren, Boston, 13 April 1772, Warren-Adams Papers, 10, MHS; Hutchinson to ?, Boston, n.d. April 1772, THLB, 27: 313–15; Hutchinson to Bernard, Boston, 29 May 1772, THLB, 27: 340; W. T. Baxter, *The House of Hancock: Business in Boston, 1724–1775* (1945; New York: Russell & Russell, 1965), 270–81. On Bowdoin see Hutchinson to Commodore James Gambier, Boston, 7 May 1772, THLB, 27: 330–31.

124. *Copy of Letters Sent to Great-Britain by His Excellency Thomas Hutchinson, the Hon. Andrew Oliver, and Several Other Persons, Born and Educated among Us* (Boston: Edes and Gill, 1773); *JHRM*, 50: 26–35; Hutchinson to ?, Boston, 16 July 1773, THLB, 27: 514–15.

125. Royall to Dartmouth, Medford, New England, 18 January 1774, *Procs. MHS*, 1st ser., 13 (1873–75): 179–82.

126. Alan Valentine, *Lord North*, 2 vols. (Norman, Okla.: University of Oklahoma Press, 1967), 1: 314, 320, 323; Derry, *English Politics and the American Revolution*, 102–3; P. D. G. Thomas, *Tea Party to Independence: The Third Phase of the American Revolution, 1773–1776* (Oxford: Clarendon Press, 1991), 62–63.

127. Bernard, *Select Letters*, i–vii.

128. [John Pownall], State of the Disorders, Confusion and Mis-government which have prevailed and do still prevail in His Majesty's province of Massachusetts Bay in America, BP, 8: 182–228; Narrative [1773], BP, 8: 229–43; List of Papers relative to the Province of Massachusetts Bay, selected from the Paper concerning Riots and Tumults in North America, laid before the House of Lords, from the 1st day of January 1746 to the present time, [28 January 1774], BP, 8: 244–78. One opposition pamphleteer claimed that the Lords' report was "solely founded" upon the information provided by Bernard and Hutchinson. *The Report of the House of Lords, to Enquire into the Several Proceedings of the Colony of Massachusets's Bay, in Opposition to the Sovereignty of His Majesty, in His Parliament of Great Britain, over that Province* (London: William Bagley, 1774), i–iii.

129. Wickwire, *British Subministers*, 146–47.

130. Shy, *Toward Lexington*, 406–7; King George III to Lord North, Queens House, [London], 4 February 1774, *Correspondence of King George III*, 3: 59.

131. Valentine, *Lord North*, 1: 319–20; Derry, *English Politics and the American Revolution*, 104.

132. *Correspondence of King George III*, 3: 85; *Commons Journals*, 34: 561, 696; William Bollan, *The Petition of Mr. Bollan, Agent for the Council of Massachusetts Bay, to the King in Council, January 26, 1774* (London: J. Almon, 1774).

133. Edmund Burke, *Speeches and Letters on American Affairs* (London: J. M. Dent & Sons, 1961), 1–63, with references to Bernard at 23, 25, 33–34, 46–47.

134. *PDBP*, 4: 71, 176, 210–11, 212–14, 221, 230, 242–59, 268, 347; *DLTH*, 1: 312; *Correspondence of King George III*, 3: 94–97. Parliamentary debates on the Port Act were printed in *BGCJ*, 16 May 1774.

135. *DLTH*, 1: 195.

136. Bernard to John Pownall, Astrop Wells, 28 August 1773, BP, 12: 285–87.

137. *DLTH*, 1: 557.

138. Quoted in Hill, *Georgian Lincoln*, 12.

139. [Lord Camden], *Considerations on the Measures carrying on with respect to the British Colonies in North America*, in *English Defenders of American Freedoms, 1774–1778: Six Pamphlets Attacking British Policy* comp. Paul H. Smith (Washington: Library of Congress, 1972), 96–97.

140. Thomas, *Townshend Duties Crisis*, 262.

CONCLUSION

1. [Hulton], Some Account of New England, 142; Mrs. Mercy Otis Warren, *History of the Rise, Progress and Termination of the American Revolution*, ed. Lester H. Cohen (1805; Indianapolis: Liberty Classics, 1988), 25.

2. The first proto-Loyalist protest was organized in Plymouth by forty friends of government three days before the Boston Tea Party. Ostensibly, they were protesting the adoption of the radical pamphlet, *The Votes and Proceedings of the Freeholders and Other Inhabitants of the Town of Boston* (Boston, 1772)—known as the *Boston Pamphlet*—for its contentious assertions of colonial rights of self-government. A printed copy is attached to the *BGCJ*, 27 December 1773, Dorr Collection, 4. The most significant protest outside Boston was in Worcester, when forty-three freeholders protested over the town's vote of approval for the *Boston Pamphlet* in May 1774. Albert A. Lovell, *Worcester in the War of the Revolution: embracing the acts of the town from 1765 to 1783 inclusive* (Worcester, Mass.: Tyler and Seagrave, 1876), 29, 35. On Petersham see Mabel Cook Coolidge, *The History of Petersham, Massachusetts* ([Petersham]: Petersham Historical Society, 1948), 86–87, 94–97; proceedings of Pe-

tersham town meeting of 2 January 1775, in *BGCJ,* 16 January 1775. On Deerfield, George Sheldon, *A History of Deerfield, Massachusetts,* 2 vols. (1895–96; Somersworth, N.H.: New Hampshire Publishing Co., 1972), 2: 678–79. For Marshfield see Petition of the Inhabitants of Marshfield and Scituate to Lt. Gen. Gage, Marshfield, 20 January 1775, *Documents of the American Revolution,* 9: 41–42; Cynthia Hagar Krusell, *Of Tea and Tories: The Story of Revolutionary Marshfield* (Marshfield: Mass.: n.p., 1976). For a full discussion see appendix to Nicolson, " 'McIntosh, Otis & Adams are our demagogues,' " 110–14.

3. Copies of the addresses are in Stark, *Loyalists of Massachusetts,* 124–32.

4. Nicolson, " 'McIntosh, Otis & Adams are our demagogues,' " 95–100.

5. *BGCJ,* 30 May 1774.

6. Coffin to Steuart, 6 July 1774, Steuart Papers, MS. 5028: 226–27; Farewell Address to Governor Hutchinson, Boston, 30 May 1774, *BGCJ,* 30 May 1774.

7. Albert Matthews, ed., "The Solemn League and Covenant, 1774," *Publications of the Colonial Society of Massachusetts* 18 (1915–16): 103–22.

8. Coffin to Steuart, 6 July 1774; *BTR,* 18: 177–78.

9. Tyler, *Smugglers & Patriots,* 217. Normally only 700 or so of the several thousand in attendance could vote. One-fifth would represent about 140 voters, 17 more than the subscribers to the address to Hutchinson.

10. Earl of Dartmouth to General Gage, 3 June 1774, "Documents Relating to the Last Meetings of the Massachusetts Royal Council, 1774–1776," ed. Albert Matthews, *Publications of the Colonial Society of Massachusetts* 32 (1933–37): 450–504, at 468.

11. Coffin to Steuart, 6 July 1774.

12. Matthews, ed., "The Massachusetts Royal Council, 1774–1776," 456–66.

13. Gage to the earl of Dartmouth, Salem, 25 August 1774, *ibid.,* 473–74.

14. Old John Erving did not resign his seat until 25 or 26 August. In October he was invited to attend the Provincial Congress, but refused and in October 1775 signed the farewell address to Gage. Gage to the earl of Dartmouth, 25 August 1774; *BGHU,* 12: 154; A List of Notes Reloaned the Government by John Erving, [1787?], David Greenough Papers, Box 5, 1789–95, MHS.

15. Brown, *Revolutionary Politics, 190.*

16. The Novanglus letters are reprinted in *Works of John Adams,* 10 vols., ed. Charles Francis Adams (Boston: Little & Brown, 1850–56), 4: 11–181, esp. 22–75. His friend Robert Treat Paine came to the same conclusion, "Reply to Massachusettensis," n.p., n.d. [1774–75], Robert Treat Paine Papers, MHS.

17. [Daniel Leonard], *Massachusettensis: Or a Series of Letters containing a Faithful Narrative of the State of Many Important and Striking Facts, which laid the Foundation of the Present Trouble in the Province of Massachusetts Bay* (Boston, 1775; 3d ed. London, 1776), 83.

18. [Thomas Bradbury Chandler], *A Friendly Address to All Reasonable Americans, on the Subject of Our Political Confusions* ([Boston], 1775), 35–36.

19. Leonard, *Massachusettensis,* 64.

20. Contemporary reports indicate that 625 other persons—counted here neither as Loyalists nor as friends of government—joined militant associations. Nicolson, "Friends of Government," 1: 353.

21. Nicolson, "Governor Francis Bernard," 35.

22. *Ibid.,* 37–38.

23. Bernard to Col. Thomas Oliver, Pall Mall, 2 October 1770, BP, 8: 123–24.

24. The Rev. Henry Caner to Bishop Richard Terrick, Boston, 25 May 1775, *Letterbook of the Rev. Henry Caner,* 62.

25. The pattern of a mainly loyal Anglican clergy and a much divided laity was

prevalent in the other colonies except Virginia, where the majority of clergy were Patriots. Overall a majority of Anglican laity and a majority of both the Congregational clergy and laity supported the Revolution. Clark, *Language of Liberty*, 296–351, 363.

26. Nicolson, "Governor Francis Bernard," 60–61 and appendix A, 68–113.

27. Paul H. Smith, "The American Loyalists: Notes on Their Organization and Numerical Strength," *WMQ* 25 (1968): 259–77.

28. Edward Countryman, *A People in Revolution: The American Revolution and Political Society in New York, 1760–1790* (Baltimore: Johns Hopkins Univ. Press, 1981); Brown, *The King's Friends*.

29. Nicolson, "Governor Francis Bernard," 34, 61; Nicolson, "The Friends of Government," 1: 333–37; 2: 353–66; David E. Maas, comp. and ed., *Divided Hearts: Massachusetts Loyalists, 1765–1790: A Biographical Directory* (Boston: New England Historic and Genealogical Society, 1980).

30. See Paul H. Smith, *Loyalists and Redcoats: A Study in British Revolutionary Policy* (Chapel Hill: University of North Carolina Press, 1964); Christopher Hibbert, *Redcoats and Rebels: The American Revolution Through British Eyes* (New York: Avon Books, 1991), 80, 235, 279.

31. Nicolson, "Governor Francis Bernard," 60–61; Nicolson, "Friends of Government," 1: 359–65.

32. Only 14 percent had their properties confiscated by the new state government. Many of the Loyalist refugees, including some who were named in the Banishment Act of 1778, were eventually allowed to return and resume their estates. See David E. Maas, *The Return of the Massachusetts Loyalists* (New York: Garland Publishing, 1989).

33. *JHRM*, 51: 189.

34. The principal state legislation concerning the Loyalists is in Stark, *Loyalists of Massachusetts*, 137–44.

35. Copy of the Act to confiscate the Estate of Sir Francis Bernard & others in the State of Massachusetts Bay, 30 April 1779, BP, 12: 315–17. The purchaser of the house and land at Jamaica Plain, Roxbury, was Martin Brimmer, a Boston merchant; the Dorchester property was bought by another merchant, William Allen. The sale fetched over £3,431 net in new emission currency. Maas, *Return of the Massachusetts Loyalists*, 292–95, 311; John T. Hassam, "The Confiscated Estates of Boston Loyalists," *Procs. MHS*, 2d ser., 10 (1895–96): 162–85.

36. Isaac Royall to James Bowdoin, Kensington, 19 November 1778, Bowdoin-Temple Papers.

37. Bernard to Thomas Flucker, Aylesbury, 1 February 1774, Henry Knox Papers, MHS (microfilm copies of originals in Pierpont Morgan Library, New York).

38. Petition of Walter Logan to the Lords Commissioners of His Majesty's Treasury, Edinburgh, 10 May 1782, Spencer Bernard Papers.

39. Bernard to Hillsborough, Bath, 24 February 1772, "copy," Massachusetts Papers, MHS.

40. John Bernard and William Gale to Messrs. Lane, Son and Fraser, Boston, 30 June 1785, Miscellaneous Bound MSS, MHS; Thwing File Card Index, MHS; Suffolk County Registry of Deeds, Record Book, 120: 41; 132: 75.

41. Higgins, *The Bernards*, 2: 325.

42. Higgins, *The Bernards*, 2: 330–31; Thomas Bernard to Scrope Bernard, n.p., Wednesday Night [16 June 1779], Spencer Bernard Papers.

43. Probate of the Will of Sir Francis Bernard, 12 July 1779. For estimates of wealth and income by social group see Marshall, *English People*, 42–43; Rule, *Albion's People*, 32–33, 40; Beckett, *The Aristocracy*, 41.

44. William O. Sawtelle, "Mount Desert: Champlain to Bernard," *Sprague's Journal of Maine History* 13, no. 3 (1925): 182–86.

45. G. E. Cockayne, *The Complete Baronetage*, 6 vols. (Exeter: William Pollard, 1906), 5: 150–52.

46. The Rev. James Baker, *Life of Sir Thomas Bernard* (London: John Murray, 1819); Frances Elizabeth King, *Female Scripture Characters Exemplifying Female Virtues*, 12th ed. (London: J. G. Rivington, 1833), v–vi.

47. Nikolas Pevsner and Elizabeth Williamson, *The Buildings of Buckinghamshire* (Harmondsworth: Penguin, 1994), 449–52.

48. He was secretary to a Royal Commission of Inquiry into Public Offices, then Buckingham's private secretary; Usher of the Black Rod, and Master of the Rolls in Ireland under William Grenville. His election as M.P. for Aylesbury—a constituency once under Grenville's influence and noted for its corrupt and contested elections—led in due course to his appointment as undersecretary of state for the Home Department under Henry Dundas. Higgins, *The Bernards*, 3: 57–159.

49. Jane married Bernard's executor, a forty-six-year-old Lincoln barrister, Charles White on 22 December 1774, when she was twenty-six. Frances Elizabeth (Fanny) was eighteen years old when she wrote a tale celebrating Jane's marriage. After two marriage proposals from suitors her own age, she eventually married the Rev. Richard King. Higgins, *The Bernards*, 1: 284; 2: 74, 240, 272–74, 291–94, 326–27; 3: 12, 29.

50. Gordon to Bowdoin, Stoke-Newington, 8 September 1786, "Letters of William Gordon," *Procs. MHS*, 3d ser., 63 (1929–30): 612.

51. Nathaniel Hawthorne, *Grandfather's Chair: True Stories from History and Biography*, Centenary ed. ([Columbus, Ohio]: Ohio State Univ. Press, 1972), 136.

Bibliography

MANUSCRIPT COLLECTIONS

United States

Episcopal Diocese of Massachusetts, Library
  Edward Bass, the Right Reverend, Papers

Harvard Archives, Harvard University
  Catalogue of Printed Books

Houghton Library, Harvard University
  MS Sparks Papers, 10
    Bernard Papers, 13 vols.
    Papers Relating to New England, 4 vols.
  MS Sparks Papers, 16
    Franklin Letters
  MS Can 16
    Hulton, Henry, Letterbooks, 2 vols.

Massachusetts Historical Society
  Boston Committee of Correspondence, Letters (photostats of originals
    in New York Public Library)
  Boston Episcopal Charity Society Papers
  Bowdoin-Temple Papers
  Commissioners of Customs in America, 1755–1777, typescripts of
    Bowdoin-Temple Papers
  Dorr, Harbottle, Collection of Annotated Newspapers, 4 vols.
  Greenough Papers
  Hancock Family Papers
  Hutchinson, Thomas, Correspondence (transcripts of the originals in the
    Massachusetts Archives Collection, SC1, 45x, vols. 25–27)
  Knox, Henry, Papers (microfilm copies of originals in Pierpont Morgan
    Library, New York)

Massachusetts Loyalist Claimants (microfilm copy of Loyalist claims in
the Audit Office Papers, vols. 13–14, Public Record Office)
[Massachusetts Papers]. Papers Relating to Public Events in
Massachusetts, 1749–77, 3 vols.
Oliver, Andrew, Letterbooks
Paine, Robert Treat, Papers
Price, Ezekiel, Papers
Quincy, Samuel, Papers
Robbins, J. M., Papers
Savage, Samuel P., II, Collection
Smith-Carter Papers
Williams, Israel, Papers
Winslow Papers

Massachusetts State Archives at Columbia Point, Boston
Massachusetts Archives Collection
Governor's Council, Executive Records, series 327, vol. 16, 1765–74

Princeton University Library
Manuscripts Division, Department of Rare Books and Special
Collections
Andre de Coppet Collection, C0063, box 18, folder 4
[Henry Hulton], Some Account of the Proceedings of the People of
New England from the Establishment of the Board of Customs in
America to the breaking out of the Rebellion in 1775, [post 1783]

Suffolk County Registry of Deeds, Boston
Record Books (CY3.13, 1205)
Deeds relating to Sir Francis Bernard and family
Vols. 98: 113; 102: 39; 108: 89; 120: 41; 122: 189; 123: 114; 132: 75

Great Britain

Buckinghamshire Record Office, Aylesbury
Spencer Bernard Papers

House of Lords Record Office, Parliamentary Archives
Main Papers

Lambeth Palace Library
Fulham Papers, American Colonial Section 6 (Massachusetts), microfilm
copies

Lincolnshire Archives
Ancaster Papers
Dean and Chapter of Lincoln, Muniments
Foster Library Collection

Lincoln Diocesan Records
Lincoln City, Records
Monson Papers

Public Record Office
  Colonial Office Papers
    Original Correspondence of the Secretary of State
      CO 5/754 (1754–83)
          755 (1761–66)
          756 (1766–67)
          757 (1767–68)
          758 (1768–69)
          759 (1769–70)

National Library of Scotland
  Charles Steuart Papers, MS. 5025–28

Nether Winchendon House, Aylesbury
  Spencer Bernard Family, Papers

Sheffield City Archives
  Wentworth Woodhouse Muniments

PRINTED PRIMARY SOURCES

Newspapers

The Annual Register. Reprinted in *Rebellion in America: A Contemporary
    British Viewpoint, 1765–1783*. Edited by David Murdoch. Santa Barbara,
    Calif.: Clio Books, 1979.
Boston Chronicle
Boston Evening Post
Boston Gazette and Country Journal
Essex Gazette
The Journal of the Times. Reprinted in *Boston Under Military Rule,
    1768–1769, as Revealed in a 'Journal of the Times.'* Edited by Oliver M.
    Dickerson. 1936. Reprint, New York: Da Capo Press, 1970.
Massachusetts Gazette. (Title varies: *Massachusetts Gazette*, 1768–69;
    Massachusetts Gazette and Boston Post-Boy Advertiser, 1769–74.)

Pamphlets

[Adams, Samuel]. *An Appeal to the World; or a Vindication of the Town of
    Boston from Many False And Malicious Aspersions*. 1769. Reprint,
    London: J. Almon, 1770.

Allen, William. *The American Crisis: A Letter Addressed by Permission to the Earl of Gower*. London: T. Cadell, 1774.

Baillie, Hugh. *A Letter to Dr. Shebear: Containing a Refutation of his Arguments Concerning the Boston and Quebec Acts of Parliament*. London: J. Donaldson, 1774.

Bailyn, Bernard, ed. *The Pamphlets of the American Revolution, 1760–1776*. Vol. 1. Cambridge: Harvard Univ. Press, 1965.

[Bernard, Francis]. *Select Letters on the Trade and Government of America; and the Principles of Law and Polity, applied to the American Colonies*. London: W. Bowyer and J. Nichols, 1774.

Bollan, William. *The Petition of Mr. Bollan, Agent for the Council of Massachusetts Bay, to the King in Council, January 26, 1774*. London: J. Almon, 1774.

[Chandler, Thomas Bradbury]. *The American Querist: Or, Some Questions Proposed Relative to the Present Disputes Between Great-Britain and Her American Colonies*. New York, 1774.

———. *An Appeal to the Public in Behalf of the Church of England in America*. New York, 1767.

———. *A Friendly Address to All Reasonable Americans, on the Subject of Our Political Confusions*. [Boston], 1775.

———. *What Think Ye of The Congress Now? Or an Enquiry How Far the Americans are Bound to Abide by and Execute the Decisions of the late Congress*. New York, 1775.

[Church, Benjamin]. "An Address to a Provincial Bashaw [Boston, 1769]." *The Magazine of History* 18, extra number 74. Reprint, Tarrytown, N.Y., 1921.

———. *An Elegy to the Infamous Memory of Sr F-B-*. Boston, 1769.

———. *The Tom-Cod Catcher: On the Departure of an Infamous B-r-t*. [Boston, 1769].

Copies of Proceedings in the Several Assemblies, in Consequence of the Resolutions of Parliament in the Last Session. [London], 1769.

Copy of the Complaint of the House of Representatives of Massachuset's-Bay against Sir Francis Bernard: With Sir Francis Bernard's Answer. Now Depending before His Majesty's Council. [London, 1770].

[Galloway, Joseph]. *A Candid Examination of the Mutual Claims of Great-Britain and the Colonies: with a Plan of Accommodation on Constitutional Principles*. New York, 1775.

[Gray, Harrison]. *A Few Remarks Upon Some of the Votes and Resolutions of the Continental Congress, Held at Philadelphia in September, and the Provincial Congress, Held at Cambridge in November 1774*. [Boston], 1775.

———. *The Two Congresses Cut Up*. New York, 1774.

[Hutchinson, Thomas, ed.]. *Collections of Original Papers relative to the Dispute between Great Britain and America*. 1777. Reprint, New York: Da Capo Press, 1971.

[Leonard, Daniel]. *Massachusettensis: Or a Series of Letters containing a Faithful Narrative of the State of Many Important and Striking Facts, which laid the Foundation of the Present Trouble in the Province of Massachusetts Bay*. 1775. 3d ed. London, 1776.

Matthews, Albert, ed. "The Book of America," *Procs. MHS*, 3d. ser., 62 (1928–29): 171–97.

Mein, John. *Sagittarius Letters*. Boston and London, 1775.

[Otis, James, Jr.]. *The Rights of the British Colonies Asserted and Proved*. Boston, 1764.

[Seabury, Samuel]. *A View of the Controversy Between Great-Britain and her Colonies . . . In a Letter to the Author of A Full Vindication*. New York, 1774.

———. *The Congress Canvassed: Or an Examination into the Conduct of the Delegates, at their Grand Convention held in Philadelphia, Sept. 1, 1774*. New York, 1774.

———. *Free Thoughts on the Proceedings of the Continental Congress, Held at Philadelphia, Sept. 5, 1774*. [New York], 1774.

Smith, Paul H., comp. *English Defenders of American Freedoms, 1774–1778: Six Pamphlets Attacking British Policy*. Washington: Library of Congress, 1972.

Laws, Legislative Proceedings, and Public Records

THE PROVINCE OF MASSACHUSETTS BAY

The Acts and Resolves, Public and Private of the Province of Massachusetts Bay, 1692–1776. 21 vols. Boston: Wright and Potter, 1896–1922. Vols. 18–19.

Bradford, Alden, ed. *Speeches of the Governors of Massachusetts 1765–1775*. 1818. Reprint, New York: Da Capo Press, 1971.

The Journals of the House of Representatives of Massachusetts, 1715–1776. 53 vols. Boston: Massachusetts Historical Society, 1919–85.

Matthews, Albert, ed. "Documents Relating to the Last Meetings of the Massachusetts Royal Council, 1774–1776," *Publications of the Colonial Society of Massachusetts* 32 (1933–37): 450–504.

Pruitt, Bettye Hobbs, ed. *The Massachusetts Tax Evaluation List of 1771*. Boston: G. K. Hall, 1978.

Whitmore, William H., ed. *The Massachusetts Civil List for the Colonial and Provincial Periods*. Albany, N.Y.: J. Munsell, 1870.

TOWN RECORDS

Boston. *Reports of the Record Commissioners of the City of Boston*. 38 vols. Boston: Rockwell and Churchill, 1876–1909. Vols. 16, 18, 20, 22.

———. *The Town Officials of Colonial Boston, 1634–1775*. Edited by Robert Francis Seybolt. Cambridge: Harvard Univ. Press, 1939.

Braintree. *Records of the Town of Braintree, 1640 to 1793*. Edited by Samuel Bates. Randolph, Mass.: D. H. Huxford, 1886.

Worcester. "Worcester Town Records from 1765 to 1774." Edited by Franklin P. Rice. *Collections of the Worcester Society of Antiquity* 4 (1881–82).

UNITED KINGDOM

Board of Trade. *Journals of the Commissioners for Trade and Plantations*. 14 vols. London: HMSO, 1920–38.

Boston, Lincs. *Transcription of the Minutes of the Corporation of Boston.* Edited by Betty Coy et al. Boston, Lincs.: The History of Boston Project, 1993.

Colonial Secretaries. K. G. Davies, ed. *Documents of the American Revolution, 1770–1783.* 21 vols. Shannon: Irish Univ. Press, 1972–81.

Crown. Clarence S. Brigham, ed. "British Royal Proclamations Relating to America, 1603–1783." *Transactions and Collections of the American Antiquarian Society* 112 (1911).

Historical Manuscripts Commission. *Report on the Manuscripts of the Earl of Ancaster Preserved at Grimsthorpe.* Dublin: HMSO, 1907.

———. *Report on Manuscripts in Various Collections.* Vol. 6. Dublin: HMSO, 1909.

House of Commons. *Journal of the House of Commons, 1715–1774.* 34 vols. London: By order of the Commons. Vols. 28–34, 1758–74.

———. Sheila Lambert, ed. *House of Commons Sessional Papers of the Eighteenth Century.* 2 vols. Wilmington, Del.: Scholarly Resources Inc., 1976.

House of Lords. *The Report of the House of Lords, to Enquire into the Several Proceedings of the Colony of Massachusets's Bay, in Opposition to the Sovereignty of His Majesty, in His Parliament of Great Britain, over that Province.* London: William Bagley, 1774.

Lincolnshire Archives. *Archivists' Reports.* Vols. 1–30. Lincoln, 1948–88.

Parliament. *The Parliamentary History of England from the earliest period to the year 1803.* 36 vols. London: Hansard, 1806–20.

———. *Proceedings and Debates of the British Parliament respecting North America, 1754–1783.* 5 vols. Edited by P. D. G. Thomas and R. C. Simmons. Millwood, N.Y.: Kraus International Publications, 1982–86.

Privy Council. W. L. Grant and James Munro, eds. *Acts of the Privy Council of England: Colonial Ser., 1613–1783.* 6 vols. London: HMSO, 1909–12.

Royal Governors. Leonard Woods Labaree, ed. *Royal Instructions to British Colonial Governors, 1670–1776.* 2 vols. New York: Appleton-Century Company Inc., 1935.

Personal Papers and Correspondence

Adams, John. *Works of John Adams.* 10 vols. Edited by Charles Francis Adams. Boston: Little & Brown, 1850–56.

———. *The Diary and Autobiography of John Adams.* 4 vols. Edited by Lyman H. Butterfield et al. Cambridge: Harvard Univ. Press, Belknap Press, 1961.

———. *Papers of John Adams.* 6 vols. Edited by Robert J. Taylor et al. Cambridge: Harvard Univ. Press, 1977–83.

Adams, Samuel. *The Writings of Samuel Adams.* 4 vols. Edited by Harry Alonzo Cushing. New York: G. P. Putnam, 1904–8.

Amherst, Gen. Jefferey. *The Journal of Jefferey Amherst . . . from 1758 to 1763.* Edited by Clarence Webster. Chicago: University of Chicago Press, Ryerson Press, 1931.

Andrews, John. "Letters of John Andrews, 1772–1776." *Procs. MHS*, 1st ser.,
    8 (1864–65): 316–413.
Bernard, Sir Francis. *The Barrington-Bernard Correspondence and Illustrative
    Matter, 1760–1770*. Edited by Edward Channing and Archibald Cary
    Coolidge. Harvard Historical Studies Series, vol. 17. 1912. Reprint, New
    York: Da Capo Press, 1970.
————. *Letters to the Ministry from Governor Bernard, General Gage, and
    Commodore Hood, and also Memorials to the Lords of the Treasury, from
    the Commissioners of Customs with sundry Letters and Papers annexed to
    the said Memorials*. 1769. Reprint, London: J. Almon, 1769.
————. *Letters to the Right Honourable The Earl of Hillsborough from
    Governor Bernard, General Gage, and the Honourable His Majesty's
    Council for the Province of Massachusetts Bay with an Appendix containing
    divers proceedings referred to in the said letters*. 1769. Reprint, London: J.
    Almon, 1769.
————. "The Library of Francis Bernard." *Procs. MHS*, 2d ser., 10
    (1895–96): 546–47.
———— [ed.]. *Antonii Alsopi Ódarum libri duo*. London, 1752.
Bowdoin, James. "The Bowdoin-Temple Papers." *Collections of the
    Massachusetts Historical Society*, 6th ser., 9 (1897).
————. "Letter of James Bowdoin to Dr. [Benjamin Franklin]. Mass. Bay,
    June 29, 1771." *Procs. MHS*, 1st ser., 8 (1864–65): 468–73.
Boyle, John. "Journal of Occurrences in Boston, 1759–1778." *New England
    Historic and Genealogical Register* 84 (1930): 142–71, 248–72, 357–82; 85
    (1931): 5–28, 117–33.
Burke, Edmund. *The Correspondence of Edmund Burke*. 9 vols. Edited by
    Thomas W. Copeland. Cambridge: Cambridge Univ. Press and
    Chicago: University of Chicago Press, 1958–70.
————. *Speeches and Letters on American Affairs*. London: J. M. Dent &
    Sons, 1961.
Caner, The Reverend Henry. *Letterbook of the Rev. Henry Caner*. Edited by
    Kenneth Cameron. Hartford, Conn.: Transcendental Books, 1972.
Clarke, Richard. "Documents Drawn from the Papers of Richard Clarke,
    1762–1774." *Publications of the Colonial Society of Massachusetts* 8
    (1902–4): 78–90.
Cushing, Thomas. "Letters of Thomas Cushing from 1767 to 1775."
    Collections of the Massachusetts Historical Society, 4th ser., 4 (1858):
    347–66.
Franklin, Benjamin. *Letters and Papers of Benjamin Franklin and Richard
    Jackson, 1753–1785*. Edited by Carl Van Doren. Philadelphia: The
    American Philosophical Society, 1947.
————. *The Papers of Benjamin Franklin*. 28 vols. Edited by Leonard W.
    Labaree et al. New Haven and London: Yale Univ. Press, [1959]–.
Gage, Gen. Thomas. *The Correspondence of General Thomas Gage and the
    Secretaries of State, 1763–1775*. 2 vols. Edited by Clarence E. Carter. New
    Haven: Yale Univ. Press, 1931–33.
George III. *The Correspondence of King George III from 1760 to December
    1783*. 6 vols. Edited by Sir John Fortescue. London: Macmillan, 1927–28.

Gordon, The Reverend William. "Letters of the Rev. William Gordon."
    Procs. MHS, 1st ser., 7 (1863–64): 291–97.
———. "Letters of William Gordon." *Procs. MHS*, 3d ser., 63 (1929–30):
    303–613.
Gray, Harrison. "Letters of Harrison Gray and Harrison Gray Jr., of
    Massachusetts." *Virginia Magazine of History and Biography* 8 (1901):
    225–36.
———. "Memoir of Dr. Jonathan Mayhew by Harrison Gray." Edited by
    Louis L. Tucker. *Proceedings of the Bostonian Society* 80 (1961); 28–48.
Grenville, George. *Additional Grenville Papers, 1763–1765.* Edited by John
    R. G. Tomlinson. Manchester: Manchester Univ. Press, 1962.
Henry, Augustus, Duke of Grafton. *Autobiography and Political
    Correspondence of Augustus Henry, Third Duke of Grafton, K.G.* Edited
    by William Anson. London: John Murray, 1898.
Hulton, Ann. *Letters of a Loyalist Lady: Ann Hulton, Sister of Henry Hulton,
    Commissioner of Customs at Boston, 1767–1770.* Cambridge, Mass.: n.p.,
    1927.
Hutchinson, Thomas. *Copy of Letters Sent to Great-Britain by His Excellency
    Thomas Hutchinson, the Hon. Andrew Oliver, and Several Other Persons,
    Born and Educated Among Us.* Boston: Edes and Gill, 1773.
———. *The Diary and Letters of His Excellency Thomas Hutchinson.* 2 vols.
    Edited by Peter Orlando Hutchinson. London: Sampson Low,
    Marston, Searle & Rivington, 1883.
———. "A Recently Discovered Thomas Hutchinson Letter." Edited by
    Mary Beth Norton. *Procs. MHS*, 3d ser., 82 (1970): 105–9.
Mauduit, Jasper. "Jasper Mauduit, Agent in London, 1762–1765." Edited by
    Worthington C. Ford. *Collections of the Massachusetts Historical Society*
    74 (1918).
Murray, James. *Letters of James Murray, Loyalist.* Edited by Nina M. Tiffany
    and Susan I. Lesley. Boston: n.p., 1901.
Oliver, Peter. *Peter Oliver's Origin & Progress of the American Rebellion.*
    Edited by Douglass Adair and John A. Schutz. Stanford, Calif.:
    Stanford Univ. Press, 1961.
Palfrey, William. "Letter of William Palfrey to John Wilkes March 13,
    [1770]." *Procs. MHS*, 1st ser., 6 (1862–63): 480–83.
Pitt, William, Earl of Chatham. *Correspondence of William Pitt, Earl of
    Chatham.* 4 vols. Edited by William Stanhope Taylor and Capt. John
    Henry Pringle. London: John Murray, 1849.
———. *Correspondence of William Pitt with Colonial Governors and Military
    and Naval Commissioners in Colonial America.* 2 vols. Edited by
    Gertrude S. Kimball. New York: Macmillan, 1906.
Price, Ezekiel. "The Diary of Ezekiel Price." *Procs. MHS*, 1st ser., 7
    (1863–64): 185–262.
Rowe, John. *Letters and Diary of John Rowe.* Edited by Anne R.
    Cunningham. Boston: n.p., 1903.
———. "Extracts from John Rowe's Diary." Edited by E. L. Pierce. *Procs.
    MHS*, 2d ser., 10 (1895–96): 11–108.

Royall, Isaac. "Isaac Royall to the Earl of Dartmouth, Medford, January 18, 1774." *Procs. MHS*, 1st ser., 13 (1873–75): 179–82.

Saltonstall, Richard. "The Saltonstall Papers, 1607–1815." Edited by Robert Moody. *Collections of the Massachusetts Historical Society* 80 (1912).

Steuart, Charles. "Charles Stuart [*sic*] and James Murray Letters, 1766–1772." *Procs. MHS*, 1st ser., 43 (1909–10): 449–58.

Temple, John. "Letters from John Temple to the Earl of Hillsborough." *Procs. MHS*, 1st ser., 12 (1871–73): 207–11.

———. "The Missing Temple-Whately Letters." Edited by Neil R. Stout. *Procs. MHS*, 3d ser., 104 (1992): 124–39.

Warren, Mercy, Mrs. "Mrs. Warren's *The Group.*" *Procs. MHS*, 3d ser., 62 (1928–29): 15–22.

Wilkes, John. "John Wilkes and Boston." Edited by Worthington C. Ford. *Procs. MHS*, 3d ser., 47 (1913–14): 191–220.

Miscellaneous

"An Alphabetical List of the Sons of Liberty Who Dined at Liberty Tree, Dorchester, August 14, 1769." *Procs. MHS*, 1st ser., 11 (1869): 140–42.

Ford, Worthington C., ed. "Some Letters of 1775." *Procs. MHS*, 3d ser., 59 (1925–26): 107–38.

Freiberg, Malcolm. "An Unknown Stamp Act Letter." *Procs. MHS*, 3d ser., 78 (1966): 138–42.

"Petition of the Native Americans Residing in London, to His Majesty George III in 1774." *New England Historic and Genealogical Register* 19 (1865): 21.

"Protestors Against the Solemn League and Covenant." *Procs. MHS*, 1st ser., 11 (1869–70): 394–95.

"The Solemn League and Covenant, 1774." Edited by Albert Matthews. *Publications of the Colonial Society of Massachusetts* 18 (1915–16): 103–22.

Secondary Sources

Francis Bernard and Family

Baker, James, The Reverend. *Life of Sir Thomas Bernard.* London: John Murray, 1819.

Bernard, Thomas. *Life of Sir Francis Bernard.* London: n.p., 1790.

Cockayne, G. E. *The Complete Baronetage.* Vol. 5: 150–52. Exeter: William Pollard, 1906.

Fiore, Jordan D. "Francis Bernard, Colonial Governor." Ph.D. diss., Boston Univ., 1950.

———. "The Temple-Bernard Affair." *Historical Collections of the Essex Institute* 90 (1954): 58–83.

Higgins, [Sophie Elizabeth] Napier, Mrs. *The Bernards of Abington and Nether Winchendon: A Family History*. 4 vols. London: Longmans, Green & Co., 1903–4.

Jones, Ruth Owen. "Governor Francis Bernard and His Land Acquisitions." *Historical Journal of Massachusetts* 16, no. 2 (summer 1988): 121–39.

King, [Frances Elizabeth], Mrs. *Female Scripture Characters Exemplifying Female Virtues*. 12th ed. London: J. G. Rivington, 1833.

Matthews, Albert. *The Portraits of Sir Francis Bernard*. Boston: Club of Odd Volumes, 1922.

Sawtelle, William O. "Mount Desert: Champlain to Bernard." *Sprague's Journal of Maine History* 13, no. 3 (1925): 168–86.

———. "Sir Francis Bernard and His Grant of Mount Desert." *Publications of the Colonial Society of Massachusetts* 24 (1920–22): 197–254.

Sents, Aeilt E. "Francis Bernard and Imperial Reconstruction." Ph.D. diss., University of Missouri, 1973.

Sexton, John E. "Massachusetts Religious Policy with the Indians under Governor Bernard, 1760–1769." *Catholic Historical Review* 24 (1938–39): 310–28.

Walett, Francis G. "Governor Bernard's Undoing: An Earlier Hutchinson Letters Affair." *New England Quarterly* 38 (1965): 217–26.

Other

Alden, John E. "John Mein: Scourge of Patriots." *Publications of the Colonial Society of Massachusetts* 34 (1937–42): 571–99.

Alden, John R. *General Gage in America: Being Principally His Role in the American Revolution*. New York: Greenwood Press, 1948.

Ames, Ellis. "The Circular Letter, September 14, 1768." *Procs. MHS*, 1st ser., 4 (1856–60): 385–88.

———. "The Provincial Charter of Massachusetts." *Procs. MHS*, 1st ser., 10 (1867–69): 370–75.

Ammerman, David. *In the Common Cause: American Responses to the Coercive Acts of 1774*. Charlottesville, Va.: Univ. Press of Virginia, 1974.

Anderson, Fred A. *A People's Army: Massachusetts Soldiers and Society in the Seven Years War*. Chapel Hill, N.C.: University of North Carolina Press, 1984.

Andrews, Charles M. *The Colonial Period of American History*. 4 vols. New Haven: Yale Univ. Press, 1938.

Appleby, Joyce. "A Different Kind of Independence: The Postwar Restructuring of the Historical Study of Early America." *WMQ* 50 (1993): 245–68.

Archer, Richard. "A New England Mosaic: A Demographic Analysis for the Seventeenth Century." *WMQ* 47 (1990): 477–502.

Bailyn, Bernard. *The Ideological Origins of the American Revolution*. Cambridge: Harvard Univ. Press, 1967.

———. "The Index and Commentaries of Harbottle Dorr." *Procs. MHS*, 3d ser., 84 (1973): 21–35.

———. *The Ordeal of Thomas Hutchinson*. Cambridge: Harvard Univ. Press, Belknap Press, 1974.

———. "The Origins of American Politics." *Perspectives in American History* 1 (1967): 1–120.

Baker, Florence. *Nettleham: A Short History of the Village*. Lincoln: n.p., 1938.

Baker, J. H. *An Introduction to English Legal History*. 3d. ed. London: Butterworths, 1990.

Bancroft, George. *History of the United States of America from the Discovery of the Continent*. 6 vols. London: Macmillan, 1876.

Barrow, Thomas C. *Trade and Empire: The British Customs Service in Colonial America, 1660–1775*. Cambridge: Harvard Univ. Press, 1967.

Batinski, Michael C. *Jonathan Belcher, Colonial Governor*. Lexington, Ky.: Univ. Press of Kentucky, 1996.

Baxter, W. T. *The House of Hancock: Business in Boston, 1724–1775*. c. 1945. Reprint, New York: Russell & Russell, 1965.

Beckett, J. V. *The Aristocracy in England, 1660–1914*. Oxford: Basil Blackwell, 1986.

Bedwell, C. E. A. "The Inns of Court." *London Society Journal* 213 (1939): 165–71.

Beeman, Richard R. "Deference, Republicanism, and the Emergence of Popular Politics in Eighteenth-Century America." *WMQ* 49 (1992): 403–30.

Bell, Hugh F. "A Personal Challenge: The Otis-Hutchinson Controversy, 1761–1762." *Historical Collections of the Essex Institute* 106 (1970): 297–323.

Bellot, L. J. *William Knox: The Life and Thought of an Eighteenth-Century Imperialist*. Austin, Tex.: University of Texas Press, 1977.

Bennett, Stewart, and Nicholas Bennett, eds. *An Historical Atlas of Lincolnshire*. Hull, Eng.: University of Hull Press, 1993.

Bentick-Smith, William. "Nicholas Boylston and His Harvard Chair." *WMQ* 93 (1981): 17–39.

Benton, William A. *Whig-Loyalism: An Aspect of Political Ideology in the American Revolutionary Era*. Rutherford, N.J.: Fairleigh Dickinson Univ. Press, 1969.

Bill, E. G. W. *Education at Christ Church, Oxford, 1660–1800*. Oxford: Clarendon Press, 1988.

Billias, George A., ed. *Law and Authority in Colonial America*. Barre, Mass.: Barre Publishers, 1965.

Blackstone, Sir William. *Commentaries on the Laws of England*. 4 vols. London: William Reed, 1811.

———. *The Commentaries on the Laws of England of Sir William Blackstone adapted to the present state of the Law*. Edited by Robert Malcolm Kerr. 4 vols. 4th ed. London: John Murray, 1876.

Boyd, Julian P. *Anglo-American Union: Joseph Galloway's Plans to Preserve the British Empire, 1774–1788*. Philadelphia: University of Pennsylvania Press, 1941.

Bradford, Alden. *Memoirs of the Life and Writings of Rev. Jonathan Mayhew*. Boston: C. C. Little, 1838.

Bradner, Leicester. *Musae Anglicanae: A History of Anglo-Latin Poetry,*
    1500–1925. New York: Oxford Univ. Press, 1940.
Brasch, Frederick. "The Royal Society of London and Its Influence upon
    Scientific Thought in the American Colonies." *Scientific Monthly* 33
    (1931): 336–55.
Brennan, Ellen E. *Plural Office-Holding in Massachusetts, 1760–1780: Its*
    Relation to the "Separation" of Departments of Government. Chapel Hill,
    N.C.: University of North Carolina Press, 1945.
Brewer, John. *Party Ideology and Popular Politics at the Accession of George*
    III. London: Oxford Univ. Press, 1976.
Bridenbaugh, Carl. *Mitre and Sceptre: Transatlantic Faiths, Ideas,*
    Personalities and Politics, 1689–1775. New York: Oxford Univ. Press,
    1962.
Brooke, John. *The Chatham Administration, 1766–1768.* London: Macmillan,
    1956.
Brown, Richard D. "The Massachusetts Convention of Towns, 1768."
    WMQ 26 (1969): 95–104.
———. *Revolutionary Politics in Massachusetts: The Boston Committee of*
    Correspondence and the Towns, 1772–1774. Cambridge: Harvard Univ.
    Press, 1970.
Brown, Robert E. *Middle-Class Democracy and the Revolution in*
    Massachusetts, 1691–1780. Ithaca, N.Y.: Cornell Univ. Press, 1955.
Brown, Wallace. *The Good Americans: The Loyalists in the American*
    Revolution. New York: William Morrow, 1969.
———. *The King's Friends: The Composition and Motives of the American*
    Loyalist Claimants. Providence, R.I.: Brown Univ. Press, 1965.
Browning, Reed. *The Duke of Newcastle.* New Haven: Yale Univ. Press, 1975.
Buel, Richard, Jr. "Democracy and the American Revolution: A Frame of
    Reference." *WMQ* 21 (1964): 165–90.
Bullion, John L. "British Ministers and American Resistance to the Stamp
    Act, October–December, 1765." *WMQ* 49 (1992): 89–107.
———. *A Great and Necessary Measure: George Grenville and the Genesis of*
    the Stamp Act, 1763–1765. Columbia, Mo.: University of Missouri Press,
    1982.
Burns, John F. *Controversies Between Royal Governors and Their Assemblies*
    in the Northern American Colonies. 1923. Reprint, New York: Russell &
    Russell, 1969.
Bushman, Richard L. *King and People in Provincial Massachusetts.* Chapel
    Hill, N.C.: University of North Carolina Press, 1985.
Calhoon, Robert N. *The Loyalists of Revolutionary America, 1760–1781.* New
    York: Harcourt Brace Jovanovich, 1973.
Cannon, John. *The Aristocratic Century: The Peerage of Eighteenth-Century*
    England. Cambridge: Cambridge Univ. Press, 1984.
Cappon, Lester J., et al., eds. *Atlas of Early American History: The*
    Revolutionary Era, 1760–1790. Princeton: Princeton Univ. Press, 1976.
Carleton, John D. *Westminster School: A History.* London: Rupert Hart-
    Davis, 1965.

Cary, John. *Joseph Warren: Physician, Politician, Patriot*. Urbana, Ill.:
University of Illinois Press, 1961.

Chaffin, R. J. "The Townshend Acts of 1767." *WMQ* 27 (1970): 90–121.

Channing, Edward. "The American Board of Commissioners of the
Customs." *Procs. MHS*, 3d ser., 43 (1909–10): 477–91.

———. *A History of the United States*. 7 vols. New York: Macmillan,
1921–32.

Christie, Ian R. *Wars and Revolution: Britain, 1760–1815*. London: Edward
Arnold, 1982.

———, ed. *Myth and Reality in Late Eighteenth-Century British Politics*.
London: Macmillan, 1970.

Christie, Ian R., and Benjamin W. Labaree. *Empire or Independence,
1760–1776: A British-American Dialogue on the Coming of the American
Revolution*. Oxford: Phaidon Press, 1976.

Clark, Dora Mae. *The Rise of the British Treasury: Colonial Administration
of the Eighteenth Century*. Newton Abbot, Devon: David & Charles,
1960.

Clark, J. C. D. *The Language of Liberty, 1660–1832: Political Discourse and
Social Dynamics in the Anglo-American World*. Cambridge: Cambridge
Univ. Press, 1994.

Cogliano, Francis D. *No King, No Popery: Anti-Catholicism in Revolutionary
New England*. Westport, Conn.: Greenwood Press, 1995.

Cohen, Lester H. *The Revolutionary Histories: Contemporary Narratives of
the American Revolution*. Ithaca, N.Y.: Cornell Univ. Press, 1980.

Cole, G. D. H., and Raymond Postgate. *The Common People, 1746–1938*.
London: Methuen, 1945.

Colley, Linda. *Britons: Forging the Nation, 1707–1837*. New Haven: Yale
Univ. Press, 1992.

Conser, Walter H., Ronald M. McCarthy, and D. J. Toscano, eds.
Resistance, Politics, and the American Struggle for Independence, 1765–1775.
Boulder, Colo.: Lynne Rienner Publishers, 1986.

Cook, Don. *The Long Fuse: How England Lost the American Colonies,
1760–1785*. New York: Atlantic Monthly Press, 1995.

Cook, Edward M., Jr. *Fathers of the Towns: Leadership Structure in
Eighteenth-Century New England*. Baltimore: Johns Hopkins Univ.
Press, 1976.

Coolidge, Mabel Cook. *The History of Petersham, Massachusetts*. Petersham
Historical Society, 1948.

Countryman, Edward. *A People in Revolution: The American Revolution and
Political Society in New York, 1760–1790*. Baltimore: Johns Hopkins
Univ. Press, 1981.

Currey, Cecil B. *Road to Revolution: Benjamin Franklin in England,
1765–1775*. Garden City, N.Y.: Anchor Books, 1968.

"Deference or Defiance in Eighteenth-Century America? A Round Table."
Journal of American History 85 (1998): 13–97.

Denio, Herbert. "Massachusetts Land Grants in Vermont." *Publications of
the Colonial Society of Massachusetts* 24 (1920–22): 35–59.

Derry, John. *English Politics and the American Revolution*. London: J. M. Dent & Sons, 1976.

Dickerson, Oliver M. *The Navigation Acts and the American Revolution*. New York: Octagon Books, 1974.

———. "Opinion of Attorney General Jonathan Sewall of Massachusetts in the Case of the *Lydia*." *WMQ* 4 (1947): 499–504.

Dickinson, H. T. *Liberty and Property: Political Ideology in Eighteenth-Century Britain*. London: Wiedenfield and Nicolson, 1977.

Dickinson, H. T., and Kenneth Logue. "The Porteous Riot: A Study of the Breakdown of Law and Order in Edinburgh, 1736–1737." *Journal of the Scottish Labour History Society* (10 June 1976): 21–40.

Dinkin, Robert Joseph. "Provincial Massachusetts: A Deferential or a Democratic Society." Ph.D. diss., Columbia Univ., 1968.

Ditchfield, Peter, and William Page, eds. *The Victoria History of Berkshire*. 4 vols. London: Institute of Historical Research, 1906–27.

Dunn, John. "The Politics of Locke in England and America in the Eighteenth Century." In *John Locke: Problems and Perspectives*, ed. John Yolton, 45–80. Cambridge: Cambridge Univ. Press, 1969.

Egnal, Marc. *A Mighty Empire: The Origins of the American Revolution*. Ithaca, N.Y.: Cornell Univ. Press, 1988.

Ellis, George. "Memoir of Jared Sparks LL.D." *Procs. MHS*, 1st ser., 10 (1867–69): 211–310.

———. "The Old Province House." *Procs. MHS*, 1st ser., 15 (1876–77): 178–79.

Fischer, David Hackett. *Paul Revere's Ride*. New York: Oxford Univ. Press, 1994.

Fitzmaurice, Lord Edmond. *Life of William, Earl of Shelburne, afterwards First Marquis of Lansdowne, with extracts from his Papers and Correspondence*. 2 vols. London: Macmillan, 1912.

Foster, Apthorp. "The Burning of Harvard Hall, 1764, and Its Consequences." *Publications of the Colonial Society of Massachusetts* 14 (1911–13): 2–43.

Fowler, William M., Jr. *Samuel Adams: Radical Puritan*. New York: Longman, 1997.

Freiburg, Malcolm. "William Bollan, Agent of Massachusetts," part 4. *Boston Public Library, More Books* 23 (1948): 168–82.

Frese, Joseph R. "Some Observations on the American Board of Customs Commissioners." *Procs. MHS*, 3d ser., 81 (1969): 3–30.

Galvin, John R. *Three Men of Boston: Leadership and Conflict at the Start of the American Revolution*. Washington: Brasseys, 1976.

Gipson, Lawrence Henry. *The British Empire before the American Revolution*. 14 vols. Caldwell, Idaho, 1936. Rev. ed., New York: Knopf, 1958–71.

Goldstone, Jack. *Revolution and Rebellion in the Early Modern World*. Berkeley: University of California Press, 1991.

Granger, Bruce Ingham. *Political Satire in the American Revolution, 1763–1783*. Ithaca, N.Y.: Cornell Univ. Press, 1960.

Greene, Evarts B. *The Provincial Governor in the English Colonies of North America*. Harvard Historical Studies series, vol. 8. New York: Longmans, Green & Co., 1889.

Greene, Jack P. *Peripheries and Center: Constitutional Development in the Extended Polities of the British Empire and the United States, 1607–1788*. New York: W. W. Norton, 1986.

Greene, Jack P., and J. R. Pole, eds. *Colonial British America: Essays in the New History of the Early Modern Era*. Baltimore: Johns Hopkins Univ. Press, 1984.

Guttman, Allen. *The Conservative Tradition in America*. New York: Oxford Univ. Press, 1967.

Hanley, Hugh. *The Prebendal, Aylesbury, A History*. Aylesbury, Bucks.: Ginn & Co., 1986.

Hassam, John T. "The Confiscated Estates of Boston Loyalists." *Procs. MHS*, 2d ser., 10 (1895–96): 162–85.

Hawthorne, Nathaniel. *Grandfather's Chair: True Stories from History and Biography*. Centenary Edition. Columbus, Ohio: Ohio State Univ. Press, 1972.

Hayter, Tony, ed. *An Eighteenth Century Secretary at War: The Papers of William, Viscount Barrington*. London: The Bodley Head for the Army Records Society, 1988.

Henretta, James A. *"Salutary Neglect": Colonial Administration under the Duke of Newcastle*. Princeton: Princeton Univ. Press, 1972.

Hibbert, Christopher. *Redcoats and Rebels: The American Revolution through British Eyes*. New York: Avon Books, 1991.

Hill, Sir Francis. *Georgian Lincoln*. Cambridge: Cambridge Univ. Press, 1966.

Hinkhouse, Fred J. *The Preliminaries of the American Revolution as Seen in the English Press, 1763–1775*. New York: Columbia Univ. Press, 1926.

Hoerder, Dirk. *Crowd Action in Revolutionary Massachusetts, 1765–1780*. London: Academic Press, 1977.

Holmes, Geoffrey, and Daniel Szechi. *The Age of Oligarchy: Pre-Industrial Britain, 1722–1783*. London: Longman, 1993.

Humphreys, R. A. "Lord Shelburne and British Colonial Policy, 1766–1768." *English Historical Review* 50 (1935): 257–77.

———. "Lord Shelburne and a Projected Recall of Colonial Governors in 1767." *American Historical Review* 37 (1931–32): 269–72.

———. "Two Colonial Governors: Thomas Pownall and Francis Bernard." *Lincolnshire Magazine* 1, no. 7 (1932–34): 209–14.

Hutchinson, John. *A Catalogue of Notable Middle Templars with brief biographical notices*. London: Society of the Middle Temple, 1902.

Hutchinson, Thomas. *The History of the Colony and Province of Massachusetts Bay*. Edited by Lawrence S. Mayo. 3 vols. 1936. Reprint, New York: Da Capo Press, 1971.

Jensen, Merrill. *The Founding of a Nation: A History of the American Revolution, 1763–1776*. New York: Oxford Univ. Press, 1968.

Johnson, Richard R. " 'Parliamentary Egotisms': The Clash of Legislatures in the Making of the American Revolution." *Journal of American History* 74 (1987): 338–62.

Jones, Edward A. *The Loyalists of Massachusetts: Their Memorials, Petitions and Claims*. London: St. Catherine's Press, 1930.

Kammen, Michael. *A Rope of Sand: The Colonial Agents, British Politics and the American Revolution*. Ithaca, N.Y.: Cornell Univ. Press, 1968.

Katz, Stanley. *Newcastle's New York: Anglo-American Politics, 1732–1753*. Cambridge: Harvard Univ. Press, Belknap Press, 1968.

Kelch, Ray A. *Newcastle: A Duke without Money: Thomas Pelham-Holles, 1693–1768*. London: Routledge & Kegan Paul, 1974.

Kemmerer, Donald L. *Path to Freedom: The Struggle for Self-Government in Colonial New Jersey, 1703–1776*. Cos Cob, Conn.: John E. Edwards, 1968.

Kershaw, Gordon. *The Kennebeck Proprietors, 1749–1775*. Somersworth, N.H.: New Hampshire Publishing Co., 1975.

Knollenberg, Bernhard. *Origin of the American Revolution, 1759–1766*. New York: Macmillan, 1960; New York: Free Press, 1961.

Krusell, Cynthia Hagar. *Of Tea and Tories: The Story of Revolutionary Marshfield*. Marshfield, Mass.: n.p., 1976.

Kulikoff, Alan. "The Progress of Inequality in Revolutionary Boston." *WMQ* 28 (1971): 375–412.

Kurtz, Stephen G., and James H. Hutson, eds. *Essays on the American Revolution*. Chapel Hill: University of North Carolina Press, 1973; New York: W. W. Norton, 1973.

Labaree, Leonard W. *Conservatism in Early American History*. New York: Oxford Univ. Press, 1948.

Landau, Norma. *The Justices of the Peace, 1679–1760*. Berkeley: University of California Press, 1984.

Langford, Paul. *A Polite and Commercial People, 1727–1783*. London: Oxford Univ. Press, 1992.

Lefavour, Henry. "The Proposed College in Hampshire County in 1762." *Procs. MHS*, 3d ser., 66 (1936–41): 53–79.

Lord, Donald C., and Robert M. Calhoon. "The Removal of the Massachusetts General Court from Boston, 1769–1772." *Journal of American History* 55 (1969): 735–55.

Lovell, Albert A. *Worcester in the War of the Revolution: embracing the acts of the town from 1765 to 1783 inclusive*. Worcester, Mass.: Tyler and Seagrave, 1876.

Lucas, Paul. "A Collective Biography of Students and Barristers of Lincoln's Inn, 1680–1804: A Study in the 'Aristocratic Resurgence' of the Eighteenth Century." *Journal of Modern History* 46 (1974): 227–61.

Maas, David E. *The Return of the Massachusetts Loyalists*. New York: Garland Publishing, 1989.

———, comp. and ed. *Divided Hearts: Massachusetts Loyalists, 1765–1790: A Biographical Directory*. Boston: New England Historic and Genealogical Society, 1980.

McCusker, John J. "Colonial Civil Servant and Counter-revolutionary:

Thomas Irving 1738?–1800 in Boston, Charleston, and London." *Publications of the Colonial Society of Massachusetts, Transactions* 12 (1979): 315–50.

McCusker, John J., and Russell R. Menard. *The Economy of British America, 1607–1789*. Chapel Hill: University of North Carolina Press, 1985.

McLynn, F. J. *The Jacobite Army in England, 1745: The Final Campaign*. Edinburgh: John Donald, 1983.

Maier, Pauline. *From Resistance to Revolution: Colonial Radicals and the Development of American Opposition to Britain, 1765–1776*. London: Routledge & Kegan Paul, 1973.

Maitland, F. W. *The Constitutional History of England*. Cambridge: Cambridge Univ. Press, 1909.

Marshall, Dorothy. *English People in the Eighteenth Century*. London: Longmans, Green & Co., 1957.

Martin, James Kirby. *Men in Rebellion: Higher Governmental Leaders and the Coming of the American Revolution*. New Brunswick, N.J.: Rutgers Univ. Press, 1973.

Massachusetts Historical Society. "Minutes of Monthly Meetings, 1791–1833." *Procs. MHS*, 1st ser., 1 (1791–1835): 2d & 3d meetings, at 5–14; 4th, 17–22; 6th, 24–27; Oct. 1794, 75; Oct. 1795, 89; Jan. 1833, 459–60.

———. "Minutes of Monthly Meetings, 1835–1848." *Procs. MHS*, 1st ser., 2 (1835–55): Feb. 1835, 31–33; Feb. 1836, 65–67; Dec. 1837, 94–96; Feb. 1847, 362–63; Mar. 1848, 383–85.

———. "Minutes of Monthly Meeting, Nov. 1864." *Procs. MHS*, 1st ser., 8 (1864–65): 76–77.

———. "Minutes of Monthly Meetings, 1875." *Procs. MHS*, 1st ser., 13 (1874–75): 451.

———. "Minutes of Monthly Meeting, Dec. 1920." *Procs. MHS*, 3d ser., 54 (1920–21): 81.

May, Henry F. *The Enlightenment in America*. Oxford: Oxford Univ. Press, 1976.

Meredith, Gertrude E. *The Descendants of Hugh Amory, 1605–1805*. London: n.p., 1901.

Merrit, Bruce E. "Loyalism and Social Conflict in Revolutionary Deerfield, Massachusetts." *Journal of American History* 57 (1970): 227–81.

Middleton, Richard. *The Bells of Victory: The Pitt-Newcastle Ministry and the Conduct of the Seven Years War, 1757–1762*. Cambridge: Cambridge Univ. Press, 1985.

———. "The Duke of Newcastle and the Conduct of Patronage during the Seven Years War, 1757–1762." *British Journal for Eighteenth-Century Studies* 12 (1989): 175–86.

Miller, John C. *Origins of the American Revolution*. 1957. Revised reprint, Stanford, Calif.: Stanford Univ. Press, 1959.

———. *Sam Adams: Pioneer in Propaganda*. 1936. Reprint, Stanford, Calif.: Stanford Univ. Press, 1960.

Minot, George. *Continuation of the History of the Province of Massachusetts Bay, from . . . 1748, with an introductory Sketch of events from the original settlement*. 2 vols. Boston: Manning & Loring, 1798–1803.

Morgan, Edmund S., and Helen M. Morgan. *The Stamp Act Crisis: Prologue to Revolution*. Chapel Hill: University of North Carolina Press; New York: Collier Books, 1963.

Mullet, Charles F. "English Imperial Thinking, 1764–1783." *Political Science Quarterly* 55 (1930): 548–79.

Murrin, John M. "Anglicizing an American Colony: The Transformation of Provincial Massachusetts." Ph.D. diss., Yale Univ., 1966.

Myerson, Joel D. "The Private Revolution of William Bollan." *New England Quarterly* 41 (1968): 536–50.

Namier, Sir Lewis B. *The Structure of Politics at the Accession of George III.* 2d ed. London: Macmillan, 1958.

Nash, Gary B. "Social Change and the Growth of Pre-Revolutionary Urban Radicalism." In *The American Revolution: Explorations in the History of American Radicalism*, ed. Alfred F. Young, 3–36. Dekalb: Northern Illinois Univ. Press, 1976.

———. *The Urban Crucible: Social Change, Political Consciousness, and the Origins of the American Revolution*. Cambridge: Harvard Univ. Press, 1979.

———. "Urban Wealth and Poverty in Pre-Revolutionary America." *Journal of Interdisciplinary History* 6 (1976): 545–84.

Nelson, William H. *The American Tory*. Oxford: Oxford Univ. Press, 1961.

Newman, Gerald. *The Rise of English Nationalism: A Cultural History, 1740–1830*. London: Macmillan, 1997.

Newman, Simon P. *Parades and the Politics of the Street: Festive Culture in the Early American Republic*. Philadelphia: University of Pennsylvania Press, 1997.

Nicolson, Colin. "The Friends of Government: Loyalism, Ideology and Politics in Revolutionary Massachusetts, 1765–1776." 2 vols. Ph.D. diss., University of Edinburgh, 1988.

———. "Governor Francis Bernard, the Massachusetts Friends of Government, and the Advent of the Revolution." *Procs. MHS*, 3d ser., 101 (1991): 24–113.

———. " 'McIntosh, Otis & Adams are our demagogues': Nathaniel Coffin and the Loyalist Interpretation of the Origins of the American Revolution." *Procs. MHS*, 3d ser., 108 (1996–97): 73–114.

Noble, John H. "Some Massachusetts Tories." *Publications of the Colonial Society of Massachusetts* 5 (1897–98): 257–97.

Nobles, Gregory H. *Division throughout the Whole: Politics and Society in Hampshire County, Massachusetts, 1740–1775*. Cambridge: Harvard Univ. Press, 1983.

Olson, Alison G. *Anglo-American Politics, 1660–1775: The Relationship between Parties in England and Colonial America*. Oxford: Oxford Univ. Press, 1973.

———. "Eighteenth-Century Colonial Legislatures and Their Constituents." *Journal of American History* 79 (1992): 543–67.

Owen, John Beresford. *The Rise of the Pelhams*. London: Methuen, 1957.

Page, William, ed. *The Victoria History of the County of Lincoln*. Vol. 2. London: J. Street, 1906.

Paige, Lucius R. *History of Hardwick, Massachusetts*. Boston: Houghton, Mifflin and Co., 1883.

Paine, Josiah. *A History of Harwich, Barnstable County, Massachusetts, 1620–1800*. Rutland, Vt.: Tuttle, 1937.

Palfrey, J. G. *The Life of William Palfrey*. Vol. 7, *The Library of American Biography*, ed. Jared Sparks. Boston: Little, Brown, 1848.

Patterson, Stephen E. *Political Parties in Revolutionary Massachusetts*. Madison, Wisc.: University of Wisconsin Press, 1973.

Pencak, William. *America's Burke: The Mind of Thomas Hutchinson*. Lanham, Md.: Univ. Press of America, 1982.

———. *War, Politics & Revolution in Provincial Massachusetts*. Boston: Northeastern Univ. Press, 1981.

Pencak, William, and Ralph J. Crandall. "Metropolitan Boston before the American Revolution: An Urban Interpretation of the Imperial Crisis." *Proceedings of the Bostonian Society* (1977–83): 57–79.

Perkin, Harold. *The Origins of Modern English Society, 1780–1880*. London: Routledge & Kegan Paul, 1969.

Perry, William Stevens. *Historical Collections relating to the American Colonial Church*. 5 vols. Hartford, Conn.: n.p., 1870–79.

Pole, J. R. "Historians and the Problem of American Democracy." *American Historical Review* 67 (1962): 626–46.

———. *Political Representation in England and the Origins of the American Revolution*. London: Oxford Univ. Press, 1966.

Porter, Roy. *English Society in the Eighteenth Century*. London: Allen Lane, 1982.

Potter, Janice. *The Liberty We Seek: Loyalist Ideology in Colonial New York and Massachusetts*. Cambridge: Harvard Univ. Press, 1983.

Pownall, Charles A. *Thomas Pownall, M.P., F.R.S., Governor of Massachusetts Bay*. London: Henry Stevens, Son & Stiles, 1908.

Purvis, Thomas L. *Proprietors, Patronage, and Paper Money: Legislative Politics in New Jersey, 1703–1776*. New Brunswick, N.J.: Rutgers Univ. Press, 1986.

Quiller-Couch, Lilian M., ed. *Reminiscences of Oxford by Oxford Men, 1559–1850*. Oxford: Clarendon Press for the Oxford Historical Society, 1892.

Reich, Jerome. *Colonial America*. 4th ed. Upper Saddle River, N.J.: Prentice Hall, 1998.

Reid, John Philip. *Constitutional History of the American Revolution*. Vol. 3, *The Authority to Legislate*. Madison, Wisc.: University of Wisconsin Press, 1991.

———. *In a Defiant Stance: The Conditions of Law in Massachusetts Bay, the Irish Comparison, and the Coming of the American Revolution*. University Park, Penn.: Pennsylvania State Univ. Press, 1977.

———. *In a Rebellious Spirit: The Argument of Facts, the Liberty Riot and the Coming of the Revolution*. University Park, Penn.: Pennsylvania State Univ. Press, 1979.

Reitan, E. "The Civil List, 1761–1777: Problems of Finance and

Administration." *Institute of Historical Research Bulletin* 47 (1974): 186–201.

Riddell, William Renwick. "Impeachment in England and English Colonies." *New York University Law Quarterly Review* 7 (1930): 702–8.

Riley, Stephen T. "Some Aspects of the Society's Manuscript Collection." *Procs. MHS*, 3d ser., 70 (1950–53): 243.

Ritcheson, Charles R. *British Politics and the American Revolution*. Norman, Okla.: University of Oklahoma Press, 1954.

Robson, Robert. *The Attorney in Eighteenth-Century England*. Cambridge: Cambridge Univ. Press, 1959.

Rogers, A. *A History of Lincolnshire*. Henley-on-Thames, Eng.: Darwen Finlayson, 1970.

Rogers, Alan. *Empire and Liberty: American Resistance to British Authority, 1755–1763*. Berkeley: University of California Press, 1974.

Roughead, W., ed. *The Trial of Captain Porteous*. Glasgow: William Hodge & Co., 1909.

Rudé, George. *The Crowd in History: A Study of Popular Disturbances in France and England, 1730–1848*. Rev. ed., London: Lawrence and Wishart, 1981.

Rule, John. *Albion's People: English Society, 1714–1815*. London: Longmans, 1992.

Schutz, John A. *Thomas Pownall: British Defender of American Liberty*. Glendale, Calif.: Arthur H. Clark Co., 1951.

Shaffer, A. H. *The Politics of History*. Chicago: Precedent Publishing, 1975.

Shaw, Peter. *American Patriots and the Rituals of Revolution*. Cambridge: Harvard Univ. Press, 1981.

Sheldon, George. *A History of Deerfield, Massachusetts*. 2 vols. 1895–96. Reprint, Somersworth, N.H.: New Hampshire Publishing Co., 1972.

Shepherd, James F., and Gary M. Walton. *Shipping, Maritime Trade, and the Economic Development of Colonial North America*. Cambridge: Cambridge Univ. Press, 1979.

Sheridan, Richard B. "The British Credit Crisis of 1772 and the American Colonies." *Journal of Economic History* 20 (1960): 161–86.

Shy, John. *Toward Lexington: The Role of the British Army in the Coming of the American Revolution*. Princeton: Princeton Univ. Press, 1965.

Siebert, Wilbur H. "The Colony of Massachusetts Loyalists at Bristol, England." *Procs. MHS*, 3d ser., 45 (1911–12): 409–14.

Smith, Paul H. "The American Loyalists: Notes on Their Organization and Numerical Strength." *WMQ* 25 (1968): 259–77.

———. *Loyalists and Redcoats: A Study in British Revolutionary Policy*. Chapel Hill: University of North Carolina Press, 1964.

Sosin, Jack M. *Agents and Merchants: British Colonial Policy and the Origins of the American Revolution, 1763–1775*. Lincoln, Nebr.: University of Nebraska Press, 1965.

———. "Proposal for Establishing Anglican Bishops in the Colonies." *Journal of Ecclesiastical History* 13 (1962): 76–84.

Stark, James H. *The Loyalists of Massachusetts and the Other Side of the American Revolution*. Boston: n.p., 1910.

Stedman, Charles. *The History of the Origin, Progress, and Termination of the American War.* 2 vols. London: n.p., 1794.

Stevenson, John. *Popular Disturbances in England, 1700–1870.* London: Longman, 1979.

Stone, Lawrence, and Jeanne C. Fawtier Stone. *An Open Elite? England, 1540–1880.* Oxford: Clarendon Press, 1984.

Sturgess, H. A. C., et al., comps. *Register of Admissions to the Honourable Society of the Middle Temple, from the Fifteenth Century to 1975.* 5 vols. London: The Society of the Middle Temple, 1949–78.

Sutherland, L. S., and L. G. Mitchell, eds. *The History of the University of Oxford.* Vol. 5, *The Eighteenth Century*, ed. T. H. Aston. Oxford: Clarendon Press, 1986.

Taylor, Robert J. *Western Massachusetts in the Revolution.* Providence, R.I.: Brown Univ. Press, 1954.

Thomas, Leslie J. "Partisan Politics in Massachusetts during Governor Bernard's Administration, 1760–1770." 2 vols. Ph.D. diss., University of Wisconsin, 1960.

Thomas, P. D. G. *British Politics and the Stamp Act Crisis: The First Phase of the American Revolution, 1763–1767.* Oxford: Oxford Univ. Press, 1975.

———. "George III and the American Revolution." *History* 70 (1985): 16–31.

———. *Tea Party to Independence: The Third Phase of the American Revolution, 1773–1776.* Oxford: Clarendon Press, 1991.

———. *The Townshend Duties Crisis: The Second Phase of the American Revolution, 1767–1773.* Oxford: Clarendon Press, 1987.

Thompson, Pishey. *The History and Antiquities of Boston.* Boston: John Noble Jr., 1856.

Tucker, Louis Leonard. "Centers of Sedition: Colonial Colleges and the American Revolution." *Procs. MHS*, 3d ser., 91 (1979): 16–34.

———. "The Church of England and Religious Liberty at Pre-Revolutionary Yale." *WMQ* 17 (1960): 314–28.

Tucker, Robert, and David C. Hendrickson. *The Fall of the First British Empire.* Baltimore: Johns Hopkins Univ. Press, 1982.

Tyler, John W. *Smugglers & Patriots: Boston Merchants and the Advent of the Revolution.* Boston: Northeastern Univ. Press, 1986.

Ubbelohde, Carl. *The Vice-Admiralty Courts and the American Revolution.* Chapel Hill: University of North Carolina Press, 1960.

Valentine, Alan. *Lord North.* 2 vols. Norman, Okla.: University of Oklahoma Press, 1967.

Walett, Francis G. "James Bowdoin: Patriot Propagandist." *New England Quarterly* 23 (1950): 320–28.

———. "The Massachusetts Council: The Transformation of a Conservative Institution." *WMQ* 6 (1949): 605–27.

Walmsley, Andrew S. *Thomas Hutchinson and the Origins of the American Revolution.* New York: New York Univ. Press, 1999.

Warden, G. B. *Boston, 1689–1776.* Boston: Little, Brown, 1970.

Warren, Mrs. Mercy Otis. *History of the Rise, Progress and Termination of* the American Revolution. Boston, 1805. Reprint edited by Lester H. Cohen, Indianapolis: Reprint Liberty Classics, 1988.

Waters, John J., Jr. *The Otis Family in Provincial and Revolutionary Massachusetts*. Chapel Hill: University of North Carolina Press, 1968.

Watson, J. Steven. *The Reign of George III, 1760–1815*. Oxford: Clarendon Press, 1960.

Welch, William L. "Israel Williams and the Hampshire College Project of 1761–1764." *Historical Journal of Massachusetts* 13 (1985): 53–62.

Wells, R. "Counting Riots in Eighteenth-Century England." *Society for the Study of Labour History* 37 (1978): 68–72.

Weslager, C. A. *The Stamp Act Congress: with an Exact Copy of the Complete Journal*. Newark: University of Delaware Press, 1976.

Western, J. R. *The English Militia in the Eighteenth Century*. London: Routledge & Kegan Paul, 1965.

White, Shane. " 'It Was a Proud Day': African Americans, Festivals, and Parades in the North, 1741–1834." *Journal of American History* 81 (1994): 13–50.

Wickwire, Franklin B. *British Subministers and Colonial America, 1763–1783*. Princeton: Princeton Univ. Press, 1966.

———. "John Pownall and British Colonial Policy." *WMQ* 20 (1963): 543–54.

———. "King's Friends, Civil Servants, or Politicians." *AHR* 71 (1965): 18–42.

Wilderson, Paul W. *Governor John Wentworth and the American Revolution: The English Connection*. Hanover, Mass.: Univ. Press of New England, 1994.

Williamson, J. Bruce, ed. *Middle Temple Bench Book, being a register of benchers from the Earliest records to 1981*. 2 vols. London: The Society of the Middle Temple, 1937–82.

Wood, Gordon S. *The Radicalism of the American Revolution*. New York: Alfred A. Knopf, 1992; New York: Vintage, 1993.

Woolverton, John F. *Colonial Anglicanism in North America*. Detroit: Wayne State Univ. Press, 1984.

Wolkins, George G. "The Boston Customs District in 1768." *Procs. MHS*, 3d ser., 58 (1924–25): 418–45.

———. "Daniel Malcom and the Writs of Assistance." *Procs. MHS*, 3d ser., 58 (1924–25): 5–88.

———. "Letters of Charles Paxton." *Procs. MHS*, 3d ser., 56 (1922–23): 343–52.

———. "The Seizure of John Hancock's Sloop *Liberty*." *Procs. MHS*, 3d ser., 55 (1921–22): 243–84.

———. "William Bollan and the Writs of Assistance." *Procs. MHS*, 3d ser., 59 (1925–26): 414–24.

Wordsworth, Christopher. *Scholae Academicae: Some Account of Studies at the English Universities in the Eighteenth Century*. Cambridge, 1877. Reprint, Cambridge: Cambridge Univ. Press, 1968. Deighton, Bell & Co., 1874.

Zemsky, Robert M. *Merchants, Farmers and River Gods: An Essay on Eighteenth-Century American Politics*. Boston: Gambit, 1971.

Zobel, Hiller. *The Boston Massacre*. New York: W. W. Norton, 1970.

Zuckerman, Michael W. *Peaceable Kingdoms: New England Towns in the Eighteenth Century*. New York: Alfred A. Knopf, 1970.

Index

Illustrations are indicated by italicized page numbers. The abbreviation FB denotes Francis Bernard.